The Education of a Gardener

THE
EDUCATION OF
A GARDENER

Russell Page

Vintage Books
A Division of Random House
New York

First Vintage Books Edition, April 1985

Library of Congress Cataloging in Publication Data

Page, Russell.
The education of a gardener.

Reprint. Originally published: New York : Random House, c1983.

Includes index.
1. Gardens—Design. 2. Landscape gardening.
3. Landscape architecture. I. Title.
SB473.P28   1985   712   84-40532
ISBN 0-394-72920-X (pbk.)

Manufactured in the United States of America
24689753
Cover photograph of background by Susan Woods
Cover photograph of garden by Curtis Taylor
Cover design by Paul Gamarello/Eyetooth Design

To my father and my mother

Preface to the new edition

This book is now twenty years old and I am twenty years older. (In 1962 I returned to England to work as a garden consultant.)

As I had hoped this book has found its place at the bedside rather than on the coffee table and its appearance in this new edition has hardly been changed. This would in any case have been difficult, as not a few of the gardens made before its publication have changed owners, become neglected or even disappeared.

One of the main interests of my work in the intervening years has been its geographical extension. In Italy I came to know and love Rome and the countryside around from Bracciano to Anzio; and then Spain came into my range – first Motril on the coast below Granada, then westwards to Algeciras and north-east to Majorca. I worked too in Washington D.C. and in New York, but returned occasionally to design one or two new gardens in England.

Two trips to Western Australia gave me a glimpse of a surprisingly different flora and fauna: kangaroos hurtling through the air like stream-lined furry Concordes and, once, a flight over a thousand miles of desert blazing with flower colour after years of drought.

Latterly I have been on occasional forays to Chile, where the snow-covered volcanic peaks of the Andes cut the sky above blue lakes and hillsides are scarlet with embothriums and forests of drimys and eucryphia.

Like other English garden makers in this century I was at first very much influenced by the work of Gertrude Jekyll and Edwin Lutyens. Over the years, working in France and Italy, my approach to designing was modified by the greater formality of classical French planning and the more sculptural approach of the Italian tradition.

Another invaluable factor for me, and one well worth study by garden designers, has been the Japanese approach to garden design. My studies, admittedly only from books, taught me much. I would make no general criticism of the composition of Japanese gardens. They depend on another heredity and another culture. But there is one aspect of Japanese gardens from which I have learned much, and that is the relationship between objects in space. Examples of what I mean by this can be found in Chinese and Japanese drawings and nearer home in Spanish still-life paintings of the seventeenth century.

Whether I am making a landscape or a garden or arranging a window box I first address the problem as an artist composing a picture; my pre-occupation is with the relationships between objects whether I am dealing with woods, fields or water, rocks or trees, shrubs and plants or groups of plants.

My understanding is that every object emanates – sends out vibrations beyond its physical body which are specific to itself. These vibrations vary with the nature of the object, the materials it is made of, its colour, its textures and its form. Any tree has twigs, branches and a trunk – the bark on a twig is other than that of its trunk – the texture of foliage varies through the seasons. So too with a stone – the material and texture of marble differ from those of sandstone or granite, and like the shape and colour of a flower or a fruit these dictate the speed and spread of the emana-tions of each particular object and thus the interplay between objects.

I have experimented endlessly with this idea. Take, for instance, a glass, a bunch of keys, and an apple, and put them on a tray. As you move them around, their impact, the impression you receive from them, will change with every rearrangement. Many of their inter-relationships will be meaningless, some will be more or less harmonious, but every now and again you will hit on an arrange-ment which appears just. Out of doors you may have a building or a tree which is a fixed point you have to accept. Such an object or even a group of objects produces a specific vibration, which may require subduing or reinforcing; and so, aware of this factor, you start composing by adding or subtracting shapes and textures and using colours and tones to achieve the impression you want to make – whether dramatic or subdued, hard or soft, harmonious, or even strident – which might be necessary as a shock in preparation for a change of mood or scale.

It is perhaps impossible to formulate the importance of such overtones. You design a garden within all the limitations of a site, of a client's requirement, the climate and the nature of the soil, of the local culture and of your own capacities as artist and technician. All of this is, with practice, relatively straightforward, but if your garden is to have "magic" you have to take your work further and give it an extra dimension. I think that awareness of the interplay between objects, whether organic or inorganic, is of major importance if your garden is to be also a work of art.

Working around the Mediterranean I gained a knowledge of garden design in Latin countries, but it was only when I first went to southern Spain in the sixties that I became deeply interested in the Moorish gardens there, though I already knew their ancestry from time spent in the Middle East.

What is left of the complex of gardens at the Alhambra and the Generalife are perhaps well enough known not to need new description. These are the best preserved, but in the villages in the foothills of the Sierra Nevada, down to the sea at Motril and eastwards to Malaga and beyond, I have found many traces of small Moorish gardens.

Next to the airport at Malaga there is a fine elaborate late seventeenth or early eighteenth century "Italian" garden of paved terraces, balustraded stairways, fountains and a quantity of statues and urns, the whole elaborate and effective. But I sensed that the site of both house and garden had been carefully chosen (as only the Moors knew how), and I set out to explore the less frequented areas of the garden where, sure enough, I found an octagonal fountain of the fourteenth century falling to pieces in a cabbage patch and a long canal-like reservoir which still feeds the later formal water garden. The Moorish influence in gardens goes right through Andalusia, noticeably in Seville and Cordoba, and there are at least three major gardens in Majorca, Raxa, Alfabia and La Granja. These and others are all well described in Constance Mary Villers Stuart's classic *Spanish Gardens*.

The Islamic culture, as such, dates from the middle or end of the seventeeth century. All its architecture, all its applied design and all its garden design can be seen to be founded on a few geometric forms: a cross, two lines crossed at right angles, squares, rectangles and two squares crossing each other diagonally. Most Islamic designs stem from this last figure which produces the endless variations and extrapolations of the octagon; though the hexagon also gave rise to a great variety of geometrical developments.

The accepted theory is that the water neccessary for irrigation was the basis of all early gardens through Persia and the deserts of Asia and the Middle East, and that the cruciform canals, the four rivers of Paradise, derived from the logical exigencies of irrigation. This is surely true as far as it goes but I suspect it is not the whole story.

If you, as did I, become interested in the origins of garden design, the need for irrigation, the hanging gardens of Babylon and the town gardeners of Pompei seem scarcely enough as historical documentation.

If water is a necessity for the cultivation of plants it has other and less easily described functions. "White" water, breaking waves, waterfalls, cascades and fountain jets are known to produce negative ions, which "clear the air" and make people feel well. At the thirteenth-century Fountains Abbey in Yorkshire, the sick-bay was built over a weir on the river which flows under the buildings. Running water has special properties easily perceptible if you choose to examine your impressions of, say a duck-pond on a village green compared with a fast-flowing stream in a narrow valley.

Throughout history garden makers, whether Byzantine, Islamic, Romanesque, Gothic or Renaissance have, consciously or not, used water for other than utilitarian ends. Water seems to have been appreciated even without being understood: why and how can an underground source communicate with the water diviner's forked hazel rod?

I once visited a villa and its garden in Umbria, not far from Assisi. It had formerly been a monastery and there seemed nothing special about it to account for its particularly agreeable and harmonious atmosphere. It had a quite ordinary kitchen garden divided into the classical four quarters by paths. Did the sense of harmony I felt perhaps derive from the fact that under the flagstoned paths were channels of running water?

By now I was hot on the trail and looking much more carefully at gardens I most admired – or should I say enjoyed – in order to see the part played by water.

The Villa Lante at Bagnaia, near Viterbo, was an obvious starting point. Here Vignola chose a wooded hillside site where high up in the woods there was a spring. We know the result – two pavilions and a great parterre with its central pool fed by a jet supported by Gian de Bologna's superb bronze figures. The water channels rush down the central staircase from the hillside, past the stone dining table and its stone benches which are uncomfortably decorated with surprise water jets. Higher up are two small flanking pavilions, and out of sight in the woods above, the spring which is the origin of the whole composition. All of this is stylish High Renaissance exuberance, which I can find admirable but not touching. Where was, where is, the magic in this place? For me it lies in an inconspicuous detail at the place where the two little pavilions above the rioting cascades act as gatehouses to the woods behind them, for round the base of each pavilion there is a narrow and unnecessary stone channel filled with running water which suggests continuity between the unseen springs in the woods above and the babbling cascades which come to rest in the balustraded pool of the main parterre.

Next I looked at the Villa Madama, Raphael's unfinished palace on Monte Mario, some distance east of the Vatican. The garden, as it stands, is simply a long terrace levelled out of the hillside with retaining walls below and above and, on a lower terrace, a large tank for water storage. In these rather empty if well proportioned spaces I found nothing to account for the singular charm of the place until I concluded that somewhere there had to be running water. Wandering through a wrought-iron gate at the far end of the unkempt terraced garden I came out to a hillside with huge old trees composed in groups as though Giorgione had had a hand in their disposition; amongst them was a rocky mound and, in a little grotto in the rock, the spring which the quality of the whole garden had made me sure I would find.

At the Villa Aldobrandini at Frascati, near Rome, from a spring in the chestnut woods on the hills behind the house, water was brought down in a simple stone channel to make a steep ladder of gushing water which feeds the Nymphaeum, whose elaborate Renaissance facade faces the Villa across the entrance courtyard.

Mid-seventeenth-century European gardens were laid out as rather simple geometric parterres, where fountains, large or small, accented the crossing of paths or the centre of a pattern of beds. To suit his patrons' tastes Lenotre elaborated these geometric patterns with curling embroideries of clipped box; but the basic skeletons of the plans he made usually depend on a pattern of water, sometimes very large. The long tradition of the geometrical structuring of gardens compartmented by the geometric use of water survived until the mid-eighteenth-century. Switzer's formal canals and the octagonal pond at Studley Royal would have been well understood by the monks of Fountains Abbey a short mile upstream.

Elsewhere in England, Lancelot Brown was encouraging his wealthy clients to tear out their splendid formal gardens and replace them with his facile compositions of grass, tree clumps and rather shapeless ponds and lakes. Such vagaries, on a huge scale, may appear irrelevant to the problems of garden designers in the latter half of the twentieth century, but I can only think that the formlessness of so many modern gardens stems from this earlier decadence.

Another reason for the frequent lack of consideration given to the underlying structure of contemporary gardens is that modern gardeners have a far greater choice of plants. The elite among them know and care for rare and unusual plants which they collect and cultivate with care and skill. However they tend to be less interested in the visual relationships of form and colour.

Faced with a garden to design I have always tried to think about the shape it might take, of how I would want to move through the area, what existing features and what necessities such as circulation might be dealt with, and at the same time remain aware of the kind of plants I wanted or might need to use – for their forms, colours and textures would to a great extent influence the basic structure. When the vegetation is going to be complex, in form and colour and variety, I will tend to make a basic plan or framework which will ensure a slow progress through the garden, perhaps to the point of avoiding any long views or vistas which would tend to draw one on too quickly to see the next change in the garden scene. It does not matter whether one is composing informally with a play of curves designed to underline the forms of individual plants or groups of plants, or whether for other reasons one needs to use a more rigid framework for the same plants which must always be kept in mind. This implies a modulation but a calculated one, in the appreciation of your plant material. You can use any plant you like and by its placing vary the impact it will make. A square block of any one subject, in sunshine, will give a different impression from the same quantity of the same plant planted informally, say in semishade. Such processes in thinking and in the realization of a garden sound laborious and difficult. In fact they are not – the mind takes the habit of considering these and other factors simultaneously; all is present, only remains the work.

With practice the whole operation becomes in a sense organic and the garden itself becomes an organic unity. If, for any reason, I need a more formal garden the process is more or less the same – the difference lies in the visual impact. Formal shapes are taken in far faster, but what you may gain in clarity you may lose in mystery.

You will quickly read a formal pattern and a symmetrically

planned garden and even move through it faster. In such gardens you will group colour differently and use both forms and colours to make clearer and sharper contrasts.

Rain, clouds and sunshine, many climates, the landscapes of the world and all its growing plants to learn about, choose from and use, the contributions of painters and architects and sculptors of many cultures to absorb and learn from – all of these can teach a gardener magic and make that gardener content.

For fifty years and more I have been a privileged man occupied for almost the whole of that time in doing what I most enjoyed – designing gardens. I only once and very briefly had a garden of my own – a plot behind a London house.

I am very aware of the hundreds of people from whom I have learnt everything I know about my chosen subject: clients, friends, gardeners, masons, labourers, contractors, architects, horticulturalists, garden owners and garden lovers, botanists, students, writers, sculptors and painters.

Known briefly or for years across five continents and in a dozen countries, all freely shared with me their knowledge with kindness, encouragement and interest.

I salute them all.

RUSSELL PAGE
1983

Contents

Illustrations

Illustrations

Foreword

I would, first of all, like to say how much this work owes to my wife who insisted that some account of a garden-maker's activities would be of interest to amateurs and professional gardeners. Her active help and encouragement at every stage and on every level alone made the book possible. I have also to thank Miss Solita Solano and Madame Kadloubovsky for their helpful editing of the first drafts, and still another old and valued friend, Mr. Roy Hay, for his invariably good advice and for his enthusiasm for the project.

Mr. Fred Whitsey has been good enough to check plant names and bring my old-fashioned nomenclature up to date—no easy task with the constant re-naming of old favourites.

I would also thank Mr. Thomas Kernan, Editor of *Maison et Jardin*, Mr. A. D. B. Wood, Mr. Sidney Newbery and the British Travel and Holidays Association for their kindness in giving me permission to use the four photographs in the book which I did not take myself. I have, in general, preferred to use my own photographs since, in spite of their technical shortcomings, they more exactly reflect the points I wished to make clear.

Lastly, I would like to thank Mr. Mark Collins and Mr. Robert Cross for their advice, their assistance and their patience.

The education of a gardener

I last had a garden of my own when I was eighteen. Since then my main occupation has been designing gardens for other people. I have worked in England, France, Belgium, Switzerland and in Italy, occasionally in Egypt, once even in Persia, and in the Eastern United States. I have also seen gardens in India, in Ceylon, in Isfahan, in the Lebanon, Scandinavia, Holland and Germany. I have planted window-boxes and cottage gardens, housing schemes for industrial workers, layouts for factories. I have worked for landowners and great industrialists, for corporations and companies, for the very rich and for the poor, for professionals and for amateurs. Through the years this has added up to a wide and special experience. I write " wide " deliberately. I know nothing whatever of many aspects of gardening and very little of a great many more. But I never saw a garden from which I did not learn something and seldom met a gardener who did not, in one way or another, help me. Perhaps if I had spent these last thirty years making my own garden I would want to share that different experience. As it is, whatever the terms or the place, however different the physical circumstances, I have always tried to shape gardens each as a harmony, linking people to nature, house to landscape, the plant to its soil. This is a difficult standard to achieve and realisation has always fallen far short of the concept. At each new attempt, I see that which is superfluous, that is, everything which clutters up my understanding of a problem must be discarded. Everything which detracts from the idea of a unity must go.

Introduction

I started to understand something about plants by handling them. It was on one summer holiday when I was perhaps fourteen that, bored with the riding and jumping competitions at a local agricultural show, I wandered off to the flower-tent. There in an atmosphere hot and heavy with the smell of trampled grass, people, animals and flowers, my attention was caught by a tiny plant of *Campanula pulla* with three deep purple bells, huge in comparison with its frail leaves and the minute pot in which it grew. It was mine for a shilling and it opened a new world for me. I had no idea what to do for it nor how to make it flourish in the cold clay of a Lincolnshire garden. So off I went to the public library and within a few days I had found friends and teachers in Reginald Farrer with his *English Rock Garden* and Gertrude Jekyll with *Wall and Water Garden*, two people who had spent a life time with plants and gardens.

All my pocket money went on rock plants. All my holidays were given to my own personal corner of the garden. I would bicycle for miles to get a basket of leaf-soil, I would steal grit, sand or gravel from roadside heaps and I would borrow a horse and cart to collect stones which were hard to come by in our stoneless countryside. My campanula died but meanwhile I had seen a picture of *Primula farinosa*, fallen in love with it and learned that it grew wild in Yorkshire. I had to lure my father who liked bird-watching, into the Yorkshire dales. There I walked miles questioning every passer-by and after a three weeks' search I eventually found an abandoned quarry starred with the pale mauve treasures that I sought.

When I was a small child there was a market each Friday in the old Palladian butter market near the Stonebow in Lincoln. The farmers' wives would drive in early in the morning, dressed in their best, with baskets of fresh butter, eggs, chickens, ducks and bunches of freshly picked mint and sage. I used often to be taken there by my grandfather's housekeeper while she made her purchases, and I remember that always, in the spring, there would be bunches of double mauve primroses and of the heavenly-scented *Daphne mezereum*. Later when my passion for gardening

14

developed I wanted these plants but could never find them in our friends' gardens. They seemed to grow only in cottage gardens in hamlets lost among the fields and woods. I gradually came to know the cottagers and their gardens for miles around, for these country folk had a knack with plants. Kitchen windows were full of pots with cascades of *Campanula isophylla*, geraniums, fuchsias and begonias all grown from slips. I would be given cuttings from old-fashioned pinks and roses which were not to be found in any catalogue, and seedlings of plants brought home perhaps by a sailor cousin—here was a whole world of modest flower addicts.

It must have been my father who told me of a certain elderly lady devoted to flowers who lived in a Victorian Gothic house almost in the shadows of the three great towers of Lincoln Minster. One day I knocked on her door. She opened it herself and stood there, tall and gaunt, with wild grey hair and the relics of great good looks, dressed in the fashion of thirty years before. " Please be careful where you walk," said the lady—a necessary warning as half the coloured encaustic tiles flooring the dark hallway had been taken up and one had to play hop-scotch to avoid a chequer board of Asiatic primula seedlings which grew in the spaces left by the missing tiles. The drawing-room was gardened in another way; ivy had been brought in through holes in the wall to garland windows, walls and ceiling with green. This lady had lived in India where, over many years, she had made lively precise water-colour drawings of flowers, musical instruments, jewels and household objects which filled a whole pile of albums. Outside, in an old sycamore tree, a rickety bamboo ladder led up to a platform among the branches which she called her " machan " though the neighbour's cat was the only tiger she could stalk. There was a rock garden too, contrived as a home for frogs, lizards and grass snakes. Finding it colourless in the winter, she had imposed on it colonies of brightly coloured toad-stools which she told me she made herself from the lids of boot-polish tins and old tooth brushes. I was always welcome. There were no set meal-times; " A little food every two hours is better," she would say, bringing me a plate of pineapple, or custard, or a sandwich.

So I gardened as I could, learning my few plants intimately, handling them, getting to know their likes and dislikes by smell and touch. "Book learning" gave me information, but only physical contact can give any real knowledge and understanding of a live organism. To have "green fingers" or a "green thumb" is an old expression which describes the art of communicating the subtle energies of love to prosper a living plant. Gradually I came to recognise through idiosyncrasies of colour, texture, shape and habit the origin of a plant and its cultural needs.

My apprenticeship to the art of garden composition was also on a small but very practical scale. I was seventeen when I was given a grass slope, a few cartloads of the local ironstone, a few bags of cement, some plants and a piped water supply with which to make a small rock and stream garden. For three months I really lived in and with this miniature world as I struggled with my pocket landscape. Each stone represented the possibilities of a cliff or a mountain top, my dribble of water could be lake or river or cascade and three pigmy junipers were a forest. A few moist and shady inches on the north side of a stone were a Himalayan bog for *Primula rosea*; a handful of grit on the sunny side of the same stone stood for a hot stony hillside in which to grow aethionema or androsace. A six inch fall of water was a Niagara and my friends who came to visit me at work I saw only as giant feet and legs, so immersed was I with my Lilliputian problems. At seventeen my keep and a new tennis racket were sumptuous extra rewards for all that I was learning about colour, scale and texture, and about plants and their likes and dislikes.

Friends passed me on from house to house while I continued making rock gardens, always learning, with scratched hands, wet feet and often an aching back. I know now that one cannot be taught to design gardens academically or theoretically. You have to learn the ways and nature of plants and stone, of water and soil

A formal arrangement of very large beds filled with pink and red floribunda roses. The lavender hedges which outline the triangular pattern also help to furnish this French garden through the winter months. The whole area which lies between house and farm-buildings is framed by yew hedges to give additional height and one or two flowering trees placed asymmetrically break the formality of the design

This flight of steps links the forecourt of a small eighteenth-century château near Paris to the formal gardens which lie below. With its flanking walls it replaces a rough grass bank. When we began to build these steps we uncovered the foundations of the original eighteenth-century steps also circular on the same spot and of exactly the same diameter

Another linking problem between a severely classical house (near Geneva) and an expanse of grass flanked by lines of chestnut trees. A straight grass bank and a gravelled area were reshaped into a bold semicircle and the grand manner of the period is suggested by the simplest means—a curling scroll of clipped box and white-painted tubs and caisses de Versailles filled with blue hydrangeas

On the south side of the same house a wall and a double flight of steps connect the house to a formal box-edged pattern. The wall is of soft grey-green sandstone capped by a harder cream limestone which also makes the steps. The simplified profile of the two lowest steps accentuates the transition from house to garden and the severely architectural walls are clothed with japanese quince, wistaria and Cotoneaster salicifolia for the same reason at least as much through the hands as through the head. England in the twenties was a good place in which to learn gardening for there was still a leisured class, already short of money but with time, culture and taste.

One of my earliest jobs was to make a rock garden in a Rutland field where the limestone of the Oolite Belt is near the surface and has provided the material for lovely villages where manor, church, farmhouses and cottages were built of fine ashlar with Colley Weston stone tiles for roofing. North Luffenham, the village where I was working, had a fine thirteenth-century church and next to it was the manor house, Caroline on one side, Queen Anne on the other. In a field beyond the orchard its owners had recently discovered the ruined walls of an old fish-pond and a spring. Through the hard frost of the spring of 1929 which continued, if I remember, till mid-April, I toiled away with a stable-boy to help me, harnessing the spring to make a streamlet running between and over stones out into the field below. We planted the garden with rooted cuttings and all sorts of plants acquired by exchange with neighbours. All through this time I was learning fast and my host, happy to find a young enthusiast who shared his passion, was always carrying me off to see gardens nearby or away on week-end visits to other garden lovers.

I learned about plants rather quickly. By dint of holding them I began to suspect from their " feel " and their appearance what kind of conditions they would enjoy and soon I began to be able to guess their place of origin. I learned their names simply by writing down in full the name of any plant I saw for the first time. Even now when I see a plant which I cannot name for the second or even for the fiftieth time, I write out the name: in the end one learns it.

It was on one of these gardening visits that I first went to Gloucestershire and came to know Mark Fenwick and his then famous garden at Abbotswood near Stow-on-the-Wold. Mark Fenwick was already an elderly man crippled by arthritis. For thirty years he had been turning a Cotswold hillside into a paradise for plant lovers. The house, rearranged by Lutyens, had a series of rather over-mannered formal terraces and gardens which had, at the time of which I write, lost to some extent their owner's interest. He had been busy making part of his hillside into a "wild" garden where several small streams and a few outcropping stones were the excuse for a huge collection of rock and water-loving plants, alpines and flowering shrubs. Morning and afternoon, Mark Fenwick would heave himself into his electric bath-chair, see that his note-book and pencil were securely fastened to his coat by bits of string, summon Mr. Tustin his head gardener, and off we would set. In spite of his bewildering collection of different plants, Mark Fenwick showed an extraordinary taste. His plants looked happy and he managed to arrange their placing with a delicate sense of colour and a remarkable appreciation of form and texture. I came to know this garden at every season, from the first young growth of *Cercidiphyllum japonicum* and the flowering of the tulip species, anemones and primulas in spring to the October scarlets of Japanese maples, the mauve of autumn crocuses and the muted tones of the heath garden in winter.

A feeling of youth and gaiety ran right through the garden and most touching of all was my host's enthusiasm, his patience with youth and ignorance, his vitality and good spirits. He seemed happy to inculcate his love and knowledge of gardening into anyone who wished to learn.

The well-watered, well-drained and sheltered valleys of the Cotswolds are good gardening country and we used often to set out over the clover-scented hills to see neighbours' gardens. Not far away, the gardens at Hidcote near Chipping Campden were reaching full maturity. Lawrence Johnston, their owner and maker, had come as a young man from the United States and had bought a small stone manor house set in green fields with no garden. Little by little, he built up the now famous complex of gardens which, in my view, rank him as a considerable artist. The theme of the Hidcote garden is a series of small enclosures carefully related in their scale to the modest house. Each enclosure was devoted to plantings where, usually, one colour predominated. The various small gardens were carefully linked and separated by long axial lines; and, so that the richness of the planting should not appear confused, grass walks or lawns hedged with yew, beech or hornbeam were used as quiet interludes. Perhaps Lawrence Johnston's most important contribution to modern gardening was his ability to combine plants in an unusual way. I remember a double border of old-fashioned roses combined with the equally old-fashioned *Paeonia officinalis*. The path between was edged with purple-mauve *Campanula portenschlagiana* and the mustard-green alchemilla which used to be called "Lady's Mantle." In this unexpected combination these old-fashioned plants seem to complement each other exactly and one sensed the result of careful thought and a good understanding of the nature of the plants involved.

I was to see more of Lawrence Johnston's work later in the forest of Montmorency near Paris, where at St. Brice lived Edith Wharton in a late Louis XV pavilion called the Pavillon Colombe. It had been built by a *fermier-général* for two sisters, supposedly his sweethearts, the Mesdemoiselles Colombe. Edith Wharton, whose little-known first book was on the then new subject of interior decoration, had filled the panelled rooms with books and eighteenth-century furniture. With Major Johnston's help, she made a garden setting exactly in the spirit of the house. A formal box garden, called the blue garden, which they made together still exists. Now its outer beds are filled with delphiniums, galtonias, anchusa and *Salvia patens* and the formal parterre in the middle with *Nepeta fassenii* and ageratum. Height is given by the blue hibiscus, *coeleste*, which have been kept clipped to about six feet high like pyramidal pear trees. From the house you walk through a wood and around a large stone-edged eighteenth-century pool to reach the flower gardens, which are again divided into compartments. Years later, opposite the blue garden, I worked with the Duchesse de Talleyrand who now owns the house, to make another formal garden with clipped yews and two fine stone vases. The beds in the garden are entirely planted with garden pinks whose silver foliage, along with the creamy stone of the vases which are set in a frame of silver santolina, are effective all the year round. From May to July there is a foam of rose and pink and white blossom and all the garden is heavily scented.

At this time I was also working in Devonshire at a great house which lay at the head of an estuary thrusting down between hanging oakwoods to the sea. Gardening in the extreme south west was altogether different. In that mild and almost frost-free and very moist climate all kinds of trees and shrubs flourish which cannot be made to grow elsewhere; in fact Devonshire gardens, full as they are of rare botanical species, seemed to me then like an exercise in Latinity. Eden Phillpotts came to the rescue with his admirable book on trees and shrubs, and another helpful pundit was Ashley Froude, son of the historian, who lived near Dartmouth and had a garden full of the rarest shrubs. Like most gardens in that region it was more interesting than effective. Nearby too was the home of the owner and manufacturer of a special gin, who, it was said, went into seclusion once each year to mix in secret the ingredients of his product. For the rest he was an expert on daffodils.

My problem here was rather special. I had to make a rocky stream and a garden which would come into flower only in autumn. This limited my choice, and the result tended to look a bit melancholy under the moist Devonshire sky; but the hunt for plants was fascinating. At that time there was an interesting botanical garden at Paignton; and Dartington Hall, where the Elmhirsts were in full swing with their educational and cultural experiments, had an excellent alpine nursery. Now the nursery has gone but the steep grass banks and the enormous yews of the fifteenth-century tournament ground have not changed; there is a fine collection of magnolias and Japanese cherries; and in the shade of an old oakwood near the house there is a garden all of camellias.

I spent most of that autumn working on my Devonshire garden. T. E. Lawrence used sometimes to come over on Sundays.

He was stationed with the R.A.F. at Plymouth only a few miles away. The ambition of the young people of the house and myself was to lure him into one of the long walks we used to take through the tawny woods along the river, or over the headlands above the autumn sea. He liked to talk of writing and music. Friends kept him supplied with books and records. Although the external pattern of his life was eccentric and escapist, his passion for seclusion was physical rather than intellectual. He had a great feeling for style in any domain; his conversation had shape, his observations point, and his comments on my garden efforts were exact and helpful. He had the gift of absorbing a subject and scenting out its problems, even though the terms of material were foreign. He was for us a legendary figure—we considered it a rare privilege to know him and, in accord with the legend, were tactfully silent on his Middle Eastern experiences, to us heroic and exotic.

Each year I spent periods of weeks and sometimes months in France. I was fascinated by this contact with a definite and stylised culture new to me and clearer and sharper than the English tradition which has absorbed and modified and welded together influences from so many different countries—Italy, France and Holland for design, and the whole temperate world for plants. In France foreign importations, whether of style or material, had only (it seemed to me) been absorbed if and when they could conform to French style. The relatively few plants cultivated, for example, were there because they could be trusted to provide exactly the colour or the form logically required.

Meeting amateurs of architecture, decoration, sculpture and furniture I slowly learned to appreciate some of the niceties of French style, and came to know a good deal about houses and gardens of the seventeenth and eighteenth centuries. The clarity of French planning, although it can at times be arid and lack mystery and imagination, was always helpful to me as discipline for my rather shapeless jungle of a mind, apt to become over-furnished with purely horticultural images and associations.

Introduction

About 1930 I spent a part of the summer trying to enliven the garden of a château near Melun. It belonged to Ogden Codman, an eccentric, wealthy and quarrelsome old gentleman who as a young man had been an architect. In his time he had built some extremely competent houses in the eighteenth century manner in New York, Southampton and Newport. When I knew him he had long since retired, and had given many years to the study of the architecture of French châteaux. He showed me some of his files—he had tens of thousands of photos of houses documented and card-indexed. He used local directories, the mayors and post offices of small villages, well-read secretaries —Geoffrey Scott, the author of *The Portrait of Zélide* and *The Architecture of Humanism* had been one—and two lemon-yellow open Hispano-Suiza cars to track down these châteaux. For each château he aimed to have, if possible, the date, the history, the name of its architect and its owners, as well as photographs and plans. Although the genealogy of Bostonian families, a parallel hobby, took most of his time, he was a mine of information and an admirable critic of style. At that time he was also completing the Villa Leopolda at Villefranche-sur-mer near Nice. Using eighteenth-century models—the Château Borelli at Marseilles, the Villa Belgioso in Milan and the palace at Portici near Naples— he succeeded in building what is perhaps the only architecturally satisfying large house on the Riviera. Built on land which formerly belonged to King Leopold II, it had already cost a large fortune when the crash of 1929 put a stop to operations. We worked on plans for a future which, for him, never materialised. Although he died only in 1948 aged ninety-five he never lived in his fine house, whose garden, I was later to reorganise for its present owners.

In the years before the war there was a large and well-to-do American colony in Paris, owning châteaux and manors among the rivers and woods of the Ile de France around Senlis, Fontainebleau, Rambouillet and Versailles. It was the fashion to decorate these with fine *boiseries* and furniture and to bring their neglected gardens into shape. In those days it was easier to find both gardeners and plants: little by little round *massifs* of red salvias set out in rough grass gave way to good lawns, herbaceous borders and a more contemporary style of gardening. One of the most charming of these gardens was perhaps the one which Louis Bromfield made at an old presbytery on the banks of the little river Nonette where it runs through Senlis before it is caught to supply the long formal water-reaches of the Château of Chantilly a few miles to the west. Louis spent hours every day working in his own garden which, bursting with roses and lilies and healthy clumps of herbaceous plants, was the despair of those who relied on paid gardeners. He had learnt much of his gardening from Edith Wharton at St. Brice, and I think his was the only garden in France where the hybrid musk roses grew— Penelope and Pax and others. They were allowed to grow into large loosely trimmed bushes hanging over the river, loveliest with their clusters of cream and white and rose-pink flowers just as the light began to fade. Planted near them, *Lilium regale*, tobacco flowers and night-scented stocks filled the evening air with scent.

At this time I was busy with the garden of a small château on the edge of the Forêt de Senart twenty miles south-east of Paris. Of creamy plaster, it had been designed with great elegance and simplicity as a hunting-box for the Comte d'Artois by Belanger who was also his architect for Bagatelle. The small park had been well planted in the romantic manner when the house was built, with one feature of great charm—a narrow winding alley of enormous plane trees leading down to a small river which bounded the property. Planted closely together, maybe nine feet apart and in wet ground, the mottled cream and green trunks of those trees leaning outwards from the path soared seventy or more feet into the air without a branch. The effect was prodigious: the carefully planned curve of the path making it look as though it ran between two gigantic palisades of growing timber. The friendly formality of the house required a somewhat formal linking with the park, and its owner, calling in a French architect, had started with the usual formal arrangements of gravel alleys, clipped box bushes and narrow beds of red flowers. These he soon scrapped and replaced with a simple wide gravel terrace and a rectangle of grass held in place by low hedges starting from the house to embrace, as it were, this modestly formal arrangement. It might have been dull had he not given life and colour to the composition by setting out stands with huge macaws whose violent scarlet and blue and green plumage and raucous calls enlivened the picture considerably.

In this garden much attention was paid to detail. Tumblers were always set ready by a spring which bubbled out of the ground below an ivy-covered grotto. Peacocks were fed each noon from the dining-room window. Indeed in France in the thirties the minor elegances of living, made possible only by a large number of servants, still existed.

In 1932 I spent a summer holiday alone in this house with a fine library of garden books at my disposal, and it was then that I began to draw garden compositions. I spent long hours each day with pencil and paper working out problems in design and interpreting the " feel " in terms of precise measurements of the many gardens I had been visiting in the previous few years. Of course I learned also how careless and fleeting had been the quality of my observation, and from then on I made it a habit to draw summary sketches of all sorts of objects as I came across them—the moulding of a pool-edge, a cornice, the panelling of a door or a detail of trellis work. This was not so much to accumulate a formal documentation, as to train my eye and mind to look and register more carefully. The few moments spent on even a rough scribble gave me a chance to absorb more fully what I was looking at. This practice of incessant drawing also helps one to express oneself rapidly and comprehensibly on paper. It is invaluable when one is trying to explain an idea to a client, or a piece of construction to a workman.

During all this time I was obliged to earn my living somehow, going wherever a few guineas might be earned by a young man of my very limited experience. Gradually I realized that I had to be based somewhere; and my base turned out to be London.

There for a time I worked in a department store which specialised in furniture, living in the pervasive smell of new carpet and linoleum and proving a very bad salesman. My next job was nearer the mark. I found a very subordinate job in a landscape architect's office designing plantings for the endless new blocks of cheap flats then being built in the London suburbs.

It was about this time that I met Henry Bath, the present owner of Longleat. He was young, gay, brimming with ideas, and devoted to the property of which he was already in charge. Together we tackled the woods and drives of the immense park at Longleat, most of which had been rather neglected for a couple of generations. The house, a renaissance palace of golden Bath stone, lies just where Wiltshire, Somersetshire and Dorset meet, in the bottom of a greensand bowl with its lakes and avenues and clumps of isolated trees and hanging beechwoods which clothe the hills all round. It is said to have been built by John Thorpe around 1600, and it had a fine formal garden in the Dutch manner added towards 1670 perhaps by London and Wise. In the eighteenth century " Capability " Brown replaced this garden by a chain of small lakes, and planted the long elm avenue, leading to the house, which only recently had to be felled. He also seems to have devised the dramatic curtains of beech trees which lie along the hill called " Heaven's Gate " where the park rises to the east towards Salisbury Plain. In the early nineteenth century Sir Geoffrey Wyatville, then busy at Wilton and at Windsor Castle for George IV, made changes inside the house and added, very skilfully, the existing stable quadrangle and orangery. Next came Humphrey Repton who made a whole series of suggestions for improving the landscape, and incorporated them in one of his famous " Red Books." In it you can see his water-colour sketches with movable slips to show how the place was and how it would look if his suggestions were carried out as in fact, at Longleat, some were though many were not.

In the middle of the nineteenth century the deer park had been planted with ugly round clumps of mixed conifers and deciduous trees, and the woods with a profusion of exotic trees and shrubs. Mauve *Rhododendron ponticum* and the common yellow azalea had rolled on through the woods like a heavy sea and eighty years later formed thickets fifteen feet high and more. *Rhododendron arboreum* had grown into good-sized trees covered with blood-red blossom in April, *Azalea obtusa amoena* made compact tables of magenta flowers, and monkey puzzles, the giant redwood *Sequoia sempervirens*, and other conifers had grown to remarkable size in the cool greensand.

We set ourselves two tasks: to revise the planting of the deer park, and to clean out and replant the Longcombe Drive which runs from the Warminster gate up a narrow valley or combe to the top of the ridge which " Capability " Brown clothed in great beechwoods and from which you look down across the park to the house. We walked the open parkland for days, marking all the nineteenth-century clumps and individual trees which we felt should come out. Once they were gone the park looked cleaner and less complicated but rather too bare. Then began the second stage, which was to increase the earlier eighteenth-century clumps where time had clearly taken its toll of trees, and to add new groups where the composition of the landscape seemed to require them. As we analysed these old clumps we were interested to see how our predecessors sited their trees, using lines or right angles or wedge shapes exactly as though they had been designing wings for theatrical scenery. These earlier planters knew well enough that the rounded forms of mature trees demand a rectilinear pattern in the first place. To plant on such a large scale is hard work. We would plan a group, marking the position for each tree with a large and stout stake, walk back several hundred yards and then make wide circles through the rough grass to judge the effect from every angle. It is surprising how difficult it is to set out even five or seven stakes so that they do not appear regimented from at least one point; and we would have to correct our siting three or four times before we were satisfied.

Next we had to decide what kinds of tree to select. With

existing clumps we had no problem: we simply completed them with whatever tree had been used in the first place. But many of the original clumps were of elm, a tree which is liable to disease, and others were of Spanish or sweet chestnut, *Castanea sativa*, which we also wanted to avoid, as young trees resent transplanting and seedlings stood little chance of survival in this open parkland. In the end we confined ourselves mainly to lime trees and beech.

In the lowest part of the park, having cleared the lakes of unnecessary islands and overgrown shrubs, we had to give them the frame and emphasis of clumps and isolated trees. On one or two of the islands we used *Populus szechuanica*, one of the best of the balsam poplars which comes from Western China. Else-where, in moist ground near the water, we planted clumps of plane trees, which never did very well, and of scarlet oak, *Quercus coccinnea*, which have flourished exceedingly and are now quite handsome trees, whose crimson-scarlet foliage is reflected each autumn in the Half Mile Pond below the house. The plane trees were the London variety, *Platanus acerifolia*. The oriental plane *P. Orientalis*, is an altogether lovelier tree but hard to come by. Its leaves are smaller and more finely cut, and, seen in the mass, the foliage seems more tightly clustered and the light plays on it in a most seductive way. This is the chenar tree which you constantly find depicted in Persian and Mogul miniatures and at Isfahan you may still see huge old specimens planted by Shah Abbas early in the seventeenth century.

The Longcombe drive was a different problem. When we started on it the road, intended as one of the principal approaches to the house, had half-disappeared, engulfed in a tide of *Rhododendron ponticum* and the scented yellow azalea. With the help of a tractor we uprooted the ponticums and burned them on the spot. Only then could we see that the ground lay level for a few yards on either side of the road and then banked fairly steeply upwards to the Beech Woods on either side. Once the rhododendrons had gone we found a few large isolated beech trees, one or two thuyas and monkey puzzles and some very large specimens of the blood-red *Rhododendron arboreum.* This sheltered valley was enclosed in the surrounding beech forest, so here we felt we could try out all kinds of trees and shrubs which would look too exotic in a wider landscape. We decided to keep the *Azalea pontica* as the backbone of our planting for its flowers and their pungent scent and for the scarlet and orange splendours of its autumn foliage. Cutting back in one place and filling in with young plants in another, we made an irregular belt of azaleas on both sides leaving wide bays which we sowed with fine sheeps-fescue grass. Then we planted the trees: libocedrus and *Sequoia sempervirens,* where we wanted large accents of dark green; tulip trees for the clear yellow of their autumn leaves; several clumps of *Amelanchier canadensis;* and liquidambars whose young growth, until they grew clear of low-lying frosts, was blackened each year by late spring frosts. In the grassy bays we added drifts of Knap Hill and Exbury hybrid azaleas in scarlet orange cream and copper, and next to one large group of the copper variety a big group of *Pieris forrestii* whose new foliage each spring is the same bright copper red. In a cooler spot farther up the valley we placed groups of some of the better red hybrid rhododendrons, though only of vigorous varieties which do not require any cosseting. Unfortunately the soil seemed scarcely deep enough for the large foliaged rhododendron species, so for variation in texture we planted *Mahonia japonica bealei* and *Hydrangea aspera macrophylla.*

Here was a fine field for two energetic and enthusiastic gardeners and now, twenty-five years later, the park and woods begin to take the many-coloured shapes we then devised for them. Near the house we did not get: Henry's father still lived there and preferred that the view from his windows should remain as he had always known it.

The Longleat estate was then very extensive and one curious part of these holdings particularly interested Henry. This was the Cheddar Gorge, which cuts into the Mendip Hills where they fall away into the Somerset marshlands towards Wells, Bridgewater and Glastonbury. I remember the first day I drove

with him into this legendary country, with the beauty of Wells
Cathedral lying close below its sheltering hills and on the horizon
the mound of Glastonbury Tor dominating the magic acres
below where the holy thorn still flourishes. Some say that here
in the marshes is the Isle of Avalon where King Arthur rests, and
the old configuration of the land round Glastonbury, the streams,
meadows, ancient trackways, mounds and markstones have even
been interpreted as the real Round Table, a giant map of the
zodiac dating from what we have chosen to call pre-history.
Cheddar and its caves have too long been a tourist attraction.
Lying where the narrow road winds down between high cliffs
and emerges into the plain, a hamlet of tiny colour-washed,
tree-shaded cottages sells teas and Cheddar cheeses and souvenirs
in a welter of rose arbours, vividly painted signs and rustic garden
furniture, all executed in a sort of nineteenth-century folk-art
idiom. The lease of one of the two caves having recently fallen in,
we drove over to see what could be done to organise the running
of this cave in a more efficient way. We started with the idea of
putting up a corrugated iron shelter for bus drivers, but our
problem rapidly became more complex and I soon found myself
faced with having to design and build a restaurant and a museum
on a thirty-foot wide strip between the cliff-wall and the road.
If this programme was within my vision it was certainly outside
my technical competence. From the outset it seemed right to
devise a building that would be long and low in order to dramatise
the cave-mouth and accentuate the vertical face of the cliff. It
was a landscape problem in which the controlling factor had to
be the site itself. Which architect would see it from this
angle?

I had, not long before, come to know Geoffrey Jellicoe as one
of the founders of the then recently formed Institute of Landscape
Architects and an authority on classical Italian gardens. Together
we flung ourselves into the difficulties and excitements of the
Cheddar project, which included hunting for the rest of the
skeleton belonging to the famous Cheddar Skull, working for
days on end in the still, damp air of the caves to floodlight them

and finally, a year later, arranging a monster firework display to celebrate the completion of the scheme. For two young designers it was a fascinating experience, since we had to work out every detail including furniture and crockery, the waitresses' uniforms, the knives and forks and even the ashtrays. Now twenty-three years later the composition still looks fresh and unmannered although, just recently, when faced with a similar problem on a smaller scale at a second cave-mouth a little farther down the road I was to handle it quite differently as it lay close among houses built in the local style. Here I decided to make my small building in rough stone with pointed " Gothick " openings for the cave entrance and windows, and to cover the whole with ivy.

This first venture with Geoffrey Jellicoe led to a partnership which continued until war put a sudden end to it. Our first major clients were the Ronald Trees who had recently bought Ditchley Park, an eighteenth-century house built by James Gibbs, architect of St. Martin's in the Fields. Its new owners were keen gardeners and they asked Jellicoe to design a formal garden as a setting for the magnificence of the house. There was no garden and Gibbs's plans revealed nothing but a suggestion for a long grass terrace along the south front of the house. From this indication the terrace was made and divided by a wall of hornbeam from an elaborate sunken garden which was laid out below the east front. Jellicoe designed this as a simple box parterre ending in quite an elaborate semi-circular fountain basin, large enough to serve as a swimming pool. From eighteenth-century stone vases water plashed into the pool, and there were alternative arrangements of fountain jets which made a series of different combinations of playing water. This was a magnificent essay in the grand manner, spoilt only by the well-scaled box garden being abandoned at the owners' request in favour of a stone-edged parterre brought from Wrest Park. This last was, in fact, an over-intricate nineteenth-century design full of acute angles and almost impossible to plant simply and well.

Ditchley has since changed hands and I do not know what

remains of these elaborate gardens. But the main lines, the levels, the hedges and the rows of pleached lime trees will still be there to indicate an exceptionally well-organised composition, worthy neighbour to the splendours of Blenheim and the little-known gardens of Rousham Park which are an early and brilliant essay in landscape layout by Kent.

By now my approach to gardening had changed. The principles I had tried to understand in the details of planning and planting I had now to apply to larger problems of composition. During these few years before the war our work covered a wide range of problems. I remember, for instance, trying to work out a general planting guide for the admirable village of Broadway for which Geoffrey Jellicoe had made a development plan. This naturally involved the preservation of the existing charming and subtle relationship between the beautifully built stone houses and cottages and the treed hedgerows and hillsides of this most English of landscapes. But this kind of planning had to be a living, growing thing (if we were to avoid making a sterile museum piece). New housing, future factories, new roads and new planting had to be designed to further and accentuate the existing harmonies. Life, even so short a time ago, was relatively leisurely so that there was time to study each angle of the main street, to suggest a clipped yew, perhaps, for one cottage garden, a pear tree for another or a clump of hollyhocks for a third.

Another project at this time was for Charterhouse School on its plateau among the nightingale-haunted Surrey oakwoods. The school had grown beyond the limits of the symmetrical group of Victorian Gothic buildings erected to house it in 1872, into a largish community: a mixed collection of class-rooms, boarding houses, playing fields with chapel, museum, library, hall, armoury, pavilions and masters' houses. In the ensuing sixty years all kinds of traditions had been evolved. Every tree, every path, every short cut was sacrosanct to a whole series of taboos (based on all sorts of ritual distinctions) rigidly maintained by the conservatism of boys and masters. All these I knew, since I myself had been at school there. My problem was to rationalise the physical relationship of the various buildings and open areas with the problems of circulation, as well as to take into account the traditional uses of every square yard. Any proposal to cut down an old tree or plant a new one required endless lobbying. Finally, helped by the taste and the drive of the headmaster and his wife, Sir Frank and Lady Fletcher, the plan was approved by the masters, by the Governing Body and finally by the Governors; and at least some parts of it were carried out.

Although I had not been endowed with the qualities that make a successful public school boy, Charterhouse and its surroundings had always interested me. Miss Jekyll still lived in her house across the valley. Sir Edward Lutyens had built his first domestic buildings in the Bargate stone of the neighbourhood. He was to go on to make a profound study of the English Renaissance and absorb the classical principles of architecture so deeply and so well that his later buildings—currently, I think, underestimated—must eventually find their place as perhaps the last examples of the European classical tradition. His odd quirks of humour, the occasional impractical arrangement of bathroom or pantry, his possibly over-architectural and over-planted gardens cannot take away from his sheer mastery of materials, of volume and of proportions, or from the originality of his mouldings and the lively beauty of so many of his buildings. It is strange to realise that he was still practising at the same time as Gropius and le Corbusier and that much of his work was contemporary with Frank Lloyd Wright's *art nouveau* constructions.

Public and semi-public planning occupied us a good deal in the mid-1930's. The chaos of haphazard buildings and ill-conceived new arterial roads were already causing concern and we were often called in to advise on remedial planting. The Roads Beautifying Association, the Coronation Planting Committee, and various other public and private bodies, were trying to create a public interest and provide at least a palliative. I think that few people either then or since have really understood the nature of the problem; nor has there ever been in England an executive authority with power to impose a solution. Public planting and more particularly road planting has been regarded in England as a garden problem; that is, a site or a stretch of roadway has been designed to be viewed from various positions or walked through, whereas the effectiveness of road-side planting is only apparent when you are driving between thirty and sixty miles an hour. A mile of one kind of planting is almost the shortest effective length.

Meanwhile, garden fashions were changing. It may have been no longer possible even in the great houses to find the footman who would carry the wicker tables and chairs, the chintz cushions and all the shining silver paraphernalia of tea across the wide lawns to the cedars' shade. But for whatever reason, and because it was partly our speciality, we were increasingly asked to design paved terraces attached to the house where garden furniture, awnings, sculpture, fountains and plants in tubs would make an outdoor living-room. The second demand was for swimming pools. This was probably due to the popularity of the South of France as a place for summer holidays and the tremendous success of Eden Roc, whose ill-designed little pool had become a world-famous rendezvous for fashionable sun-bathers. Geoffrey Jellicoe's knowledge of, and taste for, formal garden design now began to involve us in rearranging English gardens to include these relatively new features in British gardens. In France and in Italy *perron* and *loggia* were the classic focus of every country house throughout the heat of the summer months; to re-think them in an English context was interesting and agreeable.

One of the first gardens we attempted was for the Duke of York at the Royal Lodge in Windsor Great Park, a Gothic *cottage orné* built by George IV. This had recently been enlarged and was painted a pale pink copied from a Strathmore house in Hertfordshire whose colour derived in turn from the family villa near Florence. Royal Lodge again became a royal residence and was, I might say " de-Victorianised " by our making a formal approach to the house. We also replaced a grassy bank on the garden side by a wide paved terrace facing across a sloping lawn to a wood planted with the rhododendron species which were a special hobby of both the Duke and his brother, then King, who gardened across the park at Fort Belvedere. Next to the terrace, a formally planned sunk garden, with beds designed in interlocking rectangles, was informally planted with old-fashioned roses and herbaceous plants and led in its turn to a swimming pool sited where the garden joined the larger scale of the park. To give privacy without loss of scale we used the earth excavated for the pool to make a high surrounding bank of grass which gave, too, some protection from the wind and, planted with birch trees, merged imperceptibly with the park. This was a successful small composition which after twenty-five years still falls harmoniously into place.

We made another sophisticated and rather sumptuous terrace for a fine white stucco Regency villa built by Decimus Burton on the Inner Circle in Regent's Park about 1830. Here the setting was a willow-shaded lawn sloping down to the lake alive with coloured sails; beyond lay the lovely townscape of Nash's terraces seen through the trees of the park. The fine decoration of this house was based on certain late Louis XVI rooms in the Prince Bishop's palace in Würzburg; and the owner had achieved a garden opalescent with pink hybrid perpetual roses, *Salvia turkestanica*, pale blue delphiniums and many kinds of lilies. Badly damaged by bombing, this property has now become part of Bedford College, another place I was to know later when it was used during part of the war by the B.B.C. It used to be a relief to escape from endless meetings and paper work into its modest botanic garden where various kinds of plants were displayed in a chess-board arrangement of beds.

Another town garden, this time among the old pear trees of St. John's Wood just north of Regent's Park, was the cause of my making a new acquaintance who was to become a close friend and colleague. When arranging this rather small garden I found myself concerned with the decoration of the house. Several decorators had between them achieved an inconsequent muddle which needed an expert hand to create some kind of order. The owners, at their wits' end, asked my advice. I remembered the harmony and brilliance of the interiors at Ditchley Park and, although I only knew the name of the man responsible, I suggested telephoning Stephane Boudin in Paris. He was on the site in a few hours and quickly sorted out the problems and found solutions which were enthusiastically accepted. This was a fortunate meeting for me and resulted in years of our making houses and gardens together.

The particular spark which started our long collaboration was a detail in this small London garden. I had just planted a long bed with orange-scarlet, crimson, vermilion, salmon and magenta geraniums spiced with enough white to make these clashing reds vibrate together. This combination caught Boudin's eye and may have been what decided him to call me over to France soon after to design gardens to complement the interiors he was designing for houses all over France. I was accustomed to the delaying, gentle, half-spoken, tentative British way of getting things done. Boudin's approach to his clients and their problems was a revelation to me and one which happened to suit my temperament. I began to learn from him how to be clear, rapid and competent when faced with a client, how to seize on the special qualities or limitations of a site, use them and turn them to advantage; and how, too, to use words to build up a picture and create the atmosphere and impetus which will give a project a flying start. Here was a man unable to draw a line who nevertheless was able to project his vast knowledge and experience of colour and form and proportion in terms of all the technical intricacies of interior design and decoration. Knowing his own field so well, when he turned his attention out of doors, he could understand the complications and possibilities of garden design without any specialised horticultural knowledge.

Within a week of the beginning of the war our practice ceased to exist and all my modest accumulation of plans, photographs and eighteenth-century garden books went up in flames in the first London blitz a year later.

Even at the time this sudden break seemed, paradoxically, fortunate. It interrupted a certain complacency induced by a success which, modest enough, held too superficial a glitter. The next years were passed in quite other occupations: gardening belonged, it seemed, only to the past; there was no future—only the pressing present. But the patterns of war shaped themselves for me into many and distant journeys, so that I was to learn something of the shape and look of various other parts of the planet.

My gardening education made little progress in two busy years spent in the Middle East. Spare hours were rare and there was much to see and study. I walked every alley and courtyard in old Cairo with Lady Russell, who was expertly searching in the dusty confusion of decaying hovels and crumbling walls for traces of the shape and form of the fabulous Palace of the Fatimids. I studied the excellent street planting in the newer parts of the city and in Zamalek where bauhinias and the Gold Mohur tree, *Poinciana regia*, and the amethyst blue jacaranda make avenues of lively colour. In the Gizeh zoological gardens, a nineteenth-century extravagance in the form of a romantic park made by the Khedive Ismail, was a magnificent collection of trees and plants, all new to me, also a series of serpentine ponds thick with lotus, loveliest of all aquatic plants. As to the fauna, what I remember best was the lustrous slate-grey plumage of the saturnine-looking shoebill, a rare wader from Upper Sudan, and a pale pink seagull.

In Cairo itself there were all the marvellous mosques to explore and sometimes I would sit quietly in one of them listening to a sheik chanting verses from the Koran—every sound vibrant with meaning and devotion. In Cairo in those days there were still traces of a more frivolous and charming architecture: palaces, kiosks and fountains in the Turkish rococo manner which dated from the early nineteenth century. Behind all of these lay the older Egypt, the marvels of the Egyptian

Museum and the mystery of the pyramid complex which stretches out on a low rocky ridge just where the cultivated land ceases and the desert begins. Once only I was able to take the train to Luxor. If there can be peace on earth, here is its home, and to see the sun rise over the Nile Valley is a lovely experience. The orange-gold trunks of palms and the white sugar-loaf cones of the pigeon-cotes emerge from a layer of opalescent mist and slowly all turns a pale gold and pale blue, the true colours of Egypt. My first impression of Luxor, of Karnak and Medinet Habu was one of weight and terror; only after long study has the integrity, the complete wholeness of every aspect of this great civilisation come to have meaning to me. At that time, only certain minor tombs and wall paintings seemed accessible and related to human life as I could know it. Later I was to learn more of all of this from Schwoller de Lubicz and Alexandre Varille who had given years to the study of the symbology employed in every aspect and detail of Ancient Egyptian art.

One day in Cairo I ran into Feliks Topolski on his way back from India with hundreds of his vivid pen and ink drawings. He encouraged me to start drawing again and for the next three years I made rapid drawings every single day, almost all with a fountain pen, although later I always kept watercolours in my pocket. In this way I was able to absorb, by the act of recording, the endless pageant of new impressions. Ceaseless practice gave me considerable facility, so that within a few months I was able to record with skill and speed the most complicated subjects. Only later I had to learn to sacrifice this facility in order really to study and understand and depict an object in space. Meanwhile, my pictorial diary served me well.

By the end of 1943 I was sent still farther East, over the Arabian deserts to Bahrein, then famous only for pearls, down the Persian Gulf over the splintered peaks of Baluchistan to Karachi, on over the Indus to Bombay and then to Cochin with its coconut palms and fishermen, and finally over the narrow straits to Ceylon, with its ancient cities of a former Buddhist civilisation buried in the tropical forests and the thin veneer of nineteenth-century British red brick architecture which has made Colombo as commonplace as Southsea or the Bronx. My base was Kandy and there I lived in a palm leaf hut on the edge of the sacred lake. Each evening I would listen to the magnificent drumming from the Temple of the Tooth across the water. We worked in the snake-ridden Botanical Gardens at Peradeniya. As the months went by I watched the forest trees burst into flower; first a shower of yellow followed by the blossoming of each species in its turn white, or rose or mauve. I had one special pilgrimage to make in Ceylon and that was to find the Buddha with the sapphire eyes which had so impressed Ouspensky[1] thirty years before. So one day I rattled down the mountainside in the little train to Colombo to find it. It is a reclining Buddha, some thirty feet long and wholly filling the pavilion which houses it. Because it is kept freshly painted in its bright saffron robes it is impossible to divine its age. It has to a greater degree than usual the time-lessness and the life of a major work of art. For me it has the same quality as the marvellous Chefren in the museum in Cairo, though with a different significance just as the extraordinary wooden " Ka " on the first floor of the same museum seems related by its intensity and vitality to the Etruscan Apollo of Veii in Rome.

When the war came to an end I found myself in Greece and on the day Japan capitulated I was on the island of Hydra where the little glistening white-washed town surrounds a shell-shaped harbour. As the radio announced the news I remembered what a fortune-teller in the Paris suburb of Asnières had said to me in 1939: " when the war ends you will be standing among white buildings."

My wartime travels were, in their own way, an important part of my education. Although I learnt little of plants or gardening, beyond discriminating between a good and an indifferent mango, I had learnt that life can be otherwise experienced than from the European point of view that had hitherto been my only measuring stick. Sitting in a Damascus

---

[1] P. D. Ouspensky, author of *A New Model of the Universe* etc.

café, in the bazaars of Cairo or Delhi, ignorant of the meaning of the talk going on around me I learned the pleasures of silence and how to appreciate the meaning of what was taking place without the need for verbal explanation. What little I was able to see of Mohammedan life convinced me that here was a religion which taught men how to respect themselves and their neighbour and one which helped them to find a human dignity irrespective of differences in rank or wealth. Once or twice, in the Bektashi monastery on its ledge in the Mokattam cliffs above the Citadel in Cairo and again on certain evenings spent watching the Mevlevi dervishes in Damascus at their exercises I caught glimpses of the inner meaning of the Islamic approach to God. In the turmoil of Indian cities I saw humility and love working like yeast in the daily commerce of life in spite of the meanness, greed and egotism which is as strong there as everywhere else.

Then four wartime years of intense activity, new scenes, new people, new impressions were over and I found myself in London without money or occupation. The rhythms and the urgency of the previous years had become a habit and for a while I was totally at a loss in a world to which I had become unused. Chance led me to a meeting with Oskar Kokoschka to whom I showed some of my wartime drawings. He took them, or perhaps me, seriously enough to wish to help me to find a new direction through painting. Struggling under his guidance with the problem of really drawing as I did for some months, was an illuminating and cathartic experience. To study the nature and form of the object in front of me gave me back the possibility of another kind of vision and another kind of discipline, and little by little a vast weight of accumulated superficialities fell away from me so that after some time I felt refreshed and quiet because I knew again that there is a continuing reality behind the appearances and problems of everyday.

It happened that I went for a few days to Paris to renew a certain contact, one which I hoped would help me to find myself and my true place. There I also met again my friend Stephane

Boudin. Within a week he had found some work for me and so I again began to garden.

It was not easy to start again. For several years I had been, like everyone else, a small cog in a large machine. Now I had to make my own policy, take my own decisions and stand on my own legs again. To discuss lawns and flower-beds at first seemed strange enough, and I had to learn to draw garden plans all over again. My first job, which was to plan a small garden in Paris, almost gave me sleepless nights, so lost and uncertain did I feel in a profession I had for years thought of as gone for good.

At first I floundered. Then one day I heard that an old friend, André de Vilmorin, whom I had not seen for many years, was lying ill in a Paris clinic. I went to see him. The Vilmorin family have been horticulturists and seed merchants for two hundred years and have lived for generations at the Château de Verrières south of Paris. Here, round a delightful Louis XIV house in whose garden still exists Louise de la Valliere's see-saw, the family have built up a colony of gardens, seed trial grounds, laboratories, a museum and an important horticultural library. It had always been an old-fashioned family business. The villagers working in the flower-fields still take pride in their work and a deep interest in the family and its fortunes. André de Vilmorin, who was now running the business, at once asked me to join it. He foresaw that there were going to be many gardens to make. Château life was finished, people would move into smaller houses, there would be fewer gardeners and a programme of reconstruction was already under way. Besides, during the war people had become used to gardening in order to eat; and to grow their own vegetables and fruit. They would turn now to flowers but in a new way. This was the time to popularise a kind of gardening new to French people. Together we planned to launch a campaign for small gardens of lawn and flowering shrubs and hardy plants, which would be easy to maintain with or without a gardener. We would have to introduce a whole range of plants new to France and make them widely known.

Within a few weeks I was installed in a small office overlooking the Seine, in a part of Paris that has perhaps changed less than any other. It is traditionally the centre of the Paris horticultural trade. Facing the river are all the seed merchants' shops with their stalls set out along the pavement full of packets of seed and many-coloured flowers and plants. Here and there are pet-shops with cages of exotic finches, golden pheasants, pigeons and every known race of fowl. On sunny summer days the foreign tourists come to lunch in the *bistrots* nearby to enjoy the bustle and chatter of the busy street, or cross the rushing stream of traffic to hunt in the booksellers' boxes which line the parapet above the river. Just below runs the Seine, and if you go down to the water's edge you come into another world. Here grass grows between the cobblestones, there are tall old trees and men sitting hunched over their fishing rods. Under the arches of the bridges there are the transitory bivouacs of the professional *clochards* with their red wine and their rags. It is a strangely country scene and a country river with its trees and tow-path caught for a few miles between the high stone embankment walls which shut out the clanging noisy city. This is the old heart of Paris which still, like a market town, retains its commerce with the countryside and here for the next few years I was to find my place.

Part One

CHAPTER I

In search of style

Garden-making, like gardening itself, concerns the relationship of the human being to his natural surroundings. The idiom has changed from place to place and from one period to another, whether we consider the smallest medieval herb garden, a tiny formal pattern set against the curtain wall of a fortified castle, or the enormous perspectives which Le Nôtre cut symmetrically through the gentle slopes and the forests of the Ile de France. Occasionally gardens have been used for a wider and deeper intention. A handful of men working within the Zen sect of Buddhism created gardens in fifteenth-century Japan which were, and still are, far more than merely an æsthetic expression. And what is left of the earlier Mogul gardens in India suggests that their makers were acquainted with what lay behind the flowering of the Sufi movement in High Asia and so sought to add further dimensions to their garden scenes.

I know that I cannot make anything new. To make a garden is to organise all the elements present and add fresh ones, but first of all, I must absorb as best I can all that I see, the sky and the skyline, the soil, the colour of the grass and the shape and nature of the trees. Each half-mile of countryside has its own nature and every few yards is a reinterpretation. Each stone where it lies says something of the earth's underlying structure; and the plants growing there, whether native or exotic, will indicate the vegetable chemistry of that one place.

Such things show the limitations of a site and limitations

imply possibilities. A problem is a challenge. I cannot remember a completely characterless site though, for example, a walled rectangle of sandy earth in the Nile Valley with not a tree visible would seem to qualify as such. So would a stretch of flat sugar-beet field in the industrial North of France with pylons of high tension wires standing across a bleak landscape relieved only by factory chimneys on the horizon. Even so you can always turn to something for a starting point. In the first (an actual case) the hot blue sky, cloudless all the year round, offered an easy answer —shade. A garden should be devised through which one would always walk in shade. Shade implied trees. A mango grove became the main theme of the garden and all its parts and details were subjected to the over-riding theme. For another reason trees, too, were the answer in the second case: not for shade, but to bring an illusion of wilder country into a man-spoilt landscape. Time was a factor here. The house was ugly and there was little labour available for the upkeep of a garden. I chose to plant young birch trees, and now, twenty years later, the house is veiled in a haze of birches light enough not to steal the sun, while their branches and the haphazard colonnade of their silvered trunks hide the ugly view.

Unlike painting or sculpture or buildings a garden grows. Its appearance changes—plants mature, some in six weeks, some in six hundred years. There are few gardens that can be left alone. A few years of neglect and only the skeleton of a garden can be traced—the modelling of the ground perhaps, walls or steps, a pool, the massing of trees. Japanese artists working with a few stones and sand four hundred years ago achieved strangely lasting compositions. However there, too, but for the hands that have piously raked the white sand into patterns and controlled the spread of moss and lichens, little would remain.

We live under an accumulation of periods and styles and cultures. The variations of artistic expression over the whole world for the last four thousand years are available, a vast store of information making a vast confusion. Architecture has found a way out through functionalism and has largely become applied

and often splendid engineering. Painters and sculptors, struggling
to free themselves from a top-heavy load, have experimented
with association-patterns dug from the different layers of their
consciousness.

I think that creative gardening need not suffer from these,
the results of a changing, if not a disintegrating culture. It can
begin from another point. A seed, a plant, a tree must each obey
the laws of its nature. Any serious interference with these and it
must die. It will only grow and thrive when the conditions for
it are approximately right. If you wish to make anything grow
you must understand it, and understand it in a very real sense.
" Green fingers " are a fact, and a mystery only to the unpractised.
But green fingers are the extensions of a verdant heart. A good
garden cannot be made by somebody who has not developed the
capacity to know and to love growing things.

Such intangibilities are facts and a whole new world waits to
be explored. Any starting point will do—a seedling in a three
inch flower-pot to grow into a magic beanstalk up which we can
climb to open a gate into another aspect of this world, just this
world which lies around us and in which we move perhaps quite
unsuspecting of its possibilities.

Processes have always given me more satisfaction than results.
Perhaps this is peculiarly English and may explain our national
affection for a pursuit which is always changing: growth and
decay, the swing of the seasons, our inconstant weather speeding
or retarding the development of a tree or the flowering and
seeding of a plant. English gardens seem to be always in flux. The
fugitive pleasures which gardening affords seem to be enhanced
for us by a subtle and deliberate disorder that softens the emphasis
of a straight line and never allows the garden to appear static or
achieved. A climate which favours the growing of plants from
all over the world must have contributed to the fact that the
English have been pioneers in the breeding and selection of
plants and domestic animals. A native dislike for a coldly logical
formulation, or the half termination of a spoken phrase, suggests
that a subject need never be exhausted; it is always in growth;

there is always room and time for further trial and adaptation.

Gardening in England seems like a slow process of wooing growing things into giving their best. There is no finality and there would be no satisfaction if there were. In France, the contrary would seem to be true. A pleasure garden since the time of du Cerceau or earlier has been a formal pattern laid out like a carpet; it extends the formalities of the salon into the open air. A " green drawing-room " or the " shade-room," a " theatre of greenery," inevitable parts of a classical garden composition, express the nature of a French garden quite precisely. That great designer Le Nôtre, however vast and ingenious his schemes, seldom departed from this rigid concept. Measure and clarity are essential to the French garden scene.

The Italian garden of the Renaissance started as an imaginative reconstruction of a classic grove—shade for walking and conversation and a setting for antique statues disinterred and standing as reminders of a classic golden age. Italian gardens with their trees, sculpture and fountains grew to reflect, in an ordered fashion, the busy life of a crowded countryside until the early eighteenth century, when the Bourbon influence brought the French style into fashion. Then in Italy—as well as in Austria—in the German principalities as far as East Poland and Russia and south into Spain—the spacious patterns formulated by Le Nôtre for other woods and skies degenerated into tasteless layouts imposed on landscapes for which they were not suited.

For the remainder of the eighteenth-century European gardens were dominated by the English " landscape " or romantic style. This was, on the whole, more adaptable to a variety of climates and landscapes and provided a more flexible setting in which to grow new plants from countries hitherto unknown. From then until now, I would say that in Europe plant material has been of far more importance than style in the evolution of gardens.

By the mid-nineteenth century eclecticism had destroyed the growth or continuance of style and the " museum " age was well

The windows of an eighteenth-century 'gothick' cottage
orné in a Berkshire kitchen garden surrounded with old red
brick walls, give on to a box-edged flower garden designed
in the same spirit. The beds are small and are intended for
bedding-out with spring and summer flowers. Their simple
repetitive pattern makes it easy to devise all kinds of planting in harmonising or contrasting colours

British tradition sets the great country house in a green
breadth of park but the rectangular forms of a Renaissance
house were originally reflected in a surrounding complex
of enclosed gardens. At Longleat, in Wiltshire, a grass
alley, clipped yew hedges, pleached limes and cypresses
give its original significance to the architecture of a corner of
this Elizabethan building in honey-coloured Bath stone

New stable buildings on the left, beyond, 17th century English piers and wrought iron gates lead into a walled garden. In the foreground an Italian well-head in pink Istrian stone is the focus of a garden in France. Carefully studied proportions and changes in level and an asymmetrical composition weld these disparate elements into an essentially garden scene

The stone-paved terrace of a house in the forests south of
Orleans looked too large and reflected too much light into
the main living-room. I removed the central part of the
paving and replaced it with diagonal bands of stone which
outline square sunk beds planted with dwarf box
clipped flat at ground level

started. Revival followed revival. Each country reconstructed lavish replicas: Renaissance, Louis XV, Tudor. Far removed in time and in thought from the makers of the original gardens, architects and designers wallowed in a sea of superficialities, and the essential weakness of their concepts was accentuated by indiscriminate planting. It seemed only too impressive to be able to pile the gorgeousness of exotic flowers on top of formal layouts, which originally had been rich in shape but designed with a strictly limited range of plant material in mind. Since we have inherited relics of all these styles and travesties of style, it is difficult to be free of this weight of association ourselves.

Yet it may be possible even now to make new gardens—new in the sense of refreshment. We have always the old and timeless elements of light and shade, earth, stone and water, foliage and flowers. Add houses for living, paths for walking, lawns for games, terraces and loggias for sun or shelter, water for swimming, for plants or for fountains. Using these, we can make gardens if we can understand the essential nature of the place, the principles underlying the patterns, and the cultural needs that make our plantings flourish.

There is a sixth sense which can " diagnose " a situation, understand the problem and, hence, " see " the solution. With practice this " flash of intuition " can be held for more than the usual moment. Its processes can be observed and understood at the time, and they can be recalled later. This faculty is of course a capacity not restricted to gardeners or artists and, if I use quotation marks to describe it, I do so merely because it is perhaps not ordinarily taken into account.

I know that in making gardens those which come the nearest to having a sense of unity and inevitability are those in which I have managed not to allow second thoughts or distracting details to blur the original theme. In one's own garden one has, in the end, only oneself to satisfy. I have had to remember that I have been making other people's gardens and that the garden must be theirs. People's wishes and hopes and requirements are contributory factors just like a clay soil, an oak wood, or lack of water. Where I have worked well the garden will be content to be itself and bear no obvious label.

To go a stage further; where does style start? Style for the garden designer means to assemble all the physical elements of a garden scene, to blend them into a coherent whole and to imbue this whole with all the intensity or, perhaps I should say "intelligence" that he can muster, so that the whole may have a quality peculiar to itself. Such style must be contemporary since, if a composition has style, it must reflect its maker's intention and its maker is necessarily of his own day, even though he may have chosen to give his garden an idiom derived from another place or another century. Here I would like to differentiate between real style and the eclectic use of a style borrowed from another period or another place. This will be a reflected mannerism deliberately imposed: a kind of design, a way of planting, selection of material, which belongs to that period or a place.

We might consider Le Nôtre, for example, as a seventeenth-century garden stylist who planned, designed and planted his many gardens in the framework of Louis XIV's France, her architecture and decoration, her repertory of plant material, her attitude towards religion, philosophy, and social problems. All these aspects of life influenced Le Nôtre, and so his gardens have style because he designed his creations inside the terms and the formulas of his day.

In the second half of the nineteenth century certain French industrialists, and others who had become immensely rich, tried to recreate houses and gardens with all the splendour of the late seventeenth and early eighteenth centuries. They either restored châteaux or built new ones which they thought to be precise and accurate facsimiles. Round these châteaux they built, or in some cases restored, enormous formal gardens. They used the original designs for these where they existed or else made new ones based on earlier models and paid slavish attention to every detail. Many of these gardens existed until the last war and a few have even survived until now. In every case their consciously adopted style is in competition with the style which was proper to the late nineteenth century. The coarseness of a moulding, the exactness with which a plan or a detail of design follows every convolution of a carefully executed and over-detailed working drawing, the use of wrought ironwork which looked like cast-iron, again, because of a perfection of technique, all these are without the freedom and life that an eighteenth-century stone-mason or smith would have given them. So any time or in any place contemporary styles and techniques are sure to make a pastiche of a style borrowed from another period. Such borrowings are fashions rather than styles and like all fashions sooner or later become dated and unfashionable.

Between the two wars the park of the Château of Sceaux near Paris was restored and reopened as a public park. Here again we see a reconstructed Louis XIV design, but this time rather differently handled. While the main composition remains unchanged, details have frankly been reconstituted in the Beaux Arts modern manner of the 1920's. But in this case too, even had there been an attempt to copy Le Nôtre's detail more exactly, this same modern manner must inevitably have crept in and flavoured the whole restoration.

The "landscape" style of garden which started in England in the early eighteenth century has been a dominant theme ever since wherever a European influence in houses and gardens exists. It is a style which has made a wider mark than the symmetries of the French grand manner. It has from its beginnings suggested movement. Planting accentuated hills or hollows and roads or paths curl away from the house inviting a walk. Where there were terraces to the great English country house, they were entirely architectural in their purpose and designed as bases for a monumental style of architecture.

For a garden as a place of rest one must look farther afield to countries where a Moslem civilisation has perpetuated an older tradition and designed gardens for sitting in shade or sun, for listening to the song of birds and the plashing of water, and for enjoying the scents of jasmine and rose and orange. This is a passive attitude towards a garden, but in the last thirty years the idea of the garden as a rest-place holds an increasing attraction. The tensions of modern life and an entire change in our ideas of scale and of speed have made physical tranquillity a luxury. Repose has become a rarity; we may well begin to accumulate and arrange the attributes of rest like stamps or sculpture. The idea of rest seems to be found increasingly in a no man's land between house and garden. More and more the idea " garden " invades the house, or the house roof spreads out to include the garden. It is current practice in the United States to continue a pool or a flower bed into the house or to let the terrace sweep in to pave the living-room. A whole open-air kitchen accompanies the open air grill, while contrariwise the house may incorporate the potting shed. In these new relationships, plants have to play a new role; leaves replace curtains and branches become an aspect of interior decoration. In tropical and sub-tropical climates the problem is easy to solve, but in colder climates this technique is more difficult. Cold weather must divide house from garden for some part of the year and, in the new idiom, the drawing-room becomes an air-conditioned green-house where exotic plants can look oddly out of place against the bare branches and snowy streets outside.

In other conditions the Japanese have solved the problem. Centuries ago they developed a style of visual harmony through which the house with its furnishings, the garden, paintings, textiles, pots and pans were all made subject to an order of ideas.

In Europe, every object with which we surround ourselves, every proportion of architecture, table or chair, all the products of the last thousand years have in general a disconnection which makes this kind of harmony impossible. In the United States a limited and provincial European culture was already outdated a hundred years ago by the rapid growth of a new people in a new continent. Now styles from all over the world chase each other through the American scene, to be tried, accepted, modified and then discarded. A current tendency is to throw out all traditional European styles and to arrange houses and gardens so that their maintenance may take an absolute minimum of time and labour.

In the contemporary Pacific Coast style boulders, pebbles, sand, and sections of tree-trunks used as stepping-stones are the fittings of a kind of permanent stage-setting. Trees, shrubs and plants are the growing accessories. They are used to relate car-park to swimming pool, boundary fences to the landscape beyond the garden, and all of these to the house. Such formulas fulfil the demand for fairly simple maintenance and a degree of æsthetic satisfaction, though whether they will prove enduring I do not know. Perhaps it will turn out to have been one more example of a grafted exoticism in a civilisation which originally derived from Europe, and which was imposed on this vast continent rather than growing from its soil.

One of the more involved garden styles is that of the English garden at the turn of this century. If you analyse a group of important English gardens constructed at any time between 1900 and 1930 you will see that they are based on designs borrowed from every period of European garden design. Terraces, stair-cases, fountains and architecture derive largely from the late Italian Renaissance; courtyards, green plots and topiary work, come mainly from late seventeenth-century Dutch models. For parterres and the layout and design of flower beds, garden-makers went to Gothic manuscripts, to du Cerceaux or to Kip's engravings of country seats or to the embroideries of Le Nôtre. To all these stylistic or fashionable influences rich and enthusiastic gardeners added picturesque themes such as wild-gardens, alpine gardens, heather gardens and bog gardens; they used all these elements to frame the widest range of plant material ever cultivated in any one country at any one time. The spirit of this luxurious horticultural " never-never land " has continued, and has coloured most British and some continental thinking about garden design until to-day. Here is a style that, as all high fashion must, has spread and degenerated until its mannerisms now inform popular gardening magazines with their ready-made solutions for the small garden: the formal rose beds centred on a sundial, the bird baths, planted crazy paving, and other relics are echoes of the expensive and, to our eyes, perhaps somewhat blowzy formalities of fifty years ago.

Garden designers, like all artists, need nourishment; they need to exchange ideas, to study plans and photographs of new work and to visit gardens; in short, to acquire an education and a wide documentation. All these, all of the garden designer's vocabulary and art, can be either valuable or useless. It is so easy to be glib, to accumulate material, to pigeonhole it neatly and then to make a selection more or less suitable to the occasion and the site—and then to assemble a garden plan with a bird bath taken from Copenhagen, a flight of steps from Italy, some informal planting from Zurich, and a herbaceous border from Miss Jekyll. Shaken up into a new pattern these elements will titillate and satisfy a sentimental and uneducated idea as to what a garden should be. But a ragbag of styles has nothing to do with real style; for this the process of designing must be very different. The designer will have to see what lies behind the pictorial or superficial aspect of what he is studying. Is this or that feature where it is because it is necessary and useful, because it underlines some compelling rhythm or form or shape or pattern? Does it have an idea connected with form or light or shade or colour or texture; or is it merely a more or less decorative whimsy, copied from elsewhere and with no real relevance? Technical and semi-technical magazines are full of seductive photographs whose charm must be sternly rejected if one is to analyse the underlying structure and rhythms of the scene. The brain will already register the facts presented to it on two levels. The superficial picture will only make its impact on that part of the brain where passing impressions leave their mark; the results of careful and selective study leave a deeper trace.

It is not too difficult to design architectural features for a

54

garden connected with an old house, or in any setting whose period is strongly marked. You should avoid making your architectural or ornamental motifs more elaborate than the existing architecture. Nor, I think, should you use any other materials: stone or brick should be the same as those that are there already. It is easy now to bring materials from any distance, perhaps easier than to find them locally. But when the house was built, distance may have been an insuperable obstacle, and by ignoring such a factor you risk destroying the integrity and harmony of your scheme. Of course you may reject these considerations if you like, but then you must do it deliberately and make your intention quite clear. Otherwise, I repeat, stick closely to the materials already in use on the site, and in designing details try always to be at least as simple as your models.

In any house of any period you will find a simplification of handling which spreads out from the centre. Gatehouse or portico, the state apartments of a great country house or villa, the discreet emphasis of a front door or drawing-room in a smaller house, the quality of the furnishings of the living-room of a modern house: all are simplified in the treatment of out-buildings or garage. So, as architecture spreads outwards into the garden it has, historically, tended to become simpler in form and usually slightly coarser in handling.

I can of course think of at least two palaces where this is not the case. Garden gateways, pillars, urns and wrought iron at Hampton Court are just as exquisite in workmanship as any detail within the palace; yet to my mind the atmosphere of the garden suffers from the over-refinement of these adjuncts. Versailles is another enormous exception; but the park of Versailles was conceived as an extended setting for a hieratic and elaborate court ceremonial. You have to seek out the *potager* or the remains of the great wall and gateways which surrounded the whole park and the neighbouring forest of Marly to find the beautiful limestone from the Clamart quarries handled with complete simplicity. The kitchen garden walls and pillars, for example, although they respect classic proportions, are simplified to their barest expression, and wrought iron gates and grilles are of the plainest vertical and horizontal bars with never a leaf or a scroll.

Since we do not live in a period of palace building the examples I have taken may sound irrelevant. But I see too many gardens spoilt because stone is rashly introduced into a country-side where brick is the universal building material and vice versa. In the same way new materials—concrete, synthetic stone, glass, mosaic, faience and plastics—all have their uses and possibilities, but only where they are not used in a context with traditional or historical associations. To use these new materials carelessly is to risk dating a garden, for without the most brilliant and yet restrained handling they will indicate " fashion " rather than style and so will become fatally unfashionable in twenty years. Only if the garden survives a half-century or longer, might they achieve " quaintness " and have the dubious charm that the bark-houses, ferneries and felspar grottoes of a hundred or more years ago sometimes still exercise on the romantically-inclined spectator.

Statues and vases gave excitement and richness to gardens which were mainly green and devised as exercises in light and shade, in symmetry and order. Nor must we forget their significance as emblems. Flora and Sylvanus, Cupid, Niobe, Laocoön and Hercules, the classic personifications of human, superhuman and natural attributes, had a significance and a wealth of associations for the mind of renaissance man. Now they can raise only a mild æsthetic appreciation of their quality as sculpture. Their use would only seem justified in the deliberate reconstruction of a classical composition.

I find the juxtaposition of flowers and representational sculpture often too cloyingly sweet. A leaden copy of a Verrocchio boy and fish emerging from a stone-edged lily-pond under the pink sprays of a Dorothy Perkins rose differs only in quality from a painted concrete gnome fishing in a bird bath surrounded with red salvia or blue lobelia. Flowers, the ephemeral sexual display in the yearly cycle of a plant's life, are richness enough in the garden picture. To add further ornamentation is to distract. This does not mean that gateways and steps, pools, summerhouses, pots, tubs, lighting fixtures or sundials should have no place. These are legitimate fixtures and necessary elements in garden composition. I would always want to design them simply, as simply as possible, and to see that in both material and design they accorded with any buildings near. Only if the site lends itself to a garden scene which can be isolated from the general mood of the surrounding landscape would I permit myself the extravagance of a " folly," an exotic garden structure or ornament made to point or accentuate a deliberately " escapist " garden.

Let us decide to see our problem in terms of a small garden attached to a small house. Even in our changing world, stunned as we are into stupidity by the mass media of communication and uprooted by the facilities of modern transport, the human instinct to have one's own house and one's own plot of land survives as a primary aim. I am not here concerned with town planning or the landscaping of housing schemes. These are a useful and perhaps a beautiful expression of civic consciousness which respond to other demands but they do not fill the individual's need for his own land and his pleasure in its cultivation.

An average small house is likely to have an average small garden and this fact immediately suggests that we must shape and style the garden as it will be seen from the house. The importance of the house in its garden setting as seen from outside will be of secondary importance. Our ways of living differ from country to country. For a European a garden has a different meaning than for a North American. Do you want to grow your own flowers and vegetables, make a collection of plants or specialise in one or another form of horticulture? Does your garden represent just so much more living-space for pool, outdoor dining-room and children's playground? Do you want to create a pictorial composition private to yourself, or do you want to draw in the landscape beyond the garden and use your plot to make a frame for the world outside? Whatever your choice or your need, it is such considerations that will determine your limitations and so establish a first foundation for style.

In the small garden much depends on the simplicity of its theme. Even in a large garden an underlying general theme is necessary however many subsidiary themes you may care to introduce. In a quite small garden one is enough, and it should be deliberately expressed if its details are to fall into their right places and not distract. If you intend to make an enclosed garden you must plan and plant and build with that idea uppermost; if at any point you decide to open it up in any way, then this opening must serve only to emphasise the enclosure of the whole. Or perhaps you will intend your garden to be the frame and threshold of the landscape beyond. In that case your garden must reflect your " borrowed " landscape. Gardens whose purpose is to raise crops of vegetables or flowers should be firmly enclosed in formal limits whether of hedge or fence or wall, which will protect them and at the same time leave them open to the sky. In how many gardens, large and small, have I noted an indecision where one part of a garden meets the next? Flowers merge into vegetables, vegetables into shrubbery, wobbly planting tries to camouflage yet only accentuates what it is meant to hide; or colour confuses where a plain and solid green would simplify.

Scale too is also a part of style. You must establish a scale by relating it directly to the purposes to which you plan to put your land. If you would bring the landscape beyond into your garden and, as the Japanese have expressed it, " borrow " a distant hill or your neighbour's trees, you will use features which are in scale with these outside elements and at all costs avoid the " interesting " details which, in this kind of composition, can only distract. In such a context most flower-colour distracts and when there is a distant view carelessly used colour will destroy the whole meaning of the garden. Consciously or unconsciously, both eye and mind will shift from flowers to view and back again and find no rest.

The problems of scale are easier to resolve in the small gardens devoted to growing crops of flowers or vegetables. You will make paths no wider than necessary and the dimensions of your beds will emerge from the cultural needs of your crops.

Hardest to handle is the scaled-down or miniature garden. Such a garden is a *tour de force*, compelling enough in those rare cases where it works, but more usually disastrous. Certain masters in Japan who gardened, as they fenced or wrestled, prayed or arranged flowers—that is, with a different and higher purpose than the mere exercise of technical virtuosity—seem to have achieved the next-to-impossible in this microcosmic form, although I have only been able to judge from photographs, which are notoriously unreliable evidence. Nor must we forget that the viewing and appreciation of these Japanese gardens was also almost a ritual, and an essential part of their calculated and magical effect.

In the British Isles, at least, one form of miniature garden is endemic. That is the artificially introduced rock or alpine garden in all its forms, whether a bank set with chunks of broken concrete, or the faithful reproduction of a few yards of alpine scree or moraine, or an elaborate composition of carefully bedded rocks with mountain cascades and discreet and reticent planting. I too have worshipped for many years at such shrines; but the enjoyment of this kind of gardening is an act of faith. Here you must deliberately subtract yourself from the surroundings, change the focus of your vision, and enter into the small and exquisite world of alpine plants where pebbles and grains of sand have a crystalline intensity, where the flowers of gentian and eritrichium seem to contain both lakes and sky, and where two large stones and a trickle of water are as mysterious as a Himalayan gorge. But this is a game of make-believe and, try as you may by design or by planting to lead down to the reduced scale of such a garden, it remains an anomaly and thus an enemy of style.

Of course no style and no scale have any real validity. They are only measures, concepts of the mind. Consider any natural landscape, a glade among the towering trunks of great beech-trees, a rocky river bank or the crest of a wild hillside: these have their own scale, the scale either of the vegetable kingdom or of a long-distant geological upheaval. We have only to introduce into any of these scenes a line of flagstones or a thatched roof on four wooden posts, and we at once create a humanised landscape. The flagstones will be convenient for walking on, and the thatched roof will shelter a man from rain or sun. The Chinese landscape painters of the Sung period have most beautifully illustrated the relationship of the scale of man to the scale of landscape. In a wild landscape of inaccessible mist-shrouded peaks the tiny figure of a sage meditating in the shade of a tree, a boatman guiding his craft along a rushing torrent, or a traveller crossing a frail wooden bridge is enough to humanise and give scale to an entire countryside.

Thus in a small garden designed to " borrow " the world beyond its boundaries, a few carefully placed trees or clumps of foliage, an uncluttered groundwork of grass or sand or low green planting can be correctly scaled to the outer scene, while a simple seat or a few carefully set paving stones will be enough to indicate that this is a humanised landscape, in fact a garden.

We might now consider the small garden where horticulture takes second place to the pleasures and needs of out-of-door living. Yet this is not a new kind of landscape. Pliny's gardens derived doubtless from earlier Babylonian and Persian and Egyptian precedents; and the patios of the Arab civilisations were enclosed courtyards where the activities of the household took place under the open sky.

In the climates of California, Texas and Arizona (as I have already indicated) a new garden form is evolving whose pattern is moving eastwards towards Europe and south towards the Latin Americas. This formula or theme is based on the admission that space for car-parking, the swimming pool and its surround, the children's playground, the out-of-door dining-room and kitchen, and the potting-shed and salad-ground, may take up perhaps three quarters of the area. The new tendency is no longer to consider them as necessities infringing on precious garden space but as a form of gardening or, if you prefer it, landscaping.

Here seems to be a new kind of scale—relatively large scale units so inter-related as to make a composition in themselves. As all these separate elements require level space, a special style emerges from the combination of interlocking horizontal areas which may well be set on different levels. In practice these spaces have to be hard-surfaced, and thus the varied uses of stone, brick, concrete or wood flooring make their own contribution to style. The usual materials of a garden—grass and flowers, shrubs and trees and hedges—at once become as precious as islands, rare enough to " tell " in themselves. The shape and space of each unit is not arbitrary but operational. A certain amount of space is required for cooking and eating, and that space must be shaped in a workable way, as must be the area for parking and turning cars, the space for a pool and sunbathing, the adequate run-back behind a springboard, the working room for a potting shed, greenhouse or bath-house and so on. To these you must add the problems of sun and shade, of protection and the cultural require- ments of whatever plants there are. These are new needs which will scarcely fit into the traditional shapes of Western garden design. You cannot disperse these new features within the framework of flower-bordered lawns, formal rose-gardens or woodland glades. From the proper working and just relationship between each part an " abstract " kind of patterning will evolve. You may call it " abstract " in the sense that modern painting is called non-representational. But in this case the asymmetrical forms, the relation of angles and straights and curves, will be based on the need to find a pattern which is both practical and adapted to the shape and contours of the garden area.

In gardens on a sloping site these shapes become strongly three-dimensional: a flat wooden deck may overhang a lower paved level; steps, stairs and ramps act as lines of communication. In gardens which are developed in this way, the basic shapes may be rich enough and strong enough to be left alone to tell their own story and planting should be simple enough to remain in scale. Style will again emerge from the intentional contrasts of growing plants—of organic life—set against the inert and static nature of wall and paving and carpenter's work.

We must draw a very clear distinction between style and decoration. I could consider no modern garden even remotely interesting as a work of art unless it could stand as such, stripped of every single purely decorative attribute. A garden artist will only use decoration to heighten the style, that is, the idea from which his whole construction has sprung. If he incorporates decorative adjuncts and accessory details, however picturesque, which are not directly related to his theme he will run the risk of diminishing the creative quality he should be seeking.

This way of looking at garden design does not necessarily imply rigidity or austerity. It does not mean that, if the main lines of a composition are right, the detail may be left to take care of itself. On the contrary, there must be a carefully worked out sequence of relationships on an ever-diminishing scale. Every form, from the main lines of the composition down to the last small plant or bulb, must be deliberately related and any decorative element must be precious by reason of its rarity and the skill used in its choice and setting. Fashion, it is true, has turned away from realistic classical sculpture, from balustrades and sundials, from elaborate wrought iron gates and the expensive adjuncts of the pleasure-grounds of the last three centuries. Yet the misunderstanding about the use of decorative garden ornaments continues even though the fashion has changed. It is very tempting to set a group of carefully chosen and beautiful stones on a space of pebble and sand and evolve a Kyoto garden in a London backyard, or wreathe a piece of abstract sculpture with arching sprays of *Rosa filipes*, or achieve movement by a trickle of water emerging from an artfully placed clump of bamboos. Such tricks are harmless and perhaps engaging enough in themselves; but a garden designer will do well to reflect before he indulges in a *tour de force*.

I have set myself one or two simple rules. First of all, I try to put myself in my client's place and imagine that I have to spend the rest of my life with the garden which I am going to lay out—in other words, that I am designing and planting as though for myself. This at once clears the field of all kinds of fancies and conceits. If I insist on indulging in them they will either remain to reproach me or else be cleared away as evidence of my incompetence.

Next, I consider the use that will be made of a garden. Is it a city garden in view from the windows for nine or ten months in the year and, if so, how quickly would I tire, for example, of a fountain dripping throughout the dark winter months? Should I avoid planting ideas which would mean spaces of bare earth for weeks on end? For a week-end cottage, seldom to be enjoyed for more than three days at a time, my attitude to pure decoration will be more elastic; I may try to design and plant to produce a succession of small surprises to emerge into more or less prominence at intervals throughout the year.

So time becomes an important aspect of garden design in more senses than its mere passage through the seasons which bring the garden to growth, maturity, decay and rejuvenation. In the days when men could live their lives out on their own acres, they built and modified their gardens with another rhythm of awareness, with perceptions and impressions which they accumulated and absorbed gradually. Now the habits and patterns of our civilisation impose a staccato and more shallow comprehension. There seems to be time only to look, note and look away. Outside pressures distract; nourishment for our mind and feelings becomes ever more meagre. It is a gardener's pleasure, as it could be the designer's privilege, to break this crazy rhythm, to change and break the rush of time, and make the garden a quiet island in which a moment has a new meaning.

Every designer needs to experiment, to try out new ideas, but he has to choose a field for his exuberance with care. In the modern world, exhibitions can give him just this chance. Here he will work for a spectator who comes, glances or takes a longer look, and passes on. At a flower show or garden exhibition this may be an expert whose attention will be drawn by some unexpected combination of colour, some new method of presentation. At an international exhibition the spectator is so soon stunned by the diversity and quantity of visual impressions that the garden designer's subtlety and restraint are apt to pass unnoticed; only the unexpected will bring the visitor to a full stop to look and look again and be refreshed.

There are aspects of landscape and garden design in which movement and time have to be taken into account in a different way. As in a large garden, a designer will plan and plant a public park as a series of pictures which melt one into the other as they are seen by people moving at a walking pace. When he has to landscape a natural park which may cover many square miles, or a parkway or an arterial road, he must realise that the scene will flow past at perhaps forty miles or more an hour and so think of his plantings and vistas (as I have said before) in terms of yards-seconds. Too small a group of trees will appear as a point rapidly smudged off into a blur. Should he want to emphasise, for instance, the essential quality and growth of Lombardy poplars he might need a half-mile or a mile of straight road for a motorist to register and have time to enjoy their green columns, while a winding road or a sharp corner will slow the driver's speed enough for him to enjoy a smaller group of beech or maple. In hilly country, where the eye can look down into a river valley or an estuary or across to a distant panorama of hills or mountains, the designer will make openings of an adequate length. How often, driving where it would be inconvenient or impossible to stop, is one distracted by a view which opens for only a second instead of a minute or two—time to register the impression more fully. Severer critics of our modern habits and our laziness might deplore such concessions. But these are our patterns of living; why then should we not, when we can, modify or design the public landscape accordingly?

Simple stone steps lead to the paved terrace of a modern
house on a hill top above Cannes. In the strong Mediterranean light the classical shapes of rows of locally made
flower pots in pale ochre-reds give a strong rhythm of light
and shade. In winter they are filled with cinerarias and
cyclamen, which are later replaced by anthemis, geraniums
and petunias during the summer months

A detail from a terrace high above the sea near Villefranche-sur-Mer in the South of France. The colours of furniture, awnings and planting are restricted to pale blue, white and green. Wooden plant boxes painted grey-green to match the shutters of the house contain standard orange trees and the large flower pots white oleanders and white petunias

Road-scapes are a special problem and, when we have to interfere with old ones or construct new ones, we have to work within the given data; and these must include the speed of traffic. There can be few roads as successfully landscaped as those made through the hilly forest landscapes of Westchester County and Connecticut, north of New York, where the natural landscape is skilfully accentuated by considered plantings on the largest scale. By contrast, the sheer engineering skill and the brilliant grading of the wide express ways which to-day quarter Long Island are obscured by a sort of scavenger's no-man's-land—a suburban confusion which lines them for miles on end.

Each city has its underlying style, expressed in a clutter of decoration good or bad. The rock of the Acropolis was the Athenians' focus for contact with the higher powers. In Venice the sea which brought her wealth laps palace and cathedral and the city's square. In Florence architecture and statuary, bronze and marble in a vulgar confusion of masterpieces, symbolised the avid city-state. Bruges, London, New York are revealing human landscapes, each in turn picturing the lives and aspirations of her citizens.

Now a new humanised landscape common to the whole planet seems to emerge. The airport is the first visual expression of our admission that the whole world is our home. Underlying all the to-ings and fro-ings of power politics, the overhanging threats of war and annihilation, is an awareness of the new physical shape and scale in which we will live out our lives. Idlewild, Orly, Cointrin, Schipol, Cairo and Basra: these are the new centres.

Lying between snow-covered mountains, on the fringes of the great cities, alongside the sea or out in the desert, these places have a new scale. The flat concrete runways stretch away for miles shimmering in the heat, shining rain-splashed or lined with beads of light. In the distance planes fly off or alight like insects and come wailing in towards the apron; spare metallic forms tower high above the narrowed horizontal perspectives of the landscape. The airport buildings tend more and more towards an architecture which resolves the old problems of roofing and thrust and weight, by construction as bold and spare and light as the aeroplanes themselves. Car parks, conveyor belts, lines of circulation all make a new kind of pattern designed for human beings in movement, the public address systems perpetually summoning people to go from one place to another. Travellers appear freed of their accumulations of property and reduced like medieval pilgrims to a minimum of baggage; the new bazaars sell only what can be dropped into a pocket. Men, as always, are keeping their appointments in Samara, but they take a new road.

This may seem remote from the landscape architect or the garden designer and his business. But if he is an artist, and he must be, it is his business to observe life and people; he must try to understand them and select from and transmute his experience first into design and then into reality.

CHAPTER II

Notes on composition and design

The art of composing a garden is a question first of selection and then of emphasis. When I make a composition for any site, large or small, I marshal all the attributes of that site and arrange them in my mind in what I think to be their order of significance. I try to see what the site contains in itself: is it essentially flat and horizontal with receding planes which appear to be parallel to each other, or are there gentle curving slopes? Do trees and hills form rounded masses or is it a jagged broken landscape with strong vertical accents? Or have I to deal with a small plot of ground whose borders are sharply visible or a narrow strip thickly treed and with no sharply defined limits?

Just as the nature and arrangement of its vegetation will qualify a site, so will the structure and content of the soil and the lie of the land; but it is this last which will give me my first key to a suitable composition. If, for instance, I distil from the scene before me the idea of flatness, I may choose to make this flatness the basis of planning and think in terms of level spaces. This certainly would not mean my forcing the site into flat monotony; I may make many changes in level using low walls, banks and wide and shallow steps to define the different spaces, since the consequent horizontal lines will each further emphasise my basic theme. As I try out various rough sketch plans on paper, this idea of flatness will underlie and inform all my scribblings. I have to keep three dimensions always in my mind and indeed the gardener's fourth—growth in time.

Horizontals play a large part in all garden design if only because they can set a house firmly in place and suggest stability and repose. One only notices the importance of this where calm has been sacrificed for more eccentric and " picturesque " ends. Buildings or groups of buildings were invariably set on levelled spaces until the builders of the romantic period broke away from classical formulae. Linderhof and Hohenschwangau in Bavaria, Bussaco and Monserrat in Portugal, and hundreds of other châteaux, villas and palaces of the middle and late 1800's rise in tortured confusion on the peaks of jagged hill tops or are buried in a labyrinth of exotic conifers. One marvels at these strange edifices. They seem complicated and confused enough to tremble where they stand, as though they might lose balance and topple at any moment. Yet these concoctions set a style for a whole architecture of pleasure; and more modest nineteenth-century chalets and villas, Gothic, Italianate or arabesque, remain in their thousands perched on high grassy mounds or on *glacis* of laurel, to be reached by steep serpentines of gravel.

At one time, most of my practice seemed given to simplifying the settings of country houses by making level space around them, building terrace walls to replace difficult and ugly grass slopes and anchoring houses in their surroundings by horizontal patches and lines of hedging. Looking back, I remember that we stabilised, in this way, quite a variety of houses. When I was working with Geoffrey Jellicoe on the stucco Regency house in Regent's Park by Decimus Burton, where curling walks, sloping banks and clumps of laurels were replaced by a wide paved terrace and formal rose garden rather in the Repton manner. I have heard that Le Nôtre always insisted on a large space next to the house, its width equal to the height of the building from ground level to cornice. To me this has often seemed too much: if treated (as it often was and still is) as an empty expanse of gravel, so much bare space tends to isolate a building from its surroundings.

Levels play a major part in composition and usually require discreet rather than dramatic handling. I prefer on the whole to adapt my plan to the general contours of the site than make dramatic and artificial earthworks. By doing too much violence to the existing lie of the land one risks destroying a harmony which will be difficult to recapture. Since I enjoy plants, I also like working on a site where the ground rises away from the house. Such a situation enables one to see more of one's plantings, and the play of light and shade seems richer and more interesting when one looks up and through rather than down and over.

Whether the garden goes up or down, and where there is not too steep a slope, you will arrange for winding paths and broken planting if you want to keep the scale of your garden undetermined. Straight paths, retaining walls, and steps will, on the other hand, define and accentuate your design. Steps which are high and short give a staccato rhythm; when wide and shallow they invite a more leisurely promenade. If your walls are low and your flights of steps short you can use wide or narrow ranges of steps as you choose and set them either into the walls or boldly jut them out. Where retaining walls exceed five feet, flights of steps at right angles to your walls are apt to look pretentious unless your garden is in the grand manner and on the largest scale. In such places narrow flights parallel to a wall look less pompous, they are less difficult to climb, and there are many different ways of arranging them. Long flights should be interrupted by landings since more than ten steps without a break appear arduous, though a long flight is permissible for effect where it is not constantly used.

Quite small changes in level are a great help in arranging the proportions, and a retaining wall, however low, is a simple way of giving a sense of structure and vitality. To help the work of the garden a flight of steps can be broken by a sloping stone or brick ramp set in the middle, so that a wheelbarrow can be taken easily from one level to the next.

On a sloping site a breadth of level ground next to the house is essential. Without it a garden always appears to be tumbling away from, or down on to, the house. Whether the ground rises or falls I prefer terraces of different widths. If the run of the ground demands a series of terraces of even height and width, then I like to break this repetition by a different treatment at each level. One might be all grass and another have a line or two of flowering trees or a border of shrubs to make it look narrower.

Gardens laid out on terraces falling away from the house are seldom much visited. A single additional level below that on which the house stands is usually enough on steeply falling ground. Where, however, there is a series of terraces joined by flights of steps I always prefer to arrange an alternative way of returning to the house.

At the drawing-board, I work out my composition in terms of levels. I try out the proportions of each level space or compartment in relation to the next, and decide how best to divide them, whether by a wall, by steps, or by hedges or by some other method. I have to foresee, too, what vertical features will most justly emphasise my horizontal theme: there must be enough to give point but not so many as to obscure my main intention.

I remember staying many years ago in Norfolk at the house of Mrs. Villiers-Stuart, a distinguished amateur of garden design, whose studies of Mogul and Hispano-Moresque gardens are models of perceptive analysis. Beachamwell Hall was a simple country house with no architectural pretensions, set in equally simple gardens in a flat and quiet landscape, half park, half pasture. Mrs. Villiers-Stuart gave this ordinary scene the character and intensity of a garden layout in the grand manner by the simplest of devices. Where a lawn ended and a flower-bordered kitchen garden began, she set a plain but well-designed pair of painted wood-railed gates; from these a straight path led through the kitchen garden to its far end where the same gates were repeated to open into a paddock. Beyond the paddock was a little wood through which a narrow path had been cut on the

axis of the straight kitchen garden walk. Here she placed two
more pairs of gates—one at the beginning and the other at the
far end of the wood. These four pairs of simple wooden gates
were sufficient to give definite character to a rather featureless
site. This was a subtle and modest experiment in the grand
manner which exactly suited the place. This piece of design has
stayed in my mind, for it had the rarest and, to my mind,
most desirable quality of garden design—that of being a
" sketch."

It is relatively easy for any competent designer to establish
a composition, make a garden design and elaborate all its parts
down to the last detail. Europe is full of elaborate formal gardens
of all periods, from the sixteenth century on, in all the styles
which come to one's mind. I must admit that I find many of
them dull. The exceptions are those where some freak convolution in the ground has meant an improvisation or invention and,
hence, originality of treatment; or those where a special quirk
of mind or temperament has been at work, as with Robbillon at
Queluz near Lisbon, Cuvilliers at the Nymphenburg near Munich,
or the designer of the early seventeenth-century water gardens at
Hellbrun near Salzburg. But just as I like the landscape drawings
of Claude Lorraine, Fragonard and Hubert Robert far more than
the elaborate paintings which they evolved from them, so I like
garden compositions, and particularly those in the grand tradition
of formal gardening, when they are indicated rather than underlined, blocked out in their main masses but left unelaborated. I
find the *abreuvoir* at Marly, which must be one of Le Nôtre's last
works, all the more poetic for being deprived of its sculptures.
Now, in its half-ruined state, its intention and its relation to the
site is left clear and stark. It is as touching a witness as I could
wish to see of the essence of Le Nôtre's talent for form and
proportion.

Where a site suggests to me a long straight axis, I try to keep
this axis as narrow as I can, proportionately to the area I have to
deal with. Perhaps it will be a narrow path running level, or
rising and falling with the lie of the land. Should the ground rise

and then fall away out of sight from the main viewpoint the highest point may serve for a change of direction—a new alignment of the axis. But for this kind of composition the main axial line should, in most cases, be carried through as far as possible. Such straight lines focus the attention and give direction to a garden design—you may interpret them in a hundred different ways.

Harold Peto made just such an axial composition in the park at Buscot near Faringdon, where a wood runs down to meet a wide ornamental lake in a typical eighteenth-century park. From some distance back in the wood you look down a long narrow enclosure framed in yew hedges with curved and rectangular bays which repeat the formal lines of a narrow canal or rill set in grass and bordered with the simplest of stone edges. This canal reflects the sky and draws the shining levels of the lake into the wood. If you stand by the lake and look back, the lines of water and clipped grass and hedge that lead into the wood break a dull wall of foliage and invite you to explore.

As I search out shapes and themes and block them out on paper I shall perhaps give little conscious thought how I am going to express them in detail. Only as I translate these generalised shapes into a definite design will I decide whether to work out a long vista as a pathway or perhaps as a narrow and placid pool; or whether I shall need steps or perhaps a minor cascade of tumbling white water. I may emphasise the changing nature of each part of the garden through which a path passes by gates or piers or clipped or fastigiate trees. These are secondary problems of emphasis and design, and they follow from the general composition. But the main theme must be easy to read and, at each stage of the transformation of a rough sketch for a general composition into a finished design, I have to see that each added detail takes its correct place and weight, that it is a contribution and not a distraction.

I suppose all garden designs to be variations and modulations on a few basic themes. That they assume such an infinity of different appearances comes from the way they are clothed.

Gardens are, after all, made of soil and water, stone and plants. The diversity of gardens arises from the way that these materials are combined. All the other differences in appearance belong to period and place and style; they are secondary at this stage.

A fundamental design is the garden which spreads outwards from a central nucleus—the pattern of the four rivers of Paradise flowing outwards to the four quarters from the central Fountain of Life. Essential to the logical irrigation of gardens in a desert country like Persia, you see this design repeated in the canals and plane-shaded paths of the Mogul gardens as they spread from a central pavilion—the seat of honour where a monarch would take his ease.

In the sixteenth and seventeenth centuries planning a great European house became the focus for a four-sided composition—entrance court to one side, pleasure gardens, bowling greens and plots, to a second, orchards and kitchen gardens to the third, and to the fourth, stable and service yard, laundry grounds and outbuildings. By the early eighteenth century this idea of the house as a focus was sometimes pushed to extreme limits, so that you find even small houses posed on a mound with decorative parterres and alleys of pleached trees on all four sides, to enhance a composition whose justification would appear to be display for its own sake.

Chinese practice would seem to have interpreted rather differently the idea of the house as focus. Roofed pavilions and enclosed gardens are interlocked in a maze-like pattern, and each circumscribed rectangle of garden influences the surrounding buildings as they, in their turn, influence it. Much of Chinese gardening would seem to have been within walls. This led, in a way that Europe has never known, to the invention and construction of fantastic artificial landscapes within formal enclosures. Chinese gardeners made little mountains of fretted stones dragged from the bottom of an Indo-Chinese bay. They worked on each crevice and hole and carved them into even wilder shapes; they set them in strangely shaped pools canopied by the rounded glaucous leaves of lotus. These sheltered shoals of goldfish bred specially for their protruding eyes and for their waving silken fins of silver and orange, gold and black. If such are stylistic exaggerations they derive, all the same, from a genuine form of composition in which the garden spreads outwards from a central nucleus, the house. The parts nearest the centre are the most highly charged and concentrated, and as the garden broadens it loses the intensity of the centre and begins to take on more of the atmosphere of the world outside it until perhaps it merges with it.

You may find this kind of composition on many different scales. It is reflected, for example, in the natural growth of a town with one or more nuclei or centres from which spread out the auxiliary features, housing or factories or parks. It indicates a way in which to handle extensive landscape problems in cases where no dramatic set-piece could be big enough in scale except as a minor feature within a greater landscape. The scale of the Arc de Triomphe and the line of the Champs Elysées axis seem to dominate Paris; but on the larger scale of the serpentine Seine, winding its way from the built-up plains of the south and east to the woods of the Bois de Boulogne and St. Germain to the west, this long axis from the Place de la Défense to the Louvre is like a matchstick dropped on the tapestry of the city and its surroundings. To design centripetally or, if you like, centrifugally from a central nucleus leaves one with a great deal of freedom to emphasise some special aspect of a site. On a site which has no particular charm or character you can make an artificial nucleus or centre where none exists. Uusually a house is the nucleus of a private garden; but even in a small garden you might choose to leave the house on one side and employ a fine tree, a pool, a hollow in the ground or a sudden eminence as a centre which you could use as the starting-point of your composition.

Stourhead in Wiltshire comes to my mind as an important example of this sort of composition. Here the centre is far away from the house. It lies in a valley where a stream was dammed to make a lake. It is this lake which is the focus for the hanging beechwoods and the garland of pavilions and grottoes and temples which punctuate the long shaded walk around the water.

In a dispersed and hilly garden (described on p. 285) in the mountains near Turin, I could find no way to give rhythm and direction to a garden which spread in a rather aimless way. The eighteenth-century villa was so placed that I could not, as I would have liked, use either it or its immediate surroundings to establish some kind of coherence for the whole. However, at one place a small ravine runs down between steep wooded banks to join a wider valley. Across this ravine lay a wooden footbridge, built to link the high ground on either side just where the ravine opens into the valley. This bridge was a dull affair, just a planked footpath with rustic handrails made of twisted branches stripped of their bark and painted brown. I planned to develop all this part of the garden, and in the wider valley below the bridge I had already started to build a whole series of ponds. These works would look inconsequent unless I could find some pivot for them. I finally decided to use the bridge as a central feature, as it commanded both the ravine and the valley. All I would have to do would be to make it more affirmative—a point from which to stop and look—not merely a convenient passage, nearly invisible in the shade of a group of beech trees. To achieve this I rebuilt the bridge; and to link it with the Chinese rococo decoration of the house, I designed a wooden handrail on either side in a Chinese fret pattern which I painted deep ivory white, to show up sharply against the shadowy trees.

In another case I had to extend a garden of grass and high yew hedges which I had made some years previously in a rather featureless oak wood in the sandy forests of the Sologne south of Orléans. Here I was asked to add a small and easily maintained enclosure and to plant it with flowering shrubs, more particularly with shrubs for autumn colour. As the house is mostly used in autumn, this seemed an intelligent suggestion; but a small garden full of loose masses of shrubs against a background of nondescript oak trees risked looking shapeless and weak. As the site for this addition lay to one side of the main garden I would have to make it, as it were, self-centred. I had already used all the hedges, clipped yews, stone-edged pools, seats and so on necessary for a good firm structure in the rest of the garden. For this new patch I must find another focus, one, too, that would not look too pretentious or artificial. My ground was roughly a rectangle, one long and one short side bounded by an eight-foot yew hedge and the remaining two sides roughly determined by the surrounding oak wood. I decided to use one markedly vertical element as a focal point and to place this vertical point on an oval of grass outlined by the informal plantings which would fill in the rest of the space. I chose a young nine-foot plant of *Libocedrus decurrens*, sometimes called the Incense Cedar for its flame-like habit of growth and its intensely green foliage. As it ages it takes on a spiral shape like a twisted column, quite definite enough to dominate the garden. Now after three years it already makes itself felt; planted well off centre it emphasises the oval shape of the lawn and, especially in late autumn, it shines out as a green column against the tawny oak trees, the red-purple of berberis and rhus and the flaming cerise-scarlet foliage of large plantings of the pink dogwood, *Cornus florida rubra*.

Tensions of a certain kind play a large and unsuspected part in composition. As with the interrelations of patches of colour in painting, so between the solid objects in a garden certain tensions or vibrations are established around an object and between one object and another across the intervening air. This is not, I think, true of sculpture which often represents an object where the tensions are contained but between the branches, the twigs and the foliage of a tree the air in which they all exist seems to respond and become impregnated by a subtle interplay of forces. So some vitality springs from flower to flower even in a vase, and the monotony of a bunch of cut flowers all of one kind depends just as much on the repetitiveness of the same quality of vibrations between the flowers as on their colour or form. What we call voids are solids of another kind. The art of flower arrangement as practised in Japan seems to me to depend for its total effect just as much on what lies between the elements which compose an arrangement, as on its conventional symbolism or on the variety of form and texture employed.

Recently I was wandering around a garden trying to give it that life and sparkle which can only come from a sharp eye and a loving and constant attention to detail. I noticed that a twelve-foot *Magnolia soulangiana* which I had planted years before in a paved angle near the house had grown out of bounds, that its thick foliage was blocking the view, and that it looked altogether too solid. So I began to prune it, starting rather gingerly, with a twig here and there. As I worked I realised that I was working with space, carving the empty air into volumes caught in the angles of branch crossing branch and held by leafy sprays; and that here in the circumference of a small tree lay the meaning of a whole relationship between art and nature.

This was the kind of problem that the Chinese painters set themselves to resolve, giving years maybe to reflection and the contemplation of a natural scene in order, in a moment, with a pointed brush charged with ink, to paint a spray of bamboo and a bird on the wing or the flicker of a fish moving in water, and use the white paper to convey the idea of limitless space just by the way they placed a few brush strokes.

We have been considering the relations of the parts of one tree and a passing partnership between nature and artifice. In garden composition you can set in motion such relationships and tensions by the nature and spacing of different elements. If you have a happy and practical hand you will, like a cook mixing a cake, proceed by guesswork, planting a spiky tree here and a horizontally growing one there. You will contrast grey foliage against red, matt against shiny, and so on. Or you will work out a planting plan on paper, using plant descriptions as well as your visual memory. A serious composition cannot depend on intuition or on an intellectual concept alone. All the objects you are going to place require careful study. If it is a plant you must know its size, habit, colour, texture and cultural requirements as well as its place of origin, its history and the way it has been used whether commonly or uncommonly. In fact you must consider every aspect you can, and for each plant or element separately. When you come to placing, the process becomes more complicated since now the relationship between each single element comes into play and, in gardens, habitual associations quickly become boring and result in a stale reminiscence. For instance when I plant a solitary libocedrus on a lawn I try to place it so that its essential nature is evident—its general spire-like shape, its curling fans of foliage lightening from dark green near its red-brown bark to the almost yellow-green at the tips.

It was perhaps the general flame-like quality of this tree which inspired Sir George Holford to plant it at Westonbirt in association with red-leaved Japanese maples which burn in autumn like embers at its feet. This, by colour too, is a just association. The more classical cypress and flowering-tree motif is difficult to use when working with libocedrus. The pink of a peach or mauve-pink of a Judas tree must be kept away just because of the conifer's undertone of yellow-gold. If I wanted a flowering tree and the climate would allow, I might plant the shiny-leaved orange scarlet of a Chilean embothrium as the perfect foil or (more easily for most gardens) *Amelanchier canadensis*, the " shad-blow," white flowered in spring and with brilliantly scarlet leaves in the autumn. In such a case the spatial relationship between these two plants requires careful thought. Amelanchier or embothrium will form small rounded trees while the libocedrus is still young and as it will eventually tower to six or eight times their height you will slacken or increase the tension as you increase or diminish the distance between the trees. But there is another aspect of the relationship between these two objects. The conifer is hard and definite in form, the other two species rounded and soft, so that each " feeds " the other with a different emphasis. Plant two libocedrus, and the tension will be even and balanced. If you place a smaller and denser object near your libocedrus like a stone vase or a clipped box or yew, this object will become the focus rather than its far larger neighbour. It is as though each were relative points of force. The smaller and denser object of the two discloses its quality of weight in a more concentrated way than its neighbour. Were we to plant a group of delphiniums at the foot of our libocedrus we would be composing badly because the spiky form of the delphiniums in flower would stultify the scene. But you could veil the foot of the tree with a drift of snow-white azaleas because the frailty of their blossom and their loose cloudy shapes would soften the lower part of the tree whose intensity would emerge all the more strongly as the eye moved up. André Malraux once spoke to me of classical Chinese books on landscape gardening and of how the Chinese landscape-maker strove above all that his garden should reflect and symbolise not only the changes of the seasons but the passage of each day. He wondered whether it was possible even in China to induce the morning and evening mists to linger over the shallow lotus-ponds and strange shaped rocks.

I think of designing as a delicate process by which I have to translate a composition, which exists only in my mind, into a three-dimensional actuality. I have to consider all my ideal forms, the dark lines of a hedge, the rounded silhouette of a clump of trees, a ground mist of flower colour, the meanderings of a water course: and then give them dimensions, plot their exact positions and take into careful account all the practical measures for their realisation. I know how high and how wide my hedge should grow, but I must remember the extension of its root-run and how far it will throw its shadow. The effect of a clump of trees will depend on the exact position of their trunks in relation to each other and to what lies near them, as well as to the different points from which they will be seen and to their situation on the plan as a whole. And so with the flowers: do I want bright contrasts, large or small blocks, clear shapes of colour or broken wavering masses? How many plants of a kind should I group to get the best effect? I have to calculate for this in terms of square feet or yards. If these give me the dimensions of a bed or group of beds, I have to remember the height of the plants so as to adjust the width of intermediate paths and the relation of one bed to the next. Some colours carry farther than others and this factor, too, can vary with the time of day or year. Perhaps there is a water-course already there, but needing modification: the water level is to be lowered or raised, the banks eased-off or steepened; or I have to redesign the line it takes through the garden, accentuate a curve or narrow or widen its bed. These are the kind of points I must consider as I set myself to draw out the design of a garden.

Designing is a practical business and, whether as a whole or in a detail, each part must work. The width of a path, for instance, is justified only by the use that will be made of it. Nothing looks more foolish than a four-foot path which, from the evidence of a narrow well-worn tread should clearly be only two foot six or three foot wide. A bad designer will make a narrow grass verge, forgetful of the heavy cost of endless trimming, which will whittle the grass down by inches each year, until all too soon it will have to be remade. It is easy to design a garden when you are working within an established convention and have historical precedent to go by; but even then, you must analyse your design as well as your model in detail. There may be ways to simplify and eliminate costly and unnecessary detail and still keep the character of the whole.

When I have to design without a precedent, I have to ensure that every pattern, shape and dimension has practical as well as artistic justification. I must calculate the sizes of flower beds and indeed of all planting areas in relation to the need for access to each of them. Shrub beds are likely to be wide for the obvious reason that they will contain large plants. Since they are likely to need cultivation only once or twice a year their size does not matter. I plan flower beds on a smaller scale; they have to be weeded and cultivated more often and it is easier to do this work from the sides. Where there are one or more changes of planting each year, as in formal beds for tulips and annuals, four feet is

This flat and almost flowerless garden depends for its effect,
on form and the textures of foliage. Clipped yews rise from
large lawns and the shimmering curtain of a weeping-willow
hangs above an oval stone rimmed pool whose edges are
planted with large groups of *Yucca gloriosa* and iris.
(*Domaine de St. Jean, Loir et Cher*)

This old olive tree is one of several which were transplanted to give an air of maturity to a new garden in Cannes. The foliage of tree pæonies, iris and garden pinks repeats the silvery green of the olive. Such harmonies of quiet colour can give an air of tranquillity in a climate of brilliant sunshine and violent contrasts of light and shade

A combination of formal pattern and simple planting.
Santolina rings the bases of Italian stone vases and pinks
bordered with annual candytuft fill the wedge-shaped beds.
The pinks are grown from seed and only those of compact
habit and good glaucous foliage are retained

*At the Moulin de la Tuilerie a path of old russet-brown
sandstone setts leads to the garden tool-shed between wide
beds of herbaceous plants. Various artemisias, Stachys lanata
and nepeta make a soft silvery foil for the colour of hollyhocks,
aconites, asters and musk roses*

quite wide enough; for cut flowers, beds should be so narrow that no plant is out of arm's reach.

Over the years my boots have transported enough mud from one place to another for me to design with the constant idea of reducing unnecessary work and mess. You may make formal gardens, and parterres may be as extensive and complex as you like, so long as you build them up as repeats of simple, small and preferably rectangular units. Curved shapes can be expensive to construct, especially if any masonry is involved; they can be diabolical when one comes to set out bedding-out plants and bulbs. One has to be careful too with designs for formal gardens in which colour schemes will play a large part. An over-complex pattern, or one where there is a great disparity between the sizes of its different compartments, can be very awkward to work out in terms of blocks of flower colour. Acute angles too will give trouble because wherever they come they weaken the design—your flower mass inevitably dwindles to just one plant in the angles.

Even after long practice it is hard to calculate sizes and dimensions. I usually draw a large layout at one-hundredth or one-sixteenth of an inch to one foot. On this very small scale you tend to exaggerate dimensions, especially those of paths and flower beds. At the next stage I would work to double this scale and, for detailing the patterns of beds and borders and paths, one-quarter of an inch to the foot or one-fiftieth is not too large. In the garden as elsewhere, good design is simple design, whether in its general disposition or in detail. It is better to make a statement emphatically and once only. For instance, such a statement might be simple " grass " or " lawn ": then you must decide how much lawn you want to establish, its proportion to the whole garden, and its shape; in the rest of the garden, avoid odd unnecessary corners and odd patches of grass because they will only add to your work and distract from your major statement. So with flower beds. When you have settled on what kind of flowers you want to plant, decide where you want to put them, how much space they should take and then plant them, whatever they are, there and there only. Nothing is so unsatisfactory as a walk through a garden where the same plants or combination of plants keep recurring in small patches at every turn. I immediately want to dig them up, replant them all together in one place and let them tell their story fully and just once. This is, of course, a rule of thumb to which there can be brilliant exceptions. I can think of many gardens where one or two plants pervade the garden in all its parts, successfully too because they are skilfully shown off in many different aspects by the way they are combined in different weightings and in different associations with other plants.

When we come to construction and to garden architecture, design admits of no errors. I like gardens with good bones and an affirmed underlying structure; I like well-made and well-marked paths, well-built walls, well-defined changes in level. I like pools and canals, paved sitting places and a good garden house in which to picnic or take a nap. I like brickwork and ashlar and coursed drywalling, a well-timbered bridge, well-designed wooden gates, simple wrought iron balustrading or a wooden grille through which to peer. I like bands of round cobblestones quartering a gravelled space, a courtyard of granite setts, painted shutters, well-made wooden doors, trelliswork of good proportion and, rarest of all these, good garden furniture, seats and benches in wood and metal, tables of stone or slate, simple lanterns and effective scrapers.

None of these comes of itself unless one is working in an old garden and a good one. In such places I would save all the architectural elements I could, and almost certainly model any new work after the old.

Here I would wish to avoid the tired and tendentious theme of old against new, traditional against modern. Indeed, I see no place for argument, nor do I think the opposition of the two terms valid. In a traditional setting, I would design and construct in that tradition if, by so doing, I could get the effect and the atmosphere

I was after. If not, I would build in whatever style and with whatever materials best suited to the work in hand. Manorial swimming pools set in antiqued paving with half-timbered changing rooms make a thoughtless concession to an uninformed taste for the picturesque, like that weakness for crazy paving which drives even quite sophisticated amateurs to smash good paving slabs into fragments and, like Hansel and Gretel in the fairy-tale, scatter trails of them across the garden. Yet I see little sense in being too much a purist. When you design the architectural details of a garden, to follow slavishly even the best models may well make your garden look too laboured and too sententious. Garden architecture must above all be discreet. Architecturally-minded garden makers are apt to plan schemes which are satisfying and complete as constructions; but they sometimes seem to forget that a garden is a home for growing things, and that a full planting scheme, laid over an elaborately architected framework, may add up to an indigestible whole. Architectural elements in a garden design should be frank and affirmative in their mass and weight but simplified to the limit as regards their detail. In the average garden, structures of any kind, steps, walls, summerhouses or bridges, act as foils and supports for planting. Leaves and flowers, branches, tendrils, buds and berries will add their own organic decoration. Against this argument you might cite all the elaborately architected gardens of the Italian Renaissance, the sculptures of Würzburg, Sir William Chambers's Casino near Dublin, or the temples and gloriettes of Stowe or Castle Howard. But all of these were the ornaments of gardens in which flowers played little part; petrified decorations to enliven a simple setting of grass and trees, hedges and water.

Once again we come to the idea of the garden scene as a sketch, an understatement in which the architectural elements support a theme by allusion. The pitch of a roof, the broken bar of shadow under the brick nosing of a step, can be enough in themselves to suggest the mood of a garden composition and its historic or stylistic context.

When I come to design any architectural feature I do not think it is just laziness which makes me ask myself "How simply can I arrange this change in level, or, will a wall be better than a bank?" If I decide for a wall, then I must see what kind of wall will best fit in, for it must be a wall related to other walls nearby, and not a wall in fancy-dress. Or I must make a flight of steps, and at once I try to see what is the simplest and easiest way to walk from one level to the next—from where it is best to start and at what point to arrive? This decided, I must make the steps just as simply as my materials will allow. If they need a handrail, I would design one with simple vertical bars of wrought iron. Wistaria branches, or the leaves and starry flowers of a clematis, will make an ornamentation more vivid than scrolls and foliations beaten out in metal.

A discerning eye needs only a hint, and understatement leaves the imagination free to build its own elaborations. The artifacts of a garden should be summary, direct and apposite. Exact reproductions transposed from features admired elsewhere usually fail to achieve their intended effect. One glaring example comes to my mind. In front of a wing of Robillon's masterly little rococo palace at Queluz near Lisbon there is a terrace raised by some five steps above a patterned garden of clipped box hedging. These five steps are designed as a fluid series of angles and curves like a writing master's arabesques, which alternately advance and recede along the whole length of the rococo building. One day, visiting a modern garden in Italy, I found a shortish section of these steps had been faithfully copied and set without rhyme or reason to lead down from nowhere in particular into an ugly-shaped pond full of lotus. This provides as good an example as one could hope to find, of careful and loving work carried out on the basis of a total misunderstanding.

Modern materials and modern construction offer new possibilities for garden structures as well as certain dangers. The word "garden" conveys the idea of a fixed place where plants take root and grow—rest and stability are of its essence. All the airy possibilities of pre-stressed concrete constructions, wide spans, thin and blade-like structures, weight distributed on to small and widely separated points, proffer a new and fluid garden architecture. Steps and ramps will seem to skim and spiral from one level to another, a teahouse will be cantilevered over space, retaining walls of reinforced concrete will take curves and angles impossible for old and less elastic forms of construction. This fluid architecture, for all its lightness, will dominate a garden, just as surely as does the Giambologna sculpture at the Villa Lante or the cyclopean Hercules at Vaux le Vicomte, and will always contrast rather than harmonise with the garden's vegetation. I have found in practice that, when they are related to such buildings, I have to transpose my plantings into fluid, almost moving terms. White walls and terraces become sails and decks between the mast-like trunks of trees, and I find myself planting wide sweeps of simple green. Breadths of horizontally growing evergreens suggest waves lapping against a building, and the foliage of pools of low planting, blown by the wind, moves and catches the light like ripples on water. In such a frame flowers look better severed from the ground and set in transportable containers: tubs, pots and boxes. This new architecture means a new approach to garden design and one in which planting will play a secondary and supporting role.

Non-representational painting or sculpture—so-called abstract art—has, even more than the new architecture, the quality of making a new impact on a part of consciousness not trained, or at least accustomed, to perceive classical art forms. The garden designer cannot but be sensitive to this new impact. These new directions, a new garden pattern, will come in turn to reflect the intentions of the current trend of painting and of sculpture.

Burle Marx in Brazil has already beautifully demonstrated the possibilities of vegetable abstractions by a kind of painting made with the heavy texture of tropical succulents; and we have seen his followers in Europe using a necessarily thinner palette, or making non-figurative abstractions with sand and stone and pebbles.

The sleekness of new materials, surfaces of anodised aluminium or plastic, glass and highly polished conglomerates, make for restlessness since they reflect light rather than absorb it. Nor can they ever weather or take a patina, or become fields for the minute growths of moss or lichens and thus, like the soil itself, become supports for growth and in time melt into one with the garden. A designer will do well to take these aspects, too, into account if he would make use of all these new techniques. I would be inclined to reserve them perhaps for those parts of the garden designed for more frequent human occupations—for the swimming pool and its immediate surroundings, for the summer-house or shelter and the barbecue yard and, of course, for all the working part of the garden.

Preoccupied with the æsthetics of garden design, we might forget this working part, where skilful design and the intelligent use of modern techniques and materials is all-important. As a house depends on its kitchen, so does a garden on its potting shed and cold frames, its greenhouse, its compost heap and nursery beds. Here the designer works to exact dimensions: the size of greenhouse or cold frame defines the quantity of plants that they can produce. The calculation of working space and of temperatures and humidity, the required volumes of humus, sand and peat, as well as housing for tools, offer a fascinating problem in practical designing. On its expert solution will depend the future welfare of the garden and its gardener.

So often a garden is more or less designed and growing before the need for the various components of the working section become obvious and pressing. Sheds and the like are then added piecemeal, to become an inconvenient and shabby garden slum. Here if nowhere else, lies an opportunity for good compact design and the intelligent use of modern materials, for concrete floors inside and out, so easy to hose down, for plastic finishes to shelving and potting benches, for glazing, easily clipped into the aluminium structure of greenhouse or frame to save paintwork and puttying. Only good design will ensure the right placing of soil stores and ensure that no steps are wasted between potting shed, greenhouse, frames and nursery beds.

Nor will a designer use his sense of the practical only for the utilitarian parts of the garden. He will apply common sense, in the shape of directness and simplicity, as much to the design of a garden and its parts as to its construction. He will make paths that lead directly from one place to another or which meander only with definite ends in view. He will see that the size of a summer-house or shelter is large enough for its purpose before he considers its visual aspect. Where he wants to arrange a sitting-place he will choose a wooden seat with a back set to a comfortable angle, rather than an ornamental and chilling stone bench. If he wants a pool for reflections, he will make it only as deep as is necessary for that purpose; so that beneath all the charms of a garden will lie a logical and direct framework as a satisfying assurance that here good sense and clear thinking have been at work. Good design is a matter of good articulation. It is all too easy to fritter away the effect of a good basic design by working it out in inconsequent detail.

As you elaborate the main structure and break it down into its component parts it is as well to try and keep each of these in the same terms, in the same idiom, and in a carefully related scale. Here too, common sense must have free rein. An architect, shall we say, has designed a building with a new form of construction based on the combination of a simple polygonal form. Anxious for consistency, he uses these same polygonal forms for all the furniture destined for this same building. But his polygonal form becomes impractical and ridiculous when he reduces it below a certain scale and arbitrarily tries to adapt it for furniture. Yet, as if this were not already too much, he goes further, and applies this same shape as a surface decoration and ornament on walls, furniture and textiles alike. The result, however logical, looks absurd. Were I working out a rectangular theme, for instance, I would not hesitate to introduce diagonals or curves if these were justified by expediency, or if their introduction contributed to reinforce that same theme by contrast. On the contrary, a composition all curves and irregular forms might well demand certain rigidities, certain angularities in detail or some straight lines, just because these are needed to accentuate the loose forms and curving nature of the whole. I think that such " breaks," or deliberate inconsistencies, give vitality to the design of a garden; but I would always state them clearly and strongly or they will look indecisive and only confuse. In architecture or decoration you can calculate your effects exactly; in garden design, I must repeat, you have to allow for the growth of plants, which will veil and always soften your underlying design and structure.

Current practice, garden conventions and garden good taste are insidious bonds which fetter the imagination and lead to plans as insipid as they are correct. Sometimes I have to solve a garden or landscape problem which at first sight scarcely appears a problem at all. What has to be done seems quite clear and obvious, I start drawing, each element falls easily into place, and soon I have laid out a logical and facile scheme which cannot fail to look right. Yet somehow it is too easy—this plan arrived at by a logical sequence of associations—and if I have taken the answer for granted and if the scheme is carried out it will grow to reproach me and bore all who see it with its banality. There may, of course, be many reasons why I should leave it at that: perhaps it is just what my clients like, perhaps I need the fees, perhaps I have other work in hand which interests me more; but for all that, there is a small something in me which irks and will not let me rest. In such a case, if I am to be able to respect my attitude to the work I have chosen, I must tear up my plan and think again and this time differently.

Thinking differently does not come easily or of itself. I would like to lift my dull design out into another category. Perhaps I can best explain how I might set about this by describing the quality I seek as I have occasionally found it in other gardens.

I remember once, at Petworth House in Sussex, walking through the *enfilade* of reception rooms flooded with light from the rows of long windows reaching to the ground. Going to one of these windows in the long west front of the house I expected to see the rather grandiose intimacy of a typical eighteenth-century park with its rounded clumps of trees, its lawns merging into distant pastures and perhaps a lake. But no, there was only a vast, close-cropped and empty sward running far away up a long and gentle slope to a bare skyline sharp against the luminous sky. All its effectiveness lay in the utter simplicity of this great breadth of down sweeping right in to the stone base-line of the house.

This is a large example only appropriate to our problem if we can discover its principles. So let us look at a smaller garden and wander through the chain of small enclosed gardens which flank the main vista at Hidcote in Gloucestershire. At one point we come through a yew arch into a tiny square hedged-in garden filled with so large a circular pool that there is barely room for the narrowest of paths between it and the hedge. This raised pool, perhaps twenty foot across, looks all the larger for being so compressed and the unusual proportion of the whole breaks down, for a moment, the mechanism of one's habitual criticisms and judgments. One is free to accept and feel this little scene as intensely real; the pool becomes like a sea which reflects the sky and a floating leaf. A passing bumble bee and each chance-grown plant in crevices of the stone border seem to shine with a special clarity—time and space change their scale.

Such experiences are high points for a garden lover. As I see it, these scenes have two things in common. One is a deliberate disproportion: an idea or, if you will, an intention or a feeling seems suddenly to have transcended itself, to have invaded and indeed *become* the whole scene. I do not know whence comes this illumination which enables a commonplace, like a stretch of grass or a simple pool, to lift its existence and its nature, as well as our appreciation, on to another plane.

In each case there is an exaggeration of proportion, a pushing of scale beyond the limits of what might seem reasonable to enforce and enhance our comprehension. "This is this"—the maximum and minimum statement. And then there is a second common element—unity or, more precisely, a symbol or intimation of unity; a simple expression of grass or water or stone or sky, a definition of form and direction and space; a statement made, in each case, as economically and as fully as possible. Lastly in all such as these, the serious and beautiful moments in gardening, it would seem as if it were empty space, captured and held by the barest and simplest framework, which holds the secret.

CHAPTER III

Sites and themes

If I were to choose a site for a garden for myself I would prefer a hollow to a hill-top. A panorama and a garden seen together distract from each other. One's interest is torn between the garden pattern with its shapes and colours in the foreground and the excitement of the distant view. Everything is there at once and one has no desire to wander—to make discoveries. A view, too, usually means wind, and a windy garden is unrewarding.

Paradoxically, it is usually better to try and reduce the width of a view by planting it out so that from the house you see it only partially. This, if it is possible, is best done by tree-planting of the simplest kind, using only one or two varieties; a few isolated trees and hedges carefully placed quite near the house will be enough to make a frame and a foreground. Above all avoid any garden " design " or any flower colour which might detract from the main theme which in such a case must be the view. The ground near the house is also part of the frame. It can be a grass lawn or a stretch of sand or gravel. The shadow of trees or passing clouds will give it quite enough interest. If there must be flowers they should be close against the house or below a terrace wall and so only visible when you turn your back to the view. I would arrange the gardened part of the garden—flowers and shrubs—to the sides or far enough below, so that they and the view are not seen at the same time.

On such sites, I try always to reinforce the simplicity of the foreground by arranging a stretch of ground as nearly as possible level with the house. A strong horizontal line is essential to establish foreground and background in their correct places and to accent the vertical lines of tree trunks or hedges.

The degree of formality you will use will depend on the character of the house and the idiom of the landscape. For a chalet or cottage in mountain country, a few fir or pine trees and a simple planting of a horizontal conifer such as *Juniperus chinensis pfitzeriana* might be enough. In England a box hedge and perhaps a couple of apple trees or a wide lawn and beech trees would be used for the same purpose as cypresses and myrtle on a Mediterranean coast, or a line of pleached limes and a stone balustrade in the Ile de France.

On a hill-top site, I try to draw the main horizontal lines of a composition sideways. Paths or lines of trees plunging away down hill towards the horizon so often appear meaningless; although I used to know one garden at least where all these rules were triumphantly ignored. This was Port Lympne, standing high on the hillside near Hythe facing full south and overlooking the long levels of Romney marsh and the English Channel beyond. Here, Sir Philip Sassoon created a cataract of gardens. Framed in great hedges of *Cupressus macrocarpa* (short lived and now, I believe, gone) were formal parterres, a swimming pool, blazing herbaceous borders and Gothic-walled enclosed gardens bursting with rare lilies as thickly planted as lobelias. But the Cape-Dutch house and its interior were equally exotic as also were the mixture of guests and the sumptuous meals, served often out of doors under tents of white and gold brocade. Here a harmony seemed to be established in terms of incongruity, the whole swimming in the golden summer light. In this case all this gorgeousness was valid, since in its curious way it was an expression of its owner, an artist avid of colour and life, and of the generation for whom Bakst, Poiret and Sert were the arbiters of visual taste.

For me gardening is a most intimate pleasure and the garden should create its own atmosphere of peace and quiet. The landscape is its background. A view may be a surprise but should not be a shock.

The pleasures of a "*tour de force*," a garden designed in spite of the site, are apt to be transitory. Within a stone's throw of the Seine and near the Bois de Boulogne, there is a Japanese garden designed and carried out some fifty years ago. A stroll through this garden creates a certain superficial illusion, but the sky, the soil, even the way the plants grow affirm a false quantity; this does not belong here.

Contemporary taste has veered sharply away from such exoticisms which have, in fact, dominated in European gardens since the eighteenth century when Sir William Chambers's introduction of Chinese elements into English landscape gardens set a precedent for a succession of exotic styles which lasted well into this century. Such fashions were acceptable and had a certain validity for just as long as labour was available and cheap enough to ensure the total and impeccable maintenance of the illusion.

But underneath passing or superficial fashions, the main current of gardening has run strong and true, maintained by succeeding generations of gardeners who have loved plants— the country parson budding his own rose-bushes or the pioneer woman, a hundred years ago, carrying her potted begonia by covered wagon from New Hampshire to Oregon. Of this company was Gertrude Jekyll, growing and experimenting with plants as botanist and artist, and writing book after book— classics, because she wrote quite simply of what she knew and had observed. I remember her in her eighties, a dumpy figure in a heavy gardener's apron, her vitality shining from a face half concealed by two pairs of spectacles and a battered and yellowed straw hat. Discerning the principles lying behind her experiments with colour and form, versed in the nature of soil and water and growth, Gertrude Jekyll was able so to write about gardens that now, fifty years later, the principles she defined are still valid although much of her actual work was, of course, local in its application. As always in the case of a pioneer in any field, the repercussions of her influence have been differently and indifferently understood. I can think of few English gardens made in the last fifty years which do not bear the mark of her teaching, whether in the arrangement of a flower border, the almost habitual association of certain plants or the planting of that difficult passage where garden merges into wild.

In England a certain impatience with all the accumulation of centuries of garden platitudes has emerged amongst the younger designers, and when opportunities are offered they seek simplicity. The Festival of Britain in 1951 allowed them a modest chance to set out their conclusions in three dimensions. These emerged as an absorption with essential problems of texture and colour and a reticence as regards to easy effects. The feeling for a restrained use of material and the careful handling of quite tiny spaces promised well for garden design, though the fusion of so restrained an approach with the exuberant love for colour and a well-built flower, which is a national characteristic, may well take many years to evolve as a new style.

Style and site are interconnected, though at this late date in the evolution of a civilisation, when we are able to accept almost any manner of any period, style in a garden must reflect the style of the house of which it must be considered as the extension.

The discussion between the adherents of " formal " and " informal " gardening still continues. This has always seemed to me a sterile argument, offering little but a display of partial understanding on both sides. For the " informalists " I would rather say that a garden which is after all a humanisation of nature and intended to be for " convenience and delight " needs, like all man-made structures, a framework. Its different parts need connecting in some kind of order. The spaces for terraces, paths, lawns, vegetables and different kinds of planting must be related and there must be a sequence. Whether this order, this sequence of spaces be formal in its detail or not is really of secondary importance.

An exponent of the informal approach may consider that formality limits planting; that plants should grow freely as in the wild and so on, but is he perhaps a partial artist, seeing harmony only in terms of a plant's individual growth and uninterested in any other aspect of a garden?

In Europe the limits of dullness in garden design seems to me to be achieved in the decadent formality of the later followers of Le Nôtre one glance from the centre of the main axis of their dreary compositions is enough. There seems no point in setting out for a long and monotonous walk during which one will meet with no surprises and nothing of horticultural interest.

The informal " gardeners' garden " in its current form is an exact antithesis. Its shapelessness and air of general confusion leave a sense of disquiet which no number of well-planted episodes can quite dispel. Even the largest and finest are often ill-articulated. The Royal Horticultural Society's garden at Wisley comes to my mind as a series of charming incidents beautifully gardened but incoherent and unrelated to the site.

I consider that the site must control the design of a garden, just as it will, with the climatic factors involved, inevitably control the planting. We have seen how the garden with a wide view has its own limitations. A garden on level ground in a narrow valley or rising upwards from the house, is more enclosed by nature; and the quality of tranquillity is perhaps the dominant quality of all walled or hedged-in gardens. In our minds, such enclosures are associated with sixteenth and early seventeenth-century European gardens and once again the historical association or an analysis of superficial pattern may prejudice our understanding. It is also possible to think of the enclosed garden as an outdoor room decorated in this or that colour, furnished in one manner or another. These, the details of planning and planting, will be subsidiary elements which will either enhance or destroy the theme of peace and unity which, as I see it, must be a main aim for any garden if it is to be considered as a work of art.

How free this formula can leave the designer is well shown in Kyoto where, among the low wooden pavilions of temple and monastery, small enclosed rectangular spaces, sometimes no larger than a small room, have been so often turned into informal miniature landscapes, leaving wide space for contemplation. An extra dimension is offered, but the possibility of moving into it must depend as much on the inner discipline and power of concentration of the spectator as on the true freedom attained by the creators of these particular gardens, which for all the infinity of space which they suggest, rest complete within the limitations of their sites.

The English landscape is small in scale and the immediate surroundings will often give a key or clue to both the form and planting of a garden. The nature of the underlying soil, controlling the indigenous vegetation, will give an indication as to the basic planting and even the sky will help in your selection of colour and your weighting of light and shade. It is, of course, comparatively simple to ignore local conditions and, technically, it is perfectly possible to impose any kind of garden you like almost anywhere. Such gardens were frequent some thirty years ago. Wall and water gardens, rose gardens, Japanese gardens, "wild" gardens, old English gardens, Italian gardens were constructed singly or together as attributes to the wealth of their owner. Nowadays such extravagances appear pretentious and boring. Modern taste and economics seem to demand an acceptance of the possibilities already present in the site: marriage with rather than divorce from the surroundings.

Seen from the air, gardens in the wide, hedgeless croplands of Northern Europe appear as rectangular spaces enclosing orchard and kitchen gardens and a pleasure garden, either the remains of an eighteenth-century formal lay-out or, more often, a "picturesque" romantic composition, with an irregular central lawn shaded by a few large trees and curving paths and dull shrubberies set around the perimeter. From the sky, the garden seems but a conventional extension of the house, though in hillier country a more dramatic setting of terraces and steps sometimes imposes a closer connection between the garden and the countryside.

The English ideal is that no boundary should show. Even the line of demarcation between outdoors and indoors is obscured as far as possible by bringing planting up to and on to the walls of the house. In fact the typical English garden, large or small has for centuries been arranged so that as far as possible, all that its owner can see should appear to be part of his garden. To the Englishman, indoors is on the whole considered as a necessary concomitant of out-of-doors, the latter being, like the street for a Neapolitan, the place where he prefers to spend as much of his time as possible. Hence the British garden is an anteroom to the wider world of wood and field, stream, farm and hill. As a sense of private property is still strong, boundaries exist but are almost always camouflaged by a planting carefully designed to conceal any formal limit.

Here, once again, the site plays its role. The small scale of the landscape, the variety of vegetation and the different uses of small fields, woods and spinneys are reflected in a tendency towards formlessness and mystery in the shaping of gardens.

The problem for a garden-maker is always the same, and I always try to discover in what consists the significance of the site, and then base my garden theme on that. For a theme of some kind, a basic idea is essential. It will set the rhythm of your composition down to its smallest details. The factor which will suggest the theme may well be some predominating element already on the site: a level grass lawn, a group of silver birches, an apple orchard or an olive grove, a stretch of sandy gravel and heather, a beech wood, an overgrown hawthorn hedge or a chalky hillside. Any one of such elements will provide a theme and all the plan and planting should reiterate and reinforce the basic motif. In the same way the rhythm of solid and void, the weight of the plantings, the use of light and shade and harmony or contrast of texture must also stem from this original starting point. Any false quantity and the harmony will be broken. One can, technically, achieve a bed of hybrid tea roses in a heathery setting, or persuade Himalayan rhododendrons to flower in a chalky water-meadow, but in so doing one will have made such a discord that any possibility of harmony is instantly destroyed. It takes much practice to limit one's range of materials; every nursery garden and every catalogue is full of temptations. But I have found that if I could really discipline myself and boldly establish once and for all the theme that I have, as it were, extracted from the site, whether by my plan or my basic planting, I can later introduce variations and complexities in detail which will fall into place quite happily.

A few years ago I was asked to take in hand a neglected property standing on a knoll on the Moyenne Corniche high above Cap Ferrat near Nice. There is a fine simple house set on magnificent terraces, with a hundred yard avenue of huge cypresses flanking a monumental staircase which drops steeply downwards from the house. Some of the hillside had tumble-down stone-walled terraces, and most of the eighteen acres was covered with fine old olive trees underplanted with *Spiraea cantoniensis*, a huge bush of the lovely rose " General Shablikine ", rose " Safrano," laurestinus, pittosporum, laurels and other shrubs.

The site is superb, the garden was confused and lacked point and decision. As the view from the house is the dominant feature, the architecturally satisfying but over-ornamented and glaring terraces had to be made liveable, since the main terrace was to become the focus of the house. So I removed all the indifferent sculpture and, to take the glare off the terrace, substituted blue awnings, orange trees and white oleanders in grey-green tubs and huge terracotta flower pots. In summer hundreds of pots of white geraniums and white petunias stand in rows by french windows and doors and on the various flights of steps. All this arrangement is in muted greens with white and blue to harmonise with the dominating blues of sea and sky.

As it seemed to me that the secondary main theme of the site was the olive trees, I moved all the miscellaneous under-planting so that everywhere the beauty of the gnarled trunks and grey-green foliage should dominate. These trees are now set only in lawn or rough grass covered in spring by clouds of

Iris unguicularis and the common sweetly-scented yellow freesia with occasional groups of *Iris wattii* and the large leaved saxifrages. The Shablikine roses share a terrace with an underplanting of agapanthus. The roses with their coppery foliage are covered every two months with a mass of orange-pink double flowers, while the agapanthus are handsome all the year round if only for their foliage, and superb with their globular heads of hyacinth-blue flowers through July and August.

An open site with no special characteristics and no special shape is always the most difficult to deal with and it is sometimes hard to find a point of departure. So one has to look elsewhere. The problem of maintenance will usually, nowadays, impose the principle of simple forms and planting schemes which can be maintained and developed without becoming a burden. The style of a house, its proportions, and the way the main rooms are related and arranged will, almost always, suggest a mood for that part of the garden which lies near them. I usually like to collect further data by walking around the neighbourhood to see what species of plants seem to flourish in other gardens, what wild flowers grow and what trees, the way an old wall has been built or the roof-line of a barn. I find that if I make a whole series of such visual observations this fusion can throw a good deal of light on the particular problem I am trying to solve. This process requires a little patience. Looking around anxiously at everything, wondering how this or that detail can serve, leads nowhere. You have to absorb as much as you can passively and then forget it. When a little later you bring your mind back to the problem of finding your theme and your composition, it is probable that the possibilities and the impossibilities will be much clearer.

That great formal designer André Le Nôtre was singularly sensitive to sites and their possibilities. Looking out over the symmetrical and sumptuous aridities of Versailles, one is impressed but not moved: the rather featureless site has evoked no master stroke apart from Mansart's orangery and its flanking stairways. But other of Le Nôtre's plans, which still exist as gardens, show his mastery of a difficult and asymmetrical site. His handling of

Chantilly is an example. Here he left the Gothic château to one side, isolating it on a sheet of water, and built great ramps leading up to the statue of " le Grand Condé ", the apex as well as the starting point of the long T-shaped sheet of water which is the theme of his plan. At Sceaux too the château, now an ugly late nineteenth-century building, has a minor axis of its own; and the great canal, on a lower level and at right angles to the axis of the house, is only discovered at some distance from it. The high ground from which one looks continues as a steep slope flanking one side of the canal, and a break in this slope enfolds an octagonal sheet of water connected with the main canal and in its turn linked to the house high above by a whole chain of formal cascades. You can see here very well how Le Nôtre seized on an awkward site, accepted its limitations and turned it into one of his greatest triumphs.

The grand manner, however, is not only applicable to large areas. A small garden requires exactly the same approach. I used to be taught in art-school, " Know what it is you want to say then try and express it as simply as you can "—So with a garden: if you want a lawn, go all out for it. Make everything else subsidiary to the " lawnness " of your lawn. Any planting that enhances the quality you are trying to achieve is good. Any that detracts or confuses is bad. Or perhaps you want to create an impression of blue in a garden. In that case everything that reinforces the impression of blue should be used, and nothing that will diminish that same impression should be allowed, however seductive a detail it may be. This directness and simplicity demands courage and discipline. All the good gardens I have ever seen, all the garden scenes that have left me satisfied were the result of just such reticence; a simple idea developed just as far as it could be.

A generation or two ago there was a landscape architect in France called André Duchêne, famous for his reconstructions of the huge formal layouts of the seventeenth and early eighteenth centuries. The magnificent symmetries of Champs and Voisins were two of his great achievements and it was he who made the

new formal terraces and *parterres d'eau* at Blenheim in the late
1920's. These and other of his gardens had always seemed to me
extremely able exercises in a style no longer valid and, as such,
not particularly interesting. I only learned how much of an
artist their author could be when I was called in to advise on some
detail of planting at a private house in the Faubourg Saint-
Germain in Paris. In front of the drawing-room there was the
usual grass plot, gravel paths and box-edged beds of begonias,
but a vacant lot, between high buildings and on a lower level,
had been added to the garden and laid out by M. Duchêne. I
went down a narrow flight of steps into another world, a dark
and shady wood, utterly restful, with no disturbing element and
no hint that at any point one was only a few yards from the busy
street. The achievement was remarkable and the means most
ordinary. There were a few old trees which Duchene had underplanted with yews allowed to grow quite freely; ivy was
used to cover the high surrounding walls and to carpet the
ground. A gravel path wandered about in this maze of
green; and that was all. In this particular case Duchêne not
only accepted the very limited possibilities but achieved a
remarkable garden. Since it had to be shady, he made it very
shady, and since green is precious in the city he made his garden
very green and only green.

The rather hilly and dull pasturelands of Leicestershire are not
an ideal setting for a garden. But I remember a garden on a
windy hilltop in the Quorn country which has remained in my
mind as a completely satisfactory solution to a difficult problem.
The house was occupied mainly in the winter as a hunting-box.
Using its undulating grass as a base, the owner, accepting the lack
of shelter which would have made a more stereotyped garden
impossible, had simply planted drifts of low shrubs on all the
higher parts of the ground leaving wide green spaces in the
hollows. Broad masses of mat-textured evergreens like heaths,
prostrate junipers and brooms were used; everything was kept
low and there were no verticals and no violent contrasts of colour
or texture. Here I first saw the rose " Mermaid " used as a ground

cover along with the more usual lavenders and cistus and rosemary. Various small bulbs and alpines in bays between the
shrubs kept the garden alive-looking and marked the changing
seasons. This garden was interesting for all its restraint; it
remained a garden yet took its place quite naturally in this wide
view of green fields, black winter hedges and cloudy skies. Here
again one idea, compatible with the possibilities immanent in the
site, was maintained through the whole scheme, and nothing was
permitted which would weaken or distract from a very simple
basic idea.

The site has of course its impact on the smallest gardens, even
those surrounded by buildings or with other houses and gardens
nearby. In these cases one finds oneself adding up, on one hand,
the assets, on the other the difficulties or disadvantages. How
much light is there and how much shadow? Where and at what
times will sunlight fall? What can be seen from the garden that
will be distracting and were better hidden? Perhaps there are
trees beyond the boundary whose masses can be made to count
as part of the garden picture; and the shape and silhouette of the
skyline, whether near or far, will be an element affecting the
composition; any view or escape into the distance must also be
considered in case it too can serve. Where the impact of the site
is secondary, then the theme of the garden must be strong enough
for the surroundings to be kept in their correct places as such.
Any feebleness of idea in design or in planting will, because the
foreground is weak, only bring the background into prominence.

A lovely or impressive site is apt to tempt a garden designer,
make him elaborate his plans and work out sumptuous schemes
to match his setting. In such cases he would usually do better to
discipline any tendency towards exuberance and let the site tell
its own story, contenting himself with such unassuming changes
as will enhance and underline what already exists. On featureless
ground his problem is reversed for here he must impose a
complete theme and develop it so fully that the garden will be
complete in itself. Sometimes on a flat site both grass or other

ground plantings are impossible. But there remain two further possibilities: sand and water. Sand or gravel can make the base for an enchanting form of garden. A space of sand or fine gravel must not be too large or it will seem arid and monotonous. You can make it appear infinitely large, as the Japanese so often have done, by breaking it with accents of dark green evergreen foliage or a few boulders. In very small gardens, I have made irregular islands in the sand of box, clipped flat and a few inches high with sometimes a cluster of different sized box balls. The famous garden in Kyoto with its fifteen stones on a rectangle of raked sand no larger than a tennis court, bounded by a low wall and without any vegetation at all, is an expression of faith and space and time and yet *garden* in its very essence. In another manner the great sanded court before the ceremonial hall in the Imperial Palace in Tokyo becomes a garden because of two large bushes, one dome-shaped and one growing upwards and outwards, which flank the wooden steps up to the main hall, each of them enclosed in a square of trellised fence. A hot climate is no place for such a sand garden unless its pale surface, otherwise reflecting too much light and heat, be broken by shadows for the greater part of the day.

A sand or gravel space is a perfect solution for a shady garden as in a town where trees and tall buildings may rule out a lawn. In such places a simple shape in gravel bounded by thick green planting will make an outdoor living-room where garden furniture and plants in pots will give all the necessary colour.

There are sites where a house can give immediately on to water as a replacement for a lawn of grass or sand. But I think this is only a solution for a sunny climate and not for places where there is a long winter. The tanks and reservoirs essential for irrigation in Persia and North Africa, in Spain, Italy and Portugal have often been beautifully made an excuse for an enclosed garden with perhaps a small pavilion for passing summer days at the edge of the water which brings the sky so close that the cloud patterns are broken by a finger's touch. We shall see later how this theme finds its current expression in swimming pools and their place in the garden.

In thinking out a composition for a flat or an enclosed site I shall consider the possibility of keeping the middle, the centre and base low and in one way or another build up around it so as to frame the sky, steal its changing beauties and anchor it to the garden. I learned this lesson from the unknown, probably Christian Syrian architect who built the thirteenth-century mosque of Sultan Hassan in Cairo, a miraculous and bold prayer in stone whose whole meaning culminates in the square of sky caught and held between the towering walls of the central court.

There is no reason why the centre of your garden should not be an elaborately designed formal pattern if you wish. The reason why so many complications are acceptable in, for instance, the great seventeenth-century formal gardens of France is because they are invariably enclosed by hedges made of clipped hornbeam and, behind them, by a higher wall of trees; they are hollows cut out of the forest. Once such patterned gardens are set out in open ground, as they so often have been in later years, they are apt to become meaningless, distracting and ugly. In one or another way, I will usually try to keep the centre of my garden low and relatively empty; although certain sites may, on the contrary, demand a labyrinthine garden in which one plunges at once into a thicket of vegetation.

In a small garden this empty centre is almost essential. Climate will decide with what you will carpet this space, whether grass or sand or a ground cover of some kind or even water. In Europe a grass lawn is most usual, broken by the accent of a tree or group of shrubs, framed by clipped hedges or borders of bright flowers, or melting into a less formal framework of planting where broken shadow and sunlight give depth and mystery.

Where grass is too difficult to maintain, the planting of some low evergreen will give the necessary calm. In temperate climates and for a site too shady for grass you can use ivy, periwinkle, hypericum, pachysandra, asarum and other plants whose only disadvantage is that you cannot walk on them. Heaths will replace them on an acid and dry soil in full sun. In hot, dry climates there are all kinds of succulents, like aloes, mesembryanthemums, echeverias and sedums, to make opalescent carpets.

A quite different garden conception is the one in which you plunge immediately into a labyrinth of trees and flowers. This is the theme of the earliest gardens of which we have records from ancient Egypt and later from Persia. No space is wasted: trees for flowers, for fruit and for shade; rose bushes, syringas, stocks, poppies and pinks, mixed with vegetables and nut-trees—all of these planted for pleasure and use, make a scented profusion. Nearest to them in feeling are the English cottagers' gardens where a similar mixture of plants were and still are crowded close to the house within easy reach of the kitchen door and the rain-water butt.

These cottage gardens are the forerunners of the herbaceous flower gardens which, with the numerous hardy plant introductions of the eighteenth and nineteenth centuries, inspired Mr. Robinson, Miss Jekyll and Miss Willmott to create the "herbaceous border" and a new style and fashion in Western gardening.

One of the results of this development has been that garden style either became amorphous and disappeared under a welter of flowers or else a new, indigestible and over-rich element was added to an already elaborate plan. Sir Edwin Lutyens, Harold Peto and other designers of the early years of the century tried to combine formal planning and the use of a huge repertoire of plant material and produced a whole chain of sumptuous gardens.

Between the two wars, in Switzerland, Scandinavia and Germany, a new, smaller, more studied and more austere type of gardening began to emerge. This type of garden derives originally from the *art nouveau* experiments of the early years of the century; the influence of the Wiener Werkstätte reflected by a certain daintiness in the planning, and preciousness in anecdote of fountain or sculpture. Later the influence of the Bauhaus and the idea of the house as a "machine for living" spread, and the designs of their gardens became more functional and even ascetic. Their merit, for me, lies in the serious thought that lies behind them, though they appear to suffer from a certain anaemia and have a little of the neutral and timid quality of the somewhat arid houses to which they are attached. Inside perhaps narrow limits, there is frequently a great deal of invention, a composition which is easy and free and a feeling for permanence which makes them valid as gardens through twelve months of the year.

A current impulse in garden design would seem to come from the West and South West of the United States. Here houses and gardens appear less encumbered by the European tradition so firmly established in the Eastern and Southern States. The openness and vastness of the North American continent are accepted frankly and gaily. Even if the cost of maintenance precludes very large gardens, small areas seem to be handled with gusto and in a grand manner.

These current Western American themes in both gardening and decoration seem to derive most markedly from Japan. There are, of course, other considerations and factors at work but the simplification of interiors and exteriors and the use of sharp accents to create atmosphere can come from nowhere else.

Historically, garden design has always depended on man's approach to nature, different at different times and in different places. At some time or other, in civilisations now forgotten, natural science must have been so developed that there was a more or less common understanding of the essential nature of plants. This is still the case to some extent as regards certain economic plants—wheat, corn, castor oil, cocoa, quinine, rubber etc. and the names still given to plants in remote country places indicate that the qualities of all kinds of herbs and their varied usefulness to man was once very well understood. That the olive branch stands for peace, for instance, is surely not the chance survival of a poetic image but a direct, if now forgotten allusion to some active quality in the plant itself. Certain aspects of this knowledge survive in cooking and in medicine but we have almost altogether lost any instinctive understanding of plants;

the kind of instinct, for instance, which will send a sick cat out in search of couch-grass. Being able to see and sense a plant in this way and appraising a prize dahlia or rare rhododendron are essentially different attitudes.

For the past few hundred years in the Western world there seems to me to have been a change of accent. Men have ceased their research in depth, and phenomena are no longer studied as the interrelated aspects of divinity. From the fifteenth century until quite recently a vast and superficial exploration of the planet has occupied men's minds. What was there on this earth, how much of it, what did it look like and for what could it be used? Now these values seem to be changing again and for one man whose mind is trained for the new fields of research, in physics for example, there are thousands who, aware of the new possibilities of annihilation, seek a new attitude. A re-exploration of man's psychic world which began again if tentatively some eighty years ago and from a wide variety of experiments, which have included spiritualism, occultism, alchemy, astrology, psychoanalysis and the study of extra-sensory perception—a kind of knowledge new for this civilisation—a new approach to man, to nature and to God is very slowly emerging.

We live too in a museum age. We collect and classify the artificial and natural products of every known country and civilisation. All of this as well as our plant material offer a large and confusing repertoire to the garden designer. His range of information about history and styles and an extensive documentation can easily lead him to indulge in a mixture of mannerisms which is not style but merely allusion, coming as they do from the mechanical processes of mental association.

The cubist and later the " abstract " movement in painting— the dissociation of forms—had for a long time little influence on garden design apart from a few experiments in France and Germany. But now, particularly in small gardens, there is a tendency amongst many contemporary designers to break away from classical formal patterns and to use strongly marked " free " shapes. As in painting, the results vary from the interesting to the atrocious. It is a device which can have meaning only if it is made to serve an idea.

If this tendency is not in its turn to become just another " manner," it will be because it will be used as a vehicle to convey an intention.

To use the world " intention " about a garden may at first seem strange. Perhaps we can start by accepting the established pleasures and uses which a garden may afford and raise a question as to whether a garden can call up a further refinement or subtlety of feeling; of thought and of sensation. In theory there is no reason why not. An artist who could achieve a certain degree of concentration and a certain quality of perception, could organise the elements of a garden just as a man was once able to organise stone and space into the Merveille at Mont Saint Michel. Henry Adams gave years of thought and effort to trying to understand and formulate what, in fact, had been for him the violent shock on his perceptive organs of a contact with the impressions consciously built into Mont Saint Michel and Chartres some seven hundred years previously, by men trained to embody and so transmit certain aspects of the laws which govern man and nature.

Here is practice for an artist who may begin, for instance, by deciding to convey the colour " red." Red in all its vibrations and tones, everything in his garden will be deliberately planned to enhance the impression of " red." Or it may be silver and gold in movement. Or he may wish, like Monet in his studies of water lilies, to use all the possibilities of reflected light on water or he might want to convey as fully as possible the idea of " oval."

These are examples of the expression through gardening of an idea and the process may be carried further. You may find in eighteenth-century romantic gardens that the idea of expressing a mood was well understood even though often executed in a rather literal manner; ruins to convey " solemnity," grottoes for " gloom " and so on.

I have again to turn to Japan to find the expression of an

abstraction carried much further. One reads of rocks or paving-stones baptised with a poetic formula or symbolising in miniature a gorge, a peak rising from the forest, or a stretch of well-known natural scenery. Trees, for instance, are carefully trained and shaped, only to convey a certain impression when they are covered with snow. Much of this sounds quaint and fanciful, a well-defined code to provoke certain associations in the spectator, but some garden concepts have been pushed far beyond this stage. The flat garden of the Ryoangin temple in Kyoto which I have already mentioned has been given many meanings and inter-pretations, but even from photographs it is clear that here is no minor work of art but a creative act which after four hundred years conveys an experience which cannot be interpreted or brought down to the level of our habitual manner of thinking or feeling.

It is easy to make mistakes in these associations which can so easily become merely platitudes—an old idea read somewhere, copied from a photograph or seen in another garden. There is nothing wrong or necessarily ugly in using an "obvious" solution: it may well be the best answer. A mental association, whatever its source, is a valid spring for action if you can consider it in relation to as many aspects as possible of the problem in hand. Once again, you have to "see" what you are looking at, and see it as though for the first time, and, at this moment, you must be ready to relinquish your mental associations for they may well cloud the clearness of your vision. With the picture once clear, the associative process can be released again, but each time an "idea" emerges you have to call a halt and picture it with the reality, perhaps to discard it or perhaps to retain, amplify and eventually realise it in garden form.

Much contemporary garden design and much current garden planting is the result of a haphazard working of mental associa-tions. Odd experiments have been made: great mirrors have been used as *trompe l'oeil* to prolong a small town garden into a green transformation scene and a Paris roof-top garden had growing hedges that could be slid backwards and forwards; a

Louis XV marble fireplace set on a grass lawn caused much fleeting excitement not so many years ago, but the element of surprise by disassociation, even where combined with elegance, is not enough. Such fantasies are for an occasion, like the great dragons and monsters made of clipped box which emerged from the waters of the Seine for one summer day in Paris when the then King and Queen of England went by water from the Quai d'Orsay to the Hôtel de Ville.

To consider a site for a garden is to become at once involved in the problems of composition and design. People and history, styles, patterns, forms and colour, all sorts of associations and ideas come rushing in to clog one's perceptiveness or to enrich it. If the landscape or the garden, large or small, that you are going to make is not to look either academic or sentimental you have to keep all these factors well in place and refuse to allow them to interfere with your first consideration—what does the site offer in itself as a basic theme.

In open landscape you may choose to take as your starting point the outline of a hill, the curve of a river, the mass of a wood or the silhouettes of distant buildings. You will compose your scheme so that just this one factor is accentuated and that it remains dominant however complex and elaborate your design becomes. So too for a garden site whether large or small. The shape of a tree or a group of trees, a change in level, a soil with special characteristics; any one aspect will give you a starting point and on any scale you will do well to establish your composition, work out the design and study your prospective planting in just relation to this one element whose effect you wish to underline and enhance.

Few sites are utterly featureless but when, as happens, I find myself faced with one, a short walk in the neighbourhood is likely to give me many clues. Only then, if nature offers nothing, do I turn elsewhere for a theme. This I may find from a hundred sources, a client's tastes, some facet of garden design I have long wanted to experiment with, a particular kind of planting, an exploration in terms of rounded forms or verticals or a transposition from painting or architecture or music into garden shapes and colours. The sources for an "invented" garden are many and I would never be afraid to experiment were I reduced to devising a garden for a site which gave me no help, though perhaps I should at once say that in forty years of garden-making I have never yet met a site so anonymous as to drive me to such experiments.

It happens frequently that the apparent defects of a site can be turned to the garden's advantage. For instance a soil that is all sand or all clay, too acid or too limy will, if you accept its limitations, force upon you a coherent and simplified planting. The trees that you plant to hide an unsightly building may grow to become the most agreeable feature of your garden. A mound in the wrong place that you cannot afford to move or a hollow you cannot fill can be handled as charming and unexpected incidents which will add rather than detract from a formal or symmetrical scheme. Or you can use them as a starting-point and by building your scheme around them turn them to advantage.

If your site were all shade you might do well to accept that fact as a premise for all the opportunities it could offer, even though it might be easier to get rid of the shade and make a garden as sunny as it was without character.

It is well worth while to explore all the positive possibilities of an apparent defect on a site before eliminating it. Perhaps wind is the gardener's worst enemy and a windy site the most difficult to deal with. In such a case shelter becomes a designer's first objective. On any site large or small I would be generous and give all the space necessary to plant a shelter-belt. So often such shelter-belts spoil the look of a garden. Trees which will stand up against a prevailing wind may look so prominent with their wind-torn and distorted silhouettes as to belie the colour within the garden. At the risk of diminishing the size of the garden I would plant out a sufficient width on the windward side so that inside the strictly utilitarian screen of whatever trees were used to act as a wind-break there would be room for an inner planting of trees whose nature and form were related to the garden proper.

A site where the soil is barren and dry produces its own problems, for you will have to design your garden to suit the water available, and even more difficult to handle is a site which becomes over-wet in winter when plants are resting and over-dry in spring and summer when plants are making their growth and are in need of water. In these cases any elaborate gardening must be carried out to just the extent that can be properly tended. The rest of the site must be arranged with plants that can look after themselves even in these difficult conditions and these must be taken into account when you design the plan.

When you are concentrating on a site and its problems such difficulties may seem insuperable. Each garden is its own small world. Each is different; each has its own nature. Yet each is part of nature and part of a wider world. You have only, as it were, to step back a little from your immediate problems and see them in a slightly wider context, be this only the garden next-door. Your particular difficulties have been other people's too and their solutions will surely give you the indications which you will need to make a start.

A friend devised this planting for her farmhouse garden near Paris. Black and white tulips rise from a groundwork of blue forget-me-nots against a sunny white-washed wall patterned by the shadows of an old apricot tree. This makes an exceptional garden scene which has been achieved with authority and complete simplicity

A formal lily-pool lies next to the shaded patio of a country house near Grasse. It is planted with water lilies and lotus, cyperus and Thalia dealbata. Agapanthus, cannas, Phormium tenax and other foliage plants fill the narrow flanking beds. Here water adds calm to the exuberance of the architecture and planting and the reflections depth

Seen from the house a change in level marks the end of the lily-pool. Above lies the swimming pool flanked by four magnolias. In the distance a single fountain jet marks a reservoir from which a narrow water staircase runs down to swimming pool level between young pines and cypresses.
(*Photo taken 3 years after planting*)

To give interest to a gravelled area in a small enclosed garden in Paris, I set a half-standard bush wistaria on a small island made of edging-box, which is kept vigorously clipped a few inches from the ground, and two box balls

CHAPTER IV

Near the house

When I come to consider a garden plan in detail my first concern will be with the house. All that part of the garden which lies near it must be planned as carefully as the house itself. I like to work with a detailed plan of the ground floor for doors and windows, and even the proportions of the various rooms have a direct bearing on the design of the garden immediately outside. These parts of the garden are links which I try to arrange with, as it were, a double scale in mind—one related to the proportions and arrangement of the rooms inside, the other to the larger volumes and surfaces of the rest of the garden. Here, at least, whether you design formally or informally a sense of order must permeate your plan.

In these days when all styles of all periods are available, when you may be asked to make a garden for a mountain chalet, a Provençal farmhouse, a Tudor manor house or an eighteenth-century château, you can scarcely lay down hard and fast rules for a garden design. You have to accept your role as a contemporary victim of museums and art galleries, of too much print, of easy transport and the accumulated documentation of nearly two thousand years of æsthetic styles, fashions and patterns of living. To this extent the garden designer must be eclectic and able to interpret the manner of a house and link it to the outside world and somehow achieve a harmony between the two. This often involves considerable æsthetic gymnastics. " Modern " houses are perhaps the least difficult. Whether they are bold or insipid, they do at least leave the garden-maker a good deal of freedom to establish whatever scale he may choose, and a chance to compose as boldly as he likes and to use volumes, textures and colours without the pressure of historical associations.

A house with an historical style, however simplified or even debased, carries a weight of associations with it and to ignore them is usually disastrous. In such cases no brilliance will cancel out incongruities or false quantities. British gardens, sometimes so over-loaded with pictorial incident, seem often to escape this incongruity because, on the whole, the British have no strong feeling for design and prefer allusion to precision, although it must be admitted that many great nineteenth-century gardens, planned in the French manner, overloaded with Italianate fountains, sculpture and balustrading, and then planted with a British profusion of flowers are as monumentally atrocious as any artistic manifestations in history. Sometimes our taste for blurred and softened effects will result in something touching and lovely as at Hampton Court where the once trim-cropped cones of yew in the fan-shaped layout have been allowed to grow into great church-yard yew-trees and so romanticise what was originally a rather slight essay in the Le Nôtre manner. We might start with the front door as the dominant element. Whether the approach is a footpath or a road it should be direct and without horticultural distractions. The entrance is a focus or magnet drawing you towards it, and any complicated landscaping will disturb. In a car you are moving at a speed not intended for the slower pleasure of gardening, so that only the simplest effects will be legible. The garden of a private house should, I think, also be private, whether it be enclosed or giving on to a wide landscape. Ideally one should come upon it only after passing through the house.

The simplicity of the approach can be established by the easy and necessarily simple lines of drive or roadway and by the size of turning and parking space. On a small site, this area may be altogether enclosed by fences or walls and you will limit your landscaping to preserving or planting a tree or two and to a discreet treatment of the surrounding fence, wall or hedge. It is scale which will count most and the scale can be, if you like, larger than human, since it is established by the size and speed of a car. If, then, this area is so shaped and worked out that it is practical for its purpose, it should in itself satisfy the mind and hence the eye. In such positions, my personal taste inclines to a very reticent planting in which volumes and textures will be calculated to contrast or enhance the level space, and colour be limited to green foliage with perhaps a little white or pale blue. Entrances are apt to be on the north and shady side of a house, and I think that white flower-colour best accents the play of light and shade and helps to underline the note of restraint which alone will give the elegance I intend.

At this point we should consider too the back door or second entrance and contrive a space enclosed by fence, wall or hedge at least six foot high. This space should not be so large that it cannot easily be swept or hosed down and for this reason too it should, if possible, be partly or entirely paved for if it is too large it is apt to become neglected and untidy.

For any garden my first concern is to catalogue and consider as many of the practical aspects of the problem as possible. How are the owners of the house and garden going to live and how large a garden will they want to maintain? Will there be more than one gardener or none at all? Will they want vegetables and fruit and, if so, how many mouths are there to feed and for how many months in the year? Does the owner care for roses? Has he dogs and what sort? Will he be content to look at his garden only or will he give precise orders, or will he garden himself? How many hours can be given to lawn-mowing and can hedges be clipped mechanically? What is the water supply? I have to consider these and a hundred other prosaic questions if the garden is to be just and in balance. I so often find gardens that are out of scale and out of key with the pattern of their owners' lives and to be fully satisfying a garden must be more than an artistic or horticultural *tour de force*.

So now I have to weigh up these and many other factors and translate them in terms of mass and area—roughly so much ground for vegetables, so much for fruit, so much for fully kept-up garden and lawn, so much, perhaps, for semi-wild treatment. Nor must I forget greenhouse, frames, potting sheds, compost heaps which should be near the house if the owner gardens himself, farther away if he is more interested in the results than the processes and can leave these last to a gardener.

The practical considerations should come first, because I know that if I concentrate prematurely on my composition and my planting themes I will later have to return to these calculations and perhaps find myself obliged to make modifications and compromises which will weaken the directness and simplicity of my basic idea.

All of this sounds very elaborate and implies the problems of a far larger garden than is currently possible for most of us, but such questions come up whether one is handling a millionaire's acres or a week-end cottage.

I like to push even my preliminary sketches rather far, suggesting as much detail as I can by a series of shorthand indications, so that my pencil can keep up with my thinking, which, at this stage, is pictorial, but which has also to be concerned with how the garden will eventually grow.

Usually I explore with a coloured pencil, roughing in the shapes and proportions of the various parts of the garden, faint scribbles darkening suddenly where the mind and eye sense a more exact possibility. With long practice one learns to draw a plan freehand and almost exactly to scale. Here, to anyone who plans to become a garden designer, I would say, draw ceaselessly. Draw plants, flowers, shells, trees, people—learn to explore the surfaces and volumes of all forms of organic life. Draw buildings, windows and doors. Sketch mouldings and steps, wrought iron and carved stone. Always have a six-foot tape with you or pace out the measurements of gardens with your feet and make endless sketches and notes. None of this will be wasted. Watch a house going up, study carpenters, plasterers, painters, plumbers at work, just as you will watch the technical processes of gardening. This will be precious material and later you will turn it all to use.

You can only achieve the results you want by knowing what are the processes that must go to its making. A gardener's hands must be sensitive to line and volume, texture and form and temperature. One can absorb a world of experience through the tips of the fingers and the palm of the hand, and this carefully educated manual sensitivity will turn to a mastery over pencils as well as plants to make your precise intentions graphically clear or to coax a seedling into growth.

Before I begin to elaborate my composition I like to establish the circulation—the lines of communication between house and garden and for the garden itself. Paths are all-important. They should lead as directly as possible from place to place and should not be made where they are not necessary. This principle of course raises certain difficulties when you are designing a formal or symmetrical garden, but I know of nothing that makes a garden more forlorn than an unused path.

I prefer always to approach a garden through the house. One of the qualities of a private garden lies just in the fact that it is private and when I can, I like to separate the approach to a house from the garden. A path or road which runs right round a house, a commonplace in nineteenth-century planning, leaves the house as it were high and dry and destroys any possible relationship between house and garden.

Although the main line of communication with the garden is through the house, a path linking the entrance court directly with the garden will probably be necessary. By letting it twist through a shrub-planting or between hedges or through a door in a wall, I would always so arrange it that there would be no through view.

The main circulation through the garden will start and end at the terrace or paved space which is the meeting-place of house and garden. In a formal layout paths present no special problem. Direction, size and material will be part of the plan, though, I repeat, I would keep any paths other than grass to a minimum.

Paths for an asymmetrical or informal garden are far more difficult to set out, and here another aspect of garden-planning can be a help. Most houses need anchoring to their setting, and for traditional houses some formal extension of the straight lines and rectangular shapes of the building is usually the most effective way of doing so. The shapes and even the volumes of the interior of the house should find some echo on the larger, outside scale. Curved or straight walls and hedges, a line of clipped trees, a more or less formal pattern of flowers, a change in level with a bank or retaining walls are all useful devices to this end, whether they run parallel, at right angles or in a supple curve outwards from the house. It is both logical and satisfying to have a path which will underline and follow these, the main lines of your composition, in the neighbourhood of the house. If this is all you wish to have by way of path, let it end up on something— a seat, a summerhouse or a view point. A path must always lead somewhere. Curved paths are harder to manage. On flat ground it is usually better if you see only one curve at a time. Paths indicate the structure of a garden plan, and the stronger and simpler the lines they follow the better. They help to define the organic shape of your garden; an indecisive arrangement of paths will make an amorphous and weak garden, a basic error which even the most skilful planting will never be able to put right.

Its usefulness will often justify a path which in theory may appear quite arbitrary or badly traced. This is a point that I learned at Fontainebleau where, near the château, is a perfect small eighteenth-century house, the Hôtel de Pompadour. This " folly " is reached through a great formal gateway with lodges, beyond which is a very large gravelled courtyard flanked by the stable-wing on one side and a high wrought-iron *clair-voie* on the other. The whole is a very formal and distinguished composition saved from pompousness by a charming and strictly utilitarian detail—a narrow path made of two lines of squared cobblestones running obliquely across the courtyard from the lodge to the service entrance.

I think it was Geoffrey Jellicoe who, writing about Versailles, explained that the enormous width of the walking-spaces and paths there was justified by the presence of large companies of people; it is true that, empty, they look disproportionately wide. When, at Longleat, it was decided to open the house and grounds to the public and to remodel the gardens in, to some extent, the manner of the seventeenth century, we deliberately increased the scale of the rectangular compartments of the enclosed gardens round the house and linked them by paths far wider than an orthodox reconstruction of a period garden would allow. Indeed the whole exterior setting is worked out in terms of circulation for a large number of people. Even the planting and the scale of the flower beds are enlarged designedly so as to give a certain definite impression to visitors who will spend perhaps only twenty minutes on their tour round the garden. This problem of circulation is fascinating and very important in large public gardens, where the layout of roads and paths will control the rhythm and movement of crowds.

The point of a path is to be able to walk dryshod in wet weather and to have a firm footing. Paths of gravel, sand, tan, bark or stone chippings must have a firm foundation and one which will quickly drain away surplus water. But all these materials need a great deal of maintenance, though a gravel path can be laid on a tarred macadam foundation and, if the gravel is carefully rolled in, it will keep its appearance for years and demand no upkeep. For large vegetable gardens where labour-saving is important, I have found this method the perfect solution, although expensive in the first place. Brick, stone and even precast concrete slabs offer a thousand variations of texture, pattern and colour. Sections of tree-trunk make charming stepping-stones, although rather slippery in wet weather. The only paths I find invariably ugly are those made of long runs of concrete cast *in situ* which invariably " craze," those of brick-dust whose colour is usually offensive in a garden context and finally those of " crazy-paving " as it is commonly used. The *opus incertum* of the Romans, where irregular slabs of stone or lava are carefully fitted together with the narrowest possible joints, has great beauty if only because one senses the skill of the craftsman whose feeling for, and handling of, stone remains as long as his pavement exists. To drop a mass of small bits of stone and set them where they fall, and then to fill the intervening spaces with grass or rock plants, gives a restless appearance and makes a great deal of work.

Grass is, of course, one of the most sumptuous and extravagant materials for a wide path, possible only in certain climates. It demands ceaseless mowing, weeding and watering. A grass garden path is a highly perfected invention from rich nineteenth-century England. The perfect grass path, if you can take the trouble, should be made like a bowling-green. You first put a twelve inch layer of fine cinders on top of your well-dug and enriched soil and then lay thin turves of fine grass such as sheep's fescue above the cinders. In a few weeks the grass roots will have penetrated the cinders to find their food in the soil below.

It is not always easy to achieve a successful meeting between house and garden. The Mediterranean solution of a covered loggia or gallery as part of the architecture of the house is perfect for a hot climate where direct sunlight can be too intense for comfort and where even a draught is welcome. But away from a climate in which olives and orange trees flourish there are relatively few days in the year when a covered outdoor room is not chilly and uninviting. This difficulty can be surmounted by treating a loggia or summer house rather like an orangery, with openings that can be closed by glazed doors or windows, and by filling it with growing plants, preferably in tubs, pots or wooden cases.

I used to know, at Sandgate near Folkestone, an exotic white house among pines and wide slopes of grass, rosemary and flag-iris. This house belonged to people who had lived for years in Egypt and every room opened on to a covered balcony or vaulted gallery. We spent much time in one pleasant loggia giving on to a small garden of blue flowers set against whitewashed walls. The charm of this particular corner, where, wet or fine, we lunched and dined, had tea and breakfast, talked, read and worked, came from the large open fireplace which had been built into one wall. With a big log fire burning it made a delightful place to linger in on cool autumn evenings. The firelight set the shadows of groups of fine-leaved bamboo dancing on the whitewashed walls and the only flowers allowed were lilies for their fragrance: *Lilium candidum*, *L. regale* and *L. auratum*. This was all in the grand manner and very luxurious. But luxury to me is a question of elegance and elegance is always reticent. In this case elegance derived from a few objects so combined that their weight, colour, texture and nature were in just proportion.

The conventional terrace or a rectangle of paving or gravel set square and bare in front of the house is not very welcoming. Wind is the great enemy; any place where one sits needs to be protected and two walls set at an angle to each other are better than one. Even the thickest of hedges will not give quite the same protection or, in a cool climate, store the sun's warmth as will a wall; and the sunnier it is the wider the range of climbing plants that you can plant against it.

Underfoot, some kind of paving is essential. Brick, slate, marble, stone either split or sawn are all satisfactory, whether you use them alone or in combination. The details of design for the paving must depend on the style and architecture of the house. Gravel or sand are cheaper substitutes but both demand a good deal of upkeep besides being carried into the house on people's shoes. Well-laid paving can be brushed or simply hosed down when necessary. I think that any planting set into the paving in such a place is quite unsuitable. You need to be able to move furniture about without catching it in a hummock of thrift or a bushy helianthemum and your carefully nurtured carpet of thyme will be a constant target for cigarette ash.

Paving in a garden is a rewarding extravagance. The close, firm texture of brick or stone warmed in the sun or glistening after a shower is a passive foil to the life and energy of plants. Hard surfaces of paving lend themselves to endless variation in scale and you can work out all kinds of patterns, either strongly marked by your use of different materials and textures or more subtly indicated by jointing alone. I have always enjoyed stones.

As children will, I collected pebbles and during the long months of exile in a school on the Kentish coast, I spent hours searching for the mythical cornelians which were said to exist in the shingle. In the water there seemed to be agates and cornelians galore, but once dry they always turned into ordinary pebbles.

Cobblestones used to be employed for cottage garden paths, and in Rutland little slivers of the local limestone set on edge in parallel rows were used for stable yards and paths. They gave a lovely texture and surface. Then there were the beautifully constructed dry stone walls which enclosed fields and woods and parks in all the limestone country. For garden work in England old pavement slabs of York stone make a sober paving on a large scale. The same stone direct from the quarries is also excellent, particularly if it is laid " half-split, half-sawn " which gives an agreeable variation in texture. I have also used Hornton stone with its tan and slate-blue markings as well as a certain rippled sandstone which fits well in a very informal garden.

The last great English architect to build fine houses, Sir Edwin Lutyens, had a great sense of paving materials and he must have enjoyed experimenting with unusual textures. There is a terrace at Mothecombe House in South Devon where he made panels banded with stone and filled in with slates set on edge in cement, to make a striated surface which looked like a fine dark grey tweed.

France and Italy are rich in fine stone and fine pavements. In the Tuileries gardens and at Versailles Le Nôtre used a whitish limestone filled with tiny fossils from the quarries at Clamart. Burgundy provides a very fine pinkish stone which is polished to marble smoothness for an interior and then, sawn but not polished, continued for an out-of-door terrace. Around Aix-en-Provence a coarse, yellowish and easily-carved stone lends itself to garden sculpture, and thick beards of moss and maidenhair fern will soon grow on the shady side of a stone urn or fountain basin. In Northern France and Flanders textile manufacturers used to pave their factories at Lille and Roubaix with the dark grey stone from Tournai. As cement flooring gradually replaces stone in the factories you can still sometimes obtain these slabs and make terraces and paths of them, although Flanders is, in the main, a country of fine bricks.

Italy is a treasure house for the pavement lover. For over two thousand years many different kinds of stone and marble have been brilliantly used for churches and palaces, houses, streets and squares. A lovely Italian convention is the use of a band of stone to outline a paved area and perhaps to break it into compartments which will be paved either in the same stone cut to a different scale or pattern or, where something more sumptuous is needed, in another kind or colour. Even a quite small paved place in a garden may be treated in this way. A stone band will make a frame; cross or diagonal bands will give direction and scale; and the panels thus made will be filled in with a herringbone or basket pattern in brick or the same stone or, less expensively, with fine washed gravel or sand.

Good brickwork makes fine paving. In the North of France I have often used it to make a softly red carpet laid between a whitewashed brick house and a plain stretch of lawn. There, where the winters are long, grey and wet, the warm colour of brick paving and a green lawn look far more cheerful than grey stone, leafless bushes and naked flower beds. It is better to keep brick patterns simple; straight courses used horizontally, diagonally or perpendicular to the line of sight look better than complicated patterns. Bricks should always go in on edge, if only because the large side of a standard brick has a rather ugly proportion.

Granite or sandstone " setts " or *pavés* used for paving streets make a good garden pavement provided that you keep the joints between them rather wide. Set too close together these small cubes are apt to look niggling. I sometimes stop and watch the Paris paviours as they swing and place these stones with extraordinary speed and accuracy. In the old days they used to lay streets and courtyards in a fish scale design rather like inter-locking scallop shells; and occasionally one finds a granite fantasy like that design of a heart, which was set, one wonders why, by a long dead workman into the paving in front of the Institut de France on the left bank of the Seine.

In the old days all the roads round Paris were made of nine inch cubes of hard sandstone called " grés." This is the stone which makes the tumbled heaps of rocks, each with its picturesque name, in the forest of Fontainebleau. Freshly quarried, this sandstone was easily worked into blocks which gradually hardened with exposure. It was a lucky day for the Duke of Windsor, who loves stones as well as streams, when in his garden near Paris, he found the remains of an old quarry with enough stone to pave all the garden paths. We used them with fairly wide mortared joints in the enclosed garden, and spaced more widely and with grass between, in the wilder parts outside the garden walls.

I have left cement to the last either because it is the newest paving material or perhaps because I like it least. Precast cement slabs with a stone finish can be quite pleasant in colour and are very well suited, for instance, to the painted stucco houses you find in London. In such a context the smooth surface and rather sophisticated appearance of cement may look well as long as it is kept apart from real stone. A synthetic stone moulding, which, in a fit of misplaced economy, I once used for a circular fountain basin in Switzerland, looks poor and wretched next to a wall and a double flight of steps in real stone. This is because synthetic stone will never " weather " like real stone.

Concrete used to cover any large surface will very quickly " craze " unless you allow for expansion joints. Many precast coloured concrete slabs come in rather sickly greens and mauvish pinks, colours which will swear with any planting. Cream or a slightly warm shade of grey are less offensive. The most attractive and generally useful concrete paving is in the form of precast slabs in which the cement is mixed with pea gravel. These blocks are then brushed with a wire brush and washed down before the concrete hardens, so that the final surface is of small firmly-set pebbles.

In a frost-free climate, as in the South of France, I often use hand-made terracotta tiles with a mat surface made in twelve or fifteen inch squares. Their gentle variations in colour and slightly irregular surface fit in well with the local red earth and pinkish rock.

You may furnish a garden terrace in many different ways, but the style you choose must depend on the style of the house. The present tendency is away from a formal arrangement of heavy benches and tables. Lightish furniture in rattan with loose cushions is no longer as unpractical as it was, since it is now easy, at night or if it rains, to throw a sheet of some light plastic material over the lot. Scale is all important in terrace furnishing. The scale of indoor furniture cannot well be used out of doors; it will look spindly and thin. On the other hand, designs which are too massive will look gross and heavy and immoveable and are to be avoided if the terrace is not to look like a sitting place for giants. For the same reason I never like to use seats or benches of stone.

After the problems of shelter from wind, firmly set paving and suitable furniture, comes the question of shade. A wide awning to raise or lower as one wishes is the best solution. A very elegant and sophisticated town or seaside setting may demand a striped material, black, blue or green alternating with white. In such cases the stripes should be fairly wide. In the garden a plain colour is usually best, though one has to remember that colour will always fade and that blues and greens go off rather rapidly. Cinnamon brown and the red-ochre colour of sail cloth will also fade to a softer version of the original tint. If its framework is properly constructed you may have an awning twelve to fifteen foot wide which is none the less easy to wind back and forth. Its life will be extended if, when folded back, it is protected by a wooden or metal projection fixed in the wall immediately above it.

Trees make a less sophisticated, less complete but perhaps more lively protection. To look up into their flickering green is as restful as gazing into a log fire. An odd tree carefully placed on a stretch of paving can be used to soften a too formal arrangement, an apple or pear tree perhaps, or, if you will be patient, a magnolia. Sometimes a formal arrangement can be used of trees planted in line and clipped and trained to make a leafy roof. In Europe planes and limes are trained to fill out any framework. Pleached plane trees too are often to be seen in the South of France and in Switzerland. The trees are usually set about ten feet apart and the trunks kept bare of branches to about ten feet above the ground. Then, with horizontally placed laths of wood or long canes, you make a framework in the shape you wish your trees to take. As soon as the young growths are long enough they are tied down to this frame and in two or three years the branches will have accepted this horizontal position. The supporting frame can then be dispensed with and the arbour kept in shape indefinitely by an annual pruning. Lime trees have long been used in the same way. An alley, a line or a screen of pleached limes has many uses in garden and town planning but these trees are somewhat unsuitable for any place where one sits, as in late summer they are apt to drop honey-dew which soon covers everything with sticky black spots.

Arbours cut out of yew or laurel are not usually places where one likes to linger. The only arbours I have ever enjoyed were flowery ones in Portugal. There in many eighteenth-century gardens regular summer houses are shaped entirely in huge old camellias which still, after centuries of clipping, are set solid in February and March with their bright rosettes of scarlet and pink and white.

I like at least to recall the sentiment of a formal garden close to the house, though not a lavish and symmetrical lay-out that extends so largely that the house looks like the odd man left on the chessboard. I have sometimes thought that the formally patterned garden was evolved at a time when the outside world was mainly wild, unknown and incalculable; a garden pattern was reassuring, for it extended the limits of people's authority out towards the wild. In Europe the informal romantic " landscape " garden became fashionable as the exploration of the physical world began to be achieved and the encyclopædists busily set themselves to catalogue the planet's geography as well as its flora and fauna. Large formal arrangements of flowers or roses or clipped parterres demand a maintenance so out of proportion to today's possibilities and so irrelevant to our way of life, that in the rare cases when such extravagances are possible, they will still appear inappropriate. I prefer to look back to an earlier form, the *hortus inclusus*, that small enclosed flowergarden of the Middle Ages in Europe, designed wholly for pleasure in a period when all that lay beyond the walls of castle or city was farmland, heath or forest. These restricted closes, perhaps only a few feet square, were made for growing herbs and flowers—roses and pinks and columbines—not perhaps very showy by modern standards, but one can see how much they were cherished and appreciated from a hundred paintings and tapestries of the period. How exactly and lovingly depicted are the flowers of the " Dame à la Licorne " tapestries in the Cluny museum or the flag iris in Dürer's Madonna in the National Gallery in London. Often enough these small garden plots were sophisticated and luxurious compositions: flower beds were bordered with painted trellis-work and set around carved and gilded fountains which recalled those Byzantine waterworks designed to represent the Tree of Life.

A replica of this late Gothic idiom would suit few houses to-day; but the principle of a small space near the house designed for flowers in a formal way adapts itself well to contemporary restrictions.

I like to keep the pattern of a formal garden very simple and to use squares, circles and rectangles outlined by narrow paved paths and edge them, as often as not, with lavender, box, rosemary or santolina. I see them as gardens compartmented like a Persian rug, a series of simple shapes to fill with flowers in any one of a hundred different ways.

Gardens in decorative patterns, laid out as carpets or panels, have persisted through the whole history of European gardening. Knot gardens reproduced the interlaced strapwork patterns which were the convention for applied decoration in the late sixteenth century. A hundred years later, the elaborate inlaid scroll work and foliations of buhl and counter-buhl in tortoiseshell, silver and gilt bronze, found its vegetable counterpart in parterres of clipped box, coal or brick dust and white marble chippings. Nor did formal patterns entirely disappear during a century-long vogue for romantic gardens. By the early 1800s, dry-looking bands of neat plants in Empire and Regency patterns carried the formal flavour of the drawing-room into the garden; and, for all his talent and his taste for informal landscape, even Humphrey Repton worked out quite elaborate parterres to embellish formal terraces and lawns. Although it degenerated into carpet bedding and mosaiculture, pattern-gardening just survived the nineteenth century. Banished from private gardens by a shortage of cash and labour and the advent of herbaceous gardening, it still survives in public parks and gardens.

Before the First World War Lutyens and Inigo Triggs revived the taste for pattern in gardens in a relatively simplified form; many of Lutyens's designs are masterly exercises in robust patterns made from squares and circles.

This sort of garden still has its place, though perhaps on a reduced scale, since a patch of good pattern and bright flower colour can enhance the simplified stretches of a modern labour-saving garden of grass and trees and shrubs. They should be no larger than can be maintained impeccably, but their various compartments must be big enough to tell as colour without looking spotty, and the pattern should be interesting in itself during the flowerless winter months.

At Port Lympne between the wars Sir Philip Sassoon had just such a garden immediately below the house. It was an ingenious chess board—a yard square of finely clipped turf alternating with a square of tuberous begonias or marigolds. But its effect lay in the fact that the flower squares were set nine inches below the turf squares so that when in full bloom all was at the same level. It was this refinement which gave elegance to a basically simple pattern.

I have copied this principle and interpreted it in various ways.

In one garden I wanted to give interest to a stone-paved terrace which had been made particularly wide to accommodate garden furniture. The habits of the household changed, people and furniture migrated to another corner, and I had to find some simple way to enliven this overlarge expanse. I did it by taking out a rectangular panel of paving and dividing this empty panel with a criss-cross of narrow bands of the same stone to make a diamond pattern of small beds. These beds are set six inches below ground level and are planted with box, clipped flush with the paving. This makes a lively pattern of green and stone and gives interest to the paved space without breaking it up.

In Piedmont there is an austere modern house with glass walls which disappear into a floor of large terracotta tiles set in a basket-work pattern. This house consists of one big room sparsely decorated with abstract pictures and pieces of modern sculpture. Outside, the brick paving continues to the edge of a hillside thickly set with the dwarf pine, *Pinus montanus mughus*, and forty or fifty miles away, beyond the often mist-covered plain, glisten the snowy mountains. Here too, the terrace is stark and needed some decoration to relate it more closely to the great room and its contents. It sufficed to draw a zigzag shape, using the joints in the brickwork as a guide, and devise a broken maze-like pattern which I hollowed out and again planted with box.

Roses, particularly the polyantha or floribunda kinds, are good plants for these small formal gardens if you are careful to outline your underlying pattern of beds with a dwarf hedge, perhaps in such a case of lavender. The paths that make the design should not be more than eighteen inches or two feet wide and be of gravel or else be paved in brick or stone. Grass paths, which must be wide to be practical, would be out of scale and out of character. For the same reason the beds should be kept small enough to be easily accessible. Four to five feet would be a maximum width.

These small excursions into formality may be very brightly coloured. Here is a miniature garden in which to experiment with spring plantings and later with a whole range of annual flowers. Or you might want to use these formal beds for a botanical collection, or for rare plants or bulbs which require special cultivation.

On a small site this deliberately designed and deliberately coloured patch may well be flower garden enough, the rest being simply and soberly planted to suggest space. Almost always I like to set these parterres to one side or other of the house and so to enclose them that they are felt to be separate from the main composition of the garden.

At the Moulin de la Tuilerie at Gif near Paris there is just such a garden, enclosed by buildings on three sides and lying apart from and above the main garden from which it is separated by a retaining wall. Narrow paths of well-worn square sandstone *pavés* divide the whole space into a series of square lavender-edged beds planted with roses. Close at hand, yet hidden and separate from the rest of the garden, this is a convenient place to grow hybrid tea-roses which I think are better out of sight when not in flower.

A walled or partially walled enclosure near the house suggests a small garden for cutting-flowers. They are apt to look uninteresting planted out in rows in the kitchen garden, but you may well set them in a formal pattern of beds, using one variety in each bed. The beds should be small enough to cut from them without having to walk on them. I have found that this kind of garden is all the more effective if you make no attempt at symmetrical planting; an all-over pattern of squares or rectangles with no strongly marked centre will leave you free to plant a low block of blue cornflowers next to high white marguerites, or delphiniums next to Iceland poppies. Hollyhocks will not be too tall nor dwarf dahlias too small to make good neighbours. All these sharp breaks in height, weight and colour will give brilliance and vivacity to what is usually a very utilitarian and common-place kind of gardening.

I find increasingly, when designing gardens to be looked after by one gardener, or none, that I am obliged to " sketch " and, as it were, suggest a garden by carefully establishing my proportions, reaffirming them by a simple arrangement of hedges and paths, and then giving body to the whole by planting trees and shrubs which can be left to grow without demanding too much labour. Then, looking at the whole as a question of decoration, I feel the need to make some focus of interest and colour so as to tie the composition together. Any strong colour accent set out too far away from the house will likely be distracting; and so my set-piece with its firm design and ordered colour will almost always find its place away to one side but closely tied to the house and its immediate surroundings.

This principle only works on a relatively simple and open site. Often one finds a small garden so irregularly shaped and so hemmed in that you can give it a sense of space only by closing it in still further and developing the whole area as a series of compartments—separate rooms, as it were, leading from one to another so that you never see the whole garden at one time. The openings which lead from one compartment to the next will be the linking element. I would usually make these openings rather small, so that from any one room you may realise that there are others beyond, without being able to divine their shape or their contents. Where you can contrive a succession of openings along an axial line, you can achieve a deceptive air of distance. In this kind of composition it is important that hedges or walls or high and thick blocks of planting should separate each garden. Otherwise you will lose the mystery you are aiming at.

Such gardens will seem like a continuation of the house, a further succession of rooms, each perhaps quite differently decorated; yet you can elaborate each of them in a way that would appear too complicated were it larger and visible from any distance.

Keen gardeners can work out different planting schemes or make whole gardens for one range of colour or one race of plants, without having to tackle the almost insuperable problem of welding these disparate elements into the wider landscape of an open garden. One narrow path traversing half a dozen openings through hedge or wall will lead into as many different gardens, each retaining a domestic scale. Hidcote Manor is, I think, the best example of this kind of garden; and Lawrence Johnston who made it developed the same principle in a quite different context in Edith Wharton's garden near Paris. Here a wide gravel path first runs straight away from the centre of the house through box-edged grass plots where all is open and in full sun. Then it continues between high box hedges through the shade of a wood in which at one point it divides to frame a stone-rimmed pool. Where the wood ends, two pillars mark the entry to a square of grass which I later surrounded by high-clipped horn-beam hedges, and a cross-axis leads on one side into a recently made *théâtre de verdure*, where an oval of yew hedge ends in a raised grass stage with clipped yew wings. Inside the hedged oval is a smaller, sunken oval surrounded by drywalling and set out in a chessboard design with squares of stone alternating with squares of sagina. A fine fifth-century Byzantine stone vase marks the centre while, next to the yew hedge, there are narrow beds of grey-leaved plants and lilies punctuated by white buddleias grown as standards.

On the other side of the central lawn an opening leads into the garden of pinks which I have described on page 20. Beyond the grass square the main path continues to the boundary wall shaded by an over-arching alley of clipped limes and flanked by a grassy orchard of cherry and pear trees, which is starred in spring with rose and mauve and white primroses. Thus each section of this long garden is seen from the house as a succession of narrow glimpses of sunshine and shade, the full shape and treatment of each part only being evident as you pass in turn through them.

I have used this type of composition again and again, particularly in suburban gardens where houses built about fifty years ago were so often set in long narrow plots that ran back from the road. I know very few ways of planning for such strips. If you leave their length unbroken, they inevitably look too narrow; but breaking their length by a series of cross-hedges can at once give a succession of well-proportioned enclosures. The divisions, whether wall or hedge, and the openings can be treated in various ways. Where one such division is full of colour its neighbour will be all green, while high trees and shrubs might follow a flat section.

But we are being drawn insensibly too far away from the house and its immediate surroundings, on the assumption that we have acres to deal with and ample time. On a very small site, one where the whole garden area is perhaps not larger than that of the house, I would always tend to treat the whole space as one more large room which has the sky for its ceiling. Its walls would be green hedges or a tapestry of close-foliage climbing plants or a flowery design of climbing roses, clematis and jasmine. It would have paving and a panel of plain lawn or a mat of flowers as carpeting, as well as chairs and tables. Its other incidents would fill the role that pictures, vases and objects play in a room. Each shrub or small tree would be carefully selected for its shape and texture, and the flowers I chose to use would conform to a scheme of colour of which one would not tire too quickly. Sometimes one is lucky enough to hit on a formula, a combination of colour, texture and shape, which looks so inevitable and right that it becomes " classical." It is this quality of fitness for its place that I would always look for in working out the planting for such an outdoor room.

In the Duke of Windsor's house at Gif there is a cobbled courtyard with, on one side, a low range of buildings with a tiled roof and a simple rhythm of white shuttered doors and windows and beneath them a narrow flower bed. The bare spaces on the rough creamy stone walls are clothed with *Rosa xanthina* " Canary Bird," covered in spring with its single butter-yellow flowers, with a passion-flower which has survived six winters, and with purple and mauve clematis. Every summer the narrow bed at the front of the building is thickly planted with white and blue-purple petunias which surge out over the cobblestones. We have tried verbenas in mixed colours, red and white tobacco flowers, pink cleomes and other colour combinations but finally the blue and white petunias have become a yearly fixture as they so exactly suit and give coherence to the white paint and the purple clematis.

The inside of a house, even the most rigidly stylised, reflects influences coming from many quarters and many places. The pattern of a fabric, the curve of a chair-leg, the proportions of a window pane, drawn from different sources, figure as the marks of an old and rich culture. Similarly, an outdoor living-space may be eclectic in its planting and round it you can successfully use plant material that might seem too exotic farther away from the house. Shapes, texture and colour can be definite and, in the undecided English climate, planting which suggests a warmer climate will not come amiss.

The planting of a terrace or sitting place also must strike a note which will harmonize with both house and garden. For this reason I prefer not to make flower beds as such too close to an outdoor living-room. However gay the tulips in spring, the annuals and herbaceous plants in summer, there will be many months when the earth is bare and dreary. But narrow beds at the base of a wall, plantings to give emphasis or to mark the junction of terrace and garden are sometimes indispensable if one wants to avoid too sharp a contrast between the hardness of masonry and the softness of the planted garden. For these corners, in whatever country or climate, there is always a wide choice of evergreen and foliage plants. It becomes a question of choosing one's plants for their permanent aspect the year through. Flower colour is of secondary importance and we can solve that problem in another way. Box and yew, euonymus, myrtle or pittosporum will make evergreen hedges and, where height is needed, beech and hornbeam, which when clipped keep their tawny leaves in winter, will quickly give shelter. Whether for a single plant or a group the choice of shrubs which are handsome all the year round is endless, as also is the list of subshrubs. If one likes grey-leaved shrubs there is a long line of names to choose from. Lavender and cottage pinks, for instance, can give the theme for a whole planting, or in a warm climate *Cineraria maritima*, silvery gazania and othonnopsis. A quantity of good all-the-year-round plants spring to my mind, plants that can be used in many situations and combinations. The bergenias which we used to call saxifrage or megasea are handsome through the twelve months of the year with their bold leathery leaves. Although they look rather depressed in a very hard frost, a few sunny days in February or March will bring them bursting into heavy corymbs of soft pink flowers which are curiously harmonised with their foliage by the coppery crimson of their flower stalks. They can be planted in bright sun or full shade and they seem to succeed anywhere from Cannes to Copenhagen.

Viburnum davidii is another excellent low growing evergreen, always tidy and accepting sun or shade indifferently. The ordinary mahonia is a good plant too for all kinds of places where a permanent green planting can be used. This plant, as one sees it so often in neglected shrubberies, is a rather untidy shrub of straggling growth for which its honey-scented yellow flowers and subsequent grape-blue berries scarcely make amends. I learnt how to use it from that Hertfordshire garden where I saw it as a sheet of sparkling green and yellow in April. The secret is to cut it to within six inches of the ground every two or three years so that it never becomes leggy.

I often wish to use flag iris near a house as their greyish spring foliage is so lovely, but unfortunately from July on the leaves are apt to wither so that I usually plant irises along with tree paeonies in a corner likely to be visited only between April and the end of June when these plants are at their best.

Agapanthus where they are hardy, that is, where there is little or no frost, are most useful. Their dark-green strap-like foliage is always in place, they are very free flowering and their lovely umbels of hyacinth blue flowers last well over a month. More usually they are planted in tubs which can be stored in a frost-proof place through the cold months. This is the way too that

I like to use the ordinary garden hydrangeas. Their flowering tips are already formed in autumn and risk being nipped by frost; nor, except when they are in full flower, are they very handsome plants, so there is much to be said for growing them in a portable form.

The yucca family provides good plants for giving an effect of weight and permanence near a terrace. *Y. filamentosa* seems to be the hardiest and will survive even in a cold clay soil in Eastern England. The species *Y. gloriosa* and *Y. flaccida* prefer a warmer soil and climate and all are equally generous with their great spikes of creamy flowers in August. The ordinary rosemary is invaluable: as domesticated as a cat, it belongs to a warm corner against a wall, and there is a magnificent variation which I know as the Lawrence Johnston rosemary which is a laxly growing bush with flowers of a deep purple. I believe it originally came from La Mortola near Ventimiglia.

All the lavenders are admirable plants for furnishing a sunny part of the garden. They only need a well-drained soil and a light clipping after flowering. The Hidcote variety is the best among the dwarf varieties. The white and pink varieties of *Lavandula spica* have charm but seem more delicate. But the lavender is a Mediterranean plant and, in Provence where they are cultivated as a source of oil of lavender, "le lavandin", *L. semidentatus*, the black-purple variety with green foliage and *L. spic* cover whole hillsides.

If by now your protected corners are not already full, plant cistus from seed or from cuttings: cousins of the sun roses, their single flowers in mauve, white and pink sometimes blotched in deeper colour, open for a day and then drop, all through the summer. All of them are evergreen.

Although they lose their leaves in winter there are several late flowering subshrubs which seem to me to have their place in the intimate planting near the terrace. I like *Ceratostigma plumbaginoides* and *C. willmottianum* for their porcelain blue flowers in September, as well as *Caryopteris clandonensis* with grey-green foliage and misty blue flowers, and *Perowskia atriplicifolia*, the

Russian sage with almost white foliage and deep purple flowers. This is a plant to cut hard back in late April. I first saw it used to break the intensity of a scarlet orange and crimson herbaceous autumn border at Port Lympne, and, more recently, thrusting upwards from a mass of scarlet verbena at Wisley. I like to combine it with a dark red form of *Sedum spectabile*, with Japanese anemones or as a foreground for that fine autumn-flowering shrub *Hibiscus syriacus* in the blue form called *coeleste*.

Among all these shrubby plants some of the lilies will be comfortable and I know of no better place for *Lilium regale*, *L. candidum*, *L. martagon* and *L. martagon album*, *L. chalcedonicum*, or, in a shadier corner, *L. auratum*. Among the other plants they are scarcely noticeable until they break into sumptuous and fragrant flower.

I think that planting near the house or round the terrace should be bold and, for want of a better word, sophisticated: so I usually exclude plants which really require a wilder setting such as heaths and brooms and, indeed, all manner of rock plants. For the same reason shrubs and trees should have character in their form, their foliage or their flower to gain a place where they will be seen all through the year. Magnolias, for instance, always look right. I do not know a variety which is not distinguished-looking at any time. *M. grandiflora* is equally magnificent as a tree or a wall shrub, as are *M. delavayi* and *M. wilsonii*, and other deciduous species are admirable even when not in leaf. Japanese cherries I find irresistible for the sheer ravishment of their flowering and my favourite is the single white Tai Haku. *Cercis siliquastrum*, the Judas tree, should be near the house though it is seen at its best only in a climate warm enough for it to flower before the leaves appear. To see it and the white dogwood in flower together in Virginia in April is an unforgettable experience. *Eriobotrya japonica*, the loquat, an evergreen tree south of the Loire, is an excellent wall plant in England.

I often wonder why the ordinary quince tree is not more

popular. In a simple garden it graces an important position far more than an apple tree. It is rather slow growing and likes a moist place; its branches take lovely forms, and its foliage and flowers have character and charm. Another splendid and quite hardy though slow-growing tree is *Davidia involucrata vilmoriniana*. It is a very distinguished plant well worth a key place near the house, eventually to enchant with its enormous white hanging bracts which sway and turn in the June breezes. In any moist warm climate I would want to use *Embothrium longifolia* near the house. Its scarlet blossoms make it the most spectacular of all the flowering trees which will grow in the British Isles. It has almost the same intensity of scarlet as the flame tree *Poinciana regia* which sets the streets of Cairo and New Delhi ablaze each spring.

Acer palmatum shares with many Japanese plants a distinctive refinement and looks well anywhere whether in the wilder parts of the garden or in an architectural frame.

Evergreen shrubs, so useful in giving an impression of solidity and " point " to a group, or to be placed as isolated features, must also conform to a certain standard of quality. This question of quality is indefinable. Certain plants have it anyway. Others seem to possess it only when used in certain combinations. I have to suppose that this is a question of personal prejudice, and here I would say that strong prejudices are not inimical to good garden designing and perhaps one should revise one's prejudices from time to time. I know that for years, by association, I violently disliked golden privet, I think because it reminded me of the bleak and dusty villa gardens and the smell of hot asphalt of that dreary seaside resort where I was once sent to school. Then later, one late April day, I came out of the London Underground at a suburban station to see a planting of *Forsythia intermedia spectabilis* and golden privet which seemed to have caught all the intensity of spring in a flame of greeny-yellow. Later, in as unlikely a place as the Great West Road leading out of London, I was finally converted to the possibilities of golden privet when I saw corners planted with pyramidal hornbeam set in rounded clipped mounds of the privet. The harmony of colour, texture and weight and the contrast of form in this taught me to look, in the case of every plant, as to how it could be used, since by context something can be made from what may appear very unpromising material.

But rather than dwell on the possibilities of elder, privet, snowberry and other usually unlovable plants, let us return to our evergreen shrubs. Rhododendrons, magnificent in leaf and flower, are not in my opinion suitable for planting near a terrace. In such a place one seeks to reinforce the impression of a sun-trap, and rhododendrons need at least a dappled shade where the light shines across their flowers and renders them luminous and transparent. *Laurus nobilis*, the bay laurel of antiquity as essential as olive oil in Mediterranean cooking, which grows near every kitchen door from Cadiz to Constantinople, stands high on my list. Wild, it is the most graceful of small evergreen trees and in frost-free climates it makes a magnificent large hedge. Even one plant in the sunny angle of a wall is enough to evoke the two thousand years of a classic civilisation. *Eucryphia cordifolia* and its hybrid *E. nymansensis* will give the same effect in a similar situation.

The junipers known as *Juniperus chinensis pfitzeriana* and *J. sabina tamariscifolia* with their spreading feathery branches are evergreens equally suitable for breaking a too severe architectural treatment or for masking the transition from a formal to an informal part of the garden. These are shrubs which never become monotonous or tiresome however much ground one gives them. For me they have the same fascination as the sea in movement or as tree tops, seen from above on a windy day. I know of a garden in France whose owner wished to plant a sloping field as a wood and yet not obscure the view. So he planted the whole area with *Cedrus atlantica glauca* and ruthlessly beheaded them all at six feet from the ground to achieve a sea of grey-green foliage.

For terrace planting I find myself continuously coming back to Mediterranean plants: myrtles, for instance, which require a warm place, *Arbutus unedo*, and *Viburnum tinus*, the laurestinus of the Victorian shrubbery but none the less lovely for that.

The choice of pots and tubs for flowers needs the same careful consideration as do the flowers themselves. I like only the plainest pots for flowers. Terracotta vases with swags of fruit and flowers are lovely when large enough to be planted with lemon and orange trees in the more or less flowerless setting of an Italian garden; but on a small scale and filled with flowers they almost always look over-rich. The ordinary red flower-pot, so simple in shape and material, is a perfect foil for its contents. Where you need very large pots this basic shape can be elaborated a little, but not too much, by a rather bolder rim and a simple rib or moulding about half-way up. The top of any flower pot or plant container should always be as wide or wider than its base. Narrow-mouthed oil jars, for instance, look absurd planted with a tuft of flowers or foliage which invariably appears too small for the proportions of the jar.

In any paved place I like to group pots in considerable numbers. For instance, round a very large pot with a pink oleander I would put a whole ring of medium-sized flower pots planted with pink geraniums and, where there was room, I might add still another range of quite small pots with white or pink petunias. Two or three pots on either side of a wide flight of garden steps filled with bright flowers in one or two colours will make them gayer and more a part of the garden.

In the old days in Cairo this form of pot-gardening was very popular. The steps and sanded courtyard of Cairo houses often had long ranges of pots, sometimes two or three deep, filled with cinerarias or cyclamen, white anthemis, nemesias and all sorts of annuals. In Italy, too, rows of flower pots often provide the only colour in the garden. At La Loggia near Turin the entrance to the main floor is by way of a great open staircase set into the façade. The black stone steps are carpeted in royal blue, and in late autumn each step of the long double flight is set out with pots of white and yellow chrysanthemums—a gala welcome as one reaches the portico after driving through the damp and fog of the Po valley.

Pots should always, so to speak, have their feet firmly on the ground. Hung in wrought-iron containers on walls or screens they are completely out of place: as impractical and even less attractive than those old-fashioned suspended wire baskets which one used to see filled with ferns or pendulous begonias. Glazed pots are not very satisfactory for growing plants, though cacti and tradescantia can be persuaded to flourish in them. I would never use them as their shiny surface seen out of doors makes too brilliant a juxtaposition with flowers or foliage, though faience used alone can be a very lovely garden decoration. Old Arab patios are full of tiled walls and walks in blues, greens and yellows, which give a liquid coolness to these gardens of violent sunshine and shadow.

Inheriting this tradition from the Arabs, the Portuguese in the seventeenth and eighteenth centuries made extraordinary use of glazed pottery. The rococo garden of Queluz has a balustraded canal with a bridge, a pyramid and a whole series of elaborate urns all of faience, elaborately painted with sailing ships, fish and arabesques in blue, mustard yellow and beetroot red. Not so long ago, when I was in Lisbon to advise on a property, I was taken to see a deserted garden, a complete and quite large rococo " folly," with octagonal pavilions, statues, columns, fountains, benches and walls all either made of, or covered in, this same polychrome faience.

While such rareties are hard to find and not easy to move, smaller pieces are effective in an outdoor room so long as you consider that their glazed and patterned surfaces count as flowers. There is a house near Vence whose owner has for years collected faience dishes, old watering pots and olive jars, often in brown and deep moss green. These are effectively set about in a cloistered patio planted with cypresses and huge trees of *Magnolia grandiflora* whose shining green leaves have the same texture and colour as the pottery.

The energetic revival of pottery launched at Vallauris by Picasso already suggests new possibilities for garden decoration. Young potters are making large abstract pieces in garden scale. Perhaps understandably this non-representational sculpture often seems sadly out of key in any traditional indoor setting. Yet it can be imaginative, stimulating and at the same time oddly tranquil once you place it out-of-doors in a setting of leaf, stone and pebble.

Wooden boxes and tubs need as much care in their selection as pots. Except as window boxes or on a roof top, wooden containers are best used for large subjects like trees or shrubs or plants with important foliage and not for flowers for which I think pots are more suitable. The best form of plant box is the classical *caisse de Versailles* in which to grow orange and lemon trees, oleanders, and pomegranates, and other exotics which have to be taken into an orangery in winter. At Versailles there are three-hundred-year-old orange trees still growing in such cases, though the cases themselves have been renewed many times; and at the Château de Laeken outside Brussels there is one orange tree known to date from the time of Henry Quatre. The original *caisse de Versailles* is a square wooden box constructed round four corner-posts and banded top and bottom with flat iron bars. These can be unscrewed and each wooden side taken out separately, so that the roots of the trees can be treated and new soil added when needed. Sometimes these cases are very large, up to four feet high and as many square. On this scale they are only suitable for putting in the courtyard or on the terrace of the largest buildings. You may see them lining the garden paths all through the summer in front of the colossal orangery at Versailles or on the terrace surrounding the formal layout round the great fountain in the Luxembourg Gardens in Paris. For a smaller house and garden they can be made in any convenient size so long as their exact proportion is respected. They should always be an exact cube, excluding the feet which raise the bottom of the case just clear of the ground and also the finials of the four corner-posts which are usually topped by a round or pineapple-shaped knob.

The square sides can be of vertical or horizontal planking or, better still, a frame with a slightly sunk central panel. It is simpler and cheaper to have fixed iron bands, for, if the boxes are made of larch and well charred inside, they will last a good many years. I use these cases in the South of France for orange and lemon trees and elsewhere for clipped box or yew trees, for standard or bush rhododendrons and for bay trees clipped in different ways. Set out on a terrace or in front of a house, they have a dignified and architectural air and make even a bare courtyard look well-furnished. I like to paint them in white or silvery grey with black bands. Outside Christian Dior's shop in Paris small ones holding bay trees are picked out in grey and white; at Longleat the classic proportions are used for enormous cases made with slabs of grey slate. This cube shape is the best for general use, although I know of one enchanting pair of such jardinières belonging to the Talleyrand-Périgord family which are only about two feet high and triangular in plan. These date from the end of the eighteenth century and are made of grey and white marble with gilt bronze mouldings and ornaments. Although they are collector's pieces and are, of course, not for outdoor use, I would like to see them planted with clipped standard myrtles.

Where there is a good reason for having low oblong wooden flower boxes on a terrace or in an outdoor room, these should also have corner-posts for strength and be raised some two or three inches from the ground. They will not need metal bands. These too may be painted white or pale grey or even a very dark green, which can be relieved by painted bands or a trellis pattern in white.

CHAPTER V

On planting : trees

There is so often in landscape gardening a special difficulty: that gap so hard to bridge, between good design and good planting. I have known brilliant designers who were passionately keen on garden design but who had never pushed their study of plants far enough. They either used a very limited repertory of plant material or left the planting to somebody else. In the same way remarkable plant cultivators I have known, men with a vast knowledge of plants and their likes and dislikes, have rarely had any idea of how to use their plants to make a garden picture.

The gardener or designer who can combine the two is a rare bird. These are two wide fields of knowledge and a man's lifetime is not long enough to permit his reaching the limits of either. But a man whose bent is towards design should give at least as much time and attention to plants as will enable him to develop what I must call " flair." Then even though his knowledge of names and cultivation is necessarily limited, he will understand the nature of vegetable life well enough to be able to indicate the kind of planting suitable to his plan. A master, through whichever artistic medium, will, as he matures, almost certainly express himself through a limited range of whatever are the materials of his particular art. But this repertory will be the result of years of exploration and experiment. A professional garden designer, like any other artist, easily falls into the trap of a mannerism too early crystallised. By chance he achieves a happy

In the courtyard of her house near Vence, Thalia Malcolm achieved colour without flowers. Making full use of the strong Mediterranean light she used Magnolia grandiflora and foliage plants like this Phormium to compliment the forms of her collection of old Provençal garden pots and vases

At Longleat, a severe setting of mown grass, clipped yew and cut stone frames the splendour of a white peacock in full display, a lively and glorious substitute for flowers

The dressing rooms of a swimming pool near Cannes are built into a lavender-planted hillside. The pool level is deliberately higher than the terrace, which is shaded by a simple iron pergola planted with vines whose shadows make intricate and changing patterns on the handmade terra cotta squares below.

The wide curve of a gently graded garden staircase on a Mediterranean hillside. The risers of the steps are sections of pine trunks and the carefully controlled and reticent planting is of wide stretches of santolina, lavender, eriocephalum, teucrium and other sun-loving plants

result and then he becomes content to repeat the same plan and the same range of planting. It is a tremendous temptation to repeat a successful formula; but a mass-production method of garden designing can easily come to an unfortunate full stop. One day one finds oneself faced with a site to which one's ready-made recipe would simply not apply; and to re-think and re-see a problem is difficult and sometimes impossible once certain mental habits and associations have been fixed. It may be less commercially satisfactory but it is far more interesting to the garden designer to see the planting of each new garden as a new problem to which his previously accumulated data may or may not apply; to try to find new solutions for new problems rather than, so much more easily, impose his well-tried formula. But, to do this demands a good deal of patience and some of that not easily marketable commodity—artistic conscience.

To compose a planting scheme is similarly easy or difficult. Although I know from experience that a particular plant which I have often used before will do very well for my immediate purpose, I am always reluctant to decide just that it will do and to leave it at that. Perhaps there is another plant which, for one reason or another, will be even better. So once again I am obliged first to refer to that compartment of my mind which contains an illustrated catalogue of plants, and then to study plant lists and encyclopædias in the hope of finding a better alternative.

Planning will give your ground its shape and form, establish its levels and decide the disposition and nature of the elements you wish to include, but already at the planning stage your ideas about planting must begin to take shape. A painter may start his painting by a detail in one corner, a focus radiating outwards which he will eventually link to other points—other departures started in other parts of the canvas—or he may sketch in the broad lines of his composition. In both cases he will almost certainly hold his general intention in his mind's eye so that from wherever he starts the details and parts of his painting will have relation to a prefigured whole.

Whatever its nature or situation a garden is successful in so far as its composition, its patterns and its planting interlock and are related to the site. In a garden composition the various possibilities of plan and perspective, of solids and voids must be related to the plants you will use. A plan which looks all right on paper easily becomes a mockery unless the designer has his planting in mind through every stage.

A single example will perhaps explain my meaning. On a recent tour of the parks and gardens in and around Lisbon, I lunched at a garden restaurant in the middle of the newly planted forests of cypress and juniper and eucalyptus on the hilly country which overlooks the mouth of the Tagus. The restaurant is in a garden designed on a small plateau dominating the countryside around. It is a sunken garden and has a long narrow pool in a lawn flanked by drywalls and, at the far end, a pergola planted with various climbers. The plantings of herbaceous plants, grasses and aquatic plants had been most carefully studied, but almost all the plants would grow equally well in Northern Europe and you have the impression of being on the shores of the Baltic or the North Sea. Here is a competently achieved composition but one quite out of context and arousing just that sense of falseness and discomfort once expressed by a Japanese diplomat visiting a famous " Japanese " garden in Europe who, seeking to pay a suitable compliment, could only say " We have nothing like it in Japan."

The range of plants which the gardener can use has grown so large that a beginner is likely to lose his way among them very quickly. Only with time and by experiment will he accumulate some knowledge of a more or less limited range of plant material. Little by little the amateur will learn what is possible and what is not for his own garden, while the professional will have to extend his repertory to cover a thousand different situations.

There are always a great number of possibilities and one is always tempted to try too many of them at the same time. I have been lucky enough to have made many gardens of all kinds and in all sorts of places during the last thirty years, but I have not yet learned to be sufficiently inexorable with myself in this

matter of limiting my plant varieties and planting them boldly
and on the largest scale which the garden composition and the
site will allow. Yet I know that the most striking and satisfying
visual pleasure comes from the repetition or the massing of one
simple element. Imagine the Parthenon with each column of a
different kind of marble! Yet in gardening one is constantly
making this mistake. Living plants are so lovely in themselves
and their texture and colours so accommodating that one has to
go to considerable trouble to make them really clash. One tends
to devise harmonious detail and forget the whole. But a planting
patchwork however subtly worked out will always remain a
patchwork and once again the wonder of wholeness and unity
will have escaped us.

Gardens must have a theme which will not depend only on
their plan. Your aim, or one of your aims, is to suggest a
" paradise " in the terms of the elements already existing on the
site and which give it its special character, to intensify and
concentrate the *genius loci* and give free rein to a love of nature
by offering each plant the best conditions possible for its development. Here already is one of the traps into which the garden-
maker almost inevitably falls: in this situation he will tend to let
the needs of an individual plant override other considerations.
In a wild garden, composition becomes noticeably many dimen-
sional; colour is added to volume and texture to colour. And to
this you must add the procession of light and shade through the
days and the seasons, perhaps the sounds of falling water, or of
branches in the wind and the bright passage of bird and butterfly.
The sheer joy of all these is enough to inebriate any gardener.
Give him freedom to plant from many different worlds of
vegetation and his intoxication is complete. This represents a
maximum of horticultural satiety and I find that, for myself, I
must look for a subtler satisfaction.

For instance, change the scale, and the agreeable floral
confusion in an Alpine meadow will become another world.
You have only to take a magnifying glass to a wild orchid or
columbine, to the smallest plant of primula or androsace and,

at once, strength, will, design, colour and a tremendous rational simplicity invades eye and mind. These appear to me attributes of each living plant and flower and I will always want a garden to echo and stress the vitality and the wholeness of the individual elements which go to make it.

You will move into the garden as into the " otherness " of an unknown place. It will be evocative and the more so if you will contrive to keep it free from elements which recall the commonplace and all the consequent and wellworn visual and mental associations. I remember Helen Lindsay-Smith's Surrey garden where, below the house in a little valley, a sombre stream ran through the peaty mud of a swamp which was an alder wood. Maybe there was half an acre of black swamp and smooth alder trunks with their brown-green leaves and on that day the whole dark place was lighted to magic by countless thousands of carefully selected *Primula japonica* with their tiered rings of white flowers shading here and there into the palest pink.

Whatever your idea, whatever you set out to achieve in an informal garden, you will do, in the main by planting. Paths, of whatever they are made, will be wide and easy and should not, I think, twist or turn too frequently if you wish to avoid unnecessary complication. On sloping ground changes of direction may be inevitable but in general a sharp turn should occur only when passing from one section of such a garden to another. Each picture should be large in scale however limited in actual area. This largeness of scale is really a question of how simply you will express one main theme and how careful you will be to see that all the subsidiary planting and all the detail shall contribute to your main idea and not distract from it.

Any plant or genus of plants, for instance, could be your basic planting. Perhaps you have an oakwood, soil and climatic conditions are right, and you want to make a camellia garden. In this case you might compose the main lines or rather masses of your planting entirely with camellias so that through the bare spring branches of the oaks the thin broken sunlight would light up your massing of shiny dark foliage and the crystalline whites and pinks and reds of the flowering camellias. If you were to add a single yellow forsythia or the pinky-mauve or blue of an early rhododendron the unity of your garden would at once be dispersed and lost. All your other planting will be made with one intent—to enforce the effect of the camellias, so you will perhaps use as ground cover subshrubs, gaultherias and *Viburnum davidii* and *Cornus canadensis*, plants with glossy leaves in different tones of green.

Even with this limited range of planting I would go further in my search for simplification and unity. I would sharply limit my range of camellias to a very few kinds and plant these in mass to such an extent as would satisfy me that here the full nature and essence of these particular plants were presented.

There are two objections which will come to the gardener's mind. The first is that such discipline and such a use of garden space for a few brief weeks in the year is an extravagance that few people can permit themselves. I think the answer is that any piece of ground so treated may have a second flowering peak at another moment as long as it is of a different nature. In this particular case lilies might provide an answer—summer or autumn flowering, their thin stems rising from the under-planting and their flowers luminous against the now quite dark green camellias.

The second objection is that this is no new theory. True, since it is customary to mass dwarf hybrid roses, certain annuals and tulips. Gardens composed entirely of heaths have had a certain success as have the iris and other one-plant gardens. It has also become customary to make woodland plantings exclusively of rhododendrons. But I think the process may be carried much further and that the study of texture and colour in different aspects of light could result in lovelier gardens, more coherent and with more unity. A composition in terms of camellias or, perhaps, large-leaved rhododendrons is not for everyone but even the most untractable soil or site may be conjured into a unique composition if the possibilities of a severely limited range of plants are fully expressed.

In general, in any garden one should limit one's choice of plants to those that will flourish. To succeed with a rare or difficult plant is a different pleasure and another question. A garden which is a well-run clinic or museum lies outside the domain of visual harmony which is perhaps almost the chief aim of a garden designer.

It would be a treason to one's understanding to consider any plant ugly in itself. There is and must be always a complete integration between root and stem, flower, leaf and seed. I happen, for instance, to be a sworn enemy of the common elder because it thrives so well in the sour corners of neglected gardens, but I have to admit that a mature bush with its great plates of scented creamy flowers hanging over a wall, perhaps among farm buildings, has always enchanted me. In the same way most kinds of fir or spruce as isolated specimens in a garden or small park suggest to me the rather silly romantic approach to landscape gardening fashionable in the late eighteenth and middle nineteenth century, although nothing can be more lovely than a large stand of these trees in mountain country. Such personal prejudices are almost necessary in a gardener's approach to plants, and he will surely shape his world of flowers within the bias of his likes and dislikes. Once you begin to be sensitive towards plants and their cultural needs, you learn that their proper placing will usually produce a harmonious result. I stress this because I so often, for example, find lavender planted in the lush grasses of a water meadow and flag iris associated with azaleas in shade and an acid soil. And I have often met rhododendrons, rambler roses and geraniums all planted together in one sunny bed, although the first like peat and shade, the second a good strong loam, and the third a poor, starved soil.

Plants grouped according to their cultural needs will always give certain major themes for the composition of a garden or part of a garden, while, conversely, the existing soil conditions should be allowed to a great extent to dictate the species, forms and textures of your plantings. This will lead not to monotony but to coherence, and there are endless variations to be played on the simplest basic theme.

I have very often gardened in Mediterranean places where old olive trees gave the basic note with their gnarled and twisted trunks and silvery-green, sun-flecked foliage. These are patient trees which will live two thousand years in the stoniest ground. On the outskirts of the garden *Iris unguicularis* can be naturalised under them as well as freesia and the wild scarlet and blue anemones, small white Roman hyacinths and white jonquils for their scent.

Near a house I would maybe make a lawn under the olives and plant mauve wistaria, blue kennedya, yellow and white Banksian roses as well as *Rosa anemonoides* and the free-flowering fast-growing rose "La Follette" to ramp about among the branches and make swaying garlands of scent and colour. In yet another setting, taking the silvery reflections of the trees as a theme, I would plant grey-leaved shrubs to grow wild and make a thicket: rosemary, cistus, the grey-leaved teucrium so much used in the South of France, *Atriplex halimus* and lavenders. In the garden proper the same lavenders, flag iris of all kinds, garden pinks, santolina, diplopappus, *Felicia amelloides*, *Aster pappei* *Phlomis fruticosa*, various salvia species, and *Leonotis leonorus* can, make a flowery groundwork for the olive trees. If I want a bolder and greener look, bay laurels, *Choisya ternata*, the lovely late-flowering *Lagerstroemia indica*, agapanthus and tree paeonies will compose another kind of picture, always in the same basic frame of olive trees.

Farther north, a wood of pine trees might provide the theme. Under pines you may well find a sandy and slightly acid soil. If the air is moist and the shade sufficient a whole range of rhododendrons, both species and hybrids, will grow to be used either for their flower colour or for compositions based on the form and texture of their foliage. Such species as *Rhododendron falconeri*, *R. sino-grande*, *R. macabeanum* and fifty others from the Himalayas, Yunnan and Upper Burma with their stiff leathery leaves, lined with silver or cinnamon-coloured felt, make a tapestry of varied green. The endless range of rhododendron hybrids will give dappled colour in the half-shade from March until July—whites, creams, pinks, rose, scarlet and crimson and every shade of mauve from pale lilac to black-purple. As a secondary theme various species of lilies can prolong the interest of such a planting well into autumn.

Again, with the same background you might wish to use azaleas for an even more brilliant composition, though I never like to mix any of the Ghent, mollis or other species of deciduous azalea with rhododendrons. Their colouring of yellow, orange, flame and orange scarlet, the lettuce green of their young foliage and the transparent papery texture of their flowers go badly with the solidity of rhododendrons and their different range of flower colour.

Even amongst these azaleas colour has to be used with discretion. The creams, yellows and oranges are best kept apart from the rather hot pinks, and the darkest reds need white to light them up.

Perhaps the only place in Europe where *Azalea indica* can be properly grown is on the shores of Lakes Como and Maggiore. There, mixed with gardenias and camellias, they make a fantastic showing. In colder places I would use Kurume azaleas with their mounds of white, rose, scarlet and magenta. The Japanese have for centuries employed these low-growing, compact evergreens in their gardens but elsewhere it is only in the last twenty years that they have spread from a few specimens in collectors' gardens to a new use and popularity for massed plantings.

If the soil of our pine-wood is sandy or gravelly the family of heaths is large enough to supply subjects for still another theme. Here are plants for massing and grouping, varying in height from a few inches to six feet, tidy all the year round with their mats and mounds of varying greens and russets, silvers and golds. Nor is it difficult to have colour for twelve months in the year. At that moment in March or April when there is least colour amongst the heaths, the minor bulbs which will, in the main, be happy in the same conditions will star the sandy spaces between the drifts of heaths with brilliant flecks of colour. Crocus species, scillas, chionodoxas, dwarf narcissi and many kinds of dwarf wild tulips at once spring to mind.

With the same background of pines as our starting point we can continue to find idea after idea for plantings. Near the sea where the air is moist and there is little frost to brown the next year's flower-buds already formed, you might make a whole garden picture with hydrangeas, using again both species and hybrids. Or in a warm but drier climate the cistus family would make a garden of subtle scents to mingle with the resinous air around the pines. All summer long the ephemeral single flowers, of yellow, white, mauve and rose, sometimes splashed with crimson and chocolate, will cover the bushes each morning to fall again at night. I would carpet the ground of such a planting with mats of helianthemum, especially the silver-leaved varieties with single flowers of rose, white and yellow, and, for contrast, add drifts of camassia for its spikes of grey-blue flowers.

An olive grove or a pine wood, a clump of silver birch, a weeping willow by a muddy duck-pond, a swampy meadow filled with meadowsweet and flag iris, a hazel coppice or an oak wood, a rocky hillside—these are all natural settings. What may happen is that we set out with one idea and the intention of carrying it through: then an irresistible plant for which we must find a home turns up, or we are tempted to plant something to fill in a temporary gap and the discipline we have imposed on ourselves is forgotten. It is often hard to be ruthless and make the sacrifices necessary to our theme.

An untouched ground with natural features whose character can determine the planting themes of a garden is perhaps rather exceptional. The designer more often has to face other harder and less easily defined problems of site. The alteration and planting of an existing garden is one of these. If the garden is old—that is, with matured trees and shrubs already there—it is on these and any other features, such as water, walls and hedges, that he will base his planting schemes. In any garden made in the last hundred years, there will almost certainly be a greatly mixed planting. Deciduous trees of all sorts will be interspersed with a variety of conifers. Flowering shrubs and evergreen hedges of laurel, yew and privet will compete in their confusion with flower beds as well as unnecessary paths and all the minor clutter of three or four generations of garden fashions. As usual design and planting must be considered together. Faced with this kind of a problem, I first try to diminish the confusion and establish calm. My first action is to remove all the obvious rubbish, misshapen spindly trees and bushes that have lost in the struggle for light and air and food, as well as such plants as elder, snowberry or indeed any other unattractive subject which has run wild.

Once this is done you are left with plants which have grown well because the site suits them, though there will still be almost certainly too many varieties in odd and uncomfortable propinquity. But among these you will find perhaps one plant or a combination of plants which by their nature, their form, their silhouette against the sky, their colour or their texture, will suggest or become a basic theme. Their position or their relation to a house as well as to the landscape will also play an important part in the composition. Once you have cleaned away all the inessentials you might, for example, be left with a group of thuyas or cypresses. Their spires of green, blue-green or golden-green may suggest a garden whose basic planting will be mainly vertical, or contrariwise you may decide to accent their height and shape by using shrubs and trees of only horizontal habit. In the same way a group of Lombardy poplars may suggest water for reflections and the water in its turn demand water-lilies and iris to emphasise the general mood.

When I start a planting scheme for an empty site I find it easier to set up a general framework first. For one thing the larger elements, trees and hedges and shrub plantings, take time to grow. Once they are in place you can forget their temporarily meagre aspect by concentrating on your smaller scale planting.

Many people fear to cut down a fully grown tree, chiefly, I think, because they find it difficult to visualise with any clarity the consequent change in silhouette and lighting. Many people, too, are timid about planting trees and hedges, afraid they will have to look at sapling growths for the rest of their lives. So they plant fast-growing trees and hedge-plants—poplars, willows and privet—forgetting that most fast-growing plants are apt to be short-lived and have terribly invasive root-systems. I would always plant the trees which will give me the qualities I want for a given situation irrespective of their rate of growth. One so soon forgets their spindly first years in the pleasure of watching their progress, which, since leaf and branch increase by a sort of geometrical progression, is rapid enough.

The decision as to what trees to plant on a bare site requires courage too. Once I have selected the kinds of trees which I think likely to succeed I have almost always to resist the temptation to plant a mixture of my particular favourites chosen from among them: here a tulip tree, there a liquidambar, or a taxodium perhaps or a deciduous magnolia. At this point I have to be firm and remember that the prime object of this basic planting of trees is to create visual unity. Once this is strongly emphasised you can experiment with variations in detail and not lose the general sense of harmony.

On a very small site it is essential to avoid planting trees which will be too cumbrous or too greedy. Poplars, for all their rapid growth, have roots which travel far, undermine foundations and make it difficult to grow anything else for yards around. Chestnuts too make a heavy and sour shade, though on a larger site they make a handsome screen. Most of the oaks would be good garden trees since you can successfully plant under them; were they not so very slow-growing. Although they are superb as old hedgerow trees, I never plant sycamores in a garden as they are usually covered with black spot by August, when even the attractive coloured spring foliage of certain varieties will have faded to a dirty green. Many of the maples are good garden trees and their autumn colour is comparable in brilliance with that of the scarlet oak (an excellent tree in moist and acid soil). I particularly like the small-leaved *Acer campestre*, so good in combination with *Liquidambar styraciflua*, as well as *Acer saccharinum*, the sugar maple, and *Acer platanoides*. All these trees, turning yellow and scarlet in autumn, are the more brilliant for a foil of *Pinus excelsa* whose long silky needles even in young trees have exactly the right shade of blue green for contrast with the autumn-fired maples.

The red-twigged lime, *Tilia europaea*, is the best of its family for a small site. It can be clipped and trained or left free and the orange red of the young wood warms a winter landscape as do the trunks of Scots firs, *Pinus sylvestris*, although these last are rather dull when young. The Austrian pine, *Pinus nigra*, though an admirable windbreak, is rather coarse in scale for the small garden and looks clumsy as a young tree.

In a small garden, or one where I want to create a woodland air, I like to plant silver birch. They grow fast, are graceful even as small trees and fit into a wild or a sophisticated garden equally well. They seem to flourish in almost any soil and are good neighbours for other plants. I like to plant them rather lavishly, for the hackneyed group of three always looks thin, and when I want the accent of a single white trunk, I prefer to use Young's weeping birch which looks the better for being isolated.

Flowering trees of medium size will give character to a small garden, especially if you resist the temptation to use too many different kinds. An old apple or pear orchard owes its special quality to its being planted, in the main, with one kind of tree. A miscellany of malus and prunus varieties planted together in orchard pattern will never have the same charm. When I want flowering trees to dominate a planting scheme I try to select one or two varieties for my main planting, use them boldly, and support them if necessary with small groups of other varieties in the same category.

There is a wide rabbit-cropped clearing of fine turf at Longleat called the Green Drive, set in a wood of mature beech and among the tawny trunks of old Scots firs. Wanting the colour and lightness of flowering trees to fill the gap between the crimson April-flowering of huge old bushes of *Rhododendron arboreum* and the June-flowering forms of *Rhododendron loderi*, we had to decide what flowering trees to use. At first we were tempted to plant Japanese cherries in groups, using *Prunus yedoensis*, " Ukon," " Mount Fuji," "Shirofugen," and others to give pale colour along the length of the ride. Finally, although the planting extends for three or four hundred yards, we limited ourselves to one species only, *Prunus sargentii*, because it was wild enough in character for its woodland setting yet handsome enough in flower to stand in company with the splendour of the rhododendrons.

The ordinary white-flowered wild cherry and *Prunus padus*, the bird cherry, as well as its slightly more showy variety, *watereri*, will make a good simple basic planting and a setting for groups or single specimens of all the more sophisticated Japanese varieties. In the same way the whitebeam, *Sorbus aria*, with its silvery underleaves, and the common rowan will weld together a more exotic planting of the different Asiatic species of mountain ash.

The crab apple family need particularly careful planting since so many of the crimson flowered varieties have more or less purple foliage. In planting crabs I like to use a high percentage of such unpretentious varieties as the John Downie crab, the green form of *Malus floribunda* and the very late white flowering *Pyrus hupehensis theifera*, a plant I have always admired since I first saw the magnificent specimen which grows by Chobham church in Surrey. The purple-leaved plums like *Prunus pissardii* and many other red and purple-foliaged trees and shrubs require most careful placing. Nothing destroys the harmony of a garden more than the dark blotch of a copper beech or a *Prunus pissardii* seen among the green of deciduous trees. I think a copper beech can look well when, as a large specimen, it stands near a building of mellow red brick or where there is a considerable group in a setting of huge cedars, firs or pine trees. The only major experiment I have made with copper beech has been to plant it on both sides of about a mile of winding country lane near a Wiltshire village; when it finally joins overhead it should make an impressive canopy.

In the same way I think *Prunus pissardii* should be grouped only with other purple-leaved shrubs and trees. It takes a satisfactory place in a mixed planting of the purple-leaved hazel, *Corylus maxima atropurpurea*, *Rhus cotinus atropurpurea*, the red form of *Berberis thunbergii* and other plants in the same dusky range of colour. Since I have the opportunity for planting many gardens, I incline to experiment with such colour combinations though, were I restricted to a small garden of my own, I think I would be quite happy to keep purple foliage out of it.

In a very sheltered garden where magnolias will grow there are many possibilities for demonstrating their elegance. Seen at their best against a dark green background I would, for once, give them an evergreen frame of thuya, or even firs accented by the high spires of libocedrus and low wide patches of spreading junipers. I say " for once " about the thuyas because I find many of the hardy cypresses extremely hard to place in the garden. I know them to be invaluable as a windbreak and useful as a background; but their spikes break the skyline into such ungainly silhouettes that they seem to me only tolerable when growing amongst other trees at least as high as themselves. Like spruce and fir, they too may well be impressive in mass in their native forests, but I can seldom recall seeing a garden improved by their presence.

Taste varies in regard to gardens as in most other matters. I can respect another man's predilection for them without understanding it. I hope that one day I will see them successfully used.

South of Lyons, *Cupressus sempervirens stricta*, the Italian cypress, has a compact and columnar habit of growth and is a perfect foil for flowering trees, repeating a motif used for centuries in Islamic art from Persia to Spain. Planted as a hedge or screen or as individuals these cypresses give stability to a hilly site, height to a flat one and character to any garden in which they are planted.

It has become fashionable in the South of France to clip them to needle sharpness and since they can be transplanted up to forty feet high a few days' work rapidly makes a new garden look mature. In Mediterranean gardens cypresses are like trumps in bridge, enabling one to resolve the most difficult situations.

Plantings of small trees make small garden sites appear large. Large trees are useful for a different purpose. They break the stiffness of a formally designed area, make a foreground and a shade pattern where an open view lies beyond, break a roof line or canopy and make a garden of an enclosed courtyard. All these are places in which to use trees with important foliage or flowers or a distinctive habit of growth. Such is *Catalpa bignoniides* with its huge heart-shaped leaves, spires of maculated white flowers and the picturesque architecture of the branches of a mature specimen. Even though it comes into leaf very late this is an admirable tree to place in close relation to buildings or for a town square, or to centre a garage yard or garden court.

Another good tree for planting among or near buildings is *Sophora japonica* either in the foreground of a large garden or if you have place for only one tree, alone. As a mature tree its dark trunks and handsome lacework of branch and twig look well against the winter sky and its deep-green tidy pinnate foliage is set late with racemes of white pea flowers.

Planes, limes and chestnuts are trees for landscape planting on the largest scale but all three have a secondary use in smaller gardens. You can plant and clip them in formal lines and shapes, or use them singly, training them horizontally as is so often done in Switzerland with plane trees to make a pool of shade. To these I would add the small-leaved elm *Ulmus pumila* which seems resistant to elm-disease, impervious to extremes of heat and cold and as easily trained and clipped as a hornbeam. You can see this tree so used outside the main railway station in Milan.

There are many varieties of trees which take quite kindly to training and shaping. The Vicomte de Noailles at his garden in Grasse uses the redbud or Judas tree, *Cercis siliquastrum*, to arch over a terraced walk, and at Bodnant I remember a pergola of clipped and trained laburnum alternating with wistarias to make a dappled tunnel hung over with gold and mauve tassels. Recently I was asked to tackle a singularly unpromising eighth floor roof-garden—a narrow walk surrounding a canteen above a large furrier's establishment in Paris. To break up its narrow monotony, I made deep wooden cases at intervals along each side with iron arches linking them overhead. To these I tied young plants of the familiar weeping willow, *Salix chrysocoma* which even in the first year gave me a series of yellow green arches fringed with rustling trails of foliage. These would make rather inconvenient curtains very quickly had I not made my arches at least four feet higher than I would normally have done to allow for headroom.

Of all large deciduous trees I know none nobler than the tulip tree *Liriodendron tulipifera*. Many years ago, finding a stand of sapling trees I did not recognise in a deserted Lincolnshire nursery I dug one up, liking its habit and its rather curious leaves, and moved it to my own garden nearby. I met it again as a magnificent specimen growing on the lawn of the garden of Little Paddocks near Windsor Park where I worked for several years in succession and each autumn it faded magnificently first to yellow and then to orange. The finest examples I know of in England are in the woods landscaped in the eighteenth century at Stourhead in Wiltshire. It is native to the Eastern United States, and Thomas Jefferson, who adapted corn-cobs and tobacco leaves as decorative elements to Palladian architecture, planted tulip trees on the campus as part of his design for the University of Virginia at Charlottesville.

Taxodium distichum, the swamp cypress, also from the Southern United States, is another large tree of such quality and interest as to merit a key position. If it can grow by the water's edge it will eventually develop a series of knobbly and picturesque knees around its base. It does not grow very fast but even as a young specimen, with the yellow green of its young leaves which turn to clear rust red in autumn, it is well worth planting. *Metasequoia glyptostroboides*, another deciduous conifer whose discovery in China in recent years caused such a stir, is rather similar but seems to grow infinitely faster. It too appears to like rather wet ground.

Choosing the right kind of tree and planting it in the right place presents a great many difficulties. You have to calculate ahead, decide what silhouette, what weight and colour of foliage you want, how extensive a shadow can you afford and where will this shadow fall. Are you prepared to wait while a gawky young subject grows to maturity and the stature your composition requires? Planting a group you will almost inevitably set them too close for if you follow the rules your group will strike you as far too widespaced or far too small. If you plant doubly thick meaning to take out half your trees twenty years later, the twenty years will pass all too quickly and it may well be that neither you nor your successor will then find the necessary ruthlessness.

As to your choice of subjects you will again have to decide, if you are working on a large scale, whether you are going to impose a planting of trees regardless of the existing landscape and know that your planting will eventually be its own landscape or whether you will choose varieties which will blend with plantings already there. Even in cases where you are planting on quite a small scale the same problems will come up. You will have to see whether you will use species so exotic to their surroundings as to create a purely garden atmosphere or whether by a simpler choice you will bring the sentiment of the surrounding trees and woods into your garden. Then you will have to apply the same considerations to the colour of foliage. Perhaps you have the courage, the means and the space to set the spike of golden cypresses with rounded masses of purple beech or prunus, glaucous feathery junipers with golden elms or yellow green catalpas, or the flaming embothrium against a wild heathered hillside. There were many such violent landscapes made in the years before 1914 but only in certain public parks and gardens have they left a dubious progeny.

For years I have taken exception to the variegated maple, *Acer negundo*, so used was I to seeing it planted with one laburnum and one red may tree as the local nurseryman's solution for a suburban front garden. I was surprised and a little appalled when one day the Duke of Windsor said that this was a tree he liked and where could we plant some. We found two places, one away across the lawn at his Paris house in the Bois de Boulogne in the shade of some large lime trees and against a background of the mixed green shrubs—laurels, aucubas and privet—which ring most gardens on the outskirts of Paris. Here we planted a group of fifteen half-standard variegated maples which in two years grew enough to make me think even in grey weather that a patch of sunshine has been caught and held in that shadowy corner. We used them too at the Duke's mill in an angle set between high walls, a draughty corner facing north. First we planted the walls with the lovely silver variegated ivy which the French call " Marengo "; then we set a tree or two of the maple with, in front, *Elaeagnus pungens aureo-variegata* and silver and green evergreen euonymus. As ground-cover there is *Elymus avenarius* and *Eulalia zebrina*, variegated hostas, the variegated form of *Iris pallida dalmatica*, and, if there are gaps and we are lucky with the seed, we fill in with the annual silver and white leaved *Euphorbia elegantissima*. Now I find the whole corner, for long a problem, as interesting to look at as anything in the garden; and, as one never invents anything, I looked back through the ragbag of memory and associations and found that I had stored but never used until then an idea from one of E. A. Bowles's books and a description of a gold garden by Miss Jekyll.

I have very often had to design gardens for the medium-sized houses which have been and are being built near industrial towns on the Continent, houses built for the younger generation of industrialists wanting to bring up a large family in a country atmosphere and yet be close to their work. The character of these houses varies but they are often built in traditional style somewhere between a farm house and a manor, sometimes in stone, sometimes in brick. Where one is lucky the site may be on a piece of ground, an acre or two, parcelled out from a large estate with a few good trees. But more often than not up goes

the house on a quite bare site and you have to decide what trees
you are going to plant. With a modern house you are free to
consider the problem as entirely one of form and colour and
you can choose from a wide repertory, but a house whose
architecture has traditional and historical connotations will
demand a different approach. I find myself obliged to respect
and indeed to accentuate the mood and the atmosphere that the
architect has aimed at, so that I try to reinforce it by planting such
varieties of trees as I would expect to find round an old house of
similar character. Optimistically in goes perhaps a cedar of
Lebanon or tulip tree to mature a century hence, but meanwhile
I need something faster growing. In such cases fruit trees, apples
or pears, are extremely useful. They grow fairly rapidly and
help to accentuate the character of the house. Exotic conifers
or groups of shrubs are altogether too grand and too pretentious
an approach, leading one to expect grander architecture and an
ornamental garden, and, while the development of the garden
itself can be pushed as far as its owner's taste and fortune will
permit, it is usually more satisfactory to underplay the approach
and the general framework. Fruit trees, flanking the approach or
planted symmetrically as a rather formal orchard, can often give
a comfortable air; they are gay in their flowering yet give the
useful promise of fruit. If you can strike this note firmly enough,
you can, inside this frame, work freely with flowering crabs and
cherries, with magnolias and clipped lime trees or yews to make
the basis for any kind of garden that you may wish to develop.
If, on the contrary, you fail to establish a definite atmosphere for
the whole site, all your planting may easily look forced and out
of place. This principle is all the more valid in a quite small
garden where perhaps even one large-sized tree will be too big.
Half a dozen small trees all of one type or, better still, all of one
species, whether flowering cherries, crab apples, birch or mountain
ash, will create a basic mood and give character and unity—a
frame within which you can plant as you like in detail without
ever jeopardising the harmony of the whole.

I must admit I find it very hard, every time I come to plan

a new garden, to stick to this principle. The possibilities are so wide, the choice of trees so large, that I am always tempted to display too many different varieties. Caught by such diversity, I usually write in on my first planting plan a whole quantity of different trees which might be suitable and then I leave the plan to one side and, as they say, " forget " it. In fact some kind of mental process does go on and, when I come back fresh to the problem, I simplify and eliminate all but the one or two varieties of trees which will best give me the mood I want to capture and hold on that particular site.

In Flanders fruit trees seem particularly suited to the red tiles and brickwork, often white-washed, of the local type of building. Round Lille for instance pears, particularly " Doyenne du Comice," grow especially well and I have made many gardens using pear trees in different ways: as orchard trees for espaliered walks through kitchen and flower garden or pruned into pyramids in more formal arrangements. A little farther north at Courtrai, where apples flourish, I have used them in the same way— coming to a house through a true orchard of standard apples whose trunks are newly whitewashed each spring, lining kitchen garden paths with horizontal cordons and, in the garden proper, using crab apples, *Malus floribunda*, *M. eleyi* and *P. hupehensis* as shade trees for rhododendrons, azaleas or hydrangeas.

I repeat that I find it difficult to use forest trees, chestnuts, limes, beech or planes as specimen trees in a small garden. When they are there already or when for some reason you want to plant such trees, you must, I think, make them the main feature of the garden and then design and plant round them. You must work with them and never against them. It is useless to fight a battle which you can only lose in trying to grow roses or delphiniums or annuals anywhere near a large tree. Try rather, with grass or water, with hedges or with quiet green plantings, to give every aspect of your tree its full value. Try to enhance the shape of its trunk and branches, the texture and colour of its foliage, the light shining through it and the shadows it makes, so that your garden scene leads only up to this one tree. (If this is not the kind of garden you like then it is better not to attempt an impossible compromise but start afresh on another basis.) One of the minor triumphs in the garden at Hidcote, with its varied tapestry of flower colour and closely-packed foliage, is the stretch of grass surrounded by a dark yew hedge which Major Johnston designed as a setting for half a dozen secular beech trees.

In a new garden the designer may find himself at a loss, wishing to achieve an effect of bulk as soon as possible, needing to hide some ugly angle of a building or to plant an unwanted corner. One most useful tree for such places is the weeping willow. There seem to be two forms so that I always specify the yellow-twigged variety, *Salix chrysocoma pendula aurea*. It is a lovely tree, whether planted singly or as a group, and flourishes just as well hemmed between buildings as at the edge of a stream or lake. It is a tree for level ground. If planted on steep slopes, in rocky ground in mountainous country or anywhere near any conifer (except *Taxodium distichum*, the swamp cypress), it looks and is out of place. The weeping willow is a tree so satisfying in itself that it can be left to tell its story unaccompanied. A very few trees will soon cover a wide area of ground and densely enough to inhibit weeds. With a little training and pruning, it can be kept at a suitable height and still not lose its characteristic form.

One of the difficulties of gardening in our day comes, like many other problems, from the reckless speed we have imposed on ourselves. There is time only for the ready-made but because, in most cases, you cannot produce a mature garden in a few weeks, people incline to plant for quick results. I myself feel gardening as a process and a garden at any stage on any day of the year is a whole world full of interesting things.

Only scale differentiates the planting of a landscape from the planting of a garden; scale and, perhaps I should add, an even more urgent need for simplicity. In England in the early part of the eighteenth century, Brown, Kent and Bridgeman with the enthusiastic help of a group of wealthy amateurs set a standard for the siting and choice of trees for park planting in temperate climates which has never since been excelled. You have only to consider the work of their mid-nineteenth century successors who endeavoured to make landscapes with a wider and more exotic selection of trees, to see how much lovelier are the earlier parks. I think this is due to a strict sense of fitness which kept exotic varieties as isolated specimens near the house or hidden away in a faintly artificial, though informally planted, " American " garden. For their broad effects the eighteenth-century masters used only native trees—elms, chestnuts, limes and beech—for formal avenues and park " clumps " for shelter belts, for hanging woods and curtains. They used this simple material which blended so well and so inevitably with the surrounding countryside, to enhance the ground modelling and the contours of the area they were treating. They developed a systematic scenic idiom which they base very strictly on the rules of composition borrowed from such painters as Poussin, Claude Lorraine and Salvator Rosa. The analysis of any park planted in the mid-eighteenth century shows how well its designer understood the use of form. A park " clump " of three or five or a larger but always odd number of trees is never circular. They planted trees in lines or triangles or wedges in order to get the maximum effect from the rounded masses of foliage when the trees would be fully grown. In fact you can usually detect nineteenth-century clump planting: it was frequently and disastrously made of a mixture of trees, an error I have never observed in eighteenth-century work.

When I have to do large scale tree planting, and perhaps not wishing to employ the deliberately theatrical manner of the eighteenth century, I always aim at a certain coherence and unity by using one variety, or at most two, as the backbone of my planting so as to achieve simplicity in tone and in silhouette. If I use any additional varieties it will be to make a deliberately considered variation of form or texture.

It is fairly easy to exercise this kind of restraint. Once you have decided on your composition—where and why you want open spaces and where you want massed foliage and the effects of sunlight and shadow from fully grown trees—you must go the whole hog and, as a water-colourist would say, lay in the broad washes of your chosen variety. It will be time enough to add the decorative accents in the shape of contrasting or harmonising species, although as often as not you will do best to leave it at that and add nothing. In our day opportunities for private planting on this scale have become rare. Woodland planting in the British Isles at least is mainly for the purposes of afforestation and a landscaper's efforts to ameliorate the shock of acres of soft wood planted in the traditional English landscape with its elms and oaks and beech can seldom be happy. These artificial wood-lands are usually a short-term programme and are likely to be cut long before they reach beauty and maturity. The farsighted and enlightened authority or private owner who can afford to sacrifice immediate profit in favour of hardwood plantings, which will mature in perhaps a hundred years, is the exception.

But between large scale forestry and the planting of individual trees in the small garden there are intermediate problems. Roadside planting is one of these. The rules I have set myself for this are simple. Outside towns in open country I will only plant trees that are native to, or have become naturalised in, the particular area, or, occasionally, trees of the same family. For instance, in a place where Lombardy or grey or white poplars are prevalent I would feel free to use *Populus candicans* or *P. lasiocarpa*. Avenues should always be of one variety only and usually they suit only level and more or less straight stretches of road. The secret of good roadside planting is never to try to be original.

In the city smog and smoke and petrol fumes impose an unnatural limitation, otherwise a large range of trees is yours to choose from, except for conifers which grow badly in towns. Another problem is that of height and volume. It is useless to plant trees which will later have to be pruned and clipped out of shape and so lose their natural beauty. Better in such cases to use trees which you intend to clip from the start. French and German towns and villages use the red-twigged lime to make formal alleys and squares. To look their best the foliage should meet overhead and you can space the trees as closely as nine feet each way. The foliage of horse chestnuts is too large and their rate of growth too rapid for them to make satisfactory clipped and pollarded trees but you can cut them *en riviére*: that is, cut them vertically about four feet from the trunk, from between ten to twenty feet above the ground, and then let them grow freely. The finest example of this kind of planting which I know is the Avenue de l'Observatoire in Paris, where two high green walls of chestnut trained in this way continue the Luxembourg Gardens southwards towards the Observatory. You will find many other examples of this treatment at Versailles and in the park of St. Cloud. Lime trees like *Tilia euchlora* also lend themselves to this kind of handling. In Italy the evergreen oak *Quercus ilex* is clipped square to give shade in streets and in the great renaissance gardens; in Cairo a small-leaved evergreen fig, *Ficus nitida*, is used for the same purpose.

In England taste veers over the years from one variety to another. In my youth the pyramidal Cornish elm seemed inevitable in every suburb and every seaside town. The alternative was a horrid flowering mixture of red May, *Crataegus coccinea*, mixed with *Acer negundo*, laburnums and *Prunus pissardii*. Between the two wars the Japanese cherry " Hizakura " became the most fashionable street tree, especially in the suburbs and to such an extent that I find that many people no longer want this very lovely tree in their gardens. Birch and mountain ash are other favourites but, for me, they have such a flavour of wild and barren country that I find them out of place dryly lined out along the pavements.

If you were to name the common attribute of all Provençal towns and villages I think you would decide on the huge plane trees which shelter the fountain in every village square, left to grow free or clipped each year into a gnarled and curious growth. Although municipal authorities dislike them, as their falling leaves make the roadway below them slippery, planes make superb avenues if there is room for them to grow freely, as they so wonderfully do along the Quai de Bercy in Paris which runs for two miles between the Seine and the Halle aux Vins.

I have a special weakness for pink chestnuts because for a week in each year the road beneath them becomes a deep rose-coloured carpet. I like too *Sophora japonica* as a town tree because of the complex shadows thrown by its pinnate leaves and because it bears sheaves of white pea flowers as late as mid-July. In Italy umbrella pines, *Pinus pinea*, cast graceful shadows on town and country road alike. Although these are scarcely hardy in most parts of the British Isles I have wondered why the second noblest of the pines, *P. radiata* (*insignis*) is not more used in the south-west where it flourishes.

In Paris, the municipal authorities of sixty or more years ago must have employed a first class director for their parks and gardens. The Haussman boulevards and much of the late nineteenth-century town development still show traces of a good mind and good taste at work on tree planting. In one or two streets there are avenues of mature paulownias which, alas, must flower only for the benefit of those who live high up in the surrounding houses. Although I pass under them a hundred times a year I have somehow never yet caught a glimpse of their blue-mauve spikes of flowers.

I am maddened to see how the conservatism and xenophobia of French nurserymen, the lack of sufficient credits and the need for quick effects influence current French practice in the planting of new housing schemes, which seem to be restricted to Lombardy and Canadian poplars, mop-headed acacias, privet and aucubas.

The technicalities of street planting are easy to learn; the limits of height and width and the nature of the soil will indicate the possible varieties of trees from which you will have to choose. As for the æsthetic aspect I would always say: be bold and be simple. Further generations will ignore or uproot a timid conception, but they will bless you and perhaps remember you for a fine simple planting like the Long Walk in Kensington Gardens, recently replanted, or the splendid unity of the chestnut avenues in Bushey Park.

I find myself straying away from what seems to me to be one of the most difficult exercises in landscape gardening—the design and planting of a public garden or park. This is perhaps because I have never been called upon to make one, if I except the projects which I made for the very special case of Abadan on the Persian Gulf. But I have seen so many that I have drawn certain conclusions.

A city park, whose main physical purpose is perhaps to supply extra oxygen for the body, should also perhaps be an escape for the feelings as well as a refreshment for eyes tired of streets and buildings. In long established cities public parks are often the adapted remains of private parks and gardens that have been preserved as public spaces when towns started growing beyond their original boundaries. These are public parks by accident and retain more or less the character of their original purpose. Hyde Park, St. James's Park and Kensington Gardens were eighteenth-century landscape parks attached to royal palaces. The Tuileries and Luxembourg gardens too were the private formal gardens of their palaces. The Bois de Boulogne was a former royal forest preserved for game and had imposed on it a curling nineteenth-century road plan designed for riding and driving. The woods were severely cut and damaged in 1870 and are only now beginning to resume their maturity. Central Park in New York was designed by Olmsted as a nineteenth-century pastiche of an eighteenth-century landscape park, while in Washington the same eighteenth-century manner has a faintly Japanese flavour with its shallow lagoons and groves of flowering cherries. In Rome the Borghese gardens are, like the Boboli gardens in Florence, little changed from their renaissance origins as private gardens.

What is common to most of these parks is that they are islands, separate entities of green more or less enclosed by the city's streets and buildings, and as such the informally " landscaped " ones seem better to fulfil their potential purpose. The pleasures of a formal layout seem to pall more quickly. In the Tuileries, for instance, once you have paused to admire the long vista from the Carousel across the Place de la Concorde up to the Arc de Triomphe, you are immediately conscious of the strict lines of trees, the balanced parterres and the existence of the garden's limits. There is no room for the imagination to roam, there is nothing to guess at; all is orderly, logical and self-explanatory. One takes one's pleasure in such places from the accidental, the broken silhouette of tree tops seen against buildings, or the gleam of a pool or fountain perceived between the trunks of the trees. These accidental joys come, as it were, against the intention and pattern of the garden. I would not, of course, consider a formal botanical garden from this point of view, since these are intended for the systematic and orderly display of many species of plants. But I think a public park or garden, large or small, should be designed to be mysterious and as remote in its mood as possible from its surroundings. You can treat only a very large area in the grand landscape manner, since large spaces are needed to deploy massed groves and isolated clumps set in undulating grass and wide levels of water. Nothing fails so dismally as this kind of treatment on a small scale. The provincial towns of Europe are full of pathetic *jardins anglais* where a curly pool inhabited by one swan and crossed by a cement log bridge is set in a violently undulated lawn on which three or four trees appear far too large. Landscapes have their scale and you cannot violate this effectively. I know of only one small city garden which successfully intimates the grandeur and scale of a " landscaped " park and that is Berkeley Square in London with its group of great plane trees on a level lawn. The secret of its success is, of course, the proportions and architecture of the little building in the middle though its original quiet cream colour has recently been changed for a more vulgar scheme.

I should ring a city park of any size with a belt of large trees so that from inside there would be a high bank of foliage to contrast with the buildings behind and accentuate the sense of separateness between city and park. I would not want to encircle the whole area with a belt of low trees or shrubs set close to the boundary and this for two reasons: first because they usually grow badly so close to the passing traffic, and secondly because they would prevent the passer-by from feeling drawn into the park. Thick low planting would therefore lie back some fifty feet or more from the boundary with occasional openings to give glimpses into the inner park.

It would be absurd to try and outline, even theoretically, the design for a park in a single paragraph: its layout would of course depend on a hundred local factors—country, climate, soil, local customs and the amenities to be included. But I think in any case it should have one or more long vistas of open ground which with the aid of careful planting and skilfully forced perspectives would give a sense of size and distance. All the auxiliary features would lie to the sides of these main vistas, linked like a chain and composed as a series of more or less enclosed spaces, each one designed to suit its purpose.

Tree planting in a public park requires careful thought. The restraint I would exercise in almost any other context does not seem to me valid in this case. My aim would be to create an illusion and use every variation of form and colour and every texture of foliage to further the sense of remoteness and, if you like, magic, at which I should like to aim. By magic I would not infer a dazzling confusion of vegetation or a sylvan Disneyland. You can endow any site with magic if you are quite certain of the pictorial aspect you want to achieve and even the least promising site holds in itself its own possibilities. Look and look again, note and then put on one side the different elements you will have to incorporate; later, when you reach that stage, they will re-emerge to shape your thinking and your composition. Meanwhile you must go on looking and give your feelings as well as your mind access to the problem. Remember that one of your aims must be to lift people, if only for a moment, above their daily preoccupations. Even a glimpse of beauty outside will enable them to make a healing contact with their own inner world.

Nor must you ascribe such an idea to sentimentality. It is one most valid reason and justification for gardens and for gardeners.

In such a park I might imagine a glade of silver foliage; white and aspen poplars, *Salix caerulea* silvered by each breath of wind, with below them the graceful mounds of *Pyrus salicifolia* and then drifts of sea buckthorn, *Hippophae rhamnoides*, *Buddleia alternifolia* and *Cytisus battandieri*. For ground planting I would have a choice of half a hundred grey-leaved sub-shrubs— lavenders, caryopteris, santolina, tufts of silver white pampas grass and even the common blue grasses such as elymus and *Festuca glauca*.

The weeping willow *Salix chrysocoma pendula aurea* is a common enough tree, perhaps too often used as a single specimen accompanied by its classical partner a Lombardy poplar. In my park I see a large oval or round space, perhaps a children's playground, entirely surrounded by a ring of perhaps fifty weeping willows to make a swaying curtain of bright yellow green. In another more gardened part of my imaginary park, I would like to plant an orchard only of small flowering trees, cherries and crab apples, each set in a round bed which I would use for showing a hundred different varieties of tulips in the spring and follow these with low-growing annuals to make a hundred rings of bright colour through the summer.

To plant trees is to give body and life to one's dreams of a better world. There is an infinity of possibilities and it would be outside my scope to attempt to make a catalogue or book of recipes. The possibilities lie rather in your attitude and approach to the problem. Like clay for the potter, the engraver's burin or a painter's colours, trees will be the raw materials with which you will construct a landscape or a garden. To learn to handle them as such you must learn to know them from as many aspects as you can. Study them as seedlings and as young plants and learn to recognise them at all stages of their growth and at different times of year. Drawing them carefully is a special and rewarding way of learning them. Take a leaf, a twig, a branch or a whole tree. As your pencil tries, however inexpertly, to render the shape and texture of a leaf or the silhouette of a tree or the point where a trunk divides and branches, you will find that inevitably you absorb an understanding of the forces at work in the tree's growth: you will feel its nature and sense each branch as though it were your own arm. (No matter what the drawing looks like: your aim is not to make a pretty picture but to increase your understanding.) In this way you will fast acquire a kind of tree-love if, as I think, " love " is that kind of knowledge that is deeper than the superficial information accumulated by the everyday functioning of the brain alone.

CHAPTER VI

On planting : shrubs

When he comes to consider shrub plantings the garden-maker might forget his catalogues and alphabetical lists and, to clear his mind and eye, devise his own and different classification. So much has been written on shrubs, their descriptions, cultural needs and so on that one may soon become fuddled by an excess of information.

I would try to classify shrubs according to the places and parts of the garden for which they are most suited by their nature and their appearance. For example, whatever the climate and the site, there will be a range of shrubs which belong to the fringes of the garden, species whose form and habit are such that they will " mix " well with the natural growths of the place and cause no sense of shock at points where garden merges into woodland or meadow. They may, of course, have other uses too and many will find a place in the more civilised and elaborate parts of the garden. For example *Rhus cotinus*, the smoke or wig bush, is one of these: native to the rocky slopes of the Alps and South East Europe, and like many of the berberis species suitable for the fringes of a wild garden on certain sites, it is also interesting enough in its habit, its foliage and its flowering to star in an important position in a more sophisticated part of the garden. There are many different species of shrubs, that you can use as native plants, if you are sure that they will look in no way exotic in their setting. There are, indeed, certain plants for which I can find no other use. The yellow and red-twigged willows, pollarded each spring and planted in quantity, will enliven a flat wet site with their winter glow of greeny yellow and smoky red as will *Cornus alba sibirica* and other varieties, but these are plants only for distant use. Individually and seen in detail they lack interest and are altogether too dull to look more than weeds inside the limits of a garden. One can make a short list of such plants useful for blending with the indigenous vegetation on the outer fringes of the garden proper.

On the other hand there is another group of shrubs which I think are often misused, since their proper place is in an enclosed garden. These include philadelphus, weigela, deutzia and the hybrid lilacs. These plants make most unsuitable neighbours for ericaceous plants like rhododendrons and azaleas, for instance, though I have constantly seen them so used and even mixed with brooms, heathers and Japanese maples. To my mind they belong somewhere between flower garden, orchard and kitchen garden where they can be associated with such old-fashioned flowers as paeonies and lilies and pansies. They are perhaps a little dull when not in flower and so need the support of flowering herbaceous plants. But when they are in blossom they have an air of sophistication which belongs well inside the garden enclosure. Lilacs look their best and are easier to prune and keep shapely when you grow them as half-standards. For the first two or three years they will be disappointing, but after that they will make great rounded heads covered with flowers. Weigelas need grouping in mixed colours of white and pink and crimson, but they become unsightly unless you ruthlessly cut out old wood as soon as they have flowered. The philadelphus hybrids, too, are apt to grow into unmanageable thickets unless you take out as much old wood as possible each July. Both weigela, philadelphus and deutzias merit a fair space of ground in sun or even in half-shade where their effectiveness can be prolonged and strengthened by groups of the old *Paeonia officinalis* white, hot pink and deep crimson with perhaps an edge planting of *Campanula portenschlagiana* or *C. carpatica*. I would not make the same reservations about the lilac species which are quite suitable for the wilder parts of the garden,

The picturesque sweep of the pine trees suggested the oval sweep of the outer side of this pool near Cannes. Changing rooms are built into the hillside and a vine-covered pergola shades a paved space set below the level of the water: (designed with Jacques Regnault)

Water-gardening in the French classical manner. Here a small river is channelled between stone margins and two large sculptured groups mark the corners of a wide canal at right angles to the main stream

The same canal flanked with formal alleys of lime trees, which will later be clipped, ends at a wide flight of shallow steps leading down from a paved courtyard. A weeping willow shades a low building and already breaks the severity of a composition barely twenty years old

A windy day in Flanders. Across the moat which surrounds a small château trim lawns and box hedges frame the seventeenth century gate-house

as are the Preston hybrids, while the charming dwarf *Philadelphus microphyllus* fits in almost anywhere.

Rose species in the main belong to the wild garden, though amongst them again are some which have such character and colour that I use them in many different ways. I have seen *Rosa rugosa* growing as pheasant-cover in the Yorkshire dales, its single mauve-rose flowers and red hips blending perfectly with thickets of brambles. Its many hybrids though, are more strictly garden plants. Rose " Blanc Double de Coubert," "Roseraie de l'Häy" and " Conrad Meyer" are three superb doubles to use with herbaceous plantings or in a garden of shrub roses.

I have often dreamt of working in a level meadow in full sun with shrub roses, limiting myself to such kinds as are not tied by association to a more formal and enclosed type of garden. Perhaps milky-green thickets of varieties of *Rosa alba* would be the main theme or moss-green mounds of the many varieties of *Rosa rugosa*. In the first case I would add only wide stretches of *Rosa rubrifolia* for the blue bloom on its purply-red foliage and, for the same reason and for later colour of flower and leaf, the purple-leaved form of *Rhus cotinus*. For earlier flowering I would add clump upon clump of Chinese and herbaceous paeonies, blush-white and cream with *Rosa alba* or in brighter pinks and reds to announce the stronger colours of *Rosa rugosa*. For even earlier blooming I would also allow myself only two varieties of tulips, white and pale pink, but so lavishly planted as to appear naturalised. All these would make a coherent composition where colour and form would carry the underlying theme in flowering splendour from May until August.

When you classify shrubs according to the parts of the garden for which you intend to use them, your choice and scheme of distribution will be limited by soil and climate. With a warm sandy garden, for instance, you may well use the cistus family in large semi-wild plantings, but in a colder garden you may have to content yourself with one or two plants to grow below a sunny wall and bring a breath of the Mediterranean to your doorstep.

Other shrub families are more adaptable and you can use their different species and varieties in all sorts of ways and in all sorts of positions. In acid soil and a mild climate few plants are as useful as the hydrangea. The aquamarine and sapphire blue of *Hydrangea macrophylla* combined with the indigo of wet slate roofs and the dark green of *Cupressus macrocarpa* and *Pinus radiata* is a lovely combination, common enough in Cornwall and Brittany. I like to see these same hydrangeas massed in moist and shady woods where they look no more exotic than *Rhododendron ponticum*. The vinous purple red, the crimson and pink and white varieties are perhaps better inside the garden but in large masses, associated with evergreens only and in a setting of grass and nearby trees. I find their weight of flower colour altogether too overpowering for me to attempt to use other flowering shrubs or plants anywhere near them. In colder gardens or in limy soil *Hydrangea macrophylla* becomes a plant for large pots or wooden tubs to be set out near the house and either taken in or protected in winter. Many of the species are rather hardier though they all need a neutral or acid soil. *Hydrangea paniculata grandiflora*, useful for its late flowering, is a shrub for massing in sun or light shade or to use in small groups to reinforce a herbaceous planting. *Hydrangea aspera macrophylla*, *H. villosa*, *H. sargentiana* and *H. quercifolia* are all admirable plants with strongly defined foliage and a distinguished habit of growth. They are as good grouped in a wildish spot as used singly or in small groups at key-points in the garden, provided that you can give them a deep and moist soil. Here I would mention the climbing hydrangea *H. petiolaris* which is a most valuable self-clinging deciduous climber with bright brown stems, heart-shaped leaves and characteristic white flowers. Its chief merit is that it will grow in deep shade on a north wall or under trees and, given time, it will make a ground-cover like ivy.

In the last twenty years much has been written on winter-flowering shrubs many of which are interesting as plants though hardly useful for their decorative effect even where space for a group of these plants is available. There are two of these, corylopsis and sycopsis, cousins of the witch-hazel, which are rarely planted and are well worth a place in the garden along with *Viburnum fragrans, Prunus subhirtella autumnalis,* chimonanthus and hamamelis.

In Lincolnshire where I lived when I was young almost every cottage garden had a cydonia or Japanese quince growing as a clipped bush against the house wall, usually accompanied by fine clumps of polyanthus and perhaps a trailing mat of purple aubrietia and a tuft of yellow alyssum whose fragrance still comes back to me. Now the cydonias have found yet another name, but even as chaenomeles this is a race of plants which offer a wide range of possibilities for the garden designer. *Chaenomeles japonica* and its many varieties are all quite hardy and indifferent to what soil they grow in. One of their charms is that they flower in April, or even earlier in a clement spring, in a whole range of white, pale pink, coral, rose and scarlet, colours which form a useful contrast to the pale yellows, mauves and blues of so many spring flowers. These are plants to mass, mixed or by colours, up to fifty or a hundred at a time in a sunny open space where I like to see them as a cheerful and suitable groundwork for groups of the better cotoneasters such as *C. frigida* and *C. cornubia.* As they tend to throw up suckers all too easily it is simple enough to grow a large stock for this kind of planting. The chaenomeles fit well into a landscape of green fields, hedgerows and deciduous trees, but they are just as suitable for the sandy fringes of a pine wood.

In the garden proper these plants look as effective near water as they do espaliered against a wall, either alone or combined with large-flowered clematis or, as I often use them, with *Cotoneaster salicifolia* or with the pyracanthas, both excellent wall plants. To get the best display from the chaenomeles you should prune all young growth back to three or four inches to make flowering spurs and be particularly ruthless in doing this on wall-trained plants or they will soon look like a hedge. There is one species known as *Chaenomeles cathayensis,* a tall rough-looking shrub for which I have never found much use although its flowers are a pleasant shade of pink.

In the first quarter of this century plant-hunters sent back from East Asia a horde of new finds from among the cotoneaster family. For the most part I think them of moderate value in the garden picture. Many of them are apt to make unshapely bushes with leaves so small and so dully green that they give the impression of a blackish mound of twigs. They are all tough enough to stand poor ground and little attention, and I think they just pass muster when massed on the far side of a lawn and when seen from some distance. There are, of course, exceptions. *Cotoneaster horizontalis* is irreplaceable as a handsome ground cover or trained flat against a low wall. Its use for this has become so common that where you see an odd plant near a house you can be sure that it is there to hide a manhole cover. The secret of keeping it in flat fans lies in cutting off every twig or branch which shows a tendency to grow vertically.

To see large-scale plantings of cotoneasters you should go to Exbury, on the Beaulieu River near Southampton, where that gardener in the grand manner, Mr. Lionel de Rothschild, planted acres of gravelly soil with conifers, some autumn colouring trees and dense thickets of cotoneasters and berberis. Some of these, planted about thirty years ago, have disappeared, but there are still wonderful clumps of his cotoneaster hybrids, derived, I would suppose, from the more aristocratic members of the family such as *C. lactea*, *C. henryi*, *C. frigida* and others of vigorous growth and handsome fruit. In late November these plants, the best of which is called *Cotoneaster rothschildiana*, are a lovely spectacle, massed as they are with scarlet and sometimes pale yellow berries which hang on the plant until well after Christmas.

Among the medium growing cotoneasters, *C. wardii* has the twiggy look and undistinguished foliage of so many of its kind; but these are compensated for by an abundance of lacquer-scarlet berries which are very large for the size of the plant. A small specimen set close to a huge sandstone rock in the Duke of Windsor's French garden has now almost covered it and makes a startling show each November. For some reason *Cotoneaster simonsii* is very popular with nurserymen; I don't know why, unless because it strikes easily from cuttings. It is a horrid ungainly plant which I would usually exclude from any garden.

To-day I think too much accent is placed on flower colour in shrub plantings; evergreens are merely dotted about to fill in ungrateful places where something more flowery will not grow. In the eighteenth and nineteenth centuries shrubberies were invariably of native box and yew, later augmented by cherry laurel, Portuguese laurel, aucubas and skimmias. Looked at closely these shrubberies were dull affairs, but they had a certain homogenity and they gave useful colour through the long winter months. As used to be said, they "furnished" the shady edges of garden and park. Later, *Rhododendron ponticum* and the so-called *Azalea pontica* and then the first rhododendron hybrids brought flowers and colour, and the accumulation of new plants continued until the shrubbery became a shapeless rag-bag for anything bushy.

In the nineteen-twenties nurserymen began to commercialise the planting of flowering shrub borders on a large scale. When St. Dunstan's in Regent's Park was pulled down and the present Neogeorgian house was built on the site, the large Victorian garden with its trees and clumps of laurels which fitted sympathetically into the character of the park was turned into a vast lawn surrounded by a wide border of mixed trees and shrubs planted regardless of colour, texture or form. There is another example, now hideously mature, bordering the Datchet road by Windsor Castle; and the same sort of parti-coloured blight spoils thousands of gardens all over the country.

As a cathartic we might consider how to use evergreen shrubs in the garden to make a composition which will stand by itself before any flowering plants are brought in to add colour and diversity. First in Western Europe, I would place the ordinary yew, *Taxus baccata*, as an evergreen of many garden uses. You may use it as a feathery bush and then tree, to grow on through the centuries and be handsome at every stage. You may clip it into hedges from three to fifteen feet in height or give it any shape you like. Lightly clipped over each year, you can use it as a close-textured green background for other plantings or for a formal or informal barrier between two different parts of the garden. Never believe those who complain that it takes too long to grow. After the first three years it will give you increasing satisfaction which is as much as can be said for most trees and shrubs.

Box in its many varieties is the slowest-growing of our evergreens; left wild it makes a warm and satisfying greenery under wintry trees and there is perhaps no need to enlarge on its uses for hedging. I remember working in a Northamptonshire garden which had a double box hedge about fifteen feet high which you could walk under. Next to box and yew I like best *Laurus nobilis*, the bay laurel, although only in Southern Europe is it hardy enough to use freely to thicken a wood or to clip into high and fragrant walls of foliage. Farther north it needs a sheltered corner in which to make a green buttress. I think of it always as a symbol of Mediterranean civilisation and I do not like a garden to be without it.

A common shrub in all French public gardens, where it is usually planted with snowberries, privet and aucuba, *Viburnum rhytidophyllum* is a most effective evergreen which will grow to eight feet high in almost any soil, whether in sun or shade. It does the better for being protected from the wind. This is a noble plant with large rugose leaves of a warm and cheerful green, rich and architectural enough to be effective by itself or as a background for strong colour. I like to use it with the Lanarth variety of *Viburnum tomentosum*, with hydrangeas or with hypericum " Rowallane." Near the sea I would add *Griselinia littoralis* to my list of fine foliaged evergreens to use as a foundation plant round which to build all kinds of different planting schemes; and in a really warm climate the pittosporum family offer a whole range of good evergreen plants, many heavy with scented white blossoms in May or June. In such places the silver-green *Pittosporum tenuifolium*, used as a hedge or as a small tree, makes a good background for a composition built up entirely of the endless variety of grey-leaved shrubs which thrive in a similar climate.

I deliberately exclude rhododendrons and camellias from my list. The former for two reasons: firstly, because latterly in places where they thrive they seem to have monopolised the British garden; and secondly, because there exists a large and specialised literature on this subject. Camellia-growing too is a special field, though this is the most magnificent of all evergreens for a frost-free climate. I say frost-free not because camellias are not hardy but because their flowering is ruined and their growth checked by sudden changes of temperature; and in a cold climate they seem to succeed best in places where no winter sun will reach them.

Viburnum tinus, the laurustinus, seems to have gone out of fashion, although it is a most useful winter-flowering evergreen which makes a tidy bush about six feet high. Around Tours and Vouvray you see it admirably used in many old gardens as a loosely clipped hedge.

Although it is indeed slow growing and very difficult to transplant successfully, the holly is a superb evergreen plant. I like to use two thornless varieties, *Ilex aquifolium hodginsoni* and *I.a. camelliaefolia* which I first saw in Colonél Horlick's then fascinating garden at Little Paddocks near Sunningdale. Here they grew in clumps as a sombre green foil to standard Japanese cherries, a singularly handsome association of plants which I have always remembered and often copied.

All the prostrate and horizontally growing junipers are wonderful evergreens for massing in full sun. For very large scale plantings, I like to use *Juniperus chinensis pfitzeriana*, and lovely spreading feathery " Knap Hill " juniper.

You might continue to catalogue in this way, but always trying to visualise your shrubs as part of a composition, to take their place in a scheme which you will construct and plant. You must remember too that time and nature will take over where you leave off, so that you must allow room for development and select your shrubs to suit the soil.

Those few plants that I have mentioned will scarcely provoke a gleam in the plant collector's eye; but he too might not do amiss to consider his rarities in a light which might widen and increase their possibilities as material for new garden pleasures.

I remember a plant addict and brilliant gardener who had a small garden in a Rutland village. The kitchen-garden paths were lined with *Omphalodes luciliae*, a ravishing and difficult plant like a dwarf and more exquisite *Mertensia virginica*; mats of freely flowering *Gentiana acaulis* grew everywhere; under a wall there was a long and flourishing bed of the gentian blue crocus-like tecophilaea from Chile; and beyond an old orchard thick with *Lilium testaceum*, that rare and lovely cross between *L. chalcedonicum* and *L. candidum*. These were plants to make an amateur's mouth water, yet the garden was distinctly unlovely. I remember thinking at the time that, were I able to grow such plants, I would want them only if I could give them a setting worthy of their quality.

If you are a garden designer you can scarcely be a purist since a garden is by definition an artifice. To try to imitate nature exactly, just as to fly in her face, leads to absurdity. When you plant trees and shrubs, however informally, your aim is to intensify a natural ambience and to condense and underline a theme derived from nature herself.

In a Piedmont garden near Turin I have spent several years modifying and enlarging a Victorian layout on a hilly site. In one place a sharp declivity drops away from a series of terraced gardens to merge into a sloping lawn, which in turn runs down into a wooded valley. Here I found a mixed bag of planting—lime and beech trees, a large taxodium, some conifers, groups of rather uninteresting rhododendrons and azaleas and, fringing a path winding down the slope, a thicket of deutzias and philadelphus shorn regularly each winter of the following year's flowering wood. Amongst the odd plants was one large *Acer palmatum*. Having many other things to deal with, I shirked this part of the garden for several seasons until, finally, its turn had to come. The first thing to do was to clear away all the indiscriminate shrub planting and leave only the trees. This done, I saw that I had gained a sense of space but that the site lacked coherence, and that I still had an unlovely grass slope with a few haphazard trees. To change the contours and levels would have led to costly and unnecessary complications, so that I could only save the situation by imposing some planting theme which by its unity would dominate the site. As this slope lay not far from the house I did not want to close in the view by planting more conifers or rhododendrons, and rather than invent some arbitrary solution I looked at the site again and again, hoping that something already present would indicate a theme and give me a starting point. This something turned out to be the one Japanese maple which grew out of sight, hidden behind a large thujopsis. Starting a little timidly, I planted twelve more red-leaved *Acer palmatum* in all the open spaces on the upper part of the bank. When this was done I had a large enough sample to see that these trees, if I planted enough of them, would grow into a semi-transparent veil of reddish foliage which would give character to the site and be interesting enough in itself to distract the eye from the rather awkward lie of the land. In the end I planted three dozen more maples of the same variety which fill in all the awkward spaces and continue out and downwards to make a large planting, spreading on to the open lawn below. I was able to handle many other planting problems in this garden in the same way, since there were individual trees and shrubs of great interest and beauty in the congested and cluttered planting of about a hundred years ago.

Nowadays few private individuals have the space or the means to make an arboretum, a private world of trees collected for their interest and beauty like Sir George Holford's arboretum at Westonbirt in Gloucestershire with its accent on autumn colour. But a shrub garden needs less room and will reach maturity in far less time. I am thinking of a garden in which considerations of landscape have no place, an enclosed and sheltered space in which to compose a tapestry of woody plants regardless of natural associations, a garden which is frankly artificial.

I sometimes use such gardens on a small scale as part of a general garden composition in which I want a contrast of solids and voids. I made one garden in this way for a moderate-sized new house in the flat pastures near Courtrai in Flanders. In front of the house and its paved terrace there is a plain stretch of grass with two or three trees planted for shade. At the far end of this lawn I made a large rectangular pool to reflect the sky and act rather like a sunk fence or ha-ha to separate the garden from the meadows beyond. High hornbeam hedges frame this lawn on either side, the one on the left hiding the kitchen garden, while that on the right forms one side of a rectangular hedged enclosure only about 150 feet long by 50 feet wide. I designed this whole space as a thickly planted garden of shrubs only. The basic pattern is very simple. I made a wide grass path down the middle and narrow grass paths next to the hedges on all four sides. These leave a long bed about eighteen feet wide on each side of the central pathway. I divided this bed into wedges by more narrow diagonal grass paths and then planted these quite formal beds with groups of flowering shrubs of all kinds from two to ten feet in height. These make a rich and interesting planting through which you can still sense the formal pattern which underlies the whole garden. I adapted this particular pattern from the William and Mary garden which lies next to the sunk garden at Hampton Court and which was originally designed as a formally planted parterre. The design remains though the beds are now full of overgrown shrubs. Within the formal limits of my pattern I felt free to work out plantings in which I had only to consider pictorial values from close to, and thus only in terms of the details of foliage and flower and habit of growth. This is an intimate form of gardening and one which can effectively replace a flower garden when maintenance has to be cut to a minimum. If the soil has been deeply dug and well-manured and if you add a good deal of peat as you plant, occasional mulching and regular and considered pruning will keep such a garden handsome and well clothed for many years.

I turn more and more towards shrubs as an alternative to herbaceous plants because they seldom need staking or splitting up, two operations that take a great deal of time as well as skill. Used for this purpose shrubs give you the means of achieving agreeable variations of texture and form, although you cannot usually manage the sudden and recurrent contrasts and harmonies and the close and rapid changes of colour which herbaceous plantings will provide. I prefer to think of shrub plantings as exercises in the assembling of texture and shape, with leaf colour as a secondary consideration and flower colour as an additional and more ephemeral satisfaction. When there is no place for a separate garden you may design a border of shrubs, perhaps against a hedge (but not so close to it as to obscure its crisp wall of sunny or shadowed foliage) or else under a wall or simply rising from a breadth of lawn. It will be a tapestry woven of leaves from the five continents in associations that are visually pleasing but in quite a different way from the far more cautious and restrained use that one would make of them when planting for a natural or wild effect. In such a border berberis from Chile, choisya from Mexico, azaleas from Japan and ceanothus from California can be set as closely as plums in a cake. I like to use a rather heavy weighting of slow-growing evergreen shrubs— *Mahonia japonica bealei*, pieris, *Pinus montanus mughus*, *Chamaecyparis lawsoniana wissellii*, evergreen azaleas, prostrate junipers, skimmias and certain berberis, to mention only a few; for these will give interest and stability for twelve months of the year and modulate the "twigginess" of such things as *Viburnum tomentosum mariesii*, brooms, *Hydrangea paniculata*, *Philadelphus microphyllus*, indigoferas and those other deciduous shrubs whose main contribution will be for the colour of their flowers.

I find it dangerous to overload these shrub borders with heavy-leaved plants like the hybrid lilacs, snowball trees and the larger philadelphus, deutzias and weigelas; for much of the year their heavy foliage and undistinguished structure will dull the compact and lively contrasts I enjoy.

On the whole, in deciding on flower colour, I think in terms of all the different tonalities of white, pale yellow, pale blue, rose and mauve. Bright reds and oranges and violets will throw these subtler harmonies out of key; nor, in these colours, do I know how to prolong the flowering season beyond the spring excitement of rhododendrons and azaleas. The autumnal purples and magentas of the large-flowered buddleias, or the scarlets and crimsons of some of the polyantha or floribunda roses, seem to belong to another kind of garden planting.

Given enough space one can veer from greens into a stretch of grey-leaved planting with *Cytisus battandieri*, *Buddleia alternifolia*, caryopteris, perowskia, lavenders, *Juniperus squamata meyeri* and *Potentilla vilmoriniana* and, in certain situations, a cloud of red-leaved subjects will find a place. These last need either a rather formal setting; that is, they should be in the more sophisticated part of a garden or in large groups. I have a strong prejudice against spots of red foliage against a general background of green. I prefer to use these red-leaved plants that have a slightly bluished bloom like *Rhus cotinus atropurpurea* and *Rosa rubrifolia* to make long rather clouded patches of soft colour and then use the more metallic reds of *Acer palmatum atropurpureum* and the red form of *Berberis thunbergii* against this softer background. If I were working on a larger landscape scale, copper beech and the darkest form of *Prunus pissardii* would also come into the picture. I incline, too, more and more towards the use of variegated shrubs, particularly near the house or where I need evergreen foliage to light up a dark corner facing north.

Other writers and gardeners have written at such length and in such detail on rhododendrons that there is little I could add. But this is a tempting race of plants. By a judicious selection a rhododendron garden can show flower colour from March until

July. With enough peat they can be induced to survive in all but the most limy or chalky gardens; they can be transplanted at their owners' whim on almost any day of the year; and rhododendron addicts form a large class in the upper strata of British gardeners. From one garden designer's point of view this form of wild gardening has perhaps been carried rather too far and all too seldom with happy pictorial results. It is sixty years since the indomitable Miss Jekyll rightly inveighed against mixed plantings of hybrid rhododendrons and Ghent and mollis azaleas; but how often still, in gardens which are exemplars and by which public taste is formed, we see the most atrocious dissonances of colour where the enthusiast, whether amateur or professional, has ignored the reticence and discipline essential for making a garden picture. I should perhaps quote an example. Stourhead, on the borders of Wiltshire and Somerset, is perhaps the most complete and elaborate example of the eighteenth-century English landscape style remaining in this country. The original conception was in terms of water and hanging beechwoods and quiet dark green shrubberies which were enlivened by a series of architectural incidents. If you accept the style, here was coherence, dignity, scale, charm and tranquillity. At some point in the last seventy years somebody must have decided that this garden would lend itself to the cultivation of hybrid rhododendrons in all the new and brilliant colours which were then becoming available. When last I saw the garden the approach to the lake was completely disfigured, and the whole mood of the composition destroyed by enormous rounded masses of pink, crimson, scarlet and white rhododendrons. This kind of error is so constantly repeated that I turn with relief to planting long quiet stretches of R. "Sappho", R. *fastuosum flore pleno*, R. *catawbiense* or the simple and fragrant R. *luteum* (*Azalea pontica*.) Were I ever given a free hand with some of the marvellous species and hybrids that have been introduced or developed in the last twenty years, I must admit that I would enjoy using R. *griersonianum* and some of its coral and scarlet progeny in a setting of the yellow-green of a spring-time oak wood. I would use drifts of *Osmunda regalis* as their only foil before passing through another part of the wood, given entirely to rhododendrons grown only for their handsome leafage, and only then develop another planting with another series of hybrids, allied by their parentage and in all the modulations and variations of one colour.

If I have wandered rather far from the more restricted subject of flowering shrubs used as plant material and as a more easily maintained substitute for herbaceous plantings, it is because what is valid in the design and composition of a small scale planting is just as valid however large a garden composition becomes and whether it is formal or informal. The word "wild" for any form of gardening is a misnomer and can be a convenient label to excuse plantings which are ill-considered, if indeed they have been considered at all. In making a wild garden perhaps the best we can do is to deploy all the discretion and taste we can muster so that our plantings have an air of belonging. Every plant over which the eye can range should look as though it could grow naturally in that place. For this one must respect ecological, geological and climatic factors as well as the æsthetic exigencies of colour harmonies, form and texture, although these last must almost invariably work out right if the first three elements have been carefully considered. Now as I write there is in the British gardening world a rising tide of Kurume azaleas which may well tend to swamp our gardens. They are a craze already in the Eastern United States, where hundreds of varieties are cultivated and listed in the nurserymen's catalogues. These are admirable plants and even the basic "Wilson's Fifty" offers a wider choice than could be properly placed in even a large garden. I would be content to choose only four or five kinds, to plant in stretches beneath and between rhododendrons as base planting to a house or for association with other evergreens. When I use them for colour I find myself constantly returning to those coral pinks which have no trace of blue in them, to the white edged with pale scarlet and to the all-white variety called "Palestrina." Like *Rhododendron obtusum amoenum*, all the magenta, crimson, mauve and pink varieties seem satisfactory only when associated with each other and isolated from any other flower colour. Although these plants seem to stand up well to full sunlight I would always prefer to use them in a broken or dappled light. So placed they seem to stare less and take on a certain depth and variation in colour. In unrelieved sunlight they reflect light so immediately and superficially that they look almost artificial. I find myself often in sympathy with Japanese practice which consists in clipping these plants into low green mounds and preventing their ever flowering. Used in many varieties in full sun they remind me invariably of a bed of mixed cinerarias—an admirable display of colour, if you will, and most useful and suitable in a considered and very sophisticated setting, but scarcely a type of planting which one would think of placing in a " wild " garden.

If you use grey-leaved subshrubs it is easy to make a permanent planting in a sunny border or above a sunny retaining wall; but at times I find myself having to devise plantings for a less favoured northern aspect, such as the one I contrived at the Duke of Windsor's mill at Gif. Here we replaced a very steep grass bank, facing north and sloping sharply down to the shaded mill-race, with a series of narrow terraces about three feet wide which were held up by low dry walls. In the wall-face we planted London Pride and *Campanula portenschlagiana* and in the beds themselves clumps of white and pale pink Kurume azaleas to give the planting weight and body. These were set out in informal drifts running diagonally across the different levels. To lighten the general effect I added, between the azaleas groups of *Philadelphus microphyllus*, the feathery dwarf syringa which comes into flower after the azaleas, and then, to prolong the flowering seasons still further, clumps of *Spiraea japonica* " Anthony Waterer." I have found it best to cut this right down in April, as otherwise the summer's flowers open a faded pink instead of their proper cerise-crimson. In this particular planting, I filled in all the remaining gaps with polyantha primroses, using the clear rose with a yellow eye developed by Blackmore and Langdon, aquilegias in pale colours whose flowering coincides with that of the philadelphus, and groups of *Lilium regale* to bridge the gaps until the spiraea flowers in late July. Where the lowest of these walls meets an angle of the house in a particularly cold and draughty corner I planted a quite large *Mahonia bealei* for which I had never found quite the right spot. To my surprise this place seems to suit it exactly; it has grown fast and each January its thick sheaves of pale yellow flowers scent the air for yards around.

Although I would not use them in any place where they would be under one's eye all the year round, many of the old-fashioned roses are well suited for massed planting in borders or beds where you may need an effect of mass in a setting which would be rather too formal or gardened for many flowering shrubs. I like to choose the less violently rampant growers which do not need a complicated system of staking and those that I do use I like to shorten back somewhat in July after they have flowered and then in spring take out some proportion of the old wood. The first time I saw a garden devoted only to these old roses was at Nymans in Sussex, where Colonel Leonard Messel had devised a rather formal arrangement of beds set in a clearing in the woods. Although I thought the setting not formal enough, the mass effect of the mounds of foliage, the quiet colours and the extraordinary perfumes hanging heavy in the quiet air made an impression I have never forgotten. Now I like to make just such plantings but preferably in a garden enclosed, or at least backed, by a wall or hedge.

These roses vary enormously in their habit of growth, their height, their spread and their capacity to be self-supporting. For many of the gallicas and some of the centifolias one stout stake is enough. I don't hesitate to use with them some of the hybrid perpetuals for their free flowering. To get the best display from these—Caroline Testout, General MacArthur and Ulrich Brunner—I make a flat framework of laths about two foot six above the ground and tie down the long growths horizontally so that they may throw flowers along their whole length. It is complicated to interplant herbaceous plants amongst these roses but I cannot resist planting *Thalictrum glaucum*, the rue called " Jackman's Blue," *Clematis davidiana* and *Campanula lactiflora*. None of them requires staking and they all show some glaucous blue tone which underlines the milky tone of both the leaf and bloom of many of these old-fashioned roses. To relate the mass and texture of these bushes, one to another, demands the same attentive eye as for any other planting. Each variety has its own nature and its own habit and, as always, these must be respected and indeed enhanced by the way in which they are juxtaposed. In a garden of these plants their perfume will add an extra delight, so to all the spicy scents of the roses I would add the fragrance of some of the philadelphus, particularly *P. coronarius*, and then the sharp pineapple smell of *Cytisus battandieri*, whose silvery-green foliage accords well with that of the roses. In the context of this planting I would add a vertical and evergreen element by using *Cupressus arizonica*. I am particularly fond of this lovely silvery-blue feathery conifer but I find it very difficult to place. In any naturalistic planting its colour seems to make it look too exotic, but here amongst the roses its colour emphasises and completes the general harmony and its form gives a little sharp relief to the rounded masses and flower laden branches of the roses.

The more I plant and the more plantings I plan for, the more inclined I grow to restrict the range of material to be used in any one place. Such a planting as the one I have just described would suit an enclosure in a rather large garden as its flowering will scarcely outlast the two months of May and June. In those parts of the garden which are constantly in view, I like to limit myself to a palette of two or three varieties only. European gardening has nothing more satisfying to offer than a well-kept lawn set about with hedges or clipped shapes of yew or box, two simple elements of which, like good bread, one never tires. I am always looking for ways of making just such simple combinations with other plants.

Nothing gives me more pleasure than to see a good plant used with skill and taste. Not long ago I was in Olivet, a suburb of Orléans, where the long main street is inhabited mostly by nurserymen whose gardens stretch away behind the houses on the alluvial sand deposited by the Loire. I was struck by a small front garden, a ten-foot-wide strip between the house front and the road, which is planted only with a wide band of that admirable evergreen *Choisya ternata*. The house-wall which faces east seems to provide sufficient shelter to this plant which is as charming in detail as it is in the mass. Its green stems give an added richness to its foliage which has a deliciously pungent smell when crushed, while every spring it is white for weeks with its fragrant flowers. As long as it is protected from one side this is a shrub which seems to accept extremes of heat and cold and is not at all fastidious as to soil. When I can give it full sunlight I like to set it against a wall, or back it with a loose hedge of yew, or laurel or even of aucuba. At once there is a garden picture of great distinction. Anywhere south of the Loire or in the South-West of England I would like to plant in front of it a line of agapanthus and perhaps, in a cooler climate, use a thick edging of lily of the valley.

Even the most ordinary plants will take on a new significance if you will refuse the associations that spring to mind and try to see their form, texture and colour as though for the first time. In a garden near Chantilly I had to plant a rough bank some fifteen feet wide running down to a path from a twenty-foot wall which faces due north and allows little sun to penetrate. The soil was bad—heavy, wet and very limy—which meant that I had to choose such tough plant material as would stand these conditions.

After some reflection I planted the hundred-foot length of the wall entirely with quite ordinary ivy which now after three years has covered the whole surface. Next to the wall I planted groups of *Viburnum rhytidophyllum* alternating with *Aucuba japonica*, the plain green and not the spotted variety, while further still to the front I put in bushes of the large-leaved Handsworth box. All these rise from a carpet of bergenia, the large-leaved evergreen saxifrage. These are the most ordinary of plants and the whole effect of this planting, all dark green, comes from the different way each species reflects or absorbs the light. The felty leaves of the viburnum make matt surfaces as a contrast to the slight glow reflected by the smoothness of the aucubas. The box, kept compact by careful pruning, reflects light only in small points from their relatively tiny leaves, while under all these the light catches all the complex and handsome modelling of the bergenias.

Across the path where there is more light and air the box are repeated to give unity to the whole, as does a wide border of bergenia, but between and behind the box *Mahonia japonica* clipped to a height of two feet adds its light-reflecting qualities and its scented yellow April flowering. Where this border emerges into full sunlight, the planting changes again to alternate groups of *Stranvaesia undulata* and chaenomeles which flower in different shades of white, coral, pink and scarlet.

These are simple plantings, effective because I was able, as it were, to exploit the possibilities of the very few varieties which I could hope to make grow in this dank and chilly garden.

Nearby in the same garden, I had to deal with a small wood of neglected spruce which had never been trimmed. When I first saw them, their trunks supported thick columns of ivy and they were branchless to a height of thirty or forty feet. We cut the ivy at the base of each tree so as to make it die back, after which it was fairly easy to tear it off. Then we took down the worst trees to let in some light and air. Now, each year, we take out a few more spruce and replant young Austrian and Scotch pines. Here again we had to decide on an underplanting which would be simple and easy to maintain, which ruled out grass since mowing between the tree trunks would be too difficult. On the outskirts, away from the garden proper, we planted large drifts of ordinary male fern and in the spaces between them foxgloves, which have more or less naturalised themselves although we add a few young plants of the white Excelsior strain each year. To give height there are large clumps of *Macleaya Bocconia cordata* which flourish in spite of the soil. For the rest I have again used large stretches of low-clipped mahonia, periwinkles, both the large and small variety, *Hypericum calycinum* (the " Rose of Sharon "), and in one or two places near a path the admirable low-growing *Viburnum davidii* whose leaves always look glossy and healthy. Between these evergreen patches are drifts of polyanthus, mostly yellow and white, which are also spreading naturally. As these go out of flower the columbines begin. I used long-spurred aquilegias in mixed colours grown from seed and planted them by the hundred. They seem to flourish in this uncongenial soil, and to like the half shade.

I know of no garden picture livelier than this one, made of these thousands of flowers—pale yellow, cream, white, mauve, pink and rather pale orange scarlet—dancing in the broken sunlight that streams through the trees. They are in full flower for more than a month and, when they have been cut back after flowering, their neat tufts of grey-green foliage, touched with dull reds and quiet purples as autumn approaches, make a very satisfactory ground cover. Some groups of the old-fashioned white and mauve sweetly scented rocket precede the columbines and for July and August there are large patches of *Phlox paniculata*. These in two or three varieties only—pink, white and lavender—are planted near the edge of the wood because, while they like moist ground, they must have almost full sunlight. An occasional dressing of peat seems enough to prevent their foliage from yellowing in this excessively alkaline soil.

To design and plant a garden in difficult or bad conditions of soil or climate, or both, is to gain precious experience. You learn to simplify your palette and to make the most of the limited repetition of plants which you can hope to make flourish. In such cases I learnt that you must start, from the very beginning, by studying what plants you will use, because you must shape your composition and design each part of the garden with the restricted planting possibilities always in mind. In designing a garden in an easy soil and climate you are free to compose as you will, since you know that you can choose just those plants which will fulfil the purpose and place for which you intend them. But when you know that you can succeed only with certain plants, then you must compose your landscape or your garden so that you can deploy your plant material to its best advantage. For instance, in the garden I have just described there was no question of growing a wide range of interesting plants, tucking them in here and there where they would look best; I had to limit myself to four or six varieties which were likely to succeed, and because of this limitation I had to plant in broad masses, since nothing is more distressing to the eye than the repetition of the same plants in small patches. In this particular case, whether for foxgloves, phlox, columbines or for the low evergreens, I made drifts up to forty feet long and twenty feet wide. Only in this way was I able to maintain good scale among the bare vertical trunks of the spruce where I deliberately kept paths and walks wide also. Thus the proportions of the garden resulted directly from the nature of the plants employed.

Yew and box, beech and hornbeam are plants for hedges, and when I draw out my first tentative lines on paper to represent the general organisation of a garden, its boundaries and volumes will, as likely as not, be limited by hedges.

How seldom one sees a tapestry hedge, that subtle civilisation of the wild hedgerow. On the way to Longleat you pass a Wiltshire village inn sheltered by pollarded limes, which are called the Twelve Apostles, and follow a winding lane shaded by high trees. This lane announces the neighbourhood of the great honey-coloured stone house to which it leads by the carefully clipped hedge on either side. It is a low and crooked hedge of holly, beech, box and yew, a patchwork of russet and different shades of green all woven into a pattern as irregular as that of the gold and red-purple lichens on the stone arch which marks the beginning of the mile-long avenue to the house. This simple device is just enough to give a sense of expectancy and prepare the mind for the transition from village to mansion. You need no set rules for making such a hedge, save to avoid a stretch of any one plant: the more you mix them the better. In a garden you might make other experiments with copper and green beech perhaps or with holly and chaenomeles which when the holly berries have gone, will star the prickly foliage of the holly with white and salmon and scarlet flowers.

Hedges will make the living green skeleton of the garden: the rigid framework which your planting will clothe with muscles and flesh. It was from Geoffrey Jellicoe that I learned how important this could be—by watching the progress of his work at James Gibbs's domestic masterpiece, Ditchley Park. Here he established the relationship between house and landscape by extending its main façade with long ten-foot-high beech hedges which back a long grass terrace. This was enough to "place" the house firmly in its setting and make a starting point for a series of enclosed gardens to match the stateliness of the architecture. Later I tried many experiments in composition, using hedges to give "line" and form. I like high hedges which really enclose. Beech is good for these and, if you will make a rough trellis framework of the full height you wish to attain, you may train your hedge upwards on this support and only when it reaches its full height allow it to thicken and the framework to decay. I clip any hedge more than a foot high so that it will be wider at the base than at the top and thus ensure against its going thin at the bottom. This is an important practical point and, as well, gives any hedge its proper air of stability.

On the Continent you see few beech hedges; hornbeam, a closely related species, is commonly used in France, in Switzerland and in Italy, although it is sometimes difficult to establish.

Farther south in Italy the bay laurel, in spite of its rather large leaves, makes a fine high barrier, though it looks better for being cut over with secateurs rather than clipped with shears. On the Riviera I like to use myrtle as a substitute for box which is apt to become diseased. I cut the myrtle hard back only after its gloriously scented flowering, to make an impeccable and compact green hedge.

There is nothing to be gained by planting fast-growing hedges. In my experience, the faster they grow the more rapidly they decline and though you may set out with the idea that you will remove it later, a temporary planting too often remains to reproach you as the rest of the garden attains maturity. *Cupressus macrocarpa*, which in a mild climate, makes a beautiful hedge with great rapidity may last for ten or fifteen years and then, caught by one degree more frost than it can stand, become a browned ruin overnight. Privet, too, turns deciduous in a severe winter besides impoverishing the ground for a yard or more on either side. It is better to grow it as a high, spreading bush in a shady corner and enjoy the heady perfume of its small panicles of creamy lilac-like flowers. *Lonicera nitida* will clip into a neat low hedge until a heavy snowfall smashes it flat.

Roses will make a lovely flowery limit to a garden if you can give the time to keeping them in order. Among rambler roses I like to use the wichuraiana varieties, " Alberic Barbier " and " François Juranville," which keep their glossy green leaves through a mild winter, as well as Albertine for its profusion of flowers, but these rambler roses need a framework on which to grow. Occasionally one can use shrub roses to make a lax and flowery hedge: the rugosa varieties like the " Blanc Double de Coubert," " Roseraie de l'Haÿ " and " Cardinal Richelieu," are useful for their bright moss-green and matt foliage as well as for their flowers. The varieties bearing the name Grootendorst, both pink and red, produces clusters of fringed flowers like old-fashioned garden pinks, over a long period. All these should, I think, be pruned back into shape rather severely every second year, and old wood taken out when necessary. I have used *Prunus pissardii*, the common purple-leaved plum, as well as its improved variety, *nigra*, to make hedges from six to eight feet high. They require very careful pruning in the first years in order to keep the bottom of the hedge well-furnished. I like to plant a single line of three-foot plants, thicken the base with two-year-old plants, and then severely prune the whole. The small plants will then make twiggy growth to fill in the gaps at the base of the larger ones. This hedge will flower none the worse for being clipped, and it will make a lovely and unusual background for an autumnal show of Michaelmas daisies or Korean chrysanthemums. The Myrobalan plum also makes a good rough hedge in places where you might need a stout barrier. It will grow five foot wide and eight foot high but you must be prepared to clip it at least twice a year or you will find you have a line of unsightly plum trees which, every few years, will produce a huge bounty of tiny yellow plums. I have sometimes tried *Acer campestre*, the small-leaved native maple, as a hedge-plant, chiefly because of the lovely soft yellow of its autumn foliage but it is very slow growing, and were better used perhaps as one of the elements in a mixed tapestry hedge.

In the main I do not care much for unusual hedges. Most of the plants which might compose them can be better used in other ways. I think of hedges as enclosures, and it is with hedges that you may best articulate the bony structure, and skeleton as it were, of a garden. For this a hedge should usually be close in texture, monotone in colour and sharply defined in shape. I would therefore restrict myself to the classical materials: on box and yew, holly, ilex and bay laurel, beech and hornbeam, cypress, pittosporum, myrtle, lavender and rosemary.

I find I am easily hypnotised by plant-associations and tend to mix too many different kinds just to enjoy the effects of juxtaposition. Yet we enjoy a hedge just because it is a clear and simple statement, a simple form usually simply expressed in terms of one variety of plant. We have long since accepted the convention of a rose garden, an iris garden and a heather garden, and, I suppose, of a rhododendron garden. These embody a principle which could be carried further in large or small gardens old and new, nor need they necessarily be a specialist's collection of one kind of plant. One or two varieties of shrubs, carefully selected, would be enough to make the backbone or basic theme of a whole garden. I would plant them in quantity, and so dispose them as best to set off their main characteristics. I would only add other varieties in smaller patches, and only then where they would reinforce the effectiveness of the main theme. Such self-imposed limitations do not preclude original and effective plantations. I remember, some thirty years back, when he had established the main lines and themes of his garden at Hidcote Manor where planning and planting achieved a rare synthesis, Lawrence Johnston began to experiment in another way. Steeped in the site and its possibilities and having already pushed to the limit the pictorial possibilities of a conventional manor-house garden, Major Johnston freed himself from his frame and learned to handle plantings and compositions in a bold and unexpected way. For instance, on the outskirts of the garden lay a piece of undulating grass-land with a quiet view over stone-walled fields merging into the distant blue hills. Here he planted the higher parts of the ground with large groups of many kinds of berberis, red in autumn with their translucent berries and colouring foliage, which stressed in their close-textured masses of foliage the undulations of the whole site. But what lifted this scheme on to a higher plane were tufts and groups of Yuccas, *Y. flaccida*, *Y. filamentosa* and *Y. gloriosa*. Exotically Mexican, their sharp foliage and creamy candelabra spikes of flowers defied the expected and made a new kind of world, apt setting for a flock of rosy pink flamingos unbelievably wading in the shallow pond which was the centre of this garden.

This integration of three such disparate elements would seem wilful save for the sure eye which could contrast such textures and render such a scene " classical " (for I do not know what other word will do) and place such an experiment in a continuity of garden design.

CHAPTER VII

On planting : flowers

Garden lovers anywhere are certain to associate English gardens with herbaceous borders. They will imagine an improbably green lawn with a mixed border on either side with every plant in flower simultaneously from one end to the other. The mixed border of herbaceous plants has indeed dominated the British garden for the last seventy years. In its beginnings it was a device to show the beauty of hardy flowers as the alternative to a current passion for bedding out half-hardy annuals. An artist like Gertrude Jekyll made flower borders which were lovely by any count just because she was an artist and whatever she touched bore her stamp as such. She and others, professionals or amateurs, designed gardens in which flower borders were the main feature, and within a generation this new and aristocratic horticultural fashion had spread to every middle-class garden. Nurserymen have been printing plans for long-flowering mixed borders on the back page of their catalogues for some years now and herbaceous gardening in England has become a popular amusement.

But even from the early days of herbaceous borders dis-criminating gardeners sought to modify what was becoming a commonplace and started composing in a range of one colour—blue, perhaps, or yellow or white—in an effort to find a new formula for using hardy plants.

To-day in England high garden fashion has veered towards other forms of gardening, but in France and Italy and Switzerland people ask for an English garden; when one asks them how they envisage an English garden the answer is always that they want grass right up to the house and a mixed flower border. Except near the sea or in the mountains or where the air is especially moist, herbaceous borders are not a success on the Continent. For their somewhat disillusioned owners they are not bright enough for long enough, and continental gardeners will not learn their proper cultivation. The admittedly difficult problem of staking is solved by a piece of string tied so tightly that it throttles and deforms the plant, and then, in despair, annual flowers are planted in the bare spaces which grow larger year by year.

I must have seen thousands of herbaceous borders and I know I have planned and planted hundreds, though not always with pleasure. A border is often too narrow for one to plant it in depth; and herbaceous plants should have breadth of treatment since they are basically meadow flowers which should by their arrangement recall their native haunts. Then, in the best case, where you may have a fifteen or twenty-foot-wide border, this extensive and brightly flowered hay (for that is what many herbaceous plants quite simply are) has neither body nor character enough to make broad planting look other than flimsy. These are my reasons for disliking the classic herbaceous border in general, although I have and shall continue to make exceptions. Norah Lindsay, so typical of the English lady who gardens, even her hats an offering of fruit or flowers, had a special talent for handling gardens of herbaceous plants. Between the wars she moved from one country house to the next, gardening and keeping everybody amused and entertained. She rushed from garden to garden, leaving long and brilliant reports as to what should be done and what planted, all pencilled out in a large flowing writing on endless sheets of flimsy paper. For all her minor and charming eccentricities, Mrs. Lindsay could by her plantings evoke all the pleasures of a flower garden. She captured the essence of midsummer with blue and mauve and pink and white and grey or gave the pith of autumn by her sensitive combination of phlox and helenium, montbretias and Michaelmas daisies. Hers was a talent which I find hard to define. She lifted her herbaceous planting into a poetic category and gave it an air of rapture and spontaneity. I think she visualised very surely, added the unexpected species whose form and colour would shake a group of plants out of the commonplace, and then she would be on her way, leaving the rest to nature and the astonished gardener.

Norah Lindsay did not invent the trick of using grey-foliaged plants as a foil for brightly coloured flowers, but she certainly carried it so far that some of her borders looked almost opalescent. She would use artemisias, senecios, lavender and nepeta as a base for soft pinks and mauves with perhaps a few sparks of crimson. Part of her secret, of course, was to use allied and related colours together and to deploy comparatively few flowers against a great deal of grey foliage.

Strangely enough, when she attempted the same procedure with flowering shrubs the magic did not seem to work and the results, I thought, were often chaotic and commonplace.

It must be thirty-five years ago that I was taken to see her own garden at Sutton Courtenay near Abingdon. There was a dusty lovely Elizabethan timbered house and a wide walled garden which I remember as a turbulent sea of flowers. One moved along paths through a waist-high haze of pinks and greys. It was here that I first saw *Salvia turkestanica* with its rough foliage and nacreous bracts, beige, mauve and greyed-pink, used in masses as quiet foil for pink mallows and sidalceas and high old roses, bushes whose arched sprays were heavy with silvery pink blossoms. These roses were perhaps " Zephirine Drouhin " and the pink *Rosa centifolia* and " Maiden's Blush " whose slightly darker form the French call " Cuisses de Nymphe Emue ". This was the first time, too, that I learnt how much body rose bushes will give to an herbaceous planting. Since then I have usually added groups of roses to my border plantings. The strong reds of some of the polyantha or floribunda roses like " Frensham," " Donald Prior," " Cocorico," " Moulin Rouge " and " Concerto " are bright enough to place near delphiniums, and they can be relied on to flower in June when bright crimson reds are useful to set against the strong blues of anchusas and lupins.

I don't usually care for violent colour contrasts in informal flower plantings. Now and again a brilliant juxtaposition of colour will bring a low-toned harmony into life. I will group strong primary colours, reds, for instance, or yellows or blues in large patches all of one general colour with all the variations, whether slightly sharp or slightly flat, and then add one accent of a contrasting colour, but only if it is necessary to enhance the blueness or redness or yellowness of the main planting. Dark red roses, like many other flowers of this colour, are likely to look black and make a hole in any colour arrangement, so that I will often lead up to them, as it were, with a muted red or pink.

Many years ago, near the disused ironstone quarries of the outskirts of Lincoln, there was a house built like a Scots peel-tower which looked oddly out of place in East Anglia. In it came to live a family friend who was a keen and rather slap-dash gardener and determined to make the flowery best of this bleak house which looked like a Victorian stage-setting for Macbeth. In the pseudo-ramparts valerian had seeded itself to make bushy clumps of grey-green leaves and white and dulled pink and red flowers. Just below them our friend planted large clumps of pink and red polyantha roses and this accidental combination gave me a lesson in handling colour which I have since constantly found useful.

Valerian in its three colours is a first-class plant, as suitable in the wildest part of the garden as it is near the house or combined with far more aristocratic and difficult subjects. It will grow in any place that is neither shady nor wet and properly handled it will flower for months on end. It makes nice comfortable rounded clumps which need no staking. Only near yellow or blue flowers will it look like an insignificant weed. I often combine it with the white or the rather milky mauves of the different varieties of *Campanula persicifolia*, with lavender, and, for its second flowering, with the pink and the crimson form of *Sedum spectabile* with its fleshy foliage of grey-green with creamy undertones.

To consider a herbaceous border is to consider the plants that will go into it—and this may lead to the frequent and pleasurable pursuit of red herrings. I am constantly tempted to lose sight of my theme and scale in my delight in secondary details of planting. One name leads by association to another and, unless you take care, a garden in which you intend to plan for colour quickly ceases to be a unity and turns into a miscellaneous assortment of perhaps charming incidents.

The classic herbaceous border acts as an element which gives mass and colour against the planes of a lawn or the vertical line of hedge or wall. Its width is usually between eight and fifteen feet, its length anywhere from thirty to two hundred. These conventions of size and use have necessarily dictated the dimensions and weight of the clumps of individual varieties. Only so many delphiniums at a time in the back row, since phlox must come in front to succeed them, and in front of the phlox still another earlier, or later flowering and lower plant. This way of handling herbaceous plants has become so stereotyped that it is well worth while to stand back from the whole problem for a moment and try to see it from another angle. It may be that the habitual combinations are not, in fact, inevitable or infallibly successful. Perhaps the soft weedy growth of a Michaelmas daisy would be better set away from the equally undistinguished architecture of a golden rod or the lush and sappy growth of delphiniums. Here, I think, the architecture of a whole plant as an individual and the form it takes alone, or in a clump, requires consideration. If one looks at the usual range of herbaceous plants—and a quick run through a catalogue will soon recall the various shapes—one sees that relatively few of the plants are architecturally striking. We accept this defect in many plants because of their splendid flowering, but their flowering period is limited and for at least four out of the six months of their growth they are without flowers. If a haze of colour is my main object I can, and often must, fill the gaps left by plants that have finished flowering by interplanting dahlias and cannas, gladioli, galtonias and annuals. But this is a costly and elaborate process, and it takes hours of very skilled work every day to achieve and maintain a continuity in the exact colours you want. Do it haphazardly and your result will be chaotic. Plants will grow through and into each other; only the most vigorous will win their place in the sun and all your careful colour-planning will go for nothing.

I try first to look at my planting as an exercise in monochrome —to see form only and, for the moment, let the colour ride. For any given situation I endeavour to decide where I need dark, where light, where flower and foliage should glitter and where they should be matt and quiet in tone.

Almost always I find that it is quite impossible to think out even this first, colourless stage with only the usual run of herbaceous plants in mind. I will have to use foliage as part of my picture. So I add a new range to my plant repertoire: plants whose flowering is secondary to their form and texture. Funkias, now called hostas, come at once to my mind and bergenias, eulalias and ferns—these and many others for their lustre and distinction of form. In another category are all the grey-leaved plants: artemisias, stachys, pinks, catmints, rue, certain salvias, *Elymus arenarius* and *Festuca glauca*.

Even though these will greatly enrich my palette, I need still stronger accents and bolder masses and now I will choose any tree or shrubs, deciduous or evergreen, or even conifers if they will give me the forms and the depth of tone I need.

But I must not forget that I am making a flower garden, and that these new elements are to enhance and not to submerge the herbaceous plantings.

If you are going to mix shrubs or even trees with herbaceous plants you must select only such plants as have, on the whole, garden connotations. Roses, lilacs, philadelphus, hydrangeas, ceanothus and certain of the viburnums spring to mind. *Chamaecyparis obtusa nana*, clipped yew, a dwarf pine, would all make a necessary dark spot in certain contexts. Caryopteris, perowskia, lavender, grey santolina and the green form as well, *Artemisia abrotanum* (the scented lad's-love of cottage gardens), the shrubby potentillas, are some of the low shrubs I often include. The lank young flowering shoots of the garden hybrids of Buddleia add nothing to this type of planting, although I find *Buddleia alternifolia* with its small leaves and rounded form very useful. Other wild species as suitable to the sophistication of a flower border as in wilder parts of the garden are *Spartium junceum* and *Cytisus battandieri*, with its silky silvered leaves and clustered heads of pineapple-scented flowers.

Now I can begin to think and visualise in colour. The cytisus and buddleia have greyish leaves. So has *Caryopteris clandonensis*; and its clear pale blue flowers in late summer when clear blue flowers are infrequent are an added attraction. The hybrid ceanothus " Gloire de Versailles " has powder-blue flowers while those of " Indigo " are a distinctly darker blue. I like to cut these shrubs hard back in spring, as they flower on the current year's growth. The hybrid lilacs flower too early for most borders and look very dull for the rest of the year, though once in a while I would use a standard or half-standard " Maréchal Foch " or " Congo." But the Persian lilac in either the mauve or pink form is a first-class plant almost anywhere you choose to place it. Newly-planted they are miserably thin little bushes, so I like to plant five young plants together. In a very few years they will make a large mound completely covered with flowers each spring. They are particularly lovely hanging over a low wall or on a bank above a pool, reflected in the water.

Certain hydrangea species are good border plants. Their habit of growth is distinguished, their foliage handsome, and their mauve-blue, pink and white flowers suit the late autumn colours of the border. Best of all is *Hydrangea paniculata grandiflora* which you can leave to grow into a large bush with medium-sized flowers or prune each spring to make huge flower-trusses opening creamy-white and fading pink about three feet from the ground.

I have a weakness for the floribunda rose " Masquerade " whose general colour is much like a ripe yellow peach, though this may well be an acquired taste for those serious gardeners

A long canal flanked by hornbeam hedges and rows of pink horse chestnuts runs for two hundred yards from a sixteenth-century château to join the river Loing, which we had diverted to make room for formal gardens around the house, built orginally as a hunting lodge by Admiral Coligny.

A water garden in Piedmont. While the main facades of this rococco villa face north and south the main reception rooms are on the first floor of this the east front. This shallow canal flanked by double hornbeam hedges and rows of lime trees replaces a stretch of waste ground. The photograph was taken two years after planting

The same canal seen from the first floor of the house.
Lombardy poplars mark the angles of a short cross canal
and add length to the perspective. The narrower canal just
beyond will be more effective when the chestnut trees planted
on either side grow enough to give height to the rather
flimsy poplar wood which already existed on the site

High above Cap Ferrat on the Mediterranean near Nice,
Ogden Codman built the Villa Leopolda and transformed the
reservoir of this terraced hillside property into a formal pool
whose horizontal cut stone borders bisect the verticals of tall
green cypresses and their reflections.

This oval pool near Nice
is blue tiled and set in
pinky orange brick paving.
The surrounding planting is
entirely silver grey

who dislike "sunset colours." The rugosa rose "Blanc Double de Coubert" goes into every garden I make and very frequently into the flower border. Its brilliant moss-green foliage would be quite satisfying even did it not flower intermittently from May until October. The flowers are chalk-white, their petals silky and almost transparent and they have the delicious pungently sweet scent of their kind.

In places where I use very strong hot colours together, reds and oranges and certain violet crimsons, I try to reduce green leafage as much as possible and here a few plants of the red-leafed form of *Berberis thunbergii* and a bush or two of *Prunus pissardii nigra*, kept severely pruned, can make a dusky foil to the fiery colours of the flowers. Various phlox, red-hot pokers, the liatris called Cobalt, some of the dark-red early Michaelmas daisies, red, copper and orange Korean chrysanthemums gain, whether separately or together from such a background, and earlier in the year it will serve to frame breeder and May-flowering tulips, whose place will later be taken by clumps of such dark-leaved dahlias as "Bishop of Llandaff" and "Olympic Fire."

All these proposals may seem to indicate flower-gardening on a scale impossible in a small garden, and it is true that these are effects to achieve on variations of the "drift" planting which has hitherto been the conventional way of setting out the hardy flower border. In the flower garden—in contrast to the informality of the wilder part of the garden, where other considerations will come in and there will be another approach— I try to come to my planting problems as an architect. My first concern is with forms, volumes, textures and with the constructions of my plant material: then as a painter, I must deal with colour for its own sake and for the planes and recessions it will give; finally, as a gardener, I have to decide which plants I can use and in what combinations. The same approach is valid for quite small plantings in small gardens, though then I have to apply these principles even more rigorously, since each detail will count more and more as the scale of the planting is reduced. One oversized flower or plant, for instance, may easily make your whole composition nonsensical. Here I should remind myself and the reader that, from my profession, I have evolved into someone whose first thought of coming to a garden is always " What does it look like? " Then only do I start to analyse and to try and see why it looks as it does and what I would do to " improve " it. Now we are at once on dangerous ground—the quicksands of " taste "—and if, to my eye, there is something wrong I must weigh up the characteristics and the elements of the picture in front of me. Is there a connecting thread in the planting and composition and, if there is, is it sufficiently clear? If it is cluttered up by extraneous and distracting details, perhaps I have only to clear these away and to strengthen the underlying theme. Or perhaps the theme is so obvious and so heavily accentuated that it is monotonous and boring. In that case I would break it up and give it a little mystery and excitement perhaps by an asymmetrical detail added to a too rigid plan or a break in colour or form to give life to a repetitious planting.

Once I have selected and placed whatever shrubs I am going to use in my herbaceous planting I reflect on the plants themselves, and here again my first care is to look for subjects which have " architectural " merits as a whole plant. Many border plants, most of the composites for instance, are useful only in mass and for their flower colour. I use asters, anthemis, border chrysanthemums, heleniums, helianthus and similar plants only when I am working for broad effects of colour and in places where their rather dull appearance during ten months of the year will not obtrude too much.

I think the best way to start is to decide on one or two families that you particularly like or that you think will grow well in the place you have allotted for them. A coloured photograph I once saw of a herbaceous garden at Bodnant in North Wales struck me as an excellent example of this kind of selective planting. Here, in the moist climate of the Conway river estuary, *Phlox decussata* in many varieties set the theme in every tone of pink, salmon, scarlet and crimson, while clumps of cream spired yucca gave weight and architecture. Phlox and yuccas alone could make a garden interesting only in late July and August but it would not be difficult to prolong the flowering season by interplanting astilbes for June and July with *Galtonia candicans* and varieties of *Lobelia cardinalis* and *Aconitum wilsonii* for September. These are all plants which will succeed in cool damp earth, moist air and plenty of sun.

Were a garden particularly suitable for growing lupins I might choose these plants as a major theme and use them in various combinations of white and pink, pale yellow, apricot, crimson, purple and soft blues. Their gamut of colour is so special that I would be at pains to avoid using near them any hard blues such as delphiniums or indeed yellows or scarlets. Flag iris and drifts of mixed aquilegias grown from seed would emphasise the general range of colour. I think with such a planting I should forgo any later August display, except in the front of the border where *Aster amellus* amongst the aquilegias would anticipate an autumn show of Michaelmas daisies planted in drifts to hide the rather ugly relics of the lupins.

Delphiniums are an obvious choice as a theme plant for a herbaceous garden. To their vivid blues I would join the scarlet of *Lychnis chalcedonica*, the silky white foam of *Crambe cordifolia*, candidum and regal lilies and any yellow-flowered verbascum for a June garden; but I would use quantities of the dwarfer, more perpetual-flowering belladonna delphiniums to prolong the flowering season. The display would be mostly over by the end of July, nor could I be sure of a second flowering of the main planting of delphiniums. In such a case I might provide late summer colour quite simply by a fairly lavish interplanting of achillea " Gold Plate " as well as various helianthus and heliopsis to ensure a mass of yellow as a foil for any second flowering of the delphiniums; or, if labour were not a problem, I would inter-plant the delphiniums with dahlias, choosing decorative and cactus varieties with small flowers on rigid stems in whites, yellows, apricot and orange.

All these are, so to speak, recipes for colour. Garden books are full of them; but, although such arrangements are invaluable for filling in your garden design in a broad way, I am always, when working out such plans and combinations, a little reminded of those children's painting books in which the various patches of the design are marked with numbers that you brush in with colour from a correspondingly marked palette. But planting can give a profounder pleasure. Let us start with another point of view and consider some one plant that we specially like: for instance *Kirengeshoma palmata*, a Japanese member of the saxifrage family. Like so many Japanese plants it seems to me to have a special architectural harmony in all its parts. It has soft green leaves, well-articulated stalks and muted yellow hanging flowers in early autumn. Its general colour is so subtle that I must choose companions for it whose brilliance will not make my clump of kirengeshoma look insipid. I would choose perhaps the willow gentian, *Gentiana asclepiadea*, for its sheaves of soft purply-blue flowers. Between or in front of these plants I would add the low-growing *Tiarella cordifolia* since, although its white flowers will have faded by July, its crumpled yellowish-green leaves begin to be edged with red as its taller neighbours come into bloom. For interest earlier in the year I shall plant *Mertensia virginica* whose milky-blue flowers in late April or early May seem only slightly bluer than its glaucous foliage. Then perhaps all I will need to complete this grouping will be some bulbs of *Erythronium dens-canis*, the dog's tooth violet, for early spring and, if the soil is peaty enough, a few trilliums. But even now this planting scheme may still be too ephemeral. It needs more weight, so I will add a good patch of one of the large leathery-leaved saxifrages, *Bergenia cordifolia*, *B. ligulata* or *B. crassifolia*, all of which grow equally well in sun or shade. Here at once there is a change of scale, so that next to these saxifrages with their crimson flower-stalks and corymbs of pink flowers which appear in March or April I could plant hostas with their heavy grey-blue, green or green and white striped leaves and their white or dull mauve flowers in summer. Finally I would set bulbs of *Scilla hispanica*, the cultivated bluebell whose white, pink and blue-mauve flowers will fill a gap in May.

Where this planting goes deeper into the shade of the trees I would plant the small-leaved periwinkle or mahonia whose sulphur yellow honey-scented flowers look so well with the saxifrages. Such a planting could cover five square yards or fifty. Its size will depend on the scale of the garden but, whether with twenty plants or four hundred, you will be able to achieve the same mood and the same quiet harmony of subtle colour and distinguished form.

But it is just as easy to start with a more ordinary herbaceous plant, say one of the sidalceas, which grows well in almost any soil and in full sunlight. This member of the mallow family has spikes of soft rose-pink flowers and rather dull green foliage. Once again its colour demands harmony rather than contrast. I would plant next to it *Campanula lactiflora* with milky-blue flowers and, with them both, *Salvia sclarea* or *Salvia turkestanica* for its large hairy and silvery foliage and its bracts and flowers with their browny-pink, mauve and cream colours which make the whole plant look opalescent. These plants will all flower together in July. For still later flowering you could add Japanese anemones, dull pink or white. Any of the flag iris—blue veined with white, or the lavender of *Iris pallida dalmatica*—would suitably start the flowering season in May or June.

Studying one's plantings in this way, starting from any one plant and seeing how to enhance its special qualities, its flower colour and habit of growth, its silhouette, its likes and dislikes, you can weave a herbaceous tapestry on any scale: building, plant by plant and variety by variety, a texture valid at any point, as you have considered the shape and colour of each plant in relation to its neighbours. I have given two examples of soft colours, but in using a brightly coloured plant as a starting point the procedure is just the same, though in this case it is strong contrasts which will lead your plantings into a sharper harmony. Let us start with the brown-red stalks and coarse red flowers of a heuchera. I have often used this as a front row plant next to *Veronica spicata*. The gentian-blue spikes of this veronica are almost too sharp and too intense, so that I might use next to it the much lighter clear blue of *Anchusa caespitosa* and then only make a transition to the indented foliage and creamy white flowers of *Anthemis cupaniana* in order to move on towards the yellows of other anthemis such as "Grallagh Gold" and the softer blue of *Veronica longifolia*. Behind the heuchera comes the red-flowered form of valerian, *Centranthus ruber*, with its rather silvery green foliage. Ordinary lavender planted next to it accentuates this silver note and enables me to use the white plushy leaves of *Stachys lanata* in front of it and from there to start on a new series of combinations.

Since I have spoken of using flowering shrubs to reinforce herbaceous plantings, I should perhaps describe just how I like to work them in. In the Duke of Windsor's walled flower garden near Paris the flower plantings were relatively wide, and as the Duke happened to dislike evergreens in general and any clipped yew or box in particular it was difficult to know how to give weight, point and body to so wide a planting. So towards the front of the borders I planted clumps of red floribunda roses whose first flowering helps to offset the blue look of the garden in June when all the delphiniums are in flower. Farther back are plants of *Buddleia alternifolia*, bushes of *Laburnum vossii* and *Spartium junceum*. Next to *Buddleia alternifolia* I planted the flowering sea-kale, *Crambe cordifolia*, for its huge spreading head of tiny silky white flowers. Next to it, and again with somewhat silvery foliage, is the erect-growing *Thalictrum flavum* with pale yellow flowers and the delicate mauve of *T. dipterocarpum*. A big clump of single yellow hollyhocks completes this particular group.

The *Laburnum vossii*, and the spartium in the background, are planted close together to make a succession of yellow flowers. Here the colour is strong. The bright green, whip-like stems and brilliant yellow of the spartium rise above a mass of blue anchusa, "Morning Glory." Then comes the equally blue belladonna delphinium and a big erect clump of scarlet *Lychnis chalcedonica*. As the spartium goes out of flower achillea "Gold Plate" pick up the yellow theme, its flat heads set against the blue spikes of

Aconitum wilsonii, one of the few really blue flowers in the late summer border.

There are three plants of the rose "Blanc Double de Coubert" near a narrow path of squared sandstone setts. In two years these three bushes have made a thicket five feet high and six wide kept in shape by the occasional pruning of old wood. Next to them is a clump of herbaceous paeonies, deep single pink with yellow centres and the not very tall delphinium, "Pink Sensation," with *Nepeta faassenii*, the mauve catmint, and a carpet of garden pinks grown from seed, to complete the planting. This is a discursive way of building up a herbaceous planting but one which lends itself to gardens of any size.

As I go about from place to place and from country to country through the summer months I see hundreds of gardens—gardens of all kinds, small and large, well kept or neglected, gardens in the suburbs of London or Paris or Brussels—the terraced plots of the French or Italian Rivieras, the rather stodgy miniature parks of middle-class houses round great industrial cities, cottage gardens in the English countryside, public gardens in city squares, and parks in front of town halls or railway stations. I am always struck by the contrast between the stylised monotony of the formal bedding-out of annuals and "soft plants" and the dishevelled incoherence of most of the herbaceous plantings that I see. I know the causes of this contrast well enough. The formal bedding-out of annuals is almost always a routine planting, dating from the mid-nineteenth century when gardens were drawn out carefully on paper and flower beds were divided up into more or less complicated patterns, each section to be filled with brightly coloured annuals. As time has gone on, these parterres have become stereotyped and simplified until they are usually just a mass of red salvia, red and yellow cannas or zinnias or snapdragons, garish witnesses to a lack of invention and a slavery to custom.

The other kind of garden, dating perhaps from the turn of the century, is dull in a different way, filled in as it is with herbaceous plants left to grow into large and rapidly degenerating clumps.

Only in exceptional cases have hazard or, occasionally, careful thought brought about charming and memorable combinations.

Annual flowers are an ephemeral decoration expensive to produce in terms of time and labour and, in my experience, best left to the professional gardener. They do, however, give a mass effect of bright colour which few perennials can rival and so we can scarcely do without them. To grow them you need a greenhouse or at least a heated frame, as sown *in situ* they are apt to grow unevenly and are hard to thin out successfully; in my experience it is only the flimsier sorts with a brief season of flowering which respond well to this treatment.

But for all this, the designer will need annuals for certain kinds of gardening. In Northern and Western Europe there is still much to be said for a formal arrangement of beds near a house bright with flowers, to offset our grey and clouded skies. When I design such a small garden I make beds that are usually about five feet across, a convenient width for working. The design may be simply a pattern of squares or rectangles, symmetrical or asymmetrical according to the architecture and style of the house. Though I will occasionally use triangular shapes I try to avoid any angle sharper than forty-five degrees, as narrow angles are difficult to plant and always look thin. In a symmetrical garden I try to avoid a central vertical ornament or feature, which invariably renders the pattern too obvious. I prefer to place some object, a vase, a seat, a sundial or perhaps one odd clipped yew or box, elsewhere in the composition, but always where it will best give a sense of balance to the whole. I try to remember that I am making a pattern which I intend to fill with flower colour and so I avoid eccentric complicated designs which are likely to make difficulties for me when it comes to working out the planting and colour arrangement. I like to plant small gardens of this kind in blocks of colour, one colour and one variety of annual to a bed. If I have to work to a larger scale with larger planting areas, I like to use box or lavender edging to break up a large area into smaller compartments. Sometimes, if your parterre is quite small, you will do well to use only one kind of flower either mixed or in separate colours. This ensures good scale and coherence and avoids the often difficult problem of replacing one bed at a time where one variety may have faded. Even in the best circumstances you cannot be sure of finding reserve plants of just the right colour and height.

Spring planting, to which I will return later, is relatively easy. Tulips with or without an underplanting will give such endless and lovely combinations that summer bedding follows almost as an anticlimax. In most years petunias will give a good account of themselves later in the season, if you will be ruthless and shear them hard back after the first flush since once they set seed their flowering time is over. I like to use the dwarf whites and silver blues with a small proportion of dark purple or white and white-and-red-striped with some good cherry red. White, crimson and pink are harder to combine successfully as so many of the pinks have an aniline intensity and a bluish cast which goes ill with the red and crimson. There is now a whole range of good strong reds, but it is as well to see them growing before deciding on a particular variety, as some of these reds fade in the sun to a rather objectionable pink.

Mixed verbenas too are a good choice, especially in a hot summer, and you can use the scarlet and lavender blue selfs to strengthen the general effect of colour. *Phlox drummondii* do well in a showery season, but this is one of the rare annuals that does not seem to appreciate a baking. These, too, are useful mixed, though as soon as they show colour I eliminate if possible a pale ochre-yellow strain that crops up in mixtures. One used to be able to grow dwarf zinnias in separate colours and make good combinations of white, yellows and a whole range of pinks. Now this dwarf strain comes only in a rather fidgety mixture which I like less. Tall zinnias are altogether too robust for bedding-out except on the largest scale and where they will be seen from a distance.

In planning colour schemes my own taste inclines almost always to harmonies of colour or what I must call quiet contrasts. I don't care for the violence of scarlet against yellow: the clash is too strong and the two colours seem to annihilate one another unless I can add an intermediate orange. In the same way I usually use white to link (or separate) yellow and blue or blue-mauve, although an orange yellow and a pinkish mauve seem all right in opposition, perhaps because of the warm cast common to both. White and pale yellow go well together in most annuals and biennials. This is a simple combination which always looks fresh and gay. Mauve-pinks are difficult to use unless you mix them well and add enough sharp salmon-pink to prevent their looking grey. I remember a small garden in Dorest where each bed was edged with mixed cottage pinks, white, lavender-pink, deep rose and crimson, and the centres filled in with godetias and clarkias with a good proportion of salmon-pink flowers. This was a lovely combination in mid-July but it would present a problem a month later.

Working out bedding schemes is tiresome work and I must admit that I prefer to leave it to the owner or the gardener. To begin with you have to devise your summer planting in January and next spring's show in July, moments in the year when your mind is likely to be set on quite other problems. Spring planting seems less difficult—violas, pansies, wallflowers and bachelor's buttons give you a good range for underplanting tulips; and devising colour schemes with tulips is a deeply satisfying task. I find myself again and again setting white and black-purple tulips on a ground of white violas or white daisies or occasionally the darkest blue forget-me-nots. These last are rather trouble-some as they are apt to damp off in winter and their flowers fade almost as fast as those of the tulips, leaving you with a gap for the last half of May before the summer bedding goes in. Pansies and violas will carry on for weeks longer and so will *Cheiranthus allionii*, a satisfying mass of cadmium orange. This is not the easiest colour to mix with tulips and I usually choose a tall white or lemon-yellow variety or perhaps an orange. I have been tempted to try scarlet but I find this altogether too striking. I like white, pink and red-feathered white tulips on a ground of dwarf double daisies either red or white. You can add a quite strong scarlet tulip to this combination. Pink and scarlet tulips usually combine well, as do pink and scarlet dahlias later in the season.

There are a host of charming annuals for which, for various reasons, I can find little use. Shirley poppies, nemophilas, nigellas, viscarias, nemesias and eschscholtzias are among them. I think it is because some of them give a fragile look to any planting and others flower for so short a time and between seasons, so that you are obliged, if you want to use them, to have some other plant to precede and follow them. I imagine I am not alone in these views, as seedsmen's catalogues each year list a diminishing range of plants but more varieties of the longer lasting kinds.

Along with zinnias, snapdragons, china asters, sweet sultan, larkspur and cornflowers seem to be rather plants for the cutting beds than for ornamental use. I know that dwarf antirrhinums are considered invaluable bedding plants, but I seldom use them, thinking them a little dull and grey when seen in the mass.

Some tall-growing annuals will always find a place in the gaps of herbaceous borders and to old friends like larkspurs, red-leaved annual spinach and clumps of sweet peas we can add a comparative newcomer, the cleome, whose spikes of clear pink and white flowers come in very usefully to combine with the later flowering phlox in August, when most borders begin to look over-weighted with yellow and orange and bronze.

Annual flower borders as such have little appeal for me because I have never seen a successful one in any garden. Even where there is a mass of colour, the whole effect is apt to lack weight and have an air of artificiality. Such displays belong more properly to the transient atmosphere of an exhibition. I have often enough had to arrange such displays for various exhibitions and, if the preparatory work behind the scenes has been well done, I can enjoy the same pleasure as a child with a new paint box and a sheet of white paper. But even for an exhibition of pot-grown flowers I like to make a very robust framework and give the area I have to fill a strongly marked shape, often outlined with a nine-inch wooden or even a cement border painted white or in some clear strong colour which will set off my flowers. If these last are mainly in orange, yellows and scarlets and mauve I might choose cerulean blue for my edgings or else pale yellow or deep orange in cases when blue, white and mauve are the predominating flower colours.

Usually I ask for a specimen plant of every variety which I am going to use. Then, with some idea of the quantities available, I can start by thinking about possible colour combinations. As the plants arrive, setting them out becomes as it were a form of abstract painting, since with a firmly established skeleton I can lay in and interweave irregular shapes of pure colour. Each moment is an adventure as I try and link colour to colour and give to each its just weight. Sometimes an area several yards square will look dead and meaningless until I step back and see what I have left in reserve and decide just what colour to add and at which point and how much.

This has perhaps little to do with real gardening but such ephemeral occasions can refresh a designer. For once, he works with everything at hand for an immediate result, and the change of tempo is exhilarating and a challenge.

Annuals, whether half-hardy or " soft," form the main, indeed almost the only flower colour in French gardens. Perhaps this is because the French see flower-gardening in terms of colour used decoratively and not for the cultivation of plants for their individual interest and beauty. Rows of frames are a normal part of French garden equipment; and French gardeners are used to cultivating huge batches of such flowers as *Begonia gracilis*, *Salvia splendens*, ageratums and several varieties of tagetes. These they will later use to make strips or circles of scarlet and mauve and orange to the formal grass plots of a classical layout or to border the serpentine gravel paths of a *jardin anglais*. Cut flowers are provided for by a few rows of zinnias, dahlias and gladioli in the kitchen garden. Certain varieties of petunias and verbenas would seem to complete the colour repertory of a French summer garden. Extremely sensitive as they are to symmetry and balance, the French prefer red as a flower colour to set in the predominating green of a garden. Blue as a colour for flowers has no appeal and, oddly, the distinct violet-mauve of ageratum is always described in seed catalogues as blue. As it is hard to teach an old dog new tricks, I have learned much from fifteen years of designing and planting gardens in France and of limiting myself to the use of annuals which more or less comply with the conventions proper to so many French gardens and gardeners. I have, however, usually set my face firmly against scarlet salvias whose papery bracts, like those of bougainvillaea, have a tone and texture which totally destroys the effect of any other flower.

Swiss gardens are less rigidly classical. The Swiss love flowers for their own sake and employ a far wider range of plants than the French. A mountain climate gives flowers a special brilliance and anybody who is interested in the decorative use of annuals for window boxes and balconies will find much in Switzerland to interest him. Mountain villages have tiny flower gardens or none at all, but the chalets blaze with colour from every window, every doorstep and every balcony. To drive from Berne, say, through the Emmenthal is an object lesson in the use of strong colour. Scarlet geraniums, orange marigolds and nasturtiums jostle and bulge and hang from every ledge and there is a very popular petunia called " Balcon Bernois " whose brilliant violet-crimson seems just right with scarlet geraniums—a Bakst-like combination which, lovely as it is against the woodwork of an old chalet, might be disastrous in the green setting of a garden. So I have to temper my strictures against certain annuals for which I find no use, when I see a Devonshire cottage garden where fuchsias, hydrangeas and roses grow companionably out of a polychrome carpet of mixed annuals—nigellas, nemesias, nemophilas, Shirley poppies, with ferns, houseleeks and all sorts of chance seedlings flourishing in every joint of the old stone walls and steps and flagged paths.

CHAPTER VIII

Water in the garden

Running water still fascinates me as much as, when a child, I spent long summer days by a Lincolnshire beck which ran through the village where I was brought up, collecting small fish in jam pots or sailing home-made boats or building dams.

Perhaps it is in desert country that the full meaning of water becomes most clear, and it was in Persia that I most sharply realised its vitality and essence. It was a baking April day when I was stowed away in an old Dakota on the airstrip at Abadan to be flown over or rather between, the jagged mountain-ranges of the Baktiari country.

After a specially sickening lurch the engines' note changed. I realised that we were no longer climbing and so took courage and looked out. In the endless haze of the pinks and yellows and greys of sky, mountain and desert, I saw a thread of milky blue water edged with the yellow green of poplars. The thread soon became a river, the line of trees widened into groves and woods and soon this oasis flowered into the fantastic opal and turquoise domes of Isfahan.

Here, on the western edge of the high Asian plateau water is queen. Every house had a shady garden of plane trees, poplars, quinces and hazelnuts which shade great bushes of single yellow, orange, and scarlet sweetly-scented roses. A tiny stepped canal runs down the middle of the plane-shaded Charhabagh, perhaps the world's loveliest processional way, and almost every garden is set symmetrically round a central pool whose four subsidiary rills carry water into each quarter of the garden and then to the roots of every tree and plant.

Between the little shops which line the vaulted bazaars are great gates which lead into the courtyards of caravanserais, often nobly built with vaulted galleries of black and white marble. The camel caravans still come to them as in the time of Marco Polo. In each court is a pool or a formalised stream, shaded by a rose bush or a pine tree.

The courts of the incomparable mosques and madrassahs too are built around pools with wide raised rims on which I liked to sit and absorb the accumulated peace of centuries of prayer and meditation. The only noise is from the trickle of water and the piercing spring singing of the bulbuls.

Water rules too in Damascus, which they say is the oldest inhabited city in the world. You have only to put your ear to any wall in the old town to hear the sound of running water. Brought from the rivers which flow down from the Antilebanon by a series of little canals, the water is divided again and again into ever smaller rills to be carried into each house to make fountain jets in the enclosed patios, to run through the kitchen sinks and even to the Turkish baths which are a part of every fair-sized merchant's house. Beyond the town lies the oasis called the Guta where water divides tiny plots of ground planted with every kind of fruit tree. These fields are of incredible beauty in April with the blossoming trees and the scarlet of *Anemone fulgens* against the bice green of the young barley.

Water seems to course on the planet's surface as blood through the body. Flying high above the delta of the Indus, I have seen the silt and mud brought down from the mountains and deserts of Baluchistan, veined like a leaf or like a vast enlargement of an anatomical diagram. But perhaps the most extraordinary impression I have had of the nature of water was when I flew from Khartoum to Cairo, for the first time. The desert stretched endlessly, dun and rose and ochre, until you come upon the Nile, a ribbon of grey mauve where it flows a thousand miles from Aswan north to Alexandria, to bring life and vegetation to the narrow land on either bank. You can see Egypt from the air as a lotus plant, the Nile as the sap running up the green stem, the Fayoum as a leaf and the Delta as the spreading flower.

Everywhere water is connected—the smallest alpine torrent is one body with the Pacific ocean, the village brook I used to paddle in is a living branch of the Amazon and the Yangtze-Kiang, the "Wave" of Hokusai's woodcut has its link with the splashing fountains of the Villa d'Este.

Water is always in place where it is used to enhance the harmony of a garden or to relate it to its surroundings. I do not like the artificial forcing of a garden landscape and there is often a temptation to use water out of its context. I remember seeing a little-known garden, now demolished, made by Le Nôtre at the Château of Pomponne, near Lagny in the eastern suburbs of Paris. Nothing in this mild and undramatic landscape prepared me for the violence of this garden where an artificial hill at the end of the perspective was used for an arrangement of boiling cascades and innumerable fountains. Water was used in every conceivable way to make a very impressive but disquieting spectacle. One felt that it was detached from, and so ill accorded with its surroundings.

In a flat countryside I like to use water as a mirror laid on the ground to give depth and interest by reflecting trees and sky. I have learned much about the possibilities of still water in the flat lands of East Anglia, where I was born, and in Flanders where a tree or a church miles away towers against the full inverted hemisphere of the sky. In these landscapes the moats that surround old manors, châteaux and farms bring the sky down to the ground. A simple rectangle of water, in such a setting, makes a good garden boundary. I have in mind a garden in Belgian Flanders where a plain lawn runs the full length of the garden between hornbeam hedges. At the end of the lawn, where the flat pastures and the willow-lined polders begin, is a rectangular pool. Only about two feet deep, it reflects the pollarded willows and the changing skies, acts as a boundary and integrates the whole garden composition with its setting.

Another example of a simple use of water, although on a much larger scale is at the château de Mivoisin on the river Loing a hundred and fifty kilometres south of Paris. Here is a small and very lovely sixteenth-century hunting lodge which once belonged to Admiral Coligny, which stood when I first saw it, in a rather dry perspective of formal gardens. The river ran close to the house to feed an old mill, but nowhere could you sense its presence. As a new courtyard with garages, stables and gun-room had to be built, I was able to change the course of the river. Now it runs in a wide curve through the park, with a branch canalised back towards the house as a broad and formalised pool. A new forecourt, linking the main approach to the house with the new buildings, was centred on this canal. Broad cobbled steps lead down to the water, emphasising its importance in the design. At either side of the canal are clipped limes. Their symmetrically aligned trunks are reflected in the stone-bordered water, and large stone carved groups of animals mark the angle where canal and river meet.

This whole composition lies to one side of the main axis of the house, whose north front looked on to a long perspective of grass framed by hornbeam hedges and behind them a double line of chestnut trees. These ended in a rather nondescript meadow through which ran, invisibly, the river. The ground is almost flat and the far boundaries of the property left little space. But I found it possible to widen the river here into a small lake which you can now see from the house. Groups of willows and poplars accentuate the water and break the rather dull skyline. Further life is given by dozens of swans, descendants of two pairs imported from the swannery at Abbotsbury in Dorset.

Such a casual description can scarcely cover the technical problems involved. The largest and most difficult operation was to get official permission to budge a French river from its regular bed for a distance of several hundred yards. Then there were many problems of levels, complicated by the presence of a water-operated turbine in the old mill which had to provide electricity for the house and required a minimum fall. For this reason the formal canal had to be established some two feet lower than the level I had aimed at. Needless to say, no sooner were all these large and rather expensive operations finished than main electricity was brought in and the turbine became obsolete. Recently we have made a new canal which runs down the centre of the main lawn to the lake, and the flanking hornbeam hedges are now each terminated by a small pavilion. House and water are thus still more closely related.

A few miles up-stream stand the great locks built by Sully, and the Louis XIII red-brick château at Bleneau when I had a different problem to handle. This house is the remains of a fortified castle, whose moat and gatehouse still exist. I made a wide lawn inside and to one side of the house a small formal garden of box-edged beds intersected by narrow gravel paths and filled with the dark red floribunda rose " Alain." The main reception rooms, as in many houses of the period, are on the first floor; so I had to connect the great salon to the garden by a double flight of stone steps, leading down into this small formal garden. To add gaiety to a static composition, I designed the little rose garden round a series of yard-square stone-edged pools, each with its tiny water jet to sparkle in the sun with its splashing.

On the way back to Paris, downstream from Chatillon-Coligny we come to Montargis. The château here had once a famous garden of which not a trace now remains. It was one of the many gardens, now I think all gone, made by the Du Cerceau family. Many prints and drawings still exist of their designs. They worked in the latter half of the sixteenth century and their compositions though often covering a great deal of ground, must have been very gay and friendly, retaining an almost Gothic intimacy far removed from the overpowering, if majestic, scale of Le Nôtre. Their plans show great invention in that, using quite simple patterns, their gardens, however extensive and complex, remain very harmonious. In France, only the garden of Villandry, although it is a modern reconstruction, shows something of the spirit of these late sixteenth and early seventeenth-century gardens. Their disappearance has left many of the finest renaissance châteaux forlorn and sad, since the parks à l'*anglaise* which usually surround them are alien to the gaiety of their style.

The Loing is at its most beautiful in November when the tall poplars are golden yellow and the reeds and sedges glow rose and ochre and tan in the pearly sunlight. This is a countryside Sisley painted, and every brush-stroke on his canvases seems to breathe his integrity and his sensitivity.

Water in the garden, whether pond or stream, lakeside or artificial pool, offers the gardener temptations hard to resist. Before your inner eye float luscious pictures of groups of iris and primula, willows and water-lilies and a mirage of picturesque details culled from books and catalogues and exhibition gardens. Too much enthusiasm of this kind and you may quite likely damage your garden composition irretrievably. My own pleasure in finding water in a garden has so often led me into the wildest errors that I have learnt to stop and reflect very carefully before starting work. I have learnt to try always to contain my enthusiasm and see the site as a whole; water is only one factor, to be looked at just as impartially as the others. Then, I must consider whether I shall have to change the shape, the direction or the levels of the water. Its relationship to the other elements in the composition may be so dull that I may have to decide to give it greater prominence or else to reduce it to an incidental detail. Running water may involve a heightening of key, so that both design and planting should suggest light and gaiety and movement; still water demands a quieter and more static treatment. My thought is always "How little can I do?", rather than how much, to achieve the most telling result.

Since running water implies changing levels, I like at the lowest point in a garden to widen and slow up a fast-running stream, whether natural or artificial. Water which runs fast and uninterruptedly through and out of a garden may seem to drain away the garden's character. In such a case I like to widen it into a pool and give it time to pause. Carefully arranged planting, too, can give the impression of steadying and slowing down the passage of a stream. Planting on both sides of a length of running water, however charming in detail, will only accentuate the sense of movement. Plant thickly with high plants and bushes in a wide bed designed as a single unit and placed at an angle to the flow; or let the stream run through a group of flowering or other trees planted on both banks, so that there is an alternation of light and shadow, level lawns and heavy planting.

Slow-moving water, pools, canals and ponds, call for a different treatment. Trees, lawns and planting should be arranged to accentuate their static qualities. The shapes and colours reflected in the water will count for much even though you may not consciously absorb the impressions they make on you. You have to remember that every vertical accent, every rounded mass will be repeated by reflection.

Not far from Turin there is a magnificent mid-eighteenth-century villa in the high rococo manner. Being Piedmontese, its style is more classical than the rococo of the Veneto or Naples. A formal entrance court leads to the elaborate and splendid north façade, and the equally elaborate south front looks down a long lawn framed in trees. I was called in to see what could be done on the east side, where the main reception rooms on the first floor gave on to a bleak piece of level ground devoted to vegetables, a few rose-beds and beyond, perhaps a hundred and fifty yards from the house, a disconsolate spinney of Canadian poplars reaching to the boundary wall. Here was a site which demanded a composition in the grand manner and I set to work.

Fired by the splendid architecture of the house I made sketch after sketch, seeing a garden to be developed in clipped hedges and pleached trees, with fountains and statues combined into elaborate and baroque forms. My host who had retrieved the house from ruin and rearranged the interior with great discretion and taste considered my efforts with a sympathetic eye and finally said, "Yes, but these are not for Piedmont." So we set out over the rich levels of the Po valley, where the fields are squared off by countless irrigation channels bordered since the time of Virgil by pollarded willows and poplars, and I saw how the great houses are set in immense expanses of gravel with gardens merely sketched in by lines of trees or a hedge or a wall, and simplified beyond severity almost to dullness.

Now I saw that my garden should be classical rather than baroque in plan and that I could avoid any dullness and still remain in the spirit of this countryside by using spaces of water rather than of gravel. A further clue was offered me by the original name of the property, " Il Carpeneto "—the place of hornbeams.

So from the house I designed a canal running across the level ground and through the poplars to the limit of the property, with two short lateral arms about half-way down. As the total length was relatively short this canal is slightly narrowed at the far end and four Lombardy poplars planted at the four corners of the crossing with their reflections, add height and distance. The canal is set, without path or edging, in close-mown grass with a line of clipped lime trees on either side as far as the centre of the design. Beyond, through the wood where the canal is a little narrower, there are two lines of chestnuts on either side which will be allowed to grow freely and eventually form a green vault over the water.

From the house high hornbeam hedges frame the first part of the canal and the lateral arms. These hedges are doubled and between them lies a wide hidden gravel walk shaded by still another double line of clipped lime trees. In three years the hornbeams, planted quite small, have grown into thick hedges four foot through and twelve feet high. As all hedges should be, they are clipped rather wider at the base than at the top so as to give the impression of great solidity. This garden of grass, hedges, trees and water seems to me to have become timeless and inevitable. Is it because it is, in one sense, a synthesis and a symbol of the nature and essence of the place, its earth and air and water and of what I must call the humanities—the house, its period and its builders?

If hornbeams flourish here, so too do roses. In case this general scheme should seem too pompous I would add that, behind this green architecture, lies an acre of rose bushes arranged in a maze of simple symmetrical beds. Dark red climbing roses cover the lower story of the villa and its dependent buildings, and from May until Christmas great vases of long-stemmed roses in many colours make the inside of this splendid house a bower of colour and scent. Incidentally, the varieties in each rose-bed are marked by glazed faience labels copied from those of Battersea enamel which used to be hung round the necks of decanters.

Here is a garden where all is controlled. Its proportions on the flat as well as in volume were carefully studied and related. Hedges, water, gravel, grass and trees are all disciplined and limited so that each plays its predetermined part in a whole. Here there is a plan and an idea; growth and time have their inevitable place which is allowed for but always controlled.

To be able to play with water in the grand manner is an increasingly rare privilege, although in fact, in our day, bulldozers, scrapers, diggers and dumpers make the construction of lakes and canals easy, rapid and relatively cheap. The handling of water in a more modest and intimate way may well make more onerous demands on labour and time.

In the tamed and gentle landscapes of England the picturesque treatment of falling water with streams, cascades and rocks, has long been fashionable. Until the end of the eighteenth century mountain landscape was in general classified as " horrid " but about then the Lake District became a poets' haunt and then a tourists' craze and Switzerland a necessary pilgrimage for lovers of the picturesque. The gentle shores of Lake Leman suited Gibbon and Boswell, Voltaire and Madame de Staël; but a later generation preferred Zermatt and Interlaken and the falls of the Rhine at Schaffhausen which the tourist views through the blue, red and yellow glass lattices of the castle close by. Walking and gardening—those two British passions—combined to form a taste for growing alpine plants and by the end of the nineteenth century rock-gardens had become a lasting feature of British gardens. With such skilled gardeners and persuasive writers as Reginald Farrer, Gertrude Jekyll and E. A. Bowles to further the cause, amateurs began devising alpine gardens in likely and, indeed, unlikely settings. You could scarcely imagine a more unsuitable site for an alpine garden than the Thames valley; yet a vast rock garden was soon under construction near Henley, complete with a miniature reproduction of the Matterhorn. " Water-worn " limestone from the Lake District, an ugly stone out of its native setting—as it looks like a conglomeration of white concrete—has been brought south by the train-load to make thousands of exotic outcrops in flat green meadowland, and gardening journals still carry recipes for making artificial rocks from clinkers, brick-rubble and cement.

However, where there is natural stone as in the Oolite Belt, where soft limestone lies close to the surface in a diagonal band running from Lincoln through Rutland and Gloucestershire towards Bristol; in the west country and in Surrey and Sussex where sandstone outcrops occur, people have been able to make very charming rock gardens from local stone which naturally falls in well with its setting. Mark Fenwick's garden at Abbotswood near Stow-on-the-Wold in the Cotswold Hills, which I have mentioned elsewhere, contained an admirable example of a rock and stream garden which was nowhere too forced. It lay on a hillside backed to the north by a sheltering belt of trees. From a paddock beyond, a spring had been tapped and the water led through the wood to make three small rills. These found their way down the hillside in a series of little pools and shallow falls contrived with flattish slabs of the local yellowish limestone. The simple rockwork was unpretentious, and it looked as though the water had simply laid bare these gentle ledges apparently lying just below the surface. Patches of grass merged with the planting and the illusion of an alpine meadow was well sustained. Only when you examined the planting in detail would you discover that this was no ordinary hillside, set out as it was with gembright dwarf plants from the world's mountain ranges. An added delight in such a garden as this is the incidental music from the different notes of water as it fell from pool to pool, as characteristic in such a place as the noise of cicadas in Provence. To accentuate these small sounds deliberately might defeat the most conscientious builder of rock gardens, but you can count in such a garden on a background of water-song which will never be out of tune.

One of the secrets of using running water successfully and naturally in a garden is to avoid forcing it into cascades or fountains which would be at variance with the surrounding landscape. A fountain jet is apt to look out of place at a high point in a garden unless there is a hill somewhere to suggest, at least, that your jet is expressing the force of water coming from still higher ground. For the same reason a fountain or a small pond does not usually look right sheer against a background of sea or lake. In either case it will appear gratuitous or even pretentious. Water features are usually better in a hollow or at a low point in the garden. When I want water on a terraced site I try to set it so that there is enough immediate background to hold my pool or fountain in place; otherwise it will look uncomfortable and as though about to slip over the farther edge. It is impossible to give an exact rule of proportion for this particular problem, but the area of level ground beyond a pool should appear roughly twice as wide as the apparent width of water. If, as may happen, you want a pool so large in proportion to its site that this rough rule cannot be applied, then the farther side must be so planted that the vertical face of this planting will give you the necessary frame.

In gardens where there are masses of flower colour ornamental water needs very discreet handling. It will be enough if it conveys the impression of space and coolness. It should be still water, in order to reflect the colours, the greens of trees and hedges, and the procession of clouds across the sky. The play of fountains in a flower garden may offer an unnecessary and too rich overtone, as though a wedding cake were waltzing.

In a more formal garden water should tell its own tale and a pool be left unplanted. When there are many flowers and the hardness of a surface of water needs breaking, water lilies will probably be sufficient. In places when you are aiming at flatness, upright-growing water plants may give exactly the opposite effect.

Fountains or pools with carved stone margins and sculpture are so full of interest in themselves and so rich in the play of light and shadow that they need a simpler frame of grass and hedges and trees and are better without the further elaboration of flowers. The play of light on spouting and falling water and the ripple of water over the hollows and bosses of carved stone or against the flanks of a bronze statue are focus enough for any garden. The beauty and excitement of Italian renaissance gardens would be infinitely less if flowers played an important part in their composition.

If I were using water in a garden because I wanted water-side conditions, and moist soil for growing plants more than for any other reason, I would want to handle my watercourses, pond or stream very discreetly. Water would play a role secondary to my planting. Its scale—trickle or wide stream—would be designed in relation to the scale of my planting, which would itself call attention to the presence of water. Calthas, the taller flag iris, *Senecio clivorum*, various rushes, the heavy foliage of hostas and *Primula florindae* as well as the great umbrellas of *Gunnera manicata* or the lovely red leaves of the cut-leaved rhubarb *Rheum laciniatum alexandrina*—all these will indicate the presence of water lying brown and quiet at their roots. In such a setting the excitement of tumbling water would be unsuitable and distracting. Conversely, had I a rock and stream garden of my own I would concentrate interest on the relation between stone and water, on the contrast between stability and movement, between the hardness of the stone and the falling water. All my planting would be designed to stress and support this idea and I would therefore make it extremely simple. Ideally, I would restrict myself to a basic planting of one or at most two subjects for at least nine-tenths of my planted area. I would perhaps stiffen this with the flat plumes of *Juniperus chinensis pfitzeriana* or low mounds of kurume azaleas in two colours only, their flat green mass relieved by Japanese maples; or in limy soil I would use a carpet of prostrate cotoneasters or small berberis.

I have never cared for gardens where flowers, shrubs, roses, lawns, hedges, pools and streams add up to an indigestible riot of form and colour. In any garden or part of one where there is water, it may either dominate or serve as a discreet and minor feature noticeable only as a flicker of light or sound. Although water in a town garden, at least in the north, is apt to look gloomy through many months of the year, there is a garden in Paris which offers one of the best examples of its use as a dominant theme. Here there is a formal stone-kerbed pool which entirely fills the space behind a splendid house in the late seventeenth-century French manner. This exclusive use of water makes, as it were, a sumptuous yet calm back-drop for the formal entertaining for which this particular house was designed.

In general I like gardens where the presence of water is at least hinted at, even if only by the old-fashioned butt collecting the rainwater from the cottage roof, a simple wall-fountain or a stone bowl for the birds to drink from, filled, if you like, with round pebbles so that they can find a footing. Any complicated arrangement of jets is usually disastrous in a garden fountain unless it is on a large scale and in a simple setting of grass and trees or hedges. In a small pool a single vertical jet will usually be the most effective.

Playing fountains always give an air of fête and are at their loveliest and most refreshing in streets and squares. One has only to think of Rome to realise how the splash of blue-white water on sculptured stone makes the whole city sparkle. I remember Carl Milles's former home in Stockholm where a few trees, the intricate patterns of water jets, and the bronze figures of the famous merman fountain, set on a terrace high above the sound, made a most satisfactory garden in which I cannot recall a single flower or blade of grass.

Water in the garden

The charm of moving water against stone or bronze comes partly from the fluidity of the one as against the permanence of the other. I remember how difficult I found it to relate pools and fountains to their setting of painted canvas and plywood when making the Festival Gardens in Battersea Park: everything seemed to have the consistency of a meringue and I had to work out the necessary contrasts in colour rather than weight or mass or texture.

I have had quite a lot to do with streams in gardens, particularly in France since the war. People have been increasingly moving into small houses and there is scarcely an old mill house within a hundred miles of Paris which has not been converted into a week-end home.

Most of these mills had overshot wheels; so there is usually the leat and mill pond at a high level and a stream or little river below. The Duke of Windsor's mill at Gif is a typical example, although we treated it in a flowery and English manner unusual in French gardens. The leat, a long, straight and slow stream, runs along the crest of a sloping meadow towards the back of the house. The mill pond has been filled in, but some of the water still runs in its old channel under the house. The main stream drops several feet to run down round the house and rejoin the leat at the bottom of the valley. We did little to the leat except to dam it with a stone wall some way up the meadow, so that it enters the garden as a low curtain of falling water. Its banks are planted simply with largish groups of gunnera and the lovely cut-leaved rhubarb and long drifts of *Iris ochroleuca* and pale yellow hemerocallis, while nearer the house are bright scarlet patches of *Lobelia cardinalis*. Where the spill-water turns to drop over a stepped cascade into a hazel-shaded pool, a series of low, dry retaining walls hold up the steep and rather crumbling banks. These walls are planted with London Pride and *Campanula portenschlagiana* while Creeping Jenny, *Lysinachia nummularia*, trails its butter-yellow threepenny-bit flowers in the water. All the banks and flat places made by the walls are covered with low green patches of asarum and pachysandra, hypericum, bergenias and dwarf periwinkle with a few single kerrias, white and deep pink kurume azaleas and forsythias for height and spring colour. Late daffodils pierce the green ground-cover, soon followed by *Scilla nonscripta* in white, pale blue and pink. Then come the pale pink foxgloves called " Tendresse " and finally the regale lilies open their cream-pink trumpets. Thus the dark greens of the background are lighted by a succession of pale clear colour from April till July.

That part of the stream which fed the mill wheel emerges again from under the house and flows through what was the kitchen garden. Here it was a straight and muddy ditch, charmless and smelly. When we transformed the kitchen garden into a thicket of herbaceous plants, broken only by a central patch of lawn, we widened this ditch, building a wall on each side to replace the muddy banks. Then we dammed the water to make three different levels with three shallow falls. As it runs here through a flower garden, we planted its banks in a rather more sophisticated fashion with dicentra and Siberian iris and clumps of different varieties of yellow trollius. Old bush cydonias and wistarias give height and character, and for later summer there are astilbes, crimson lythrums, phlox and the orange yellow *Senecio clivorum*.

The main stream winds down the valley towards the house, twisting round an occasional great sandstone boulder, its only planting the natural growth of herb-Robert, yellow flag iris and meadow-sweet. Where the streamlet from the cascade joins it and the garden proper begins, it flows under two little bridges, then along under the wall of the enclosed flower garden to pass out of the property through a water-gate in the shade of a group of weeping willows. In this part of the garden, where the stream runs close between the rock garden and the walled flower garden, there also seemed little need for planting. Its steep banks, the huge rocks which occasionally interrupt its flow and the shadow of the two little bridges give interest enough. So we contented ourselves with clearing out the nettles and brambles and establishing a few colonies of the Himalayan *Primula florindae* whose great cowslip-yellow umbels blend happily with the native growths.

Any garden with a wide view of the sea is another kind of water garden, although it is not often seen and considered as such, as problems of wind and shelter and planting tend to take precedence over this inescapable fact—the presence of the sea. Where the sea is land-locked or where there is only a glimpse of it between the folds of a hill, there is no special problem. But, for the composition of a garden, a broad marine horizon makes a horizontal bar as unchanging and implacable as a factory roof and as difficult to handle. This is particularly evident where the site is set high and consequently the horizon line lies high also. At sea level, breaking waves and the incidents of the foreshore—rock and sand, or, as so often in the Mediterranean, pine trees—make it relatively easy to absorb the seascape into the garden composition. A seaside garden on high ground is the most difficult to manage, because there is often nothing in the middle distance to give perspective.

Once again you have to consider the whole problem of the site. Perhaps you will want to reduce the breadth of the view by heavy planting or hedges, and so render any openings you leave more precious. Or else you may decide to treat sea and sky as patches of changing, opalescent colour caught in a tracery of tree trunks and branches; or again, as light contrasted with the massing of heavy foliage and its shadows. Or perhaps, more austerely, you may wish to accentuate the line of the horizon and repeat it with horizontal terraces, low hedges and parallel paths. In the face of so much space and light you must find solutions which are bold, definite and without hesitancy. Any confusion of ideas or treatment in such a place will be doubly evident. Less formally, you can create your own foreground with low rolling masses of planting to recapture in vegetation the distant waves. In this case I would always work with a palette of greens, blues and greys with some white and avoid, at all costs, pink, red, scarlet and orange, because they will only destroy, by contrast in colour, the links and harmonies you are trying to establish.

You will find in a maritime climate many plants suitable for these informal plantings. Atriplex, sea buckthorn, lavender and rosemary, grey santolina, teucrium and caryopteris—there is a long list of grey-leaved shrubs. Beside the Mediterranean the silky grey leaves of echium with its sea-blue flower spikes and the white foam of anthemis will match the sea and sky, and you can replace them perhaps by sea hollies and gypsophila on a colder shore.

A problem to me for years was a small Mediterranean villa garden at Cap d'Ail, which falls precipitously from the house to the sea sixty feet below. I had to make something of a few stunted pines, very steep steps, and narrow ledges of soil amongst sharp rocks. Finally I planted the blue fleshy-fingered kleinia to hang down all the exposed faces of rock, and, remembering the high-flung white spray of stormy days, filled the whole garden simply with white anthemis. Covered for months on end with white marguerite flowers, this is a successful planting, sufficiently in scale with the sea and simple enough to give full value to the twisted pines which shade it.

It is only in the last thirty years that swimming pools have become a part of the garden scene. Before that they were vast utilitarian affairs in concrete or white tiles, built for communal use by schools or municipal authorities. After the First World War it gradually became the fashion to have a private swimming pool. The first garden pools, in Europe at any rate, were rather clumsy and apt to mar rather than enhance the garden. They were almost always very large and rectangular, surrounded by yards of paving with complicated scum troughs which kept the water level eighteen inches below the margin. Heavy ladders and cumbersome diving boards further deprived them of any charm. And in those days, before the employment of filters, you had to choose between icy cold but clean water and something warmer but apt to be clouded with algae.

Swimming pools of this period were often given an exotic and pointless setting and were labelled "Hollywood." Gold and green and blue mosaic, marble or plaster columns, white wooden "pergolas" and masks spitting water seemed the inevitable decoration. But if many swimming pools were made hideously functional others began to be considered as part of a planned layout. At Trent Park just north of London, Sir Philip Sassoon built a long blue-lined pool between wide borders of blue and white flowers with a pleasant orangery in apricot-coloured brick at the end. At Lympne he made a more adventurous experiment, surrounding a square pool with stone balustrades and cypress hedges, and placing the water-line so high that it was almost on a level with the horizon.

I think that a swimming pool is most satisfactory when treated as part of the general composition but isolated as a separate compartment. Where it is close to the house it is best concealed, or partly concealed, by wall or hedge. A deserted swimming pool, seen from the house in winter, is far from enticing; and except in an almost tropical climate, a pool is more attractive and usable when it enjoys some privacy and protection from the wind.

Except for the most informal of holiday houses a pool in close connection with the house has certain disadvantages, and it is advisable to have separate facilities for changing and dressing. Your swimming pool will always be a magnet for the neighbours and their children, so that access and a dressing-room independent of the house are essential if entertaining people is to be a pleasure rather than a nuisance.

Small pools can give at least as much pleasure as large ones if they are carefully thought out. The pool must be deep enough in one place for diving from a springboard but elsewhere shallow enough to give foothold; a pool too deep to stand in comfortably is forbidding and unattractive. When there are small children a separate paddling pool will save increasing the size of your pool by a large " shallow end." For most people, the main object in having a pool is, after all, to be able to take a dip and lie around in the sun. Overhanging trees, heavy planting and grass too near the edge are to be avoided, nor do I like pools set in too large areas of arid paving.

The level of the water in relation to the surround is important. Very often a scum trough runs right round a pool, a foot or so below the paved edge, and the surface of the water is that amount lower than the surround. This is uninviting for the bather and plain ugly to look at. The water level, when the pool is not in use, should be kept as high as possible. One can sometimes even contrive to have a paved sitting place below the water level, a device which enhances one's sense of contact with the water. I first noticed this in a sixteenth-century room in the old palace at Cintra where a rectangular pool, intended for swans, lies immediately outside the windows and is higher than the floor level inside. The same effect is even more marked at Bacalhâo, some miles south of Lisbon. Here there is a sixteenth-century white-washed country house or *quinta*, whose monumental outside staircase and onion-shaped cupolas are covered with peacock-blue tiles. In the grounds there is a rectangular tank for irrigation, perhaps a hundred by fifty yards square, enclosed at one end by an arcaded loggia with three high-roofed pavilions. The floor of this arcade is about two and a half feet below the water level, so that from inside the light shimmers off the water and the reflected trees and hills are the more sharply defined because of the unusually low angle of vision.

Many people prefer sea water to fresh, a taste easily catered for at the edge of the sea where a constant stream can be pumped through the pool. But on one occasion I was asked to make a salt water pool in the South of France three miles from the sea and some six hundred feet above it. As the old feudal salt tax still exists we had to get special permission to fill tanker-trucks from the sea—but only in Nice harbour and under the eye of the custom officials—and then cart it up the mountainside. Filter plants had to be specially made to take the sea water. Emptying

*A Paris garden seen from above. A small area heavily shaded
by trees and high surrounding buildings precluded grass.
Surrounded by a box-edged green planting planned for form
and texture rather than for colour, this oval gravelled space
serves as an additional out-of-door reception room*

The large pool in this garden to the West of Paris was all that remained of a formal layout of about 1700. This new composition is expressed in simplified terms. Lime trees, hornbeam hedges and grass—all relatively easy to maintain—replace the elaborately designed box parterres which must once have existed here

Looking back across the pool to the miniature Regency château whose charming roof belies the formality of its period. The retaining wall and circular stairway replace a grass bank. The nineteenth century romantic tree planting on the right has its younger counterpart to the left and both are kept in place by the formal framework of hornbeam hedges

The elegant Faubourg St. Germain in Paris is a quarter unfavourable to plants and flowers. A damp cold soil and heavy shade necessitate the use of grass, water, gravel and the toughest of evergreens. This simple garden relies on the play of light and shade and a single fountain jet to give sparkle to a severely classical design

the pool was equally complicated. Letting the water out through the ordinary drains would risk lawsuits with all the owners of the carnation fields and olive groves which lay between the property and the sea. In the end it has proved simpler to fill the pool each year with fresh water and then dump four tons of sea-salt into it. When it has to be emptied the water is drained into tanker-trucks and taken back to the sea.

Nowadays it is possible to build a pool in any shape which suits its setting or conforms to your design. Though a rectangular pool will fit in with a formal frame there are many sites to which it is difficult to adapt so stiff a shape. I do not much care for circular pools in any context: they seem always so final, so monotonous and so lacking in direction. An oval, particularly what is called a " gardener's oval," is a most adaptable and successful garden form which has a mysterious charm and always looks easy. Its shape differs from wherever you look at it: from one angle it will appear more or less elliptical, from another almost circular. It can be treated austerely or with great sumptuousness, formally and symmetrically or in a setting of " free " curves or " abstract " forms. It can appear as a " moving " form or it can be made to look static.

Straight edges of water require careful handling; they can have the severity, the immutability and the monotony of the sea where it meets the horizon. Long straight lines of water used in a garden emphasise the forms and colours reflected in it. With the artificial nature and colour of a swimming pool, reflections may look distorted and false, so that angles and lines require careful consideration.

Free-shaped pools, which seem usually to work out in a bean or kidney shape, have recently become popular. These loose forms need careful treatment, especially in the case of a small pool, in order to achieve a fair length for those who like to swim. Very often a pool which starts as a rectangle at the deep end, where it will be anchored to the site by a stretch of paving, can end in a curve at the shallow end. This can be a happy compromise: rectangular at the business end where the swimmers are apt to group themselves, while the far end has a freer line designed to link the pool to its surroundings.

Hitherto filter installations, whether for fresh or salt water, have been cumbersome and extremely expensive to instal. Happily the latest filter plants are scarcely more bulky than a couple of oxygen cylinders, and scum channels can be replaced by a " skimmer " little larger than a dish, while a very small electric pump takes care of the circulation.

Lining a pool is another problem. Marble, which can be cut in quite large sizes, is admirable for elaborate and regularly shaped pools; but it is, I think, far too sophisticated a material for a pool in a normal garden setting. Coloured tiles, from three to five inches square, are also suitable so long as they have a slightly matt surface. Glazed tiles look far too shiny and do not stand up to winter frosts. Small squares of glass mosaic are as popular as they are expensive, but their colour is usually ugly and their tiny scale is out of place in the open air. All these tile or marble finishes are expensive, but once installed need no replacement. Paint is an alternative, but a pool may need repainting every second or third year. Once again the choice of colour presents difficulties. I like white, as the general colour tone will then be a quiet grey-green. Green is a dangerous colour if there are trees or grass anywhere near. A greenish or turquoise blue is better than cobalt or ultramarine, which will again look false in most outdoor surroundings. I have nothing against black or navy blue or a dark bottle green in suitable circumstances; and had I to make a heated open-air pool in the snow I would be tempted to imitate the scarlet of the open-air pool at Sestrières.

Undoubtedly pools in the near future will be either made of or lined with plastic. Prefabricated plastic pools, which are both cheap and easy to assemble, are already available, but they are inclined to be ugly in colour, and shape. A pool set in a wide expanse of bricks paving has just been built near Turin on a hill looking across to the snow-covered chain of the Alps. Both the surrounding paving and the pool are heated and the latter has been lined with specially moulded panels of blue plastic. By some happy accident the colouring process went a little wrong—at least by the manufacturers' standards. The result is lovely—the colour is in the broken and streaked tones of lapis lazuli.

The surroundings of a pool need careful thought. It has too long been the custom to put the average swimming pool in a waste of paving or cement. This usually destroys the proportions of the pool itself and gives a monolithic effect altogether too large and heavy, and disastrous in anything intended as a garden frame. Nevertheless, any form of paving round a pool should be close-set, smooth enough to be agreeable for bare feet, yet not so smooth as to be slippery. Sawn stone, brick, terracotta tiling where there is no risk of frost, and even some forms of pre-cast cement blocks, will all serve and you can elaborate the patterns of paving to suit the theme and setting of your pool. Two materials used together, brick and stone for instance, are apt to look too complicated for a swimming pool which, though it can have a decorative use in a garden, should not be dressed up as an ornamental feature to the extent of suppressing its function. In using brick paving it is sometimes difficult to know how to deal with the edge of the pool. A brick on edge will be hard on the feet and could easily crumble away in frost. At the Leopolda in the South of France I was able to obtain specially hard-baked bricks with rounded corners for the edge of the oval pool, whose colours matched exactly the warm orange of the other paving. In another garden, near Grasse, where I had to deal with the same problem, I brought the tiled lining of the pool up and over the edge and set a narrow band of these tiles right round the border of the curving pool flush with the paving of pre-cast concrete blocks. With stone paving there is no problem because the edging stone can be cut just as one wishes.

Usually there is no need for a wide strip of paving along the sides of the pool. Three feet should be quite enough for mattresses and garden furniture. In general, paving should slope very slightly downwards and outwards from the edge of a pool and there should be some arrangement for drainage at the outer edge. But this slope must be imperceptible or the pool will look illogically high. If the filter-plant is adequate it will be able to deal with any rainwater or splashings which may run back into the pool from paving which is level or even slightly sloping towards the water.

Where there is a sharp enough change of level close by to make access easy, it is sometimes convenient and practical to put the filter plant at a low level by simply extending the excavation made for the pool and placing the plant in a cellar at one end. Usually the easiest solution is to fit a small machine room into the bath-house building, but the newest filter-plants are small enough to fit into a box little larger than a dog kennel which you can easily conceal behind a hedge or a low wall. I always prefer movable spring-boards and ladders that can be lifted out of their sockets and taken away in the winter.

A swimming pool at the edge of the Mediterranean would appear redundant; but the roads are so crowded in summer and a quiet place for a sea bathe is so hard to find that most houses of any consequence have their own pools. A few years ago I was asked to make a pool on a hillside at Le Cannet just behind Cannes. The small and simple house looked over a steep slope where a semi-circle of magnificent old pine trees, their trunks leaning in every direction, fell away on either side to frame Le Souquet, the old citadel of Cannes, on its rock above the harbour two miles away. The owner wanted a large swimming pool, with its own big living-room, changing-rooms and a kitchenette, all sited well below the house. My first object was to accentuate the swing of the pine trees, to make the pool as little visible as possible from the house, and to hide its accompanying pavilion altogether. In front of the house a wide terrace shaded by olive trees and enlivened by pots of many-coloured geraniums is all there is of sophisticated garden. We did not want to break up the site with a complicated series of terraces and staircases, so we decided to plant the slope below the terrace entirely with iris and lavender, white santolina and grey-leaved senecios, cinerarias and teucriums. As the planting melts away into the shade of the pine trees, I made its dominant greys merge into the green foliage of myrtle

and agapanthus, *Spartium junceum* and white and pink oleanders.

The pavilion, with its three arched openings which lead into
a big vaulted living-room, is built into the slope so that it is all
underground except for the façade. It is hidden from the house
by the *maquis* planting which continues over its roof. The
paved terrace in front of this shaded loggia is in turn shaded by a
light metal pergola or *tonelle*, which is covered in summer with
hanging garlands of morning glory. In a few weeks this plant
covers the metal framework and hangs down in garlands and
fringes of ultramarine and sky-blue bells. This terrace is sunk
three steps below both the normal ground level and the water
level of the very large swimming pool. The shape of the pool is
interesting. The side next to the terrace is straight, cutting
across the general oval shape of the pool, the length of the oval
lying parallel to the building. From the house you only see the
far side of the pool whose curves repeat in reverse the sweep of
the trees against the sky. The curve of water is edged with a
band of stone; beyond, since grass was impracticable, we made a
lawn of the creeping verbena, *Verbena teneva*, which in May and
June becomes a sapphire carpet. A wide and stepped path
which runs down-hill from the house to the pool swings
away to one side of the house, describing a semi-circular course to
turn inwards towards the pool in a curve which repeats and
reinforces the dominant motif of the site.

In another pool in the South of France, this time in the
foothills near Grasse, I had a rather special problem to solve. The
site lay to the north of the house whose two wings sheltered a
pillared and vaulted loggia. Originally, the ground had sloped
gently upwards from the house into a small wood of evergreen
oaks and pine trees through which you caught a glimpse of the
high ridge of mountains beyond Grasse to the north-east. But an
enormous hole had been made in the rocky ground. It was a
rectangle some hundred feet long by thirty wide, five feet deep
next to the house, and perhaps twelve at the far end which we
rounded. Worse still, all the excavated stony soil had been

evenly banked round this gaping hole, leaving steep, barren and unpromising slopes. The original intention had been to make a vast swimming pool but it had hung fire for some years since it promised to be a dull and tremendously expensive operation.

A pool made to fill the excavation entirely would have come right up to the loggia which, being on the shady side of the house, was much used. It was the owner, Jean Prouvost, who first suggested making a quite small swimming pool at the far end of the excavation so as to leave the loggia free from the splashings, wet bathing dresses and all the impedimenta of swimming. When I started to make sketches it seemed logical to raise the level of the bathing pool by a few steps, so that it should not look too deeply sunk and so that we could have the necessary head-room to incorporate a filter plant under the paving at one end of the pool. This pool and its surround took up about one third of the total length. At first we planned a flower garden to fill the intervening space between pool and house, until we hit on the idea of a long and shallow canal. One of the reasons which led us to this decision was maintenance. The kind of formal flower garden we envisaged would demand a good deal of attention if it were to be perfect. A shallow canal planted with water lilies would pretty well look after itself. So I drew out new plans. To-day, a low stone retaining wall which I have planted entirely with the sky-blue *Plumbago capensis* frames the whole composition. Below the wall a paved path leads to the slightly higher level of the bathing pool. The whole of the centre is taken up by the canal and a yard-wide bed on either side filled with plants whose foliage harmonises with the water-plants in the canal itself. These include pink and yellow water lilies, *Thalia dealbata* with its lance-like leaves and spiky mauve flowerheads, cyperus and—the glory of any pool—the pink lotus *Nelumbium nelumbo*. I know of no plant that gives me more pleasure than the lotus, with its circular glaucous green leaves so often with a dewdrop caught where stem and leaf meet, with the architectural splendour of its pointed soft pink petals and with the strange beauty of the seed pods, like cones with flattened tops pierced with about eighteen holes, each enclosing a hard round seed. At first, while the whole seed head is still green and moist, each seed is held firmly in a little socket which becomes looser as the head dries and the seeds eventually fall out. The lotus is a constantly recurring motif in Egyptian wall-paintings and sculptural reliefs as it is in Chinese painting. I do not know how hardy it is in the British Isles. Continental practice is to empty the pools in which it is grown and to cover the roots with a thick layer of straw or bracken to protect them through the winter. At Grasse, where several degrees of frost are not uncommon in winter, we do nothing and all the lotus came through the hard winter of '55-'56 quite undamaged.

Although the main lines of the water garden are very simple, even severe, the planting both in the water and the two beds either side, is as sumptuous as I could contrive.

Agapanthus, cannas, clivias, bergenias, nandina and hostas now grow thickly along the sides of the little canal and seem to merge with the foliage of the water plants. At the far end a low retaining wall marks the higher level of the swimming pool, and on its face three small marble masks spout three jets of water to feed the lower pool and give the faint murmur of running water so agreeable in a hot climate. On top of this wall four rococo terracotta vases recall the rather grand eighteenth-century decoration of the house. The swimming pool itself is lined with blue tiles and set in a fairly wide area paved with pre-cast concrete slabs, with the pebbled aggregate exposed. A feature of this pool is a wide ledge just below the water level which runs the length of each side so that bathers can sit in a few inches of water. Portholes set with lights in the end of the pool nearest the house make it glow at night with a gently suffused light.

So that the swimming pool should not appear too detached in mood from what is essentially a garden composition and so as to prolong the perspective, I flanked the pool with four large *Magnolia grandiflora* set symmetrically in the paving on either side. When all this was done only the stony banks remained to be treated. The long bank beyond the pool runs up to a reservoir which is invisible from below. Again so as to accentuate the effect of length, I worked out a narrow central water-staircase down which flows a thread of tumbling white water from the reservoir, to fall between thickly planted bushes of dark green pittosporum which I clipped into low green mounds. A single jet in the reservoir above, and pointed cypresses which flank the cascade, accentuate the perspective still further and give an excuse for a little discreet indirect lighting at night.

All this adds up to a rich and complicated scene which needed a quiet frame to keep it in place. So I planted all the surrounding slopes thickly with evergreen oaks, cypresses and pines, both umbrella pines, *Pinus pinea* and Aleppo pines, *Pinus halepensis*. These trees will eventually thicken and make a dark green wood to frame the sparkling liquid heart of the garden. Meanwhile, as an underplanting to cover the white limy soil, we have planted stretches of rosemary, hypericum, the green-leaved *Santolina viridis*, as well as bay-laurel, *Laurus nobilis*, *Pittosporum tobira* and *Viburnum tinus*.

This garden for the holiday house of a great industrialist, in the somewhat overcharged setting of the South of France, might look altogether too luscious in a different context. In a less elaborate garden planted walls, neatly clipped hedges and lawns with an odd tree valuable for its shadows should provide an adequate setting for a swimming pool. Awnings, cushions and mattresses will give colour more apposite than that of flowers, while the new small pools prefabricated in brightly coloured plastic need an even more reticent setting.

Part Two

CHAPTER IX

Town gardens and others

Church or mosque, town hall, a fountain playing in the sunlit square and at most a ten-minute walk in any direction through narrow streets, to bring you through the cool shadow of a gate immediately into a countryside or orchards and gardens and little fields—this is my ideal city. The old town of Damascus or Aix-en-Provence, or townships like Wareham in Dorsetshire, St. Paul-de-Vence and Moret-sur-Loing seem to me to demonstrate a perfect urbanity. But my work has caused me to live mostly in London or Paris whose inordinate sprawling over the last two hundred years has exercised the minds of planners and in the main defeated them from Sir Christopher Wren to Le Corbusier.

Private town gardens in our day are a luxury whether for the Londoner who tries to create an air of country or for the Parisian forming flowers and trees into the decorative elements of an outdoor salon. Lacking any social or civic sense of a Utopian kind, I have considered plans for garden cities, *villes radieuses*, satellite towns and such, as development schemes where the distinct meanings of city and country are already confused. This is a field that can be frustrating to the point of heart-break and I must admit I have preferred to limit myself to such garden tasks as I could see taking physical shape. Indeed my only major contribution to townscape was the intentional frivolity of the Festival Gardens in London's Battersea Park.

My first concern in attacking a town garden is to be quite clear as to the result I am after. Do I want to recreate a country scene within the limits imposed by the site or is it my aim to create an outdoor room open to the sky? Or it may be neither of these and I may find it necessary to make a back-drop, scenery to be seen and judged only through the window, an artificial landscape made to underline and enhance the mood and decoration of an interior. More entertaining as problems in design are those town gardens where trees and buildings and the skyline beyond the limit of the garden are " borrowed "—brought into the garden which is then designed entirely as a foreground.

First of all, in the town as in the country, a wise garden-designer will study his site in silence and consider carefully his clients, their taste, their wishes, their way of life, their likes and dislikes, and absorb all of these as factors at least as important as the ground that lies in front of him. But it is with the ground that he will then start. In London the disadvantages of a clayey and starved soil full of brickbats will be offset by a tree or two in or within sight of the garden, as well as relatively low surrounding buildings and some freedom from pests and plant diseases. In Paris the soil is usually cold, stony and limy and the buildings are much higher with a consequent loss of light.

London has grown slowly into a great city from the gradual overlapping and mingling of a whole periphery of villages once separated by meadows and woods. In spite of the sophistication of its parks and squares, landscaped in the eighteenth-century manner, the city still wears a faintly bucolic air, one which the Londoner, a transplanted countryman like Englishmen anywhere in the world, cherishes and fosters. The spirit of the village green remains, the Nelson column is still a sort of monumental maypole and Greenwich and Hampton Court suggest picnics, fish suppers and boating parties, rather than the magnificence of palace architecture. I remember how one year the gardens of Lambeth Palace were a forest of ice-cream-coloured hollyhocks; and there is that noted but secluded garden, hard by South Kensington Station, which is as wide and flowered as some canon's close in the precincts of a country cathedral.

The typical London " village " of St. John's Wood, an early nineteenth-century suburb, where doubtful ladies were once set up in style in stuccoed and painted villas, but now become more respectable in neo-Georgian red brick, is still bowered in the ancient pear trees which must have given it its name. In the City, amongst ruins of the blitz, buddleia, willow herb and seedling trees soon sheathed the calcined brick and hung over fortuitous ponds where wild duck have nested. Tradition has preserved Charles the Second's aviary a stone's throw from Downing Street.

The London garden owner and designer will scarcely be able to ignore the impact of this mood and he can treat his garden, however small, as an isolated piece of a jigsaw puzzle which, joined together, makes an essentially country scene.

Forty years ago the Londoner's back garden was far less interesting than it is nowadays. Charming relics of Victorian days, little carts laden with boxes of seedlings, snapdragons and petunias, with geraniums often packed around a waving panache of kentias, went about the quiet sunny streets in May so that householders might buy a few flowers for their cat-haunted patches. I think it was the appointment of Thomas Hay—a famous Scottish gardener with an equally renowned moustache and a great deal of enthusiasm—as Superintendent of the Royal Parks, which started a tremendous revival of interest in London gardens. Mr. Hay was soon busy replacing soot-laden shrubberies in Hyde Park and St. James's with massed plantings of herbaceous and half-hardy subjects. An ardent experimenter with recently introduced plants, he delighted the public with drifts of *Meconopsis betonicifolia*, the blue poppy which ever since his day has been as ardently worked for and, in town at least, as difficult to succeed with as the philosopher's stone. He first showed in London parks *Lilium regale*, incarvilleas and a host of other exotic plants. Regent's Park caught the fever and added a long avenue of Japanese cherries, wide herbaceous borders and Queen Mary's Rose Garden. Seeing what could be done, Londoners took heart and practised public and private gardening with varying results, some of them singularly unhappy. Building speculators made helter-skelter rock gardens in Westmorland stone at the feet of poorly built blocks of flats, and metropolitan boroughs have made unsuitable experiments with drywalls, crazy paving and painted gnomes and mushrooms at busy traffic intersections and in eighteenth-century squares. Against the increasing tide of shoddiness to which such efforts contributed, banks, clubs, government offices and the premises of big business, always impeccably maintained and often painted in the clear pale colours which give a special charm to the London scene, blossomed with brilliantly planted window boxes. Latterly, the war-time disappearance of the miles of wrought and cast-iron railings has been the excuse for a further and ill-advised gardening push and the stunted and blackened yew and holly hedges and pre-doomed attempts at planting rhododendron species as green barriers have been as unsuccessful as they were well-intentioned.

I have had little experience in designing the typical small London back garden with its long narrow shape running between six-foot walls of yellowish London stock brick, though chance led me to make one or two rather larger gardens in which there was some room to manœuvre.

One was for a modern red brick house in the Georgian manner with a semi-circular entrance façade giving on to a forecourt with space enough to turn a car. Behind the house there was enough garden to make a wide paved terrace and a simple lawn, and to some old pear trees I added a pyramidal hornbeam, a maidenhair tree, *Gingko biloba*, and rhododendrons and lilies in the shade of a boundary wall. To give light and gaiety to the forecourt and to repeat the sparkle of the white-painted sash windows, I covered it entirely with white marble chippings and against the house planted *Clematis montana* which was later trained into horizontal swags at first floor level. As a base planting I restricted myself to a hedge of white and pale pink camellias, perhaps a risky choice but they flowered well since I planted them in peaty soil and in shade. On the garden side, ample wall space and full sunshine enabled me to cover the house with *Ceanothus dentatus* and rose

" Mermaid," a favourite combination of mine in powder blue and pale sulphur yellow.

A good grass lawn is not an impossibility in London, provided it is not much walked on, and it suits, I think, the mood of the town and gives an irreplaceable sense of space and ease. London flowers are flag iris, pinks, hollyhocks, all sorts of bulbous flowers and particularly lilies of many kinds. Many evergreen shrubs take hardly to the smoky air which clogs their pores. I prefer to use deciduous flowering shrubs which more gaily herald the arrival of spring in a town garden. Climbing roses like the London clay and such strong growers as *R. filipes* with its single creamy flowers and the almost evergreen " Alberic Barbier " rambler will quickly grow twenty feet where a green cover is needed.

The very small dark plot perhaps only a few square feet, in the heart of the city appears, at a gardener's first glance, an almost hopeless problem; that is, if he has hopes of gardening it in the conventional sense of the word. But such sites are really quite easy to transform if one looks at them from a different point of view. One has to garden them by allusion, first of all creating a sense of space and volume and then emphasising the mood towards which you are aiming. Walls colour-washed white or pale blue will catch and hold the light, while dark blue or a deep ochre red will absorb it and give depth and mystery. There is trellis, whether of painted wood, raw chestnut slats or bamboo, to use against the walls to give scale with as much or as little formality as you choose, and overhead a framework in similar materials can be used to filter the light or to veil adjacent high buildings. In so small a place I would pave the ground entirely with stone or marble, slate or brick. All of these will be the framing and organisation of the space and a minimum of planting will suggest the idea of green and growth. Against a dark wall variegated ivy will give the effect of dappled sunlight, while the complex green architecture of a single bush of *Fatsia japonica*, for instance, will be best seen against a light background. A vine, the grape vine or the large leaved *Vitis coignetiae*, will grow quickly to make overhead shade or garland a hard edge of wall. Happily there are a lot of plants with bold foliage which will thrive in such gardens. I remember a dark cobbled yard in Asolo near Venice surrounded by high walls which became entirely a garden for being outlined by a double row of aspidistras in pots. In Florence in May a few Japanese maples or big spreading azaleas, all in pots too, make a garden of the shady architecture of every palazzo courtyard. At Encombe, near Folkestone, echeverias in pots were the sole decoration of a white-washed loggia, and a small inner court was given all the qualities of a garden by a single clump of bamboo planted in one corner. The Mediterranean countries as well as Japanese and Chinese tradition are obvious sources of ideas for this kind of gardening, but with a careful consideration of each element, its shape and its colour, one can compose gardens all the more satisfying for being free of hackneyed associations.

In Germany and the Scandinavian countries, particularly in Denmark, much thought and study has been given to the design of the tiniest gardens whether in towns or round the small huts or summer houses in which people spend their week-ends in the suburbs or, as near Copenhagen, along the sea-shore. Designers have evolved a whole series of themes to symbolise a wide landscape and concentrate the idea of natural growth into a very small space. With a single birch tree and an ice-worn boulder, a pool and a clump of rushes, they seem to capture and hold the spirit of the Baltic landscape. The principle is admirable and the interpretation justifiable in that geography, but there has been a tendency, in climates where nature is less harsh and dry, to reproduce the same themes executed with the same elements with less happy results, since this kind of planting copied literally is no longer valid in another climate.

Nor has England entirely escaped this fashion. The South Bank Exhibition in London in 1951 showed us several gardens interpreted in terms of patches of cobblestones set about with weeds. This is an understandable revolt against the commonplaces of an unachievable " riot of colour " and acres of ill-executed " herbaceous border " which have been the common-

This Paris roof garden tops an elaborate duplex apartment full of fine furniture and objets d'art. As a simpler modern composition would have made too sharp a contrast, I used a Chinese-Chippendale fret pattern for a wooden summer house painted in glossy dark green and white

Beyond the balustrade which repeats in wrought iron the pattern of the pavilion lie the tree tops of the Bois de Boulogne. Only the Eiffel Tower in the distance breaks the green horizon. Plant boxes are filled with tulips and pansies in spring followed by petunias, usually white, and geraniums

places of current English gardening, but in a world of easy transport and the rapid dissemination of ideas any fashion or style, however authentic, becomes quickly vulgarised and, as it were, diluted. This is an inevitable decadence which cannot be remedied by plagiarising. The introduction of foreign and exotic fashions will but add to the general confusion, as apparent in garden design as in architecture, painting, sculpture and music. A wide knowledge of historical and contemporary styles and of plants and the techniques of design and execution can now, less than ever, be considered an adequate education for the landscape architect. All of these are necessary, but if he is really searching to be an artist he will have somehow to approach every problem with as truly an unbiased eye as he can manage. He must with impartiality and " freshness " consider each stage of his work and of his thinking, and never accept the facile solutions that his knowledge and experience will suggest until he has tested them against what I must call his artistic conscience.

One day my friend Kokoschka, showing me a portrait he had been engaged on for five years, told me that he started work each morning feeling fourteen years old, knowing nothing, with everything as though seen for the first time, each process of his painting a new and vivid experience. I have thought much about this, sometimes succeeding in bringing this attitude to my work, more often betraying it, though I try at least to keep it as a constant aim.

As London and Paris are differing worlds so are their gardens. Paris gardens, private and public, are seen as a decoration to be admired, whereas in London I feel that they are primarily a vehicle for an English love of cultivating growing things. The seventeenth-century Place des Vosges, the Tuileries and the Luxembourg, with their orderly compartments, were patterns to be enjoyed from the reception rooms of the *piano nobile*, or long, shaded alleys and terraces for promenading in society. Even the calculated informalities of Second Empire picturesqueness, as in the Champs-Elysées and the Parc Monceau, are incidents caught in a network of straight avenues regularly lined with trees. An instrument was clearly used for tracing the curved roadways which make the old wild woodlands of the Bois de Boulogne as regimented for the pleasures of the Parisian as were the long straight rides and *pattes d'oie* which formalised the hunting forests of the Bourbon kings.

Private gardens in Paris have always reflected this preoccupation with gardens as an orderly display in which elegantly dressed people would move amongst a clipped and static arrangement of trees and intricately clipped box parterres. Eighteenth-century engravings show bird's eye views of the Faubourgs of St. Honoré and St. Germain with garden patterns, almost identical, filling the rectangular plots of different sizes belonging to these smart quarters of the town. Relatively few of these gardens remain as they were. Haussmann's straight boulevards cut through most of them and the six-floored apartment houses built in his time and since have deprived almost all the rest of air and light.

To have a garden in Paris you must live in the Faubourg St. Germain or out where the suburbs of Neuilly and Auteuil fringe the Bois de Boulogne. Most of the gardens in the Faubourg St. Germain are damp and airless, overshadowd by chestnut trees and high buildings. A very few remain with traces of their former pleached lime-alleys and centre paths bordered with what were once *parterres à la française*. The larger Paris gardens, including the Elysée, the British Embassy and the Hotel Matignon, were transformed into undulating lawns and serpentine paths in the mid-nineteenth century, when colour was provided by beds so steeply raised as to be almost conical. Called *corbeilles* these beds were designed thus for a more prominent display of bright scarlet and yellow bedding plants. This type of gardening still survives in public gardens in provincial towns.

The adventures in applied decoration launched by Poiret and Bakst, which culminated in the Decorative Arts Exhibition of 1925, as well as early cubist painting, were reflected in certain

Paris gardens in designs whose intersecting rectangles and triangles of gravel, paving, grass and flowers repeated the currently fashionable motifs of paintings, fabrics and wallpapers. I know one large garden in this manner which is bounded by a high fence of mirrored panels set at angles like a screen to repeat indefinitely the confusion and angularities of the flower beds. In still another smaller garden of this period, which I was asked to modify, a central rectangle of flowers was surrounded by alternating and repeating lines of box-edging and bands of gravel which covered the whole site.

This garden in the Rue de l'Université lies behind a Regency *hôtel particulier*, set like all houses of any consequence of that period " entre cour et jardin." It houses a magnificent collection of pictures which included the ravishing pink of Manet's " La Prune," portraits by Delacroix and Toulouse Lautrec and two superb Goyas. The garden is just the width of the house's façade, a sober enough architecture, though showing some of the curved exuberance of its period. It was a melancholy garden, heavily shaded by one large tree and high buildings, and suggested nothing so much as the burial place of a favourite horse. I think its owners and I studied it for two years before finding a solution, and one distinguished French architect strongly advised against any change, saying it was an excellent example of its period!

The problems were many and commonplace. The site was just too large to be treated as a terrace and too small and too shaded for a conventional garden of grass and flowers. Besides, a successful lawn in a small Paris garden is so often, as it was in this case, impossible. A continental climate, with its cold winters and hot summers and the lack of moisture in the air, make a close springy turf impossible to attain. You can, if you must, sow a lawn of ryegrass each spring which at best will look as sparse as a balding head and, under trees, be no more than a muddy patch. French rain seems more leaden than English, and French lawns seem quite unable to absorb it. Since inside this particular house one could see only a dank tree against the dark, windowless walls of the high building beyond, I thought to devise some kind of central walk to increase the garden's apparent length and to enable one to look back from its far end at the charming facade. Trapped in my mind by eighteenth-century garden conventions, I employed every variation I could think of but never convinced my clients or myself. For three years I continued making sketch plans until I was told, " Something must be done—what would you do if it was your garden? " The simplicity of the question asked at that moment somehow washed away all the complicated play of associations which had been cluttering my thinking and a solution shaped itself in my mind instantaneously. Now three central steps lead down from the narrow stone terrace in front of the shuttered French windows of the ground floor, giving on to an oval of gravel which fills most of the garden and repeats the curves of an *oeil de boeuf* in the façade. At the far end of the oval three shallow steps in a re-entrant curve rise to the foot of the one big tree, and there is a raised space framed in trellis and decorated by four cast-iron Directoire urns. These are painted the darkest green, set on high bases and filled in summer with white hydrangeas to light this dark corner. The trellis is planted with variegated ivy to suggest the flicker of light, and behind it young variegated maples, *Acer negundo variegata*, for which I at last found good use, will grow to serve the same end. The gravel oval brings light down to the ground and chairs and tables make it a cool sitting place in summer. Its form is outlined with a wide thick edging of small-leaved box accented at the angles of the steps by large flattened box balls. The whole of the rest of the garden is planted with shrubs so that only the oval counts. This shrub planting is composed of enough evergreens, such as rhododendrons, skimmias, pieris, aucuba, *Viburnum rhytidophyllum* and laurustinus, as will make it look furnished in winter, while forsythia, philadelphus, deutzia and Persian lilac are grouped to mark the arrival of spring. The only flower colour is from white tulips and narcissi and *Lilium regale* among the shrubs and pots of palest pink regal pelargoniums which line the steps of the terrace in May and June.

Nearby, in the Rue de Varenne, I was called in to reorganise a large and neglected garden lying one storey lower than the reception rooms of a fine Louis XVI house, which gave on to a narrow terrace supported by a rough stone wall. The only way of reaching the garden from the terrace was by a kind of iron fire-escape. The garden, when we started on it, was full of untidy sycamore trees, muddy gravel paths and masses of variegated aucuba, but there was space and sunshine and I kept enough trees at the far end to hide a blank warehouse wall some six stories high. It seemed a pity to destroy the aucubas so I transplanted them to make blocks against the ivy-covered walls on each side of the garden. Here, their speckled shiny yellow leaves give a colour which I have accentuated by alternating these clumps with groups of forsythia. A low box hedge limits the shaded far end of the garden and a single jet of water from a circular pool set flush with grass makes a wavering thread of light. The rest of the space is filled by a lawn, with straight paths on each side limiting the shrub planting and increasing the apparent length. Three long flower beds parallel to these paths on each side insist on the yellow which is the colour theme of this garden, for they are planted in spring with tulip " Golden Harvest " followed later by pale yellow tuberous begonias.

The wall of the basement and the extraneous iron staircase remained to be coped with. A stone staircase in keeping with the house meant two long monumental flights and enormous expense. Finally we covered the wall and boxed in the iron staircase with a fairly close trellis. Now they are welded together by an all-over covering of *Pyracantha lalandii* and *P. rogersiana* which, clipped close to the trellis, make an admirable dark green base for the building. They are covered with white flowers in May and then with their orange and scarlet berries which usually last until after Christmas when hard weather drives the birds to eat them.

Paris gardens call for a firm framework and very simplified planting. Loose shapes and a complicated range of plant material look far too confused when seen from an orderly French interior.

A symmetry, however simplified, is usually the most suitable form. In these surroundings, flowers tell best as sharply defined blocks of colour. Cultural difficulties and their brief flowering period rule out herbaceous perennials, so that one finds oneself restricted to spring and summer bedding-out. This is less a limitation than an ardent gardener may think. He can use violas, pansies, daisies, forget-me-nots, tulips and hyacinths for more exciting combinations than the habitual rose and blue or scarlet and yellow. In Paris in summer the unattractive semperflorens type of annual begonias are popular because they are easy to grow. I think them ugly with their fleshy salad green leaves and mean flowers of acid pink or faded red, just as I dislike the other popular favourite, *Salvia splendens*, although I have occasionally seen even these difficult flowers put to good use as dot-plants veiled in the purple of massed *Verbena venosa*. But there are tuberous begonias which will succeed in town gardens. In white, flesh, coral, orange and yellow they can be mixed or used singly, provided you avoid the dark red shades which will only count as so many gaps in your planting. In the Paris sunshine geraniums flourish as also do zinnias, which look strident when mixed but velvety and rewarding if massed in one colour at a time.

A garden striking to a casual visitor is not usually a garden to live with and I try to avoid any trick effects in a private garden, since even a mild shock of surprise is opposed to the idea of tranquillity which I consider more than ever essential in a city garden. But sometimes only such a deliberate *tour de force* can reconcile existing elements which are too disparate.

One quite small garden on the edge of the Bois de Boulogne presented just such a conundrum and drove me to find a very far-fetched solution. You must imagine a ground-floor flat giving on to a rectangular strip fifty feet wide and perhaps fifteen feet deep from the windows to the ivy-covered fence separating it from the road. In each of the far corners was a semi-hexagonal summer house of bamboo made in pseudo-Japanese manner and covered with wistaria. The interior of the apartment had just been decorated with cream painted Louis XV panelling, each room opening directly on to the garden which, consequently, had to serve as an additional reception area. There was literally no room to make even an allusion to the eighteenth-century interior, so I decided to keep the two little pavilions and build my garden round them. First of all I made a narrow band of paving against the house to link the french windows, and this band of cut stone continues round a small central patch of grass. All the rest of the garden is in fine gravel edged with a freely curving foot-wide band of round black pebbles set in mortar. Clumps of bamboos and azaleas frame the two pavilions and the Japanese theme is underlined by one or two bush wistaria and Japanese maples growing out of little patches of flat-clipped box designed as irregular dark green islets in the gravel. Oddly enough this crass mixture of styles and themes appears valid. Each window frames a different garden picture and the flat treatment increases the apparent size of the whole.

I enjoy designing austere gardens, using a very limited and simple range of materials and trying to create a harmony by carefully adjusted proportions. A small garden near the Trocadero, attached to a large and very formally arranged house, is again a rectangle enclosed by high trellised walls. You reach it through a room used only for receptions which gives directly on to the upper third of the garden lying some three feet higher than the rest, from which it is separated by a retaining wall, a very simple wrought-iron balustrade and a central flight of steps. This upper level is entirely paved in squares of white marble and the high walls are clothed only in the marbled green and white variegated ivy. Green ivy covers the walls and trellis surrounding the lower garden. This is filled by, again, an oval of grass set in a broad frame of cut stone paving carefully worked out with radiating joints. All round is a planting entirely in green and white, which includes *Philadelphus microphyllus, Deutzia gracilis, Hydrangea paniculata grandiflora, Viburnum tomentosum mariesii,* as well as snowball trees, rhododendron " Sappho " and green box bushes and also a few white narcissi or, for later, white tobacco flowers. This garden was designed for outdoor dining and dancing, a sober but rather elegant green and white frame for gala dresses. It was made some years ago and I sometimes wonder whether anybody has ever been in it except myself and the gardener who keeps it tidy.

Another Paris essay in the grand manner was a garden I made in the Rue de l'Université for Madame de Jouvenel who had been French Ambassadress in Rome. She asked me to make a garden of dark green with lots of clipped yew trees and one which would recall Rome. Her house was very splendid, full of Chinese porcelain and fine eighteenth-century drawings, while the garden was the usual rectangle running parallel with the house but only about thirty feet deep and more than usually dark, with the house on one side and walls thirty-five feet high on the other three.

Since it would have taken years to cover such tall walls with climbers, I had to build a steel framework to support huge cases three feet wide and three feet deep which are set against the wall some twenty feet above the ground. A close trellis masks these cases and their supports, so that the effect is of a second wall stepped back half-way up against the back wall. Ivy planted at ground level as well as in the cases was not long in covering the trellis and large bushes of yew, laurel and box grow freely in the cases to break the monotony of the high enclosing walls. This high-level planting is stepped down on both sides towards the middle of the back wall where I built a stone portico round a fountain niche to mark the axis of the garden. The garden itself was worked out as a box parterre and given relief and interest by a quantity of clipped specimen box and yew trees. This bare description can only try to situate the elements of such an arrangement. Time has allowed the ivy to grow up and fall again in curtains; clipped yews, so dryly balanced when newly planted, have grown into an easier asymmetry, and sunlight and shadow blend the whole into a rich tangle which might have been there these last two hundred years.

I have never been entirely convinced that roof gardens have much charm nor can I ever think of them as being really gardens. Growing on a roof-top trees and flowers seem too far separated from the ground in which they should be rooted. The New York roof gardens I saw filled me with admiration. and the parterres of tulips on the roof of Radio City I thought very impressive, perhaps because they were grown in the teeth of a climate which is intolerable for gardening. But only in Rome does a miscellaneous pot-grown greenery seem to fit, perhaps because in this hilly town the flowery roof-top of one house is often the garden or terrace of the one above.

I have only made one roof garden in Paris. This was for Marcel Boussac who intelligently preferred a sunny duplex apartment looking out over the Bois de Boulogne to the darker stateliness of a *hôtel particulier* in the Faubourg St. Germain. At either end of his roof-top two small pavilions house the staircase and a small summer dining-room, and there is a wide view over the tree tops of the Bois, from the Eiffel Tower to the east right over to Mont Valerien. At the back, to the north, between the two pavilions were only roof and chimneys. To hide these and to link the two pavilions and break the wind I designed a sort of loggia or covered gallery in trellised woodwork; and wings of ivy-covered trellis project on each side to hide the neighbouring buildings and concentrate interest on the wide view to the south. The marble-paved terrace is hedged and compartmented by simple wooden boxes painted dark green and filled with scarlet geraniums and white petunias, varied by several large terracotta vases planted in the same way. It would be a rather conventional scheme were it not for the treatment of the pavilion or gallery, which is designed in the " Chinese Chippendale " manner, its rather elaborately fretted panels painted in glossy white and black-green like the plant boxes.

Any originality of design on a roof is usually controlled by the weight of earth it can carry. One is usually limited to an arrangement of flower boxes which should be as capacious as possible if you are to avoid the laborious, costly and messy business of having to change the soil too often. For this reason, having seen that there is adequate drainage material in the bottom of all the flower boxes, I prefer to fill them with a mixture of good heavy loam and manure. Plants in boxes, especially ever-greens or hedging plants, are gross feeders and a light-textured soil is apt to get impoverished and dry out very rapidly. I have never attempted to use high trees on a roof. Even where enough root room can be contrived they are soon the wind-racked ghosts of what they should be. Low clipped hedges and very bright flowers are usually a planting sufficient to frame the view and give some illusion of a garden.

Le Corbusier lives on the far side of the Bois on the top floor of an apartment house of his own building. I once spent a fascinating morning in his huge studio whose every element had been most carefully studied and worked out, where " there was a place for everything and everything in its place." It seemed an over-severe and logical setting for a man whose conversation was imaginative and at times even poetical. Then we went on to the roof to see the garden, where Le Corbusier had been content to spread earth and, as he said, leave the birds and the wind to do the rest. So here were tufts of grass and weeds, dandelions and willow-herb and even young laburnum trees—a wild and haphazard growth from seeds blown there by the wind or left by birds. Le Corbusier's architecture, like his painting, seems to express a search for form only. His buildings strain away from their surroundings like complicated box-kites scarcely tethered by a string. I had often wondered how I would garden round one of his suspended buildings. Now I knew.

Paris and the Ile de France must be considered as the centre and starting point of the formal French garden. A few years ago circumstances led me to an essay in the grand classical manner, though I worked exclusively with grass, water, clipped hedges and trees to recapture the spirit of the period without the costly complications of box parterres and endless gravel paths.

Thirty miles to the west of Versailles lies a minute Louis XV château called Le Moulinet. Its central part is *en lanterne*, that is only one room thick, and comprises the salon with its original panelling and overdoors, said to be painted by Boucher. Two small and lower wings project forward on either side and the charm of the house lies in the complexities of the mansarded roof, partly tiled and partly slated, and the cornice which sweeps down in curves to meet the lower levels of the wings. When I first saw the Moulinet there were still a few traces of a fairly elaborate Louis XV formal layout; but time had reduced these to a series of simplified cascades along a narrow watercourse which runs parallel to the entrance drive and a large *pièce d'eau* lying on the north axis of the house, some hundred yards from it and at a considerably lower level. This pool lay in a neglected orchard which had been originally a kitchen garden. Still farther away in the same direction a semi-circular *bosquet* of pleached limes terminated the main axis at the limit of the property.

As the house is raised a short flight of steps above ground level and the whole garden slopes away on this side, there is a wide view over the Ile de France, a view of villages and low, wooded hills and fields spread under the pale blue skies and chasing pearly clouds which give this countryside its special charm.

The formal pool, newly cleaned and edged with stone, was very large in scale and demanded a quite formal setting and, at that, one in which perspective should play its part to relate the small scale of the house to this relatively large sheet of water and the wide skies above it. The first thing to do was to give the pool a spacious and level setting of grass. This involved considerable levelling. First of all I had to make a court from a sloping lawn. Then the lawn itself had to be broken by two shallow banks with steps to bring it down to the level of the pool. Beyond the pool the ground was again graded down to another small circular pool which had once marked the centre of the kitchen garden. Beyond this again a central path continued to the half-circle of old pleached limes at the farthest end of the garden.

The next stage was to frame these levels of grass and water. This I did by an extensive planting of hornbeam hedges now some ten feet high. After running straight down either side of the first sloping lawn, they widen to form semicircles round a huge poplar and a young forty-foot specimen which I planted to balance it. Level with the large pool, the hedges are set still farther back on each side and here I doubled them to enclose a wide grass walk shaded by two lines of clipped limes. Then, beyond the pool, they return towards the centre and continue down either side of the next sloping lawn which is considerably narrower. Finally, beyond a small round pool, the perspective is reduced to the width of a gravel path, bordered by philadelphus and old-fashioned paeonies.

I planted groups of wellingtonias, sophoras, willows and scarlet oaks in the right foreground of the composition to balance eventually an existing clump of large trees to the left, and beyond and below, rows of lime trees have been planted behind the hedges, to be clipped or not when they are large enough. The site of the former kitchen garden at the far end of the perspective has been planted as a wood of lime trees with an undergrowth of hazels, hornbeam and wild strawberries.

The south façade of the house, with its characteristic curved cornice, its charming fenestration and its carved figure set high in a niche, gave on to a rough meadow sloping upwards to a low hedge cutting the sky. To the east side a wood comes close to the house, while to the west a similarly planted wood lies a hundred feet farther back. The formality and rigid symmetry of the house looked lost in this quite unbalanced setting, so once again it was necessary to find a simple but drastic solution.

The first thing to do was to place the house firmly in its setting by a simple paved terrace whose low retaining wall repeats the curved sweep of the cornice. This gives, by three steps, on to a space of level ground and a wide path running parallel and close to the house clear from one wood to the other. Then the meadow had to be regraded to make a perfectly plain lawn, sloping upwards to the horizon but less abruptly than before. At the far end a shaped grass bank rises to the original level at the boundary.

In order that the house should be in the centre of the composition, I planted, on the right of this lawn, four rows of lime trees, parallel to and at the same distance from the house as the wood on the left, and behind these I set another high hornbeam hedge to conceal a tennis court and a swimming pool.

This house and garden had an unexpected charm due to the original and rather unusual conflict of scale. I do not know another eighteenth-century house so small, almost miniature in all its parts, with so large and spacious a garden scheme as this must have been. A contemporary drawing shows the house surrounded by a moat in addition to the over-large pool and the little cascades and the woods pierced by formal alleys—all in the manner of Louis XIV. To make a garden faithful to the original scheme and mood, yet one that would not be overpowering, set a series of problems which I finally resolved, as best I could, by keeping the main " lines " clear and even obvious, while using hedges and pleached lime trees in such a way as to give a sense of enclosure and mystery. It was important that no single unit should appear too large and that one would always be drawn into each part of the garden in order to see what lay beyond.

There is always something just and exact to be sought for in any garden composition and in one detail, in this garden, I had a curious proof of this. I puzzled for a long time as to how to arrange the stairway which had to lead down into the garden from the entrance court in front of the house, replacing an untidy grass bank. Looking down from the house to the larger scale of the garden, it seemed as though any large simple flight of steps would do, but looking back from the garden towards the house, with its tiny wings and miniature pediment, it was clear that such a large flight of steps would be entirely out of scale. Finally I worked out the circular steps you see illustrated between pp. 240-1, and when we came to dig the foundations for them we found in exactly the same spot the original foundations for a circular staircase of exactly the same diameter.

Whatever the contours of the site, the underlying shapes of a garden can scarcely be too simple. This rule holds good whether you are making a severely architectural garden extending from a formal house and carried out with a limited range of plant-

material or whether you want a frame, formal or informal, for a
rich and varied planting. One of the most brilliant gardens I know
was designed as a setting for a formal house in the late eighteenth-
century manner at Roubaix in the North of France, where the
landscape is marred by industrial development. The plan is
symmetrical. A long rectangle of grass runs outwards from
the house, framed by twelve-foot hedges of clipped hornbeam.
Half-way down its length, and set in the grass with no stone
margin, is a square of water marking a cross-axis invisible from
the house, which consists of two lateral arms also of grass and also
framed by hedges of hornbeam. All the area behind the hedges is
planted as a wood. There are no distractions, no gravel paths,
no sculpture and no flowers. The effect is always restful and the
existence of the cross-axis is felt rather than seen from the house
in a way which gives the garden a certain mystery. Nothing
could be simpler or more effective.

The memory of this garden has often helped me when I have
found myself getting involved in over-elaborate and complicated
designs for important gardens.

Nowadays even in France I am seldom asked to design a
formal classical garden. People prefer the informality of a country
cottage and you now have to go many miles outside Paris if you
want to find a small and simple property which does not cost a
fortune. The Ile de France has many little rivers and for some
years now old watermills for conversion have been at a premium.
They are often picturesque enough and to design gardens round
them is always interesting work, but their situation usually makes
these gardens damp and cold and especially liable to late spring
frosts.

The mill garden near Chantilly mentioned in Chapter VI presented a tough problem. The mill house is built against an eighteen
foot high embankment which is faced with a stepped drywall of
huge squared stones. Part of the garden and the road are on the
upper level as is also the entrance of the house. Two floors below
the mill stream, almost a little river, runs under the house and
away across the flat water-meadows. At right angles to the stream

the embankment stretches for almost two hundred yards. Incidentally, once cleared of its growth of ash saplings and nettles and carefully planted, it has become certainly the highest and longest flowered dry wall that I know. At the far end this wall merges with the ruins of a monastery and the original monastic mill. Here the main stream comes into the property, and there used to be a ford. The water at this point is wide and winds about in the shade of the fine old trees which shelter the stone ruins. Amongst the trees are mineral springs which were formerly bottled and sold as Chantilly water, and at some time in the nineteenth century, they were enclosed in a kind of grotto made of flints and old bottle ends.

It seemed unnecessary to modify the course of either of these two streams, the one coming from under the house and dashing away across the sunlit meadows, the other winding and shaded.

The garden on the lower level of the property is extremely simple. Below the long stepped wall is a very large herbaceous border and then a wide lawn with occasional trees which merges into a small shady wood mainly, alas, of fir and spruce. This wood surrounds the ruins and a grassy clearing with some fine yews which lies immediately in front of the roofless, gothic monastery mill.

Next to the house we confined the stream between dry stone walls and set a line of large stones from the ruins to act as stepping stones. Then we planted *Spiraea cantoniensis*, and clumps of small-leaved box as a permanent foil to violas and tulips followed by annuals. This rather sophisticated planting is confined to the few yards nearest to the house: the stepping stones and a low weeping cedar mark its limit. The upper garden between the embankment and the boundary wall is a long narrow strip of ground which proved easier to deal with. I divided it into four rectangles. The first one is of grass with a cobbled central path which leads from the front gate to the house. The only planting is of pyracantha trained flat to the surrounding stone walls, and box clipped low and flat as a base line to the house.

The second rectangle is also grass to set off an old leaning apple tree and two simple beds of the scarlet floribunda rose " Moulin Rouge". The third enclosure is square and divided into lozenge-shaped box-edged beds set out in spring with white and dark blue pansies and in summer with white and scarlet petunias. Yew hedges frame this formal carpet of colour and four yew pyramids give height.

The last enclosure is longer than it is wide. On either side of a central path narrow beds are usually planted with tulips for May followed by scarlet verbena, mauve ageratum and dwarf orange marigolds. On either side, behind these strident mosaics of colour are narrow cross-beds filled with all kinds of flowers for cutting.

To give this succession of gardens unity and scale I made yew buttresses at regular intervals against the boundary wall and planted the wall itself with climbing roses scarlet and crimson, white yellow and pink, keeping each panel to one colour only. On the inner side I planted the great retaining wall thickly with pinks and alpine phlox, campanulas, valerian and wallflowers to make the whole height of the wall a tapestry of flowers. Above it a low wide wall just high enough to sit on runs the whole length of the upper garden. Isolated clipped yews planted at the same intervals as the buttresses against the outer wall gave scale and height.

CHAPTER X

Switzerland and Italy

I went to Switzerland to garden for the first time just after the war. I was called to the Château de Bellerive on the lake-shore near Geneva, a great rectangular stone building with a fine tiled roof and flanked by two fifteenth-century towers. This old castle had its own harbour set in from the lake and an old water-gate, and had once been the port of entry and the storehouse for salt for the kingdom of Savoy. Facing west, it looks over lawns and fine trees across the lake to the long ridges of the Jura Mountains.

The layout of the garden presented no very complicated problems. I had to cut out old and dying trees and get rid of an overgrown box parterre which I replaced with a simple lawn and, against the boundary wall, a wide border of flowering shrubs. This border was some twenty feet wide by one hundred feet long and I worked out the planting entirely in white-flowered shrubs, with clumps of *Juniperus chinensis pfitzeriana* and the dwarf pine *P. montana mughus* to give it weight. Towards the back I used white lilacs, snowball trees, *Viburnum opulus sterile*, philadelphus and white *Hibiscus syriacus* for later flowering with, further forward, *Hydrangea paniculata grandiflora*, *Viburnum tomentosum mariesii*, *V. carlesii*, *Rosa rugosa*: " Blanc Double de Coubert," white brooms and white Kurume azaleas. Towards the front I planted *Deutzia gracilis*, *Philadelphus microphyllus*, *Viburnum davidii* and clumps of grey-blue leaved hostas and among these I set white Pacific delphiniums and *Lilium regale*.

The summer afternoon light reflected off the lake can be so intense that, to break it, we planted the far end of the lawn with a thin screen of silver birch and tall-growing shrubs such as tamarisk and *Rhus cotinus*, in both its purple and green-leaved forms.

I learned on this trial run in Switzerland with what care the Swiss construct and maintain their gardens. After the war years of doing without, it was an eye opener to see work so meticulously executed. The cost was and still is tremendously high, but you can count on first-class workmanship. Holes for plants are dug well and deep enough, there is no stinting of peat or manure, and you can choose all the large specimen shrubs you need from nurseries that are well stocked and well cultivated. Stone masons make a fine, exact job of paving and steps, paths are properly drained and plumbing properly laid. Gardening on the Lake of Geneva would be pure delight were it not for the *bise*, that wicked, searching wind which blows right down the Rhone Valley from Brigue to Marseilles where it turns sharply east and becomes the *mistral*, the drying bane of every garden in the South of France.

From Bellerive I went across the lake to a ravishing property called the Creux de Genthod. This small and exquisite house is one of the few surviving buildings by J. F. Blondel. It was built about 1730 for a clergyman of the old Genevese family of de Saussies. Blondel's original plan showed a very elegant yet simple house with a pediment on its two widest façades and a flat roof, which its prudent builder changed to a tiled pitched roof in view of the inclemencies of the Geneva climate. He built it in the lovely green sandstone called *meulasse* which used to be dragged out in the form of boulders from the bottom of the lake. Now, I think, no longer used, this stone was the characteristic building material for the whole lakeside in the eighteenth century.

The house with its sash windows, so unusual for a French house of that period, was set on a grass mound. Its entrance is to the south, and, as was customary in all renaissance houses, the salon was planned to face due north, down a long stretch of grass towards a large rectangular pool long since filled in. This area, now a rough lawn, is flanked on each side by four rows of horse chestnuts, brought laboriously by ox cart from Lyons, a hundred miles away, soon after the house was first built. The east façade looks out from its eminence over level ground running towards the lake two hundred yards away, and here formerly was a walled kitchen garden which obscured the fine view of Mont Blanc. When I went to see the André Firmenichs to whom the house now belongs they were perplexed. They had turned this east side of the house into a library which is the main living-room and had cleared away the kitchen garden using its fine gate-piers and wrought-iron gates elsewhere, to make a lawn which was enclosed with yew hedges and punctuated by a series of very large clipped yews brought from an old garden in Geneva.

The problem was how to link the house to this garden by something other than the ugly grass bank on which the house was perched. At first I was rather daunted; I saw at once that this was a severely architectural problem and that I would have to devise a walled terrace and a flight of steps to connect the level of the house with the long, hedged garden below. I knew too that I could not trifle with architecture of this quality. For this side of the house I eventually designed a long simple wall in the same green sandstone as the house, rising to sitting height above ground level on the inner or house side. From this, the upper level, a flight of steps leads down from each side to meet below at the centre. There was much discussion as to whether we should design wrought iron balustrades for the wall top and the steps. Finally I decided that it would be impossible to design or execute iron work of the quality that the architecture of the building demanded, and furthermore that anything so intricate would distract attention from the fine view of the Alps and Mont Blanc. So I topped the main retaining wall with a parapet wall and flanked the steps too by a very low and wide parapet that ends in two comfortably fat scrolls. The removal of the bank left quite a space between the foot of the new wall and the lawn; and here I devised a simple arrangement of box-edged beds centred on a stone-rimmed pool which lies exactly on the axis of one of the chestnut alleys on the north side and a plain barred wooden gate which marks the entrance to a small walled garden to the south.

So that the terrace wall might not look too severe or too new, I planted it alternately with *Cotoneaster salicifolia* and chaenomeles. These are kept flat to the wall and severely pruned to encourage them to flower and fruit, and to prevent them from veiling the wall too heavily. But the composition still needed a little more permanent decoration. After much searching we found in England a set of six stone vases which, although they dated from the seventeenth century and came from the Cotswolds, looked as though they would suit the architecture exactly. Happily they did and we were able to set them out at intervals along the top of the wall. At about the same time André Firmenich bid for a bronze group by Bourdelle that was coming up for auction in a Paris sale. This early twentieth-century fountain group of a boy and a goat, now placed in the centre of the round pool, looks as though it had been designed two hundred years earlier for just that position.

But Jean Firmenich is a Scotswoman and felt lost without a walled flower garden; so to the right, on the axis of the fountain and the chestnut walk, we set our white-railed wooden gate in the high wall which led into what had been a wood yard. Here we contrived a simple courtyard laid out with panels of fine shingle set in bands of cobblestones to give good scale. At the far end of this yard, under two large chestnut trees, a tiny eighteenth-century wooden pavilion, also brought from England and lined with old pine panelling, serves as a summer house. We repainted it in white and Naples yellow and, to light up this shady part of the gardens, we added tubs of pink hydrangeas. On one side this court opens on to a traditional walled herbaceous flower garden round an oval of grass. To give this garden extra life Jean found two painted wooden donkeys from a roundabout and made panniers for them which are now filled in summer with trailing geraniums.

But I still had to deal with the immediate surroundings of the house. So as not to distract from the elegancies of the architecture, I devised a very simple arrangement of areas of fine pea gravel and panels of grass: for colour I relied on carefully placed plants in tubs and cases. On either side of the entrance to the house, I placed wooden cases, *caisses de Versailles*, (described in Chapter IV) painted white and banded with black iron, to hold standard bay trees. On the east or lake side, smaller round wooden tubs are planted with agapanthus, and each year we fill the stone vases on the parapet wall with white geraniums and the white trailing scented petunia called " Satin Blanc ". In front of the north façade of the house, with the three arched windows of the salon which give on to the long length of grass shaded by the ancient lines of chestnut trees, I made a deep semicircle of gravel, re-shaped the bank into semicircular form and planted on each side, and running down the bank, rococo curves of box-hedging a yard high and a yard thick. Around the semicircle of gravel stand more huge white *caisses de Versailles* planted with bushes six feet high and as much through, of bright blue hydrangeas which last all summer until the first frosts tinge them with copper-green, turquoise, mauve and cinnamon. The Creux de Genthod is as complete and charming a composition in the eighteenth-century manner as I know. It is compact yet spacious. Its panelled rooms are filled with books and flowers and pictures and there is laughter and the noise of children till the whole household moves down to swim and sail from a summer house by the lake, and the little house is left tranquil in its garden setting through the summer afternoons.

Another year I was in Geneva again, this time to make a new garden round a remodelled house set high in a hillside park full of fine trees and looking once again over the lake of Mont Blanc. This house is without architectural interest but has two gigantic plane trees which shade the facade on the lake side. Here I could not build a terrace wall as it would have blocked the view from the main rooms in the centre of the façade. But as I needed a horizontal base line for the house, I made a paved space above a steep grassed slope, and flanked it by walled terraces at either side which project to enclose the trunks of the great planes and make shady sitting places. To the side of the house I had to build a high retaining wall and fill in the sharply sloping ground. Once levelled it became an oval of grass surrounded by wide beds of herbaceous plants. These are reinforced by clumps of polyantha roses, Persian lilacs, *Spartium junceum* and some of the newer hybrid buddleias. Beyond, in the shade of some large beech trees, are rhododendron hybrids interplanted with ferns and hostas, tiger lilies, astilbes, *Iris sibirica* and *Senecio clivorum*. The soil of the Geneva area is apt to be somewhat limy, full of rounded pebbles and rather sharply drained. I have learned to grow azaleas and rhododendrons by excavating the whole area to be planted two feet deep and lining the hole with two thicknesses of rabbit wire before filling in with peat. This seems to discourage wandering tree roots and prevent the peat from slipping away.

The lady of the house asked me for a garden full of flowers and shrubs in the " English " manner; she was, as usual, surprised that herbaceous plants do not remain in flower for three months on end. Taking her at her word I did my best, but when, among the Michaelmas daisies, I planted *Callicarpa giraldiana* for its panicles of bright pink-mauve berries, I evidently went too far and she remonstrated: " Out with your horrible English zizis! "

In this garden Swiss thoroughness and Swiss costliness reach extremes. I decided to make a fairly large formal forecourt in the angle formed by the two wings of the house on the entrance side and to carry it out in pea gravel framed in bands of cobblestones. There was much discussion as to how best to do this, for the whole family drive the largest American cars, dash up to the front door far too fast and then slam on the brakes. Such a procedure would all too soon wear down a normal gravelled finish, so it ended by our setting every individual tiny pebble in colourless bitumen, a technique which took weeks and cost a great deal of money. But now, after several years, it shows little signs of wear.

Animals were a problem in this garden. The daughter of the

house accumulated them. There were six or eight bad-tempered dogs to which I was as allergic as a postman, a couple of deer chewed a magnificent hornbeam hedge to the core, and a miniature flock of sheep demolished a long length of laurel hedge. Worst of all was a monkey who was frequently attached by a chain to any one of four magnificent clipped yews which I found for the forecourt. In a few weeks they were wrecked.

On the way across the park up to the kitchen garden there is an outstanding *Davidia involucrata vilmoriniana*, the " dove " or " handkerchief " tree which must be forty or fifty years old. It is a wonderful sight in early June and I try to time a visit each year to see it covered with its huge white hanging bracts turning in the wind. I was allowed to remake all the kitchen garden paths in asphalt covered with fine pea gravel and then edge them with a border of cut stone from the Valais. In spite of the large initial cost, this saves one man in the garden, since there can be no weeds and there are no edges to be kept tidy.

Although a wall encloses three sides of this kitchen garden, I had to devise some kind of boundary on the fourth side which joins the park. As I did not want anything too stiff, I planted a long hedge of mixed pink and red " Grootendorst " roses. This is a hybrid rugosa rose with smallish double flowers whose petals are pinked like a clove carnation. It grows to make a thick well-furnished hedge about six feet high and four feet through, and it flowers continuously from May until September.

As the park does not extend as far as the lake side, we decided to build a swimming pool, a tennis court and changing rooms at the highest point of the property beyond the kitchen gardens. Here you look out between the trunks of a group of fine mature pine trees across over the falling ground and the lake to the mountains. It is such a dramatic view that eventually I designed a more important building with a large living-room, with a wide window which disappeared by touching a button. The position of this window dictated the floor plan of the building. Behind it is a tennis court framed by hornbeam hedges twelve feet high. In front, and some six feet below the building I placed the swimming pool, protected along its north side by the building and, to the east, by a low retaining wall and a yew hedge. The south and west sides are left open to the view and, at the south-west corner, the rectangular pool breaks out towards the lake in a semi-circular bay. Although this pool is only about forty-five feet long, its simple lines and the careful modelling of the grass banks and lawn around it give it a certain breadth of scale which I hope links it worthily with one of the most breath-taking views in Europe. The necessary steps and the springboard fit into metal sockets so that they can be removed in winter, leaving the pool as a decorative feature.

I came to know all the garden contractors and nurserymen in the Geneva area well. They have excellent foremen and good Italian labour; they are well equipped and very competitive. A telephone call brings a gang within a couple of hours, to prune trees, to clip hedges, or to start construction on a garden project. If I want special plants, there is happily an English lady who lives alone far down the lake and who grows all kinds of odd plants for her own pleasure and to sell to the Lausanne flower shops. I go sometimes to see her in her little house full of Pekinese dogs, family souvenirs and tennis trophies. Birds fly in and out of the house and she swears that at dawn they bring her the day's news.

Later, Prince Aly Khan decided to build a small stone house in the eighteenth-century manner on one of the few remaining plots of land between the main Geneva-Lausanne road and the lake. The house lies some sixty feet back and a little below the road, and about the same distance from the water edge; and there was not a tree or a bush on the site. The Prince was someone whom the world's Press decided to glamorise, so I had to design a garden which would keep the reporters at bay and give some privacy to this foursquare house. After a good deal of thought I built up the top half of my narrow strip of sloping ground to road level, so that, through the main gate and behind the garage which borders the road, there is a parking space; this I hedged round with yew to make a second screen. A flight of steps and

a narrow path lead down to the front door and all the intervening space I planted thickly with birch trees. Now, after only
three years, there was a respectable coppice of birches and from
the road you could only guess at the house's existence.

Hornbeam hedges are a speciality of the Geneva region. You
can buy them any size from three to twelve feet high, they start
into growth at once and after their first year make a shapely hedge.
Elsewhere I have found them slow starters and difficult to transplant. It seems best to move them in mid-April just before they
shed the previous year's leaves. The Prince's garden is surrounded,
except along the water's edge, by just such a hornbeam hedge.
Inside it, grass with a few isolated trees and clumps of flowering
shrubs, run down to the water's edge. A simple pattern of beds
set in grass and filled with " Cocorico " roses and edged with
nepeta lies to one side of the house, and a thick belt of shrubs and
trees shields the garden from the road and attenuates the noise of
passing traffic. I know of few things in the garden that can be
as meaningless and unattractive as a planting of mixed shrubs.
Each time I have to devise such a planting I oblige myself to find
a simple theme and stick to it. In this case I decided to use hollies
and cotoneasters, *C. frigida*, *C. salicifolia* and *C. cornubia* as well
as *Viburnum rhytidophyllum* for my main planting, calculating on
a simple play of green foliage and red berries. These are growing
well and will soon make an eight feet blanket against the road.
To make a taller accent and hide a neighbouring building, I
planted three quite large *Chamaecyparis nootkatensis pendula*.
Next to these on the side boundary of the property is a large
group of red-foliaged shrubs. I used the red-leaved form of
Rhus cotinus for height towards the back as well as *Corylus
maxima purpurea*, the purple-leaved hazel; and a colony of about
twelve red Japanese maples, *Acer palmatum atropurporeum*, grow
to the front of this group from a groundwork of the reddish
Berberis thunbergii and *Rosa rubrifolia*. This last is one of my special
favourites. Its soft red foliage has a glaucous tinge, the red
veiled, as it were, with mauve and a soft silvery green to which its
brief flowering brings just the right note of mauve-pink. In this

garden I added a patch of the low-growing *Rosa mutabilis* to add a little sparkle with its mahogany-red stems and its flowers which are orange-red in bud opening to yellow and fading to mauve-pink. Had there been room, I would have added a few plants of *Indigofera giraldiana* because, although its foliage is silvery green, its wands of pinky mauve flowers bloom at the same time as the fluffy pink inflorescence of the rhus. But this was a small garden and I had to find room for a few trees for the shade indispensable in Geneva's summer heat. So down by the lake we made a wide hole in the gravel and filled it with clayey loam for a weeping willow and also near the water I planted a swamp cypress, *Taxodium distichum*. Nearer the house I placed three *Magnolia soulangiana*, a tree I cannot resist although I know that in three springs out of four a late frost will brown its early canopy of white waxy flowers. I plant it just the same for the lovely twisting forms of its elephant-grey trunk and branches and the distinction of its oval, lettuce-green foliage. Like all the magnolias, this is a plant which has " drawing " in every twig and leaf.

In a small, bare garden such as this I could easily have fallen into the temptation of planting a few fast-growing trees; but since it *was* so small I felt that it must be precious, so I choose too a tulip tree, *Liriodendron tulipifera*, slow growing but early showing its distinction. Not far from it I added three liquid-ambars and a group of pink dogwood, *Cornus florida rubra*, all planted in pure peat. These were for autumn colour. In a continental climate (and good autumn colour can be relied on every year in Switzerland) the dogwood turns a bright cerise scarlet, while the underside of each leaf remains the palest silver green.

While I made this garden—slowly, because I had to wait for the builders, (and making any garden till the plasterers have finished their work means doing everything twice)—I was called across to make a factory garden on the other side of Geneva. The factory is a handsome building designed on very simple lines, with a long triangular wedge of ground lying away to one side of it. To provide shelter from the *bise* and to hide an ugly, built-up hillside, I planted a triple row of Lombardy poplars as a boundary on one of the long sides of the triangle and designed a large, roughly triangular, reflecting pool on the lawn which covers most of the site. Next to the building, rectangular zig-zag beds of scarlet polyantha roses accented by clipped pyramids of yew, repeat the mood of the architecture in plant form. For the rest, there is a spinney of silver birch and a few carefully placed groups of Cedar of Lebanon and Scots fir.

I have never cared for intimate gardening near factories or large public buildings. The scale and idiom of domestic gardening are out of place. Wide approach roads, parking areas and long roof-lines demand the simplest garden treatment if you are to retain scale. You must plant boldly and extensively and, whether you are looking for vertical, rounded or horizontal forms, you must repeat them until they convey their message as unmistakable as the building itself. Here on the industrial side of Geneva, where the Arve in its deep gorge joins the Rhône, you sense the closeness of the mountains—with the whaleback of the Salève on one side and the long ridge of the Jura falling away to the Bellegarde gap on the other—and you feel you must plant boldly.

Next on my list came the Villa Deodati on the outskirts of Geneva where Byron once lived. This never matured as a job, but I spent a happy day or two exploring the garden possibilities for the lovely, late eighteenth-century house with its sober colonnades and magnificent wrought-iron balustrades. Unfortunately previous owners had ripped out all its eighteenth-century panelling and decorated it to resemble a transatlantic liner of sixty years ago.

Perhaps as you read you will imagine quiet months spent gardening in Swiss tempo, collected and thoughtful, with time to study every detail. In fact these years were rather like a club-sandwich with, as intermediate slices of bread, nights spent in the train. The layers between were gardening in Paris, in the South of France, or maybe in Italy, in Switzerland or in Belgium. For some years it was quite usual for me to spend four successive nights in a sleeping-car, rushing from one job in hand to another in a different country and a quite different climate. I might leave

Geneva and an old-fashioned country rose-garden in the evening, to wake up at Nice and have to be ready to deal with the problems of planting in the sea-swept limestone of the Cap d'Antibes. From there I would rush to Grasse to plant terraces of tuberoses and jasmine under the trunks of an old olive orchard, and in the evening perhaps catch a plane to Rome to design a hotel garden near the Villa Borghese. The next night might find me in the train for Verona or Venice or Milan, or back to Paris just in time to leave again for Lille or Brussels to deal with other clients, other gardens, another climate and another vegetation.

But now we are in Switzerland, so perhaps we can go slowly along the lake side through Coppet and Nyon, Rolle and Morges, beautifully built small towns with green sandstone houses lining the wide streets, often with shutters diapered in bright colours and window boxes and fountains flowing with petunias, geraniums, salvias and marigolds. The undulating countryside rising towards the Jura conceals a hundred little châteaux, mostly of the eighteenth century, which combine elegance and solid comfort. The château, with its nicely detailed doors and windows, is usually set back between its *dépendances*, the farm buildings. Usually there will be a wrought-iron gateway between stone pillars and a great stone fountain to give an air to the court-yard between the buildings.

Past Lausanne the mountains close in on the lake and you travel between terraced vineyards into the Valais. Each time I go through on the way to Italy I long to take the little train that climbs a steep valley to the right to Zermatt. Here was the Riffelalp Hotel perched high like a Tibetan monastery just on the tree line above a forest of Arolla pines with the great obelisk of the Matterhorn, its peak like a pyramidon—the point where heaven and earth meet, magnetise and interpenetrate. But we must go on through the Simplon, past Pallanza and Stresa with their famous garden shrines, the Isola Bella and the Isola Madre, down into the Lombardy plain with its rice fields and endless irrigation channels lined with poplars and willows. Turning west, we come to Turin, set on the river with its wooded hill behind, and, farther on, the great amphitheatre of the snow-capped Alps.

I first went to Turin to make the waterpiece I have described elsewhere for Count Rossi at La Loggia. This work led to my being asked to rearrange the grounds of a country house in the foothills of the Alps beyond Pinerolo. The villa is a mid-eighteenth-century house elaborately decorated in the robust and highly coloured Piedmontese style. From a low ground floor, once storehouses and stables, a spacious double stairway leads up to a wide gallery, with stucco decorations in the Chinese manner of the period, and a series of reception rooms. The garden was relatively small, entirely enclosed by a high wall and so thickly planted with ornamental conifers and laurels some eight years ago that you might have imagined yourself in a suburban garden in Streatham or Neuilly or Brooklyn. Wherever there was level ground there was a formal box parterre, six of them, some terraced and all set out with endless rows of ugly terracotta vases and white marble fountains and statues. For years the gardener had been planting conifers and adding odd beds, usually full of scarlet salvias and geraniums. When I arrived he had been there for over fifty years.

My first aim was to open up the site in order to get the shape and feel of the landscape. This involved a long and desperate struggle to get rid of some of the overcrowded trees. Each spruce, each monkey puzzle had been planted by this same gardener who grew gloomier and gloomier as one by one they went. In the end I was able to eliminate all the formal gardens, put all the statues and pots out of sight, get rid of endless winding gravel paths which led nowhere, and see daylight. Things already looked better. Between fine cedars and beech trees you could now look out across to the mountains and the winding valley; and behind the garden rose the dome of a fine baroque church built by Juvara. Beyond this church rises a steep hillside with its woods and terraced fields and little farms hung against the sky like a great tapestry, its patterns changing their colours with the seasons.

What we had achieved so far whetted our appetites for more. The boundary wall round the garden was far too close. A public road just beyond it led to the church, so we had to build a new road to sweep round the property in a far wider arc so as to reach the church from another side. Down came the wall and all the new ground gained was surrounded with a fence and hedge of the thorny maclura. Our intention was to grass these thirty acres sloping away from the house, planting trees in clumps or individually so as to make a " picturesque " park in the spirit of the house and a foreground for the mountains. We planted young cedars and weeping beech, silver limes, maples and chestnuts. But for an intermediate period only—that is, until these trees grow large enough to count—we have planted a regular orchard of standard apple and cherry trees, under which crops of hay and alfalfa make good use of the ground.

Behind the house the ground falls rapidly away to a steep and narrow valley below the great hill. This valley, too, was walled off and further hidden by a line of plane trees. Beyond the wall, in the floor of the valley was a rocky stream, a torrent of water when the snow melted in spring or after a storm, a mere trickle in the hot summer months. Down came this wall too, and the plane trees, and we took over and enclosed the valley and the steep wooded cliff beyond.

A little ravine under great beech trees runs down through the garden under a rustic bridge to join this valley. Here I started gardening in earnest, making wide beds of peat and planting the ravine with rhododendrons, kurume and Exbury azaleas, magnolias, Japanese maples and all sorts of plants which might thrive in this moist, shady and sharply drained position. In the darkest shade I used bergenias, *Vinca minor* and clipped mahonia with masses of *Scilla nonscripta*, daffodils and muscari to give spring colour; I used, too, another admirable ground cover which you are likely to find in every Italian garden from north to south. In Italy they call it convallaria and in France

" turquoise "; but it looks to me like a dwarf ophiopogon with its characteristic narrow leaves and tiny club-headed mauve inflorescence and it grows happily in sun or shade.

The main valley was altogether a larger problem. Attracted as always by the presence of water I decided to make a very simple water garden on a fairly large scale. The valley ran down-hill so rapidly that we first had to build a succession of dams with the local stone so as to form a series of pools. These dams —and there are eleven of them—vary from three to nine feet in height and make eleven pools varying from twenty to fifty feet in length. To take away the artificial look I thought it would be best to let a year of spates and storms bring down silt and stones so that the ponds might take on a natural look. I had not, however, reckoned with an August cloudburst higher up the valley which swept away all the first season's planting and many tons of topsoil and peat. We remedied that by building a larger dam out of sight higher up the valley and from it we brought a concrete pipe a yard wide and set underground to carry off all the surplus water. This made it possible to maintain an even flow for the cascades which fall from pond to pond.

We carried out all this work with local labour. All Italian workmen seem to have an inborn skill with stone, and to know instinctively how to build. On this garden project they had a tendency to elaborate their work, point all the stone work with cement and, in fact, " ornament " it in their fashion. This made difficulties at first but, once they got the hang of the work I wanted, I was amazed at the rapidity and skill with which they could translate a rough sketch into a solid construction: walls, waterfalls, steps and paving seemed to go up almost as fast as I could draw them or rather set them out on the spot. When it came to placing rocks near the cascades, to conceal the dam walls which form the underlying skeleton of this garden, things went less well. I asked for boulders to be brought from the nearest river bed, meaning to place them one by one at the foot of each cascade. When next I came on to the site I found that several truckloads had been dumped under the waterfalls at the head of each pool. Each one had to be laboriously dragged out again before I could begin the work of placing them.

When I came to plant this valley I had to go far afield to find what I wanted. Modern gardening in Italy in general follows nineteenth-century practice, and in almost every tiny villa garden you are likely to find several cedars and *Magnolia grandiflora* growing into each other, so closely planted are they; while the more sophisticated amateurs of modern architecture make gardens with the three birch trees, irregular pool, short run of planted dry-walling and bed of floribunda roses which are the common-place of " modern " European garden design from Stockholm to Palermo. The nurserymen naturally build up their stocks for the planting of this kind of garden, so that their repertory is limited. Only at the Villa Taranto at Pallanza has Captain Neil McEacharn a very large collection, and from his hand-list I was able to check what would be most likely to succeed in this garden and order plants from Holland and England.

As the valley is on the outskirts of the garden and has already a sufficiently dramatic form, with its steep, wooded sides and series of pools widening as the valley floor widens, I decided to limit the waterside planting to drifts of *Iris sibirica*, hemerocallis, lythrum, astilbes and here and there large patches of *Senecio clivorum* and *Hydrangea quercifolia*. For shrubs there are groups of *Rhus cotinus*, brooms, *Rosa hugonis*, *Rosa moyesii*, *Viburnum tomentosum mariesii*, *Spiraea cantoniensis* with some berberis and cotoneasters and several wide plantings of *Pyracantha coccinea* which, though hard to get started, once established grows well on a dry and stony slope. The wooded cliffs on the far side were in bad shape. All I could do was to eradicate the brambles and the acacia stools and plant thickly with very small plants of beech, hornbeam, silver birch and Scotch fir. As these grow and crowd each other we will be able to thin them out and group for the eventual effect we want. On the valley floor I have planted groups of *Robinia hispida* and Japanese cherries, liquidambars and scarlet oak and *Taxodium distichum* for the moister places, some weeping birch and a few conifers and evergreens. Groups of

Pine trees, the sea and the rocky cliffs of Beaulieu in the distance make a landscape which needed little gardening. Clumps of the white blue-eyed dimorphotheca soften the edges of a path which runs for half a mile along a hillside planted with lavender and rosemary, lentisk, medicago, myrtle and other aromatic natives of the South of France

Garden architecture can seldom be too simple. The play of light and shade, the shape textures and colours of vegetation and the patina given by time and use will be quite enough to enliven and enrich the plainest constructions. This simple flight of steps carefully built by a workman who understood the nature of the local stone leads from the wilder parts of the garden to the wide terrace in front of a house near Cannes

Pinus nepalensis and *Pinus sylvestris* mark bends in the valley, several libocredrus make vertical accents and wide-spread plantings of *Juniperus chinensis pfitzeriana* cover some of the steeper banks near the waterfalls, while broad-leafed hollies such as *Ilex aquifolium camelliaefolia* will eventually make a shining dark-green foil to the deciduous plantings.

I was unaccustomed to the climate in this mountain valley; so I proceeded rather slowly, trying a few new plants each year to see how they would stand up to the very hot summers, September downpours, and a brief but sharp winter when there may be three feet of snow for a month or more. In late February primroses and dog's tooth violets burst into full flower the moment the melting snow uncovers them. We are trying out camellias, and young plants of some thirty different varieties are growing in a nursery bed in the shade of a group of beech trees. If, as seems likely, they do well, they will form the main evergreen planting in the shadier parts of the valley.

One of the charms of gardening in Northern Italy is that you can keep your garden in flower until December. Once you are above the fog belt which, for weeks on end through the winter, seems to shroud Milan and Turin, and indeed all the valley of the Po, the sunny autumns prolong themselves until the turn of the year and you can make a garden bright with pansies, floribunda roses and, in particular, the Korean chrysanthemums. Farther north, in France, Switzerland and England, these last will look so sodden and discouraged by late October that you eventually decide they are not for the open garden; but often in Turin or Verona I found gardens brightly massed with their yellows and creams, oranges, pinks and reds until mid-December.

The town of Turin has its own rather austere charm. The great curve of the Po breaks a rectangular street plan and across the river you see the " hill," a small range of thickly-wooded eminences dotted with villas, many of them of the late eighteenth and early nineteenth century. Piedmontese architecture and decoration of that period looked for inspiration towards Paris rather than the south, but they have an Italian exuberance of

colour and form. Without the wealth and the means to produce
the exquisite materials and craftsmanship of their French models,
Piedmontese craftsmen made enchanting use of painted furniture
and painted decorations. The Chinese taste, for instance, came
late to Turin and you may find many houses whose reception
rooms are decorated with a late Louis XVI *chinoiserie* in brilliant
blues and yellows, lacquer reds and acid greens. The House of
Savoy, whose capital it was, built a series of extravagant palaces
and country houses, Stupinigi, Raconigi, Veneria and Moncalieri
as well as the royal palace in Turin itself; now parts of the city,
particularly along the banks of the Po, have the sober elegance
of a townscape by Belotto.

A new park beautifully planted along the river bank will
extend this urbane landscape and increase the open spaces of a
town which is growing rapidly in size and population. In the
centre of the town whose open spaces are, in the main, severely
arcaded piazzas lacking trees or gardens, the municipality take
every opportunity to plant flowers very much in the old-
fashioned nineteenth-century manner but impeccably well done
and with a great deal of invention. In front of the main station
with its Victorian-Turkish facade there is a square with a few
fine trees and a great fountain jet. Here formal pyramids of
foxgloves are set out in the grass, followed by Canterbury bells
or preceded by tulips in continuations of colour carefully thought
out and different each season. The first cleomes I saw were in
Turin, decorating a traffic roundabout, and even lamp-posts,
well mossed round, are turned in summer into twenty-foot
columns dripping with begonias.

One garden in which I worked on the " hill " near Moncalieri
gave me a great deal of pleasure. This was at the Villa Silvio
Pellico, named after the nineteenth-century poet whose home it
was. To reach the house you drive up under magnificent cedars
and libocedrus set in an immaculate sward of " Monza grass,"
that fine agrostis which grows thickly enough to make a lawn
impervious to weeds. The main block of the house, of tawny
orange stucco, has the good simple proportions of the late

eighteenth century, and there is a rambling wing and a chapel in 1830 " gothick " added. This part of the house is shaded by fine old conifers and a vast paulownia at whose foot a fine Chinese stone Buddha sits in contemplation. The lawn in front of the house stops at the edge of the hill which falls sheer away to the flatness of the plain, hazy in the sunlight.

When I first saw this garden, a steep bank beyond the lawn gave on to a very ugly sloping kitchen garden with badly-sited cold frames and many diagonal paths. To replace all this I devised a simple series of horizontal levels bordered by hornbeam hedges, in order to make a garden which would be interesting seen from above but which would not distract too much from the distant view. For this reason and to simplify the problems of maintenance I used water lavishly on each different level to make a connected series of simple stone-edged pools reflecting the sky. Once I was quite clear in my mind what I wanted to do about this part of the garden, we went ahead, levelled the ground, and built the pools, the low retaining walls and the steps. We even planted the hornbeam hedges before tackling the difficult problem of how to handle the steep bank and link the upper level to the new garden. I had to contrive a staircase that would drop some twenty feet and I had very little space into which to fit it. Eventually I made a very simple double staircase in three flights, starting outwards from the centre at the top and meeting again at the bottom. The steps are stone, with risers into the classical Roman profile. I colour-washed the stone-capped retaining walls and parapets in the same tawny orange as the house. Jasmine and trachelospermum will eventually cover them and the cypresses, bay laurel and box bushes planted on either side and in the central well will soften the severity of the architecture and, I hope, make the whole composition quiet and unassuming.

Farther east, near Verona, I rearranged the garden setting of a great villa on the foothills looking out over the plain of the Veneta. Here, to reach the Villa Musella, you drive up a mile-long avenue of great cypresses which zigzag up the terraced hillside between wheat fields and vineyards. At the end of the avenue stand superb eighteenth-century gate piers below the high wall of the terrace garden. Skirting the wall, you drive through a wood of *Magnolia grandiflora*, trees fifty to sixty feet high with their glossy leaves, brown-felted underneath and great waxy, lemon-scented flowers. This noble wood is all the more unexpected since between the trunks you see the nearby mountains, snow-capped for six months of the year.

The villa, when at length you reach it, offers a series of architectural surprises. The entrance façade is nineteenth-century Gothic, decorated with niches and bland, life-size statues of anonymous medieval heroes, their empty stare directed across the wooded valley of tulip trees to the mountains beyond. Turning a corner you pass in front of the east side of the house, a low and distinguished sixteenth-century stone façade. The south side offers only a bleak stucco building of about 1890 while on the west side which faces the main garden terrace, the building becomes a fantasy of pink and white and yellow stucco with mock-Oriental, horseshoe-arched windows and a chapel belfry designed as a minaret. Nor is this all. Close by stands a huge, ivy-covered cube surmounted by a dome of wire netting. This is a sixteenth-century aviary designed by San-Michele with a severely classical Doric arcade. You have to imagine this aviary separated from the house by a dreary stretch of gravel and dominating once again a wide view of the plain. Beside it is the formal garden which extends outwards from the house and back towards the cypress avenue. This garden is very simply arranged with rectangles of grass and some large cedars and monkey puzzles.

This extraordinary mixture of architectural styles and the bleakness of this flat garden set high above the plain were rather daunting. The first thing to do was eliminate the yards of gravel which made the whole scene so arid, whether under the hot summer sun or in the long cold winter. This was fairly easy, as I could re-adjust the proportions of lawn and gravel, but even when this was done, the villa and the aviary remained unrelated and somehow uncomfortable in each other's presence. Finally I decided that I would be guided by the volume and the superb proportions of the aviary, and that it should be the dominant theme for the composition. I achieved this by applying the principle that you cannot have too much of a good thing: so why not double the effect of the aviary by making a very large formal pool to reflect it? Although this pool is ninety feet long by twenty feet wide and has a band a yard wide of cut stone round it on which I have set out great terracotta jars holding century-old lemon trees, it appears none too large in its setting. The wire-netting dome, or cupola, of the aviary suggested still another idea. I would put floodlights in each corner of the building and so at night make the dome look like a floating bubble of light and it too would be caught and reflected in the pool.

You may consider this kind of work, these alterations to existing gardens, as perhaps of little importance; but I find it absorbing. I like to find an odd house and its garden with something basically wrong, some major error in design, perhaps something incomplete or some mistaken alteration. Indeed I find these problems more stimulating than a blank canvas, where I might have an entire composition of house, garden and surrounding landscape to organise from scratch.

Somewhere in a spoiled or incomplete or even plain ugly garden lurks the *genius loci*. Like the detective in a thriller, I have to decide from the data surrounding me, which are the right clues to follow up, what I can suppress and what veils the true character of that particular place. Sometimes, to clear away a few trees or shrubberies will change the whole atmosphere of a garden; sometimes there is some basic fault in the shape of the ground which, because it was not clearly seen in the beginning, has defeated every subsequent effort to organise the garden. These misfit gardens are almost always of nineteenth or twentieth-century origin. Until the end of the eighteenth century, gardens however simple, generally have a just relation to the houses they were made for. But later "improvements" may have destroyed the original proportions and frequently, when I start to reshape an old garden, an old tree, the foundations of a wall or the relics of an overgrown hedge will indicate that I am rediscovering the original composition.

In Italy every town and house—I might also say every hillside —is a palimpsest of two or three thousand years of building and decay. Each style and period is overlaid by its successor. One would have to be singularly insensitive to the possibilities of one's craft if one failed to reassemble and reformulate from the thousand hints and indications that wait within the range of one's eyes.

CHAPTER XI

The South of France

I first came to the Mediterranean in 1928, waking up in the train early on an April morning to see King René's castle at Tarascon, the rushing waters of the Rhône and the shimmering gold-greens of poplar trees. I had not long left school and must, I suppose, have absorbed something of my classical education to find myself excited at coming at last to the sea on which Ulysses and Aeneas had wandered. I had no precise idea as to where I would go and after passing St. Maxime I was prepared to get out at any place that looked pleasing. It was the ticket collector who suggested Beaulieu. I stayed there a month greedily absorbing the reality of the Mediterranean scene, and seeing and touching plants I had known only through my reading. I used to walk to Villefranche and Eze, and around Cap Ferrat, once or twice taking the tramway which ran along the coast road from Nice to Monte Carlo. In those days the Riviera was still mainly a winter resort. People installed themselves in their villas for three months and Cap Ferrat, like Cannes, was mainly colonised by the garden-loving English. I soon found my way into some of these gardens; "Les Bruyéres" where the aged Duke of Connaught had made a collection of rare trees; and the three Italianate villas "Sylvia", "Rosemary" and "Maryland" built early in the century by Harold Peto very much in the Florentine manner and each with an elaborate and beautiful garden.

When I went back to garden on the Riviera in 1947 all this

had changed. Restrictions had eliminated the English colony, their villas were either bombed or deserted or had been bought by the French, the Belgians or the Swiss. The South of France is now a summer resort and new gardens must be mainly designed for summer. People open their houses for ten days at Christmas and perhaps for as long at Easter, but the real season runs from June to September. This makes gardening an exercise in prolongation. Spring comes early to the south with almond blossom and *Jasminum primulinum* in February, the peach trees flower in March with *Iris unguicularis*, the tazetta narcissus, Roman hyacinths, rainbow-coloured anemones and, on the acid soil behind Cannes, the woods are a thicket of mimosa. April and May see the flush of roses: white and yellow banksias, the climbing " La Follette " and " Garibaldi," " Safrano " and the rosy-apricot " General Schablikine " which makes huge bushes and seems to flower afresh every six weeks throughout the year. In sheltered corners at Beaulieu and Mentone May brings the great purple vigandias, the paulownias and the rarer blue jacaranda into flower, and colour-washed walls flame with the scarlets and pinks of pelargonium and sheets of the difficult magenta of the ordinary bougainvillaea. After June the problem of flower colour becomes more acute, but lantanas in white, yellow, orange and pink flower on steadily, and agapanthus and *Plumbago capensis* give a welcome note of blue. In acid soil the lagerstroemia is a most useful flowering shrub for August and September.

You can grow a large range of plants along this coast where soil and climate vary considerably every few yards; but nowadays there are all too few enlightened amateurs and you have to go far to find an interesting collection. Up at Grasse which is degrees cooler than the littoral, indeed too cool for the blue spikes of echium or even orange trees, the Vicomte de Noailles has a spring garden full of Japanese cherries, iris and espaliered Judas trees. In a small sheltered valley garden on the Cap d'Antibes Basil Leng grows tree paeonies and rare South African bulbs and nelumbiums; and on Cap Ferrat M. Marnier-Lapostolle has a garden with an enormous collection of aquatics and cacti.

At Beaulieu Doctor Arpad Plesch has filled his hot terraced hillside with exotic fruit-bearing trees from all over the world; even *papaya*, the pawpaw, fruits here although a plastic cover stands ready to hand in case of a cold spell. The local nurserymen serve an undemanding clientele and content themselves with a limited range of plants, most of which they import from the lower Loire or from Italy. They appear unwilling to bother much with propagation, so that when I am making plant lists I use the catalogues of growers in Angers and Pistoia. I know that from these two places I will get any plants out of the common run. In the hills grow many kinds of cistus and lavender and all the scented plants of the *maquis*, but like the indigenous myrtle— so useful for making a scented flowering hedge—none of these can be bought.

All this makes garden planting difficult and slow, and I have had in the last ten years to establish a kind of network between gardens from one end of the coast to the other. I get the gardeners in each garden I have worked in to propagate everything of interest in their particular garden, so that I can arrange the exchange of plants from one to another.

The first garden I tackled after the war was high above Cannes next to the Observatory on the peak of a windswept hill of volcanic rock, with only a thin skin of dry and slightly acid soil, but with superb views over the whole coast from the Cap d'Antibes across the islands and the bay of Cannes to the sharp peaks of the Esterel Mountains in the west. The small and rather complicated house hung over a series of small and meaningless terraces dropping steeply down to the surrounding woods of maritime pines with a silvery undergrowth of the common mimosa, *Acacia dealbata*. As Arthur Sachs, the new owner, was remodelling the house, I was able to have something to say about its external appearance and its immediate surroundings. We gave it a very simple, creamy-white façade with pale grey shutters, and the plainest of wrought-iron balustrades for the upstairs terraces. I planted the whole of the sunny side of the house with my favourite " Mermaid " rose and wistarias. Below them, some four feet above the garden, runs a stone-paved terrace and here, in a niche between two windows, I placed an eighteenth-century porphyry urn on a pedestal which serves as a fountain to suggest coolness in the heat of summer. This terrace and a covered loggia in the angle between salon and dining-room make an outdoor living-room with simple garden furniture and a row of orange and lemon trees in large terracotta pots as well as dozens of small flower-pots filled with salmon and white geraniums or white anthemis. Below the terrace I made a stretch of lawn ending in a four feet myrtle hedge above a high retaining wall. This wall, some eight feet high, replaces the three or four stepped terraces which formerly fell away from the house. To level the ground I had to bring in truckloads of sandy alluvial soil from the valley of the Siagne ten miles away, so that this is the only place in the garden where there is more than a few inches of soil. How well plants can grow in this light loam you may see from the umbrella pines in the photograph which was taken two years after they were planted (between pp. 144-5.)

This is a garden which commands a rather overpowering view. You look out over the green lawn between the trunks of the umbrella pines, carefully placed to divide the view into two or three separate scenes. What flower colour there is lies below the retaining walls or away to one side of the house and even so these blues, whites, a little lemon yellow and a great deal of grey foliage seem bright enough in this setting of sea and sky. My first care was to transplant half a dozen very large olive trees and set them in a groundwork of lavender, *Cineraria maritima*, black-eyed milky-white dimorphotheca, garden pinks, *Felicia amelloides* (*Agathaea coelestis*), agapanthus, and echiums. For later summer I have planted the powder blue *Ceanothus* "Indigo," sky blue *Plumbago capensis*, white and yellow lantana and we supplement these with white and blue-mauve petunias. Only where there is no competition with the view did I allow the strong reds of geraniums, some salvia species, and the various scarlet orange and pink climbing bignonias, known as *B. buccinatoria*, *B. tweediana*, *B. capensis* and *B. ricasoleana*. High hedges of clipped cypress flank the garden and provide a frame for the informality of the planting, while at key points individual cypresses make vertical accents. Nowadays it has become the fashion to clip such cypresses each year into needle-like spires sometimes thirty or forty feet high. This is an expensive amusement but it does give a good " finish " to a well-kept garden.

The swimming pool is set well down below a high retaining wall and surrounded by cypress hedges. Thus, although close to the house, you cannot see it since I do not usually like to set a formal pool against a seascape. The whole garden, in fact, is a series of small terraced rectangles supporting and framing the house which rises on its eminence out of the surrounding pine wood. Under the pines I had reinforced the undergrowth of " wild " mimosa with some of the better varieties, such as *Acacia motteana* and " Clair de Lune ", which, with their silvery blue foliage, and their mounds of scented fluffy blossom, prolong the flowering season from January until the end of May.

We may drive down to the Cap d'Antibes, a rocky finger pointing south into the Mediterranean, its structure of great geological and hence ecological confusion. Here, formerly, among the wind-blown pines, stood just one hotel and the Château de la Garoupe, a large property where that family of good gardeners, the Maclarens, had built a house and made a large but simple garden in the aromatic scrub. Gradually other people acquired land and built houses, each, I must say, uglier than the last, until now the Cape is so built up that the smallest patch of barren rocky shore fetches an astronomical sum.

Eastwards towards Nice, along the edge of the sea, the glorious view of the snow-capped Alps will be hidden in a very few years by a continuous line of ugly apartment houses. But once past Mont Boron, beyond Nice, you come to the unspoilable bay of Villefranche and the more settled air of Beaulieu and Cap Ferrat. On the Moyenne Corniche and overlooking Cap Ferrat and the bay of Villefranche is the Villa Leopolda which I have already mentioned. Here, amongst other things I was asked to design a small and secluded swimming pool so that its owners and their guests could have a quiet retreat away from the grandeur and formality of the house. The great terraces and monumental cypress-lined stairway of the villa, and the wide panorama on the sea side of the house, are so large in scale that a pool here would have been irrelevant and even impertinent. On the entrance side of the house a tank 200 feet long and thirty wide with a curtain of great cypresses and urns, statues and fountains would have been just as monumental and unsuitable a neighbour for a small pool. This is a hilltop garden and these, for all their wide views, have one great disadvantage. When you leave the house you have always to go downhill and then you have to climb back again. For this reason I wanted to make a pool more or less on a level with the house and not too far from it.

A few yards from the main house there was a gardener's cottage which had been turned into a guest-house; an unpretentious, colour-washed building with the usual roof of Roman tiles. The end which lay farthest from the main house had no windows and was perched on a steep slope above an olive orchard. Dividing up a ground-floor room to make dressing-rooms, I pierced a door through this blank wall which now opens into a tile-roofed loggia built across the whole end of the little house. This loggia in turn gives directly on to a small oval pool which measures thirty-four feet along its greatest length, parallel to the house, and about twenty-seven feet across in the other direction. It is lined with blue tiles and surrounded by a paving of small orange-red bricks. High walls, continued out from the house repeat the curve of the pool for about twenty feet on each side; and a metal *tonnelle* planted with vines repeats the same curve and casts a dappled purple shadow over the brick paving.

As the pool was to be level with the house and the ground sloped sharply away there was little excavation to be done. But I had to construct a fifteen feet high curving retaining wall on the side away from the building to bring the ground level up and complete the general oval form where the wing walls leave off. This wall is set some eight feet beyond the paved surround to the pool which leaves a wide bed for planting. I planted this bed with grey-leaved shrubs which are clipped into roughly rounded forms. Atriplex, teucrium, lavender, santolina and othonnopsis make cushions of blue-grey and silver-green which repeat the rounded shapes of the olive trees beyond and below. Here, on a site which has so many splendid views, there is no view; only a shimmering wall of grey-green foliage and the pale sky.

On this part of the coast we are again on the limestone rock where although mimosas grow with difficulty we are away from the mistral. At Eze the tangerine trees are famous for the quality of their fruit; against the purplish rock bougainvillaeas, geraniums and bignonias swear brightly at each other in every clashing pink, purple, scarlet, crimson and orange; and in sheltered corners the huge lettuce-green fronds of banana trees show above the high garden walls.

From Cap Ferrat we could drive up to the Moyenne Corniche and then down again through a wild valley so clothed with pines that it looks like a Sung painting, to come to Cap d'Ail and a large and rather unusual garden. Cap d'Ail is a steep rocky hillside between the Lower Corniche and the sea. Half-way down the hill the railway emerges between two tunnels and a steep and narrow lane goes down from the main road to the sea between large and ugly villas, all built at the turn of the century when Cap d'Ail was a fashionable suburb of Monte Carlo, full of Russian grandees. Here, down near the sea, is a rather uninteresting villa bought by Fanny Heldy, now Madame Boussac, at the height of her operatic fame. After the last war Monsieur Boussac acquired the large garden of the nearby Eden Hotel with its asphalt paths, cement balustrades made to imitate logs, and old-fashioned lamp standards which lit up the winding paths which led down through rocks and pine trees to the station. He also took over a long, narrow strip between road and railway, in order to connect these gardens with his own house. To the Eden garden he was able to add two other large adjoining gardens, one with a ruined four-storied villa at its highest point, built on a balustraded terrace over an artificial grotto from which a spring feeds a series of pools and a little watercourse, all designed in the florid manner of the turn of the century. It was in 1947 that I was asked to look at this jigsaw puzzle of properties and see how best to garden them. At first I thought it all chaotic, very ugly and unmanageable, and for almost two years I declined to deal with it and told my client why. But after several visits and as many refusals I began to " see " the area and its qualities, and with the help of a sympathetic head gardener and six men I set to work and spent three years developing this rather extra-ordinary site. Extraordinary for me, because I decided that it would be impossible to destroy the period air without under-taking earth-works on the largest scale. I saw that the style of the garden suited the general atmosphere and that, instead of trying to eliminate this old-fashioned idiom I would do better to intensify it. Further, as the property was only used around Easter, I decided to cram it with sheets of all the bright flowers which are traditionally associated with the Riviera spring.

Let us start one April morning from the villa down by the sea and make an imaginary tour of the garden. We cross a new bridge over the road from the first floor of the house into a small and steeply terraced garden that used to be full of vegetables. Here, to avoid any major construction work and to give character, I planted fifty or sixty cypresses of heights varying from fifteen to forty feet, some in groups and others singly. Clipped each year into sharp points like exclamation marks, these dark spires make the main theme for what was before a formless patch of hillside. The cypresses are underplanted with sheets of the bright gentian blue echium and the low retaining walls are covered with the violet blue pea-flowered kennedya, blue *Felicia amelloides* (*Agathaea coelestis*), the blue Swan River daisy, white dimor-photheca with its dark blue splash on each petal and, next to the path, masses of blue cinerarias. On the steeply rising slope behind the cypresses a group of mimosa, *Acacia cyanophylla*, has grown rapidly to hide a high wall, which supports the twisting roadway, with its domes of silvery blue foliage and yellow flowers. Once across the bridge the path turns sharp left through this little garden and for half a mile follows the embankment between the railway and the road below. Here we have planted hundreds of young pines, pittosporum and rosemary to make a simple *maquis*. Where retaining walls hold up the path, they are covered with trailing sheets of mesembryanthemum of different kinds, including a very dwarf variety (which I have not been able to identify) with minute fleshy foliage which in April covers itself with trailing sheets of tiny pink flowers. Eventually the railway disappears into a tunnel and the path turns and climbs to the right along the foot of a steep pine wood intersected by winding paths—the so-called " park " of the Eden Hotel. Here among rocky outcrops which bake in summer in this particularly hot corner of the coast, we divided and replanted by the thousand the old tufts of aloes which had been neglected for years. I must admit to not knowing their botanical names, being happy enough to see four or five different kinds of flower spikes in orange, scarlet and copper every spring.

Climbing up the hill on this hot April morning, we reach the main part of the Eden garden. I had to reduce by a yard or two the width of the paths which wind around and up and down through the wood. Fifteen feet is all very well for public use but looks rather bleak in a private garden. Then I had cut down a whole host of overgrown pittosporum and agaves and other uninteresting shrubs so as to expose the beauty of the twisted pine trunks and the green canopy they make overhead. But sharp changes in level, and the knobbly little retaining walls which held up the paths as they corkscrewed up and down the hillside and its rocky outcrops, still looked far too complicated and fussy. The only way to calm it all down was to plant very simply and on the largest scale. So, section by section, we trenched the whole garden wherever it was possible, added enormous quantities of slow-acting sheep manure, and repaired or renewed the water pipes. I had first to try and conceal the road and the vast and ugly façade of the hotel at the top of the site. This I did by planting eucalyptus or *Cupressus macrocarpa* wherever I could find room along the upper length of the garden. Then, to make the wood gayer in the spring, I filled each clearing among the pines with groups of mimosa *Acacia cyanophylla*, *Acacia* " Clair de Lune ", *Acacia motteana* and half a dozen others. Now from February until the end of April they flower and flower and fill the wood with their strange and lovely scent.

I had to treat this garden as a wild garden. I did not wish to add any heavy tropical foliage to the fine needles of the pines, and the work entailed by intensive Riviera flower-gardening over the whole four acres of this wood would be more than could possibly be managed. But first I had to cover the bare ground beneath pines and mimosas. I chose simple perennials and sub-shrubs which could be renewed from cuttings every few years, planting them in wide-spreading patches, often as much as sixty feet by twenty, of a single variety. For silver I used *Cineraria maritima* and the more finely-cut and whiter foliage of the variety called locally " Le Diamant," as well as ordinary lavender. I used too the green leaved lavender, *Lavandula semidentata*, which seems to produce its violet-black flowers every six weeks if you clip it over after flowering, and also a single-flowered oak-leaved geranium known locally as " geranium sauvage ". This is a particularly lovely plant with deep green foliage and deep scarlet or clear scarlet-pink flowers without a hint of blue. I also used large sheets of *Iris unguicularis*, which usually starts flowering in December to become a carpet of lavender blue in mid-March, as well as the common purple flag iris and several very large patches of zonal pelargoniums. These are grown afresh from cuttings every second year and here I have mixed them using whites, pinks, salmons, scarlets, crimsons and magentas for their bright sparkling in the dancing lights and shadows of the pine trees.

As we leave the wood and come to the more intensively gardened part of the property we pass through a wide planting of coronilla, in April brilliantly yellow against the curious tawny yellow clumps of medicago. Then the garden becomes more sophisticated with a series of pools in elaborate artificial rockwork. There must have been a mason, who specialised in this work sixty years ago, along the coast. He worked with surprising skill and

The figure of Neptune and a semi-circular fountain pool
terminate the cross-axis of a garden near Turin constructed
entirely in stone, water and gravel with hornbeam and box
hedges. The only upkeep involved will be an annual hedge-
clipping and an occasional raking of the paths

This is the main axis of the garden shown on the preceding
page. The flight of steps which replace a steep and high
bank are designed to suit the early nineteenth-century villa
which lies so far back on the higher level that only the upper
floors are visible. The robust detailing of the steps emphasises
the deliberately simplified handling of a formal composition
in a neo-classical manner

The same garden seen from above immediately after planting.
The surrounding hornbeam hedges will eventually be kept
at eight foot high. The garden replaces an ugly slope given
over to cabbages and cold frames and acts as an introduction or
foreground to a wide view over the valley of the Po. To fit
in with an existing cross slope the garden extension to the left
of the central pool is higher, while that on the right, with its
Neptune fountain, is several steps lower

At the Creux de Genthod a lawn and yew hedges replace a former walled kitchen garden which blocked the view from the south side of the house across the Lake of Geneva to Mount Blanc. The formal rose garden replaces a long grass slope which ran dully down from house to lawn

a good deal of taste to build grottoes, cliffs, waterfalls and groups of rocks. He made these with wire netting and moulded his coloured cement over it with such geological versimilitude that the results are surprisingly effective. Here his work forms a backbone for an extravangantly coloured hillside—orange with dimorphotheca, gazanias, marigolds and nemesias; blue with cinerarias, violas and agathaea; pink, mauve and purple with double stocks, *Primula malacoides*, *Primula obconica*, cyclamens, bachelor buttons, ivy-leaved geraniums and more cinerarias. The air is heavy with the scent of the wild white freesias which have made dense colonies and invade even the gravel paths; and in wet places near the pools there are clumps of white arum lilies. The violet pea-flowered kennedya from Australia tumbles over the rock-work, threading its way through pink " La Follette " roses and the yellow *Jasminum primulinum*. And on one of the few level patches oranges, lemons and grapefruit make a little orchard of rounded standard trees above a carpet of blue and yellow pansies.

This garden is broken and shaded by a rather mixed collection of trees. There are palms, the large-leaved Japanese pittosporum, a few olives and bay trees and a very large grevillea. Together with the large rocks and broken ground these make a complex pattern of light and shade. As the garden relies entirely on annual flowers, I vary these each year, nor do I attempt a carefully worked out colour scheme. The patches of colour are large and set out in drifts as much as fifty feet long, woven one into another as the lie of the ground suggests.

This tangle of flowers lies at the foot of a twenty foot cliff of artificial rockwork clothed with bougainvillaea, roses and jasmine and topped by a balustrade. Above is a flat sanded terrace decorated with two olive trees and a few carefully placed cypresses, and at one end is a small summer house with a tiled roof crowned by a pigeon-cote. From its wide windows you can see the flower garden below falling sheer away to the Mediterranean. This is really a freak garden, only interesting as being perhaps the last of its kind.

By contrast, a little farther back along the coast at Eze-sur-Mer, I made a swimming pool which I had to think of as a severe exercise in landscape design. The Villa Isoletta is a house of no particular architectural distinction, built on a narrow and precipitous strip of ground perhaps fifty feet wide hemmed in between the railway and the sea. Formerly the only access to the house was by a footpath across the railway tracks and a steep flight of steps down to the front door at first floor level. The ground floor gives on to a wide paved terrace shaded by an enormous and beautifully spreading pine tree, while the garden proper stretches away to one side for two hundred yards in a series of narrow terraces. Opposite the house and connected to the mainland by a narrow causeway is the islet which gives the house its name, a hump of rock covered with stunted pines. About a hundred and fifty feet long and twenty-five wide, it rises from the sea to a sheer rock face about twenty feet high at its farther end.

When, some years ago, the Duchesse d'Acquarone bought the villa her first thought was to make a swimming pool on the island, a project which we let drop for several years, partly because it was more important to tackle first the problem of access to the house, and partly because of the difficulty of making a pool in this inaccessible spot. However, a few years later a plague of jellyfish, which made bathing in the sea hazardous and disagreeable, decided us to build a swimming pool at the highest point of the islet and three hundred yards from the nearest place to which we could bring building materials by truck. By cantilevering the paving-surround out and overhanging the sea, we were able to contrive a pool about thirty-six feet long by about twenty feet at the widest part. The shape was dictated by the site, and the slight overhang which we were obliged to make in order to be able to walk round the pool helps to keep out the fishermen and picnickers who cannot resist a dangerous scramble round the rocks below.

This was the first and only time I had to make a pool with the sea all round and the horizon as the dominating theme. It was like designing a pool for the deck of a liner, and it was thus that I decided to treat the problem. The sparse and distorted trees, struggling to live in the arid rock, lay behind the pool and I could not count on any effective and picturesque accidents of planting or of light and shade to help me. Here, with only the sea and sky, colour too presented a problem: a blue or green pool would look wonderful in clear, sunny weather, but, whenever the sea was not bright blue, strong colour would look badly out of key. Finally I decided to line the pool with pure white cement to which the sea water that is constantly pumped through the pool gives a greenish cast. Now, whatever the weather and the colour of the sea and sky, the pool faithfully takes on the same tonalities. For the same reason the paving round the pool had to be as pale as possible so as to harmonise with the pinky cream of the limestone rock and not, in this situation, look too elegant. It was this last factor which decided me against a paving of cut stone and in favour of fifteen-inch squares of pre-cast concrete made of fine pea-gravel and pale ochre-red cement. Before each slab was quite dry it was brushed down with a wire brush and washed so that the aggregate of fine pebbles was exposed. This makes a good non-slip surface, and the general colour tones in with the surrounding rock, just as the water in the pool matches the sea and sky. So limited was I for space that on two sides of the pool I had no room to build a parapet wall; so, just as on the deck of a yacht, I set slim white iron posts supporting horizontally stretched white nylon ropes.

This pool worked out so well that the next year we took advantage of another hollow in the rock, this time under the pine trees, to contrive dressing-rooms built below ground level. The flat roof, paved and railed in like the swimming pool, makes an additional and shady sitting place.

From Eze it is only a few minutes to Monte Carlo, that strange architectural eruption opposite the old Grimaldi castle on the rock of Monaco. The Casino and the buildings surrounding the " Tapis Vert " form an architectural group which must be unique, except perhaps for those nineteenth-century boom-towns which moulder on the fringes of the Brazilian jungle. At one point I was asked to take the Monte Carlo parks and gardens in hand. This was an entertaining offer since the problem was unique. The gardens were laid out in the 1880s strictly in accordance with French landscape practice of that period. They consist of a symmetrical central rectangular perspective with small informal parks on either side, set out with serpentine asphalt paths which curl around lawns hollowed in the middle and mounded out towards the path edges. "Corbeilles", raised round or oval beds, are scattered indiscriminately over these lawns and I found many planting plans of the period showing various mosaic patterns devised for two or three annual changes of bedding-out plants. The peculiarity of these gardens is that in the original plans only evergreen trees and shrubs had been admitted. The idea of making this rule was to ensure that the gardens would look entirely exotic and tropical as indeed in their peculiar way they must have done when they were extravagantly planted with cannas, caladiums and all the other tropical and sub-tropical bedding-out and "dot" plants of the period.

But meanwhile seventy years had slid past, the motor car was invented, parks and gardens were nibbled into to make parking space, new buildings in later and less baroque styles sprung up along the skyline, trees decayed and were not replaced, slightly raised beds grew conical from yearly accretions of soil, the original tribes of gardeners had been heavily cut down—in short, listlessly directed, the gardens had degenerated. Like the rest of the Côte d'Azur Monte Carlo enjoyed until 1914 a clientele who came for three months to live in the greatest extravagance and luxury. The rich still come from all over the world but they stay three days instead of three months, while the "season" lasts from Christmas to October. Besides the rich, thousands of tourists who want to see the scene of these legendary past splendours and have a modest gamble, pour in perhaps just for a few hours. To transform this decayed layout into a pleasure garden for this new world, was a temptation for a garden designer, although a few months later the whole intention and my rather controversial projects were liquidated when the then administration of the oddly named " Société des Bains de Mer " which owns and runs Monte Carlo was replaced by a less adventurous management. I had barely started a preliminary tidying up before the *status quo ante* was reinstalled. As it was, each dead or dying tree which I managed to remove was the subject of angry comment in the local papers, so that I had to get this part of the work done early in the morning when nobody was about.

Although little actual work was carried out, I enjoyed the most interesting part of the job which was the thinking-through of the problem. I decided that, since few people stayed for more than three or four days, Monte Carlo should always appear *en fête* and have the glamour and gaiety of a Coney Island de luxe. The peculiarity of the original planting gave the central complex of gardens an air of belonging nowhere; the impression one has is scarcely even Mediterranean, nor is the mixture of palms and huge ficus trees reminiscent of anything else. It seemed to me that I should have, by my planting, to " place " these gardens firmly in the Mediterranean scene and furthermore, in Provence; and that people who came from more inclement climates should enjoy mimosas and orange blossom, magnolias, oleanders, roses and all the flowering climbers which do so well along this coast. There would have been umbrella pines and cypresses, olive trees, geraniums and iris, freesias, violets and carnations, anemones and indeed every plant I could think of which might give the visitor at any time of the year a concentrated impression of colour and scent. He should have the pleasure of seeing growing the flowers he knew only from the florist's shop.

The main feature of the Monte Carlo gardens is the central lawn running uphill from the Casino, flanked on each side by a line of palm trees long past their best, alternating with the uninteresting and ugly sterculias, which have been wrongly pruned for years so that they are like caricatures of trees. I planned to suppress the lawn which lies ploughed up and fallow for months each year and is sown just in time to look green for Christmas. With it would go the mean beds of beetroot-coloured cyclamen which are supposed to enliven it from Christmas until March. In place of all this I proposed an illuminated cascade with a constantly changing pattern of water jets set between umbrella pines and *Magnolia grandiflora.* In front of the Casino I planned to transform the grass oval known as the "Camembert" into an elaborate fountain designed in the same bastard-baroque manner as the Hotel de Paris and the Casino itself. The small park to the west of the central vista I saw as a Provençal garden where flowering trees, shrubs and bulbs would give a year-long procession of colour and perfume. The valley garden to the east with its watercourse and pools would lend itself to a more exotic treatment with palms and cycads, aralias, phormiums, arums, Victoria Regina water lilies and all the tropical-looking foliage plants I could collect and make grow there. Still farther to the west where the ground falls steeply from the Casino to the railway station, which with the railway line itself will shortly be moved entirely, I planned car parks so as to leave the central vista clear, and in front of the Casino a considerable grove of umbrella pines and an amphitheatre for open-air spectacles, theatre and concerts. This programme seemed to me a logical garden interpretation of the theme of pleasure which is the curious and, perhaps as with Las Vegas, unique reason for Monte Carlo's existence.

I suppose it is inevitable in a life busy with garden-making that, as the years go past and the variety and range of work increases, there must be a certain percentage of jobs which are started and left unfinished, or planned and never executed. When I was young and just starting I must admit to counting these as personal failures. I either resented or regretted them, since either my pride or my pocket or both were hurt. Now I have come to regard them as exercises. I cannot feel impoverished if I have studied a problem, whatever the financial or physical result. Perhaps I have found that their solution has enriched my skill and enlarged my experience, and if the work has not been carried out I am none the poorer. Or it may be that I failed to find an answer to a problem and, when I look back, I think that this is because

I have failed to understand the client and his wishes or—and this can happen too—I have not been in sympathy with either. On these cases—since one can only be pliable within certain limits—I look with indifference if not relief, knowing that had I continued with them the misunderstanding would have increased and been reflected inevitably in the garden. Indeed there are in existence quite a few uneasy garden compositions whose awkwardness and lack of harmony exactly demonstrate disagreement, compromises and lack of mutual understanding between their owners and myself. Finally, I have learned to judge at a first contact whether or not I shall be able to carry a garden through. If I can neither give nor receive the comprehension that will be needed, I prefer to go no further. I would advise any garden designer to defend his point of view if he really knows what he wants to do with a given site. In some cases, feeling prodigal of invention, you may be able to produce a whole series of sketch-plans of alternative ideas; but I have found that these will usually throw any but a very expert client into confusion so that it is better to limit oneself to two only. A client may think he knows better than you, and indeed he may; but then this will be no job for you and you would do well to abandon it at once, before you find yourself doing things against your own judgment and the whole affair ends by your client telling his friends that all his mistakes are your fault. However attractive a problem of design and composition may be, there may come a moment when one has to decide whether one will compromise and make concessions to a client's wishes against one's own judgment or give up. I have learned that the latter is the best procedure. One's name attached to a garden which is not as one would have wished it may possibly gain clients who saw nothing amiss with it; but it will just as surely lose you other clients with surer taste and judgment. This may sound all too easy but of course it is not, and that kind of assurance only develops after perhaps many years of stumbling, and with as many disappointments as successes.

CHAPTER XII

For the public eye

I suppose that your true gardener considers his gardening as a personal pleasure and private struggle although I never knew one who would not enjoy showing and sharing his successes. In the old days, even thirty years ago, local flower shows and neighbourly visits brought renown for a garden in a relatively limited circle. The head gardener on a great estate might be pundit and judge for miles around; it was he who had the means to acquire and try out new plants which gradually, by seed or cuttings, found their way from his four-walled kitchen gardens and ranges of glass into the nearby villages. But nowadays cars and aeroplanes, print, radios and television have begun to make gardens and flowers a mass entertainment on a huge scale.

Already in the seventeenth century certain royal gardens were designed to attract and impress large crowds. At Versailles, for instance, the French royal family lived, for the greater satisfaction of their subjects, a life almost entirely exposed to the public eye, playing cards, dining and dancing, even dying and giving birth under the eyes of anyone who cared to go and stare. Here Louis XIV and Le Nôtre planned the huge complex of gardens as a series of state rooms and galleries open to the sky, with " cabinets ", such as the " Salle du Bal de Madame de Bourgogne " and the " Labyrinth " (where Aesop's fables were illustrated by sculptured groups in gilded lead) as enclosed spaces for more exclusive entertainments. In the eighteenth century

German princelings too, aping the Bourbon manner, built vast but stodgier rococo palaces and gardens to impress their subjects who were sometimes half-ruined by the cost of these constructions.

The wealthy and well-connected tourist, in those days usually British, would have access to any garden he might wish to see and he might return to his own country seat with French or Italian statuary; or—on a visit abroad—he might lay out for his host a park in the English manner and so help to establish the fashion for English gardening which has persisted on the Continent until now. Later, shaken by the events of the last quarter of the eighteenth century, European royalty were to live more privately, nor were they any longer the only spenders of public monies. Many royal and other gardens and parks and hunting forests passed into public possession, and the garden owned by public authorities came into being.

The end of a developing architectural style, the absence of the personal taste, talent and idiosyncrasies of the individual patron, the beginnings of bureaucracy and the age of museums made the nineteenth century, after 1830, a period of recapitulation and reproduction; and there started from then on a style-less century. Old models made of new materials were moulded by the coarse processes of early methods of mass production. Cast iron replaced wrought; stucco and cement replaced stone, asphalt replaced paving; and even plants were selected and hybridised to produce colours as similar as possible to the newly-discovered aniline dyes. Now time and fashion have half-persuaded us that the products of the nineteenth century have both style and charm; but I see only a coarsening of forms, materials of inferior quality and a total lack of direction. Central Park, New York, is a stunted travesty of an English eighteenth-century park struggling to survive on the ancient and sterile rock of Manhattan Island. The Empress Eugenie's efforts to encourage the arts caused her to order lumpy copies of the most elaborate pieces of mid-eighteenth-century furniture. Sir Joseph Paxton, although a brilliant designer of cast-iron structures, made a series of heavy-handed gardens which combined the more obvious compositions of Le Nôtre and " Capability " Brown, while Nesfield and Sir Charles Barry worked with all too much gusto on garden themes in the manner of the Italian Renaissance. In Paris, Haussman picked up projects originally made by Percier and Fontaine for Napoleon and drove axially-planned boulevards relentlessly through the town in all directions, destroying thousands of beautiful houses built " entre cour et jardin ". Incidentally, this system of town housing where only a small proportion of a site was built on was one of the most delightful solutions for town planning ever devised. More happily, Haussmann planted his boulevards with trees which conceal the atrocious ugliness of the apartment houses built at that time.

Of the Paris public gardens, the Luxembourg and the Tuileries remain on the whole as they were designed for their royal owners. All the others, like the Bois de Boulogne, are French nineteenth-century versions of the *jardin anglais*, the " picturesque " eighteenth-century landscape, embellished with strips and circles of scarlet flowers and cafés and restaurants of glass and painted cast-iron lacework—nineteenth-century architectural symbols for pleasure.

As the world's supplier of manufactured goods, Western Europe grew richer and richer and surplus money found its way into the endowment of hospitals, universities, schools, art galleries and even gardens. Enormous glasshouses were added to Kew Gardens. Leopold II of Belgium constructed some eight acres of greenhouses at Laeken high enough to shelter fully grown palm trees and connected by long glazed corridors where you can still walk between palisades of ferns, fuchsias and climbing geraniums. Old botanical gardens belonging to Europe's universities, which had existed for centuries as workshops for a few savants, now splendidly enriched, began to draw visitors and create a new public of flower gazers.

The town of Ghent, thirty miles from Brussels, lies in an area of acid sandy soil and has long been a horticultural centre. In 1836 the flower growers of this town got together and founded the *Floralies de Gand*, a quinquennial exhibition of their skill as growers of *Azalea indica*, tuberous begonias and hot-house plants; and, I believe that, except for the war years, this exhibition has taken place every five years since its inception. Now housed in a permanent building, each show attracts more than a million visitors and for ten days endless crowds move slowly among a welter of forced azaleas in white, pink, salmon, scarlet, orange and crimson. There are huge specimens of these plants a hundred and more years of age which, they say, walk to the exhibition by themselves so often have they been on view. Each time I go I recognise a large teddy-bear, a sofa and an armchair made entirely of pink and salmon blooms, which grow more voluminous at every showing. Originally this was an exhibition for specialists and technicians; now it is a pilgrimage for millions who go, as to the Pyramids or Lourdes, to be astonished. Valenciennes, an industrial town on the edge of the coal-mining areas of Northern France, has long had a flourishing horticultural society whose members are mostly coal miners. A single eight-acre pavilion was built to hold the last one, held in 1954, and the crowds were such that extra wide gangways and one-way circulation proved quite inadequate.

I find these exhibitions interesting as they offer a new and different challenge to the garden designer. You have to make a show sufficiently arresting in design and in colour to catch and hold the spectator's eye, already perhaps saturated with the dizzying effect of a half-acre of massed azaleas or orchids. You have to arrange your plants so that replacements are easy, because such exhibitions usually last ten days. The cost of filling, say, a site of a thousand square yards is so high that your exhibition must be made sufficiently interesting horticulturally as well as æsthetically if it is to win one of the substantial prizes which are usually offered and which help to pay the expenses.

I have several times arranged " gardens " for such exhibitions, which, in France and Belgium at any rate, usually take place at the end of April. This suits the azalea growers of Belgium and the Dutch bulb growers but precludes the use of most annual and perennial flowers. I learned this to my cost one year at Ghent where I had to deal with an exiguous site. Wondering how on earth to compete with the violent colours I knew would surround me, I decided to make a splash with a small field of ordinary pot-marigolds using lemon and orange with singles and doubles. This meant growing them from seed and having them in flower by the twentieth of April. So, the autumn before, I had to take my seed to the French Riviera and find a grower who would devote two large greenhouses to growing several thousand marigolds. By the fifteenth of April they were magnificently ready, row upon row of pots full of plants in bud and just ready to open in the spring sunshine. Three huge trucks were carefully filled and dispatched on their three days' drive to Ghent where they arrived in a north wind and showers of sleet. The flowers were badly shaken by the journey and the change of temperature, but I had nothing else so I planted them out. The buds drooped and fell or never opened; my field of orange and yellow looked as lively as a neglected bed of lettuces. This taught me, the hard way, to have several strings to my bow, to avoid trying to have plants too far out of season and to avoid any plan or design which would require a given quantity of any single plant.

At Valenciennes, the following year, I learned another lesson. I had to design a large island site of perhaps twelve hundred square yards, a quarter of which was taken up by a large irregular pool and another quarter by grass. The rest was to be planted with half-hardy annuals: pansies, violas, forget-me-nots, double daisies, wallflowers, cheiranthus and stocks as well as with Ghent and mollis azaleas, flowering cherries, rhododendrons, various evergreens to give weight and masses of tulips, narcissi, hyacinths and lilies of the valley. All these plants arrived in their thousands and were unloaded on the site after their hundred-mile journey by road. The site was bare earth which was handed over to me ready dug. When we came to plant we found that the digging had been very superficial and that it took minutes of hard work with a trowel in the hard-beaten gravelly soil to scratch a hole big enough to take each plant in its pot; and for most of the small pot plants you had to allow from fifty to sixty plants per square yard. My unfortunate plantsmen had to work hard with aching backs and wrists for three days to get the plants in on time. Now I have learned to cover my site with at least a foot of sand or peat so that all my potted plants can be laid out and dropped in easily and fast.

My first major experience of garden-making as a spectacle was in 1950 and 1951, when I was asked to design the Festival Gardens at Battersea Park in London for the Festival of Britain Exhibition. The site, the South Bank of the Thames opposite Chelsea, was once a marsh which was filled in and made into a public park in the nineteenth century. It was well laid out and planted and its quiet alleys had enjoyed a certain vogue when bicycling first became popular.

One of the aims of the Festival of Britain was to inaugurate a period of development for the South Bank and the idea of the Festival Gardens was to create an open air resort on the lines of the Tivoli in Copenhagen. There were to be restaurants, theatres, a boating lake, cafés and an amusement park, all in a garden setting. This was no new idea for London. In the eighteenth century there were several such gardens. Ranelagh, Vauxhall and Cremorne were the most famous, but by the middle of the nineteenth century Cremorne, the last of them to survive, became so raffish that it had to be closed.

The job of arranging these gardens and their various features and distractions was handed over to James Gardener and myself, with a free hand to arrange the general layout and to invite more or less whom we liked to design special features. We were limited only by the talent available, by the difficulties of construction and of finding materials in an " austerity " England, and by a more than modest budget.

James Gardener had been a designer for Cartiers, the jewellers. From there he had graduated into the field of display and industrial design and had recently established his reputation by his brilliant designing for the " Enterprise Scotland " exhibition held immediately after the war. Tremendously inventive, he had the lightness of touch and the fantasy which this kind of assignment demanded. He could draw anything and understood very well the possibilities of wood, glass, metal, plasterboard, paint and canvas. His designs, however fantastic, always took the technical possibilities of his materials into account, so that his various constructions were " functional " in a real sense—that is to say, they " worked." His competence was such that no emergency really flustered him, he was ready to work all hours, and he held the respect of every workman on the job, since he knew their technical problems at least as well as they did. Although we worked together unremittingly for eighteen months, I do not remember a single disagreement.

The ground allotted to us covered thirteen acres. Next to the Thames, on the north side of the site, was a narrow strip of grass with a few isolated trees. South of this strip was a double line of fine old plane trees on either side of a wide carriage-way. South of this again was a thick belt of trees, with nondescript shrubs beneath them, planted on a bank that sloped down to the general level of the main part of the site, which lay some eight feet below the level of the roadway. This, the main area, was roughly a rectangle bordered by trees and had been used as a cricket ground. There were neither roads nor paths in this low-lying space and later we discovered why.

Our first task was to establish a general composition, incorporating the various features and facilities we proposed, for the approval of Sir Gerald Barry, the Director General of the Festival. Taking the longest axis that we could find, which lay to the western end of the site at right angles to the river and to the existing road, we decided to create a main vista to draw visitors down into this area from which they could wander off to explore the various subsidiary features. The principal feature of this part of the design was a wide flight of steps leading down into a piazza with colonnades on either side. Beyond the piazza was to be a canal as large as we could make it and this was to bristle with fountains and lead to some terminal feature. Elaborate waterworks and frequent firework displays would make this the main visual attraction of the exhibition. At right angles to the canal we decided to keep a large quiet space of lawn running eastwards with the sloping bank to the left. Beyond this lawn we planned to have some formal arrangement of gardens ending in some sort of building or screen—it eventually turned out to be an aviary—beyond which would be a small boating lake and the fun fair, scenic railway and so on. The two main entrances would lie at either end of the existing roadway. There would be ample walking and standing space in the piazza and all round the canal, and, leaving the central lawn and gardens as a sort of island of green, the main circulation would follow the perimeter of the site. The road parallel to the river would be the main promenade with incidental attractions set among the trees on the south side and a row of small shops alternating with the great plane trees on the north or riverside. The level ground, about fifty feet wide between trees and river, we planned to treat as a garden with a small theatre, a restaurant, a café and various kiosks to give it life. We projected a pier too as an additional entrance point for people arriving by river-boat from the main exhibition down-stream.

Working till all hours of the night in an attic office, snatching a cup of coffee and a dubious sandwich when we could, we arrived at our general scheme through a sea of tracing-paper. We made and discarded sketches as we went along, until we were able to present a plan for which we felt we were prepared to fight if necessary, as well as a whole series of sketches and perspectives offering different suggestions for the treatment of the various parts of the design. At this point, the choice of Gardener as chief designer and myself as having sole charge of landscaping had not yet been entirely settled; but our scheme established our positions since it was thought out much further and more practically, than some rather hazy propositions had been from other sources.

Once our design was accepted, our next task was to make a list of the various amenities which we had to incorporate on the site. A permanent theatre or concert hall and a permanent restaurant were wanted, which would remain in the park after the exhibition was over. There had to be many other restaurants of differing categories, including a small and relatively luxurious one to encourage the " carriage trade " to dine overlooking the river. This was England, so there had to be facilities for providing endless cups of tea and under cover at that, since nobody could guarantee that we would have a fine summer. There was to be an old-fashioned music hall, a dance hall, a miniature railway running through the grounds, and a small " zoo " of baby animals to amuse the children. Ideas, designs and their designers flowed in from all sides and, through the next weeks, struggling with costs and endless committee meetings, we finally established a list of features and the designers responsible for each of them. A general contractor and a firm of architects were also chosen to carry out the main services, road construction and the permanent buildings. Even with this team of experts however we were quite unable to establish the indispensable priorities. First among these was, of course, to get roadways constructed so as to have access to every part of the site. When the high equinoctial tides raised the river level to the brink of the embankment, water seeped through and waterlogged the whole of the low-lying central area; and, the contractors having contented themselves with hastily-made temporary roadways, we would not infrequently find we had as many as forty lorries stuck axle-deep in a sea of mud.

Once we had decided on the shape and proportions of the main vista and the canal, we had to consider its decorative treatment as an architectural scheme. Finally John Piper, the painter, devised with Osbert Lancaster a " Romantic Gothick " architecture with an arcaded colonnade and towers on either side of the piazzas made of bamboo, plywood and tubular scaffolding, painted crimson, ochre and black and peopled with ingenious statues made like baskets from pliable rattan bamboo. Osbert Lancaster also designed two tall obelisks to flank the canal and arranged the fountain jets and the huge decorative screen, also of painted bamboo, which was to terminate the main vista.

This retaining wall and steps at the Creux de Genthod were designed to form a base line for the charming Regency architecture of the house. Below the wall box-edged beds are planted with the pink floribunda rose "Distinction" and accented by clipped box bollards. White geraniums and white petunias fill the 17th century English stone vases and lead troughs on the parapet above

Flower beds are centred on a circular lily pool with a gilt bronze group by Bourdelle which oddly suits the style of the house as well as the scale of the garden. I found the elaborately clipped specimen yews in an old garden in Geneva

I took over the riverside strip, where Guy Osborne made a
charming little eighteenth-century theatre in the Vauxhall
manner, painted pale blue and white to match the kiosks and
small shops which lined the roadway between the plane trees.
I designed these small shops to look like blue and white striped
tents supported by bamboo poles at the corners. I had found the
idea in a French watercolour of about 1760 of a garden fête, at
St. Cloud where a long line of striped tents alternated with the
trunks of a straight avenue of trees. In order to create a sense of
enclosure for the riverside strip, this line of little shops (which
still exists, although now painted in different colours which, to
my mind, has destroyed the unity of the scheme) was linked by
white-painted trellis. On the level strip next to the river we
designed kiosks for tobacco, sweets and so on, also as striped tents,
and I worked out the garden pattern as a chain of curving flower
beds bordered by a low white bent-wire edging. This idea I took
from an eighteenth-century jardinière. As I had decided to keep
this whole area white, blue and yellow, the only flowers I planted
were twenty thousand yellow tulips for the May opening of the
exhibition. It was a hard struggle to get these beds prepared six
months ahead of time with workmen everywhere, roads and
paths unmade, and the various buildings scarcely started. However we got the edgings in and the tulips planted by October and
since we crisscrossed every bed with barbed wire, every tulip
survived. As the exhibition finally opened only at the end of May
it was lucky that I chose a late-flowering variety, " Golden
Harvest," and as it turned out to be a late spring they were still
in their full glory in the first week of June.

My horticultural problems for this exhibition were many.
London parks are on the whole magnificently planted and I did
not want to repeat the kind of planting that people could see
every day. The Festival, too, was intended to bring foreign
visitors to England, so I hoped and worked to make the Festival
Gardens a shop window for British horticulture. One of my first
ideas was to include a small enclosed garden so designed that it
could be planted each month with a different range of flowers:

rhododendrons and azaleas in May, roses in June, herbaceous plants in July and so on. Mr. A. Simmonds, then secretary of the Royal Horticultural Society, did everything he could and, in particular, helped me to organise meetings of the leading nursery-men and horticultural journalists so that I could explain my projects and enlist their aid. As it turned out, I was unable to get enough support and so I decided to do the best I could alone to show British flowers and yet keep inside my budget. This is where the remarkable Mr. E. R. Janes comes into the story. I had asked Mr. Simmonds to suggest somebody who could take charge of the collecting and raising of all the plants I wanted to use. These would necessarily include thousands of annuals for bedding out, all of which would have to be sown, grown on and brought to the site in relays throughout the season, so that certain parts of my garden could be entirely replanted with plants in full flower in a few hours.

Mr. Janes was then an elderly man who had just retired. For years he had been with Suttons, the famous seedsmen at Reading, and it was he who every year used to arrange those marvellous stands of annual flowers at Chelsea Show—peaks and valleys and grottoes blazing like a prismatic bonfire with the most superbly grown plants—petunias, clarkias, salpiglossis, nemesias, tobacco flowers and indeed almost every annual you can think of. We managed to find a minute office for Mr. Janes and we worked happily together until the gardens were completed fifteen months later. I spent much of my time in my shabbiest clothes, as often as not calf-deep in mud, urging on the work all over the site. It was a relief to come back to the office and find Mr. Janes, impeccably dressed in his old-fashioned dark suits, with his painstaking way of working, calm, slow-spoken and infinitely methodical. Having started life as a gardener's boy, he had a wide experience—indeed I have never met anyone who knew so much about flowers and how to grow them. Every minute I spent with him was precious and over the months he taught me a great deal about the technique of arranging flowers and plants for exhibition. He had too a remarkable sense of colour and he

322

explained to me how to get brilliant effects by the lavish use of white and pale yellow. As I have come to learn when arranging exhibitions indoors or under cover, mauve and blue flowers have a tendency to look grey and bright reds are apt to look black, whereas whites, yellow and clear warm pinks look sparkling and luminous.

With Mr. Janes at hand I went ahead with my plans, confident that he would criticise my choice of plants or colour, from both a practical and æsthetic viewpoint. I based my plans on quite simple principles. Every pavilion or structure should have a setting of bright flowers either in window boxes or in formal beds set close to them, and these flowers would be changed every month or so, as they went out of bloom.

There would be one formally-planned garden to make a compact and brilliantly coloured pattern at the end of the central grass lawn. All the old shrubberies under the trees on the banks and along the roadway would be cleared out and replanted with groups of flowering shrubs such as rhododendrons, azaleas, philadelphus, hydrangeas and viburnums. This section covered quite a lot of ground, so I decided to use with the shrubs any perennials which would give breadth and weight by the importance and interest of their foliage. Extra colour would come from tulips, lilies and gladioli which I would place as accents of colour in a setting where texture of foliage was to count more than flowers.

Since Regent's Park already had a superb rose garden, I decided to use only floribunda roses to make blocks of crimson and pink near the formal flower garden. The site was already fairly well planted with mature trees, so I did not have to cope with one of the worst problems for exhibition layouts on a bare site—to find enough large trees, transport and plant them, pay the huge prices that such work necessarily involves, and then struggle to make them survive. As the gardens were not to open until late May there was no sense in planting flowering cherries and crabs which, even though a little flimsy, do give some account of themselves the first year after planting. Flowering shrubs however presented a real problem. Large bushes, even if I could find them, would transplant badly and sulk for a year or two, nor would small, transplantable stuff make any effect the first season after planting. The exception is of course the rhododendron family. While I was exploring the nurseries between Sunningdale and Woking which specialise in rhododendrons, King George VI happened to suggest that a weeping spruce, *Picea breweriana*, would look well in the gardens. This led to my receiving a letter from the Exbury Estate saying that Edmund de Rothschild would be happy to offer us a rather large specimen from a group planted by his father. Thus I came to revisit the marvellous oakwoods of Exbury that slope down to the Beaulieu River near Southampton, where, before the war, Lionel de Rothschild had kept an army of gardeners hybridising, growing and planting out hundreds of acres with a thousand different species and varieties of rhododendron. By now these plantings were growing overcrowded and I was able to select as many huge bushes as I wanted of magnificent rhododendrons. I chose them mainly for the quality of their foliage, though I included some of the later-flowering hybrids. As all rhododendrons are easily transplantable and as I had refreshed my tired London clay with at least a foot of peat and many tons of cow manure, these rhododendrons flourished and flowered as though they had been there for years.

Always interested in foliage plants, I decided to plant a wide irregular band of glaucous-leaved hostas from one end to the other of the main road, on the shady side beneath the trees and in front of my shrub plantings. These were to make a sheet of grey-green which I intended to break by leaving circular spaces at intervals to be planted as spots of colour with tulips, followed by lilies and gladioli.

I cheerfully asked Mr. Janes to write to a suitable nurseryman and order five, or perhaps it was ten, thousand *Hosta sieboldiana glauca*. The reply came offering fifty. We wrote further letters, back came offers of twenty or of five plants. This was in early May and the Chelsea Flower Show would open in two weeks' time; so there I went knowing that every nurseryman in the country would be represented. After three days' canvassing, everybody knew this lunatic who wanted every hosta in the country, and so insistent was I that a good many of the nurserymen hid when they saw me coming. Eventually, by accepting any kind of hosta from abroad and from private gardens, sometimes in hundreds, sometimes in twos and threes, I raised nearly enough. Happening some years later to drive through what is left of the gardens, I was happy to see the magnificent effect of huge vigorous clumps of hostas which had flourished marvellously in the intervening years.

To carry out the work of garden construction, I had been able to choose a firm of garden contractors whom I had known for years. They put an enterprising and energetic foreman in charge who had a rather temperamental nature, knew a great deal about gardening, and who quickly recruited a gang of young Londoners who worked for him devotedly in often the most trying conditions. Like many young cockneys they were tremendous dandies in their off-time, indulging in elaborate and costly hair-dos and vying with each other in their highly coloured fancy waistcoats, narrow trousers and elaborately Sherlock Holmesian sports jackets; their comments on the sartorial tastes of the various important visitors who came to inspect the site were often comical.

All through a long wet winter we struggled to make our gardens in the mud and confusion of an exhibition slowly taking shape. The one piece of formal gardening at the east end of the great central lawn was constructed first: this was a rectangle raised three steps above the level of the lawn and bordered by low retaining walls on the other three sides. Above the walls were large formal beds of scarlet and crimson floribunda roses alternating with clipped yew trees to add a little height and weight. The garden itself was a parterre of quite simple lozenge-shaped beds all edged with the soft grey of clipped lavender. By October, although the soil was almost waterlogged, the garden was ready for planting. I had chosen to fill it for the opening with nothing but pure white tulips, so in they went. When February came, wanting to see how they were doing, I dug up first one bulb and then another to find that they had all rotted—thousands of them—and that my white garden had failed. Luckily Mr. Janes, whom no emergency daunted, produced the necessary quantity of superbly grown white double stocks just in time for the opening. Later in the summer the garden was blue with lobelia and the white-eyed blue-mauve verbena called "Loveliness," and in the late summer these were followed by a crimson and scarlet scheme composed of that fine red verbena "Lawrence Johnston" and my favourite foxtailed celosias in orange, scarlet and crimson. Down the wide path which led through the middle of this garden we put perches for brilliantly coloured macaws.

As the weather remained open though very wet, we started in February to plant perennials around the edges of the main shrub plantings. One planting particularly pleased me. The base was the handsome round-leafed *Senecio clivorum*, a giant groundsel with golden orange flowers. With it I planted large clumps of tiger lily and the late blue-flowered *Aconitum wilsonii* and for earlier flowering there were clumps of variegated hosta and various astilbes.

Colour was the most important visual element of the Festival Gardens. Except for the permanent brick concert-hall and restaurant, both rather lumpishly designed in red brick, all the buildings and pavilions were built in the lightest and cheapest materials available. Near the crimson, black and gold of the main vista was a restaurant made mostly of canvas and designed as a half-circle, each bay painted in successive colours of the spectrum. The dance-hall was a huge fluted canvas cone striped in scarlet and yellow. Under the trees on the long bank Guy Osborne designed an absurdly charming grotto decorated inside with fluorescent paint. All the buildings in the riverside strip were in combinations of turquoise and cobalt blue and white with occasional accents of black and lemon yellow. A secondary piazza at one end of the main road, which served as a concourse at the entrance to the Fun Fair, had a fantastic painted décor like Alexandre Benois' setting for *Petrouchka*, and behind the small boating lake was a painted screen suggesting a small fishing village. Round the site ran the miniature railway, its little stations, locomotives and carriages designed by Emmet with his customary cock-eyed late Victorian fantasy. You must imagine all this against the mammoth looming chimneys of Battersea Power Station.

Usually in designing gardens you use colour in a setting of green hedges and grass and trees, against the stone or brick or wood of a permanent architecture or the colours of rock and hillside. Here at Battersea, against acres of exuberant colour and fantastic painted arabesques, conventional planting or even solid patterns of flower colour could have entirely the wrong effect. In a normal architectural setting flowers give a sense of transience. Here, unless very carefully handled, they would look too serious.

From the beginning I had tried to understand the nature of the problem and little by little as the general texture and atmosphere of the gardens emerged I began to see how, for the visitor, they would represent a few hours spent in a wildly frivolous world—a visual escape from the drabness and restrictions which had been our daily fare for twelve long years. This was to be a fête!

Finally I saw that I must mix my flower colours, plant in wide pools and drifts, let pale pinks overlap into clear lemon yellow, interplant orange with red-purple and use every device I could so that texture, colour, size and shape would combine to make all the flower plantings sparkle, shimmer and seem to move in contrast to the bright, flat and static surfaces of paint.

As the spring of 1951 advanced the ground still remained waterlogged, but I could delay no longer. The great central lawn, still a sea of mud, had to be turfed and the last perennials planted. To get an even, well-drained surface on which to lay the lawn, we brought in truckload after truckload of fine cinders and spread them nine inches to a foot deep over the whole area,

and then unrolled the turf directly on to the cinders. Within
two weeks the grass had grown together and sent its roots down
through the cinders, and we had an excellent lawn. Then came
the time to set out the herbaceous plants; our lavish use of peat
made planting easy and, although we were planting almost a
month late, the plants took hold immediately. We used a lot of
lupins, for their satiny rainbow colours would suit the mood
of the gardens. Interplanting them with thousands of gladioli
in a wide range of colours, we were able to cut these lupins back
after their first flowering and, the gladioli giving colour in the
interval, the lupins had time to grow and flower again in
September.

The last week of May before the opening was hectic but
hugely enjoyable. Mr. Janes had been working quietly and
steadily for months and now, as van after van came on to the site
and thousands of annuals in full bloom and superbly grown in
pots were laid out on every available clear space, I realised what a
magnificent job he had done in organising the sowing and
raising of all these plants. We spent a whole week setting them
in their places. Teams of men were carrying and placing them
as we directed, while others followed on immediately to set them
in the ground. By the evening before the opening day all were
in place. In these last days I was learning every minute from Mr.
Janes how to mass flowers and how to mix colours to get the most
brilliant effects. We made hillsides and valleys of shimmering
colour using large quantities of white, pale pink and clear yellow
broken by rivulets of pale blue or mauve. I remember a fantastic
planting of yard-high salpiglossis in warm reds, tanny browns,
gold and violet, backed by the cinnamon plumes of the incense-
perfumed *Humea elegans*, and another drift of white and pink and
glowing red-crimson tobacco flowers that melted into clumps of
crimson and white lupins. As you walked round the paths leading
from pavilion to pavilion every bend revealed a new and
unexpected mass of flower colour, backed by huge bushes of
salmon and rose rhododendrons, so that, a little dizzy from this
kaleidoscope of colour, it was a relief to go back to the riverside

strip with its green trees and its urbane blue and white buildings in what appeared as a shapely field of yellow tulips.

Such was my first essay in gardening for a wide public and on a grand scale. In this kind of work many of the factors usual to garden-making simply do not apply. The limited duration of an exhibition implies a garden without the element of growth: there is no time to wait on nature. The ordinary joys, the slow growth of a hedge, the procession of unfolding buds, blossom, seed and falling leaves, have no place here. Subtleties of planting, the pleasure of a climbing rose tossing its flowery clusters through an apple tree or the rounded bosses of an old box hedge trimmed by time and loving shears to a calculated irregularity, belong to another world. For an exhibition one has to work with one's palette prepared ahead, like a painter boldly massing colour and composing in shapes and patterns calculated to appeal and make their mark (and one has to remember this) on a moving target, the spectator. Ordinarily one enjoys a garden by stops and starts. It is seen as a series of pictures from fixed vantage points, a window or doorway, a terrace or a seat or in a leisurely stroll, as one stops to examine a plant more closely or to pull up a weed. In exhibition gardening your composition will be seen as though moving and turning at the walking pace of the crowd as it passes.

This is one reason why I find myself designing freely flowing shapes for such gardens. Even on a formal or rectangular site curving shapes of grass, water and planting can underline the idea of movement and incidentally make it possible to achieve a whole series of different effects in a very limited space. A formal symmetrical design means that you have to assure yourself of an exact number of plants of a given kind or colour to fill the fixed dimensions of your pattern and this in turn means that you must arrange for nearly double the number of plants you will actually use. In an ordinary garden accidents, gaps, failures and minor mistakes of all sorts can be accepted as part of the waywardness of nature, but in an exhibition it takes more than an ordinary amount of skill to make poorly grown plants acceptable and half a dozen such can mar the whole work.

I like to think of exhibition planting as an exercise in three dimensions, just as I do the planting of an ordinary garden. The form and proportion of all the elements I am using, whether water or grass, pebbles, stone, bushes, trees or flowers, and the shaping and modelling of the site, must add up to a combination of voids and solids which are satisfactory in themselves. Only then can I be sure of the next stage when texture and colour come into play. In practice I find that my general plan on paper carries me little further than the outline of my site and a rough idea of the proportions for the different elements—paths, planting, water, grass and so on. With the outline blocked out, I next consider vertical planes: slopes, hollows, steps or ledges, the stems of trees and the weight and height of hedges and shrubs. I find I cannot make these come to life on paper; I need to feel them on the site, whether indoors or under the sky, and they become clear to me only as I move about sensing where a flat area should be set against a block of high planting, where I will need transparency, how a curve in the ground plan should be accentuated by a contrapuntal or complementary curve in the planting, where to accentuate vertically and where to use a strong horizontal.

The " Salon des Arts Ménagers " is a sort of Ideal Home Exhibition which until this year has always taken place at the Grand Palais in the Champs-Élysées. There is a large basement to this building which the organisers of the exhibition had hitherto tried not too successfully to exploit. One part of this basement is an oval of about 1500 square yards which is filled with supporting columns and piers and lies directly under the central cupola of the main hall. Icy cold, with only a ten foot high ceiling and artificial lighting, it was a damping proposition as the setting for a flower show in the third week of February, usually the coldest moment in the Paris winter. There had to be flowers and vegetables and two shops, one for selling seeds and the other for horticultural sundries. Four huge piers, big masonry columns and a dozen cast-iron pillars had to be circumvented and six deep bays surrounding the central oval had to be utilised.

The first year that we tackled this curious setting I made an informally shaped island in the middle, thickly planted with a polychromatic mass of tulips, hyacinths, cinerarias, pink Kurume azaleas with dark conifers for contrast and clumps of yellow forsythia and the double pink flowering plum, *Prunus blireiana*. I had to make a false ceiling of stretched pale-blue cotton into which I set a large number of spotlights. The columns and piers, once they too were painted in the same pale blue, became less obtrusive. The two deep bays on either side I turned into semi-circular niches, also painted in sky blue and floored with grass set out with crimson and white double daisies. In the middle of each niche I put an old leafless apple tree, one gilded all over and the other silvered, laden with real fruit, both apples and pears, painstakingly attached with nylon thread. Of the other recesses, two became shops with blue and white striped awnings and two more were filled with more flowering cherries and forsythia against a background of conifers.

With all Paris caught in the coldest winter for years, this brightly-coloured cave proved a huge draw and we were encouraged to continue the following year. This time I kept the semicircular pale blue niches as background for two little circular kitchen gardens with formally designed box-edged beds set out with vegetables which we had had grown in pots and flown in from Algiers. To give these *potagers* a little height and fantasy, I added pyramid pear trees whose bare twigs were first lacquered bright scarlet and then hung with real yellow pears. The centre of the site was taken up by an oval pool surrounded with pink and white azaleas, hyacinths and cinerarias; and the two remaining bays were filled with flowers and flowering shrubs, one with every tone of yellow, orange, scarlet and crimson and the other in blues, mauves and whites with a little violet purple and pale lemon yellow. For these bays I again used tulips and cinerarias, azaleas, hyacinths, daffodils, *Primula obconica*, *Primula malacoides* and clumps of sweetly smelling lily of the valley, France's flower of good luck.

Each year we have to make a new composition for this difficult site. You approach it past a series of small stands selling furniture polish or patent tools for making carrots look like rosebuds, and rows of gas stoves, refrigerators and the like. One year I decided that the entrance, between bare walls of rough masonry, was altogether too bleak; so we made wooden frames containing moss sandwiched between two layers of wire netting. With these frames we built a series of arches to make a kind of pergola and then set to and clothed them all with twigs of green box, thickly set and then clipped to look like topiary work. It was an endless business to make them, but this series of green arches set in perspective made a very alluring frame for the brightly coloured flowers beyond.

French exhibitions have always had a weakness for statuary and among the chrysanthemums or orchids or vegetables of a flower show you are sure to come up against a larger-than-life stark naked lady in white plaster. Even in a real garden I usually deplore the juxtaposition of statues and flowers, preferring stone vases, obelisks or sundials, since flowers and figures seem altogether too rich and indigestible a mixture. In our underground garden however the unrelieved masses of flower colour need to be, as it were, humanised and given point by the contrasting effect of some artifact or other. Sometimes I use a pool or a fountain but now, more often, a piece of abstract sculpture.

These strange, rather amorphous forms, whether in wood or stone, bronze or plaster, seem to me very well adapted to an out-of-door garden either in a simple setting of grass, water, trees and hedges or as a static note in a turbulent sea of flower colour. They have none of the mythological associations which caused renaissance gardeners to people their gardens with a world of classical allusions; nor have they the debased sentimentality of the blowzy cupids and graces set among pink rambler roses in the great gardens of fifty years ago. They fill, rather, the place of those carefully selected rocks which Chinese and Japanese

gardeners have always prized as an accent in their garden compositions, and in my underground garden I find I can use the
oddest products of the Paris abstract sculptors even in a quite
classical and symmetrical layout as long as they carry none of the
connotations of the human form. It was interesting to see in the
1958 Brussels Exhibition how often abstract sculpture was used
with a plain stretch of grass or paving, to give the feeling of a
garden to courts and open spaces arranged without flowers. An
eight-foot sphere built of rough stones balanced on the paving of
a hall in the Austrian section gave exactly the same sentiment as
the three magnificent rocks, which the Japanese imported and
set with such skill against a plain panel of wall at the entrance to
their exhibit.

The Brussels Exhibition brought me another opportunity.
We were asked by the High Commissioner of the French
Pavilion to work out a scheme for an area lying on one side of
the French Pavilion. The site was a difficult one; roughly
triangular, with its longest side bounded by one façade of the
pavilion, a hundred-foot high wall of corrugated plastic built on
a framework of tubular scaffolding. The end of the triangle was
barred by an elevated roadway carried on huge concrete piers
some forty feet high, and betwen these piers the view was blocked
by an ugly three-storied beer-hall attached to the Vatican exhibit
and the oddly named " Civitas Dei Brasserie ". The third side of
the triangle returned from the viaduct to the end of the pavilion
in the shape of a roadway which was eight feet higher than the
level of the garden at the far or the viaduct end. Thus, my wedge
of ground was bounded by the pavilion on the left, the viaduct
at the end, and a steep bank rising to a large group of chestnuts
and the roadway on the right.

The " modernity " of the surrounding constructions and the
asymmetry of the site left me with little choice. The architect of
the French pavilion, a vast and, I think, rather far-fetched experiment in modern construction, demanded, thanks I suppose to

some hark-back to the Beaux Arts training, an axial composition with a central fountain and all the conventions of a formal layout. After one look at the muddy site I saw that this solution would be out of the question, so I turned for inspiration to certain paintings by Braque. At the far end of the pavilion, near the viaduct, was a large though subsidiary entrance, so wide walking-space, leading from this door to the narrow end and exit from my triangle, was essential. The scale of the surrounding buildings was enormous and money was limited; so I finally devised three loose island shapes, two of them firmly outlined with a foot-high concrete edge to raise my plantings out of harm's way, while the third, near the entrance, was to be a shallow pool lined with turquoise blue paint. For the pool I intended a metal mobile whose different elements would be kept in motion by the play of water jets against them. Unfortunately, in the end neither money nor time nor a suitable sculptor could be found to carry out this last feature which I had hoped would bring animation and lightness to an overpoweringly heavy setting.

The bank and the high ground towards the road and the viaduct I quite simply grassed, planting birch trees to break the massive architecture of the viaduct and reserving all colour for the island beds. Having coloured my concrete edges in blue, I thought of planting these islands, designed with bays and promontories and curved as bones are curved, with free inter-locking shapes of contrasting flower colour. As the exhibition opened in late April, my first planting was orange *Cheiranthus allionii*, white, blue and lemon-yellow violas with white and pale yellow tulips carefully grouped as a counter-theme.

This worked very well in practice. Seen from the viaduct or from the road, these quite large pools of sharply contrasted colour were exciting and lively even in this exhibition setting where every building competed in extravagance of colour and form. In June, when the first plantings had faded, I followed them with white, rose-pink and crimson petunias which were succeeded in August by dwarf-bedding dahlias in white, yellow and apricot orange. To give weight to these flat patches of colour, I planted in each island several golden yews clipped into circular bosses about three foot high and five foot in diameter.

Flower pilgrimages have developed vastly since the days when Londoners would repair to Bushey Park on " Chestnut Sunday," to Hyde Park to see Tom Hay's tulip borders, or to the Flower Walk in Kensington Gardens. Now perhaps the largest, gayest and most popular flower jaunt in Europe is to Keukenhof in Holland. Here in the middle of the bulb fields a group of enterprising growers clubbed together to buy one of these small, slightly undulating sandy parks which are set like islands among the flat polders. This little park had ponds and great beech trees surrounded by irregular hummocks and hollows covered with thickets of young birch and alder. In the last few years the whole site has been planted with every kind of spring bulb grown in Holland; and every year millions of visitors flock to see crocus and daffodils, grape hyacinths and every known variety of tulip planted formally and informally, by the acre and in every imaginable combination. For me the master-stroke is a canal of blue muscari six yards wide and a hundred long cut through a spinney of birch. As if the rainbow colours of the garden were not enough, all the plantings are seen against the fields beyond which make a solid backcloth of rose and scarlet and yellow.

This is an extraordinary experiment in publicity and in flower culture and suggests a new field for the tourist industry, a new scale and a new concept for public gardening, as well as a new and profitable opening for the horticultural trades of any country.

I had gone to Keukenhof to decide what range of tulips I could use for the Paris *Floralies* to be held in late April, 1959. For the first time an international flower show was to be held in Paris itself. The idea had long been under discussion but had been held up for lack of a suitable building. Now a new exhibition hall for industrial and technical exhibitions was rising fast at the Place de la Défense, the first building of a new development scheme which will eventually be almost a new city lying between the western extremity of Paris and St. Germain.

When I first went to look at the new building the roof was still under construction. I found myself in a labyrinth of steel scaffolding, a spider's web of metal tubing that Piranesi would have liked to draw, rising a hundred and fifty feet to support the vast ribbed concrete roof. The building is triangular and its roof rises from ground level at the three corners to its full height in the centre like three curved triangular scallop shells. This roof covers some eight acres of floor space and has no supporting columns. The inner arrangement of this strange domed space is very simple. Thirty feet above the ground and supported on concrete columns is the main floor, broken in the middle by a hexagonal well or opening, and three additional decks flank the three vertical sides of the building which are entirely of glass. The site for which I had to plan was on the ground level and was just that hexagon, covering some 850 square yards, that lay immediately under the central well of the main floor. Here I had a clear space rising 150 feet to the apex of the roof, and the main floor formed a gallery from which you could look down on our site.

This was a stimulating and difficult setting, first of all because the garden I would have to make would be seen almost vertically from the main floor as well as from ground level. It was an island site. Each side of the hexagon measured sixty feet and there was a concrete pillar at each angle. I saw at once that no symmetrical or formal composition would do. It would be too easily readable from above; nor could I break up my island space with paths as once again, from above, people moving along these paths would inevitably destroy the unity of the garden. Further, it would be technically almost impossible to cover the whole of this large area with flowers since that would involve some 50,000 plants in pots and that, in turn, would mean preparing double that quantity. Besides, at ground level, the spectator would lose everything except the twenty feet nearest to the eye. I at once rejected the idea of using grass to reduce my planted areas to reasonable proportions, because I knew that there would be large lawns in other exhibits. Besides, grass would

On the lawns around a low tiled country house on the sandy woodlands of the Sologne twenty miles south of Orléans, the informal planting of interesting trees as well as formal clipped yews and loose clumps of yuccas and blue Siberian and yellow-flag iris make a harmonious garden link between the house and woods.

Under a 150-foot-high vault of the Palais de la Défense exhibition hall in Paris, this was the hexagonal centrepiece of the first French Floralies in April 1959. It covered 850 square yards. A curving pool was lined with patterns of black, white and grey pebbles. The planting was an intricate patchwork of a hundred different varieties of flowers—fifty thousand plants assembled with one aim only—to enchant.

The Italian architect Nervi built the new exhibition hall in Paris, and his superb building called for and got a unique display. Braque influenced me in the forms and the various greys of the pebble-patterned pool. It had taken a year to bring a unique collection of plants to flowering perfection. For all their seeming careless profusion, colours, textures and forms were carefully interrelated so that no horticultural anomalies should occur to shock the keenest horticulturalist.

Steps, however simple, do much to humanize the garden. Any garden scene perhaps static in itself comes to life where path and steps suggest movement forward into another area to be explored.

look too absorbent and too dull as the centre piece of this superb building, which for all its technical audacity and brilliance is so beautifully scaled that, in my view, it is as classical a concept as a Gothic cathedral of the Ile de France or Mansart's orangery at Versailles. For this reason I felt I must avoid any garden architecture, any vertical construction or any historical idiom or association. Eventually, and long before putting pencil to paper, my reflections led me to decide that I must convey the idea of something completely free and, as it were, moving. I must also, in the midst of so much architectural clarity and logic, suggest mystery. What were the elements (and these must be natural elements) that I could use? Trees and plants, stone, sand and water. The idea of water seemed to fulfil all the conditions I had set myself or which the nature of the building imposed. So I decided to make my main theme water—the whole site water—rimmed and islanded with flowers.

It was at this point that I could begin to sketch and let my pencil search out, within the hexagon, the shapes of a wide pool to cover the greater part of the area with curves that would make a satisfying and complete form seen from above. At ground level the same curves would offer bays and promontories, capes and inlets to hide and reveal new perspectives from each side as the visitor made his way around the site.

On paper I seemed to be experimenting with "abstract" forms. In fact there came to my mind the Braque ceiling in the Louvre with its free white shapes like seagulls, enclosed in the formal compartments of renaissance mouldings and cofferings. But behind this again lay a purely landscape concept, deriving perhaps from the fifteenth-century Zen gardens in Kyoto, particularly Soami's garden at the Ryoangin monastery, a formal rectangle where sand and a few stones capture a sense of timelessness and infinite space. And so the garden concept grew, nor was it so highfalutin' as it sounds. If it had a meaning and its own mystery, this lay in the centre—an empty space of water gently rippling above raked sand. Towards the edges the water lay between islets and bays of flowers while for the spectator, whether outside or above, I intended and achieved a rainbow of flowers, colour and form, a brilliant barrier which his perceptions could pierce and see beyond into the heart of the matter.

Although the exhibition was to last for only ten days the pool, a mere nine inches deep, had to be made of reinforced concrete, which from above would look dead and blank. I did not want to paint it and so falsify all the flower colour, but I had, nonetheless, to consider it as a painter might a blank canvas. Once again I remembered the Japanese technique of suggesting a lake by the use of sand and pebbles. Oddly too, the " collage " paintings of the early cubist masters came into my mind as well as certain paintings of the Normandy coast by Braque and Derain, and I decided to make an underwater design in pebbles and sand. So from Dieppe came lorries full of carefully selected pebbles, large and small, black and grey and white. These I laid out in loose rounded shapes to accentuate the curves of the islands and bays and suggest the movement of water. I filled the remaining space with fine river sand carefully raked to suggest the ripples of moving water. Seen from above, before I filled the pool with water or began the planting, the pond shape made a satisfying pattern whose outlines, textures and colours prefigured in sand and stone the forms of the planting.

I had earlier realised that all these curves would need some sharp accents and some suggestion of weight; so I had gone to the forest of Fontainebleau and marked in red paint boulders of various sizes. Eventually on to the site came two enormous trucks filled with these glacier-worn sandstone boulders, some weighing over two tons and all of them with a marvellous patina of brown and orange lichens. In fact my first job on the site was to mark out with a bag of lime the shape of the pool and then at once place each rock, either to accentuate a promontory or to stand isolated in the water. All of them were placed in such a way that they bore a definite relation to each other and to the design as a whole. I had no thought of this being in any sense a rock garden. Each stone was there as an object in itself, and, when they were all placed and the pool made, I had already, as I had hoped and intended, a three-dimensional composition complete in itself. This sense of completeness, at various stages in the making of a garden, has always been for me a sure test of the validity of a composition. In this particular work I was able to apply this test several times. The first time was when I had placed my rocks in relation to the shape of the pool. The next stage was when the pool was completed and its pebbled floor set out. Then came the placing of a little grove of white-trunked birch trees in young leaf, the dark accents of prostrate junipers and dwarf pines, each placed in the most careful relationship to the rocks and to the surfaces of water as were the huge plants of *Rhododendron sino-grande*, *R. falconeri*, *R. macabeanum*, and *R. calostratum* which I added next. I had chosen these and other large-leaved species for the texture and form of their foliage, to give height and to act as a foil to the brilliant flower colour which was to fill all the land masses of the composition.

I used these rhododendrons, as well as some hybrid sasanqua camellias, as breaks or frames mainly at the angles of the hexagon. In this way I tried to ensure that from each of the six sides of the garden you could look inwards and across a quite different land-scape. Some of those appeared mainly as planted areas with a glimpse only of water and rock and the farther shore. But on two opposite sides the water came close to the edge of the site and you saw water-views broken by flowered islands. From no one point could you see the whole of the garden and as you walked round you could seldom see the opposite boundary of the site. Only from above was the general form visible, but from such a height and at such a distance that you no longer had any exact sense of scale. The crowds surrounding this intricate mosaic of water and rocks, trees and flower colour, looked as remote as people seen through the wrong end of a telescope.

But this was a *Floralies* and people were coming to see flowers and colour *en masse*. For ease in working I had surrounded my site with an edging about a foot high and filled in all my planting areas with from twelve to eighteen inches of peat so that all my flowering plants in their pots could be planted rapidly and easily.

Deliberately, I had made no planting plans since only when my plants were actually on the site could I be sure of just what varieties and what quantities I would have at my disposal.

Preparing plants for an exhibition is an extremely complex operation. You have to start at least eighteen months ahead and calculate for at least double the number of plants you plan to use. Bad weather, bad luck, a single error in months of cultivation can easily eliminate thousands of plants. On this occasion, a very early spring meant the too early flowering of some five thousand tulips of twenty different kinds and colours which I had carefully chosen at Keukenhof the year before. Only by building screens to keep off the sun were we able at the last minute to retard sufficiently a host of other plants.

Previous experience of this kind of difficulty had warned me. This time I arranged, before I started planting, to have delivered to the site a dozen or so pots of every plant I planned to use with a list of the quantities of each available. Thus I had my whole palette under my eyes and could decide on associations of plant, form and colour by setting down a pot here and a pot there as colour notes round which to think.

Then only I gave the word to start. Truckload after truckload of plants, some fourteen thousand pots in all, came on to the site hour after hour. Each plant, individually wrapped, had to be unpacked and ranged in rows round the site, ready to be picked up, set out and finally, planted.

I worked as I usually do in harmonies of one colour, starting under the birch trees with Exbury azaleas in orange and yellow and the young growth of Japanese maples—*Acer palmatum*—and the yellow-green fronds of *Osmunda regalis*. With these I planted large clumps of Jan van der Graaff's lilies, the orange " Enchantment " and especially " Golden Clarion " which, although Mr. van der Graaff himelf doubted whether we could force it so early in the season as the end of April, we succeeded in getting into full flower, each plant some five foot high. Under the lilies and azaleas came sheets of polyanthus primroses in yellow, orange and red with one large patch of blue primroses to enhance the sulphur yellow of the " Golden Clarion " lilies.

This composition, mainly of flame and orange, took up the whole of one side of the hexagon. I continued through to the next with a large planting of orange, scarlet and lemon-yellow Iceland poppies and red, orange and cream ranunculus which merged into sulphur yellow antirrhinums, late double yellow narcissi and clumps of the scarlet tulip, " Holland's Glory." At the next corner a huge rhododendron shaded a patch of white hydrangeas, marking the beginning of a planting of all green and white, white *Lilium longiflorum*, white hydrangeas and white columbines above a carpet of green and white leaved hostas, white bachelor's button daisies and white *Primula obconica*. These whites, in turn, merged with mauve primulas, blue and white cinerarias and blue hydrangeas, while the next angle was blocked by a clump of huge bushes of *Rhododendron obtusum amoenum* covered with violent magenta flowers.

As the planting proceeded I had constantly to climb the sixty steps up to the main deck to look down on it. I soon saw that, from above, the normal spacing between each plant left it isolated against the black peat, and that I would have to pack the plants much closer and use considerable masses of cinerarias and hydrangeas to produce broad effects of colour which alone would give sufficient weight seen from that height and distance. These are not plants I much care for and once downstairs again, I had to be very dexterous in veiling and qualifying these groups with lighter plantings to avoid the rather vulgar effect of both the cinerarias and the hydrangeas in large masses. Once past the magenta rhododendrons, I made a large planting of cinerarias, shading from magenta down to very pale pink with just enough brick red to give life to all this rather saccharine colour. On one of the islands which lay close by, I concentrated on white violas and daisies with blue hydrangeas, yuccas for their foliage, and a few white broom; and next to the stepping stones which led to this island I placed in the water a dozen huge plants of arum, more for the rich green arrows of their foliage than for their flowers.

So, taking side after side, I moved from colour to colour. After the cinerarias, crimson and pink and white Kurume azalea "Palestrina" were grouped with white and pink *Primula malacoides* under a large "Amanagowa" cherry. Then came a clump of *Rhododendron augustinii*, its milky blue emphasised by bushes of rhododendron "Blue Tit," white *Deutzia gracilis* and again the white azalea "Palestrina." These merged with a field of the double tulip "Peach Blossom," with *Dicentra spectabilis* and great clumps of white, pink and deep red astilbes. Nearby lay another island which I planted with pink and white *Primula malacoides* and more Peach Blossom tulips and then, finding that it looked a little too sweet, I peppered the whole of this planting with more scarlet "Holland's Glory" tulips.

By now we had almost reached the last corner and the sixth side of the hexagon. The key note was struck here by a huge plant of rhododendron "Naomi" in the full glory of shell pink bud and fainter pink flower; with a hybrid sasanqua camellia "Eddy" of almost exactly the same tone next to it. In their shade I planted a large patch of cyclamen in white, shell pink and salmon. Beyond them, on ground rising to a large rock overhanging the water and set off by the noble fronds of two cycads, was an underplanting of polyanthus primroses in palest salmon and rose pink with the pink and white tulip "Her Grace," and on the rising ground nearest the big rock fifty or sixty hippeastrum with their huge trumpets of greeny white, pink, scarlet and scarlet and white striped. By now we had reached the east side where the water comes close to the boundary and from where you can look clear across between the islands to the far side. In the immediate foreground were clumps of clipped box balls of different sizes in the bright emerald green of their new foliage. I grouped these like colonies of mushrooms among massed white gloxinias and lilies of the valley and young fronds of maidenhair fern. Then remained only the planting of a clump of bamboo and the creamy-white *Rhododendron johnstoneanum* to link this exotic and scented planting to the birch wood and the azaleas with which I had begun this coloured world of flowers.

We had worked for a month some twelve hours a day in the noise and dust of a scarcely finished building. Now, clean and tidily dressed, we stood watching the first distinguished visitors come trickling in—a trickle soon to become a flood. People stood eight deep around the gallery above, eight deep around the site below. They seemed silent, almost as though hypnotised, absorbing this fantasy of form and colour. For ten days this continued and the thick cement dust, stirred up by three million feet, settled like dirty snow on all the flowers and on us as we sprayed and watered and renewed each plant that faded. I knew that we had achieved a real success, more interesting to me than the Grand Prix d'Honneur and all the other prizes awarded for this garden, when I heard more than one person say that in spite of the crowds they had felt themselves alone in it.

In Paris a minor copy of the spring splendours of the Keukenhof has been attempted in the park of Bagatelle in the Bois de Boulogne. But France's most important horticultural achievement since the war has been a remarkable series of roses developed by the Meilland family and others. The gravelly soil, the insignificant scale and the dreary layout of the once famous rose gardens at Bagatelle, where international rose competitions are held each year, make no public appeal. It would not be difficult to find ten or twenty acres of suitable soil in an attractive setting near Paris in which to plant roses deliberately as a spectacle on the largest scale, which would inevitably attract the thousands of existing rose lovers and create as many more.

With their quite special climate the shores of Lake Maggiore in Northern Italy, between the Simplon and Milan, have been famous for their gardens for centuries before Captain McEacharn built his hundred-acre gardens near Pallanza. These gardens started as a private venture for growing a catholic collection of rare and exotic plants which might flourish in this moist and clement air. Now semi-public, it attracts a large number of visitors in spite of its very special nature. I could imagine finding a large and picturesque site, and there are many such, on the shores of this lake and making a spring garden festival, drawing all Europe to see massed acres of gardenias in full bloom and hill-sides blazing with mounds of *Azalea indica* white, mauve, pink, purple, scarlet and magenta, since this is one of the few places in Europe where these two plants flourish in the open air.

In England towns and suburbs and villages are so filled with flowers that any excursion is as if through a garden. Every gate-way, every opening through a wood suggests that a hidden garden lies just behind, as so often it does. The country is filled with gardens, large and small, almost all privately owned and most willingly shown to anyone who cares to seek them out. For years now most of the more important private gardens are open to the public from time to time. As object lessons they seem to have greatly raised the general standard throughout the country, at any rate as to the variety and quality of plants grown. In a country whose climate is so marvellously suitable for cul-tivating a huge range of plants, the lack of form in almost every garden is an understandable defect; nor is there one great public garden designed and planted on a large scale as an object lesson. Kew Gardens are based on the original picturesque landscape designed and ornamented by Sir William Chambers and any formal elements are nineteenth century in their shape and detail. Only at Hampton Court is there a public garden which exemplifies changing garden styles with its formal flowery sunken garden, its seventeenth-century layout of canals and avenues set in an eighteenth-century landscape park, and its fifty year old herbaceous borders.

For the last thirty years important English gardens have developed along one line only. Formal flower gardens, the traditional acres of fine mown lawns and wide herbaceous and superbly planted borders have almost disappeared along with the skilled labour and money necessary for their upkeep. Horti-cultural taste, economics, and the mania of a generation of rich and influential garden-lovers have together informed and renewed a taste for the informal woodland garden. This is of course a return to the British eighteenth-century predilection for "naturalistic" gardening, now no longer dependent for its interest on laurel shrubberies, grottoes, temples or summer houses, but ablaze with rhododendrons and azaleas, primulas, iris and astilbes, flowering crabs and cherries and a thousand shrubs and trees to flare with the bright fires of autumn. The range of material and the wealth of colour available are overwhelming, and the amateur can scarcely be blamed if he mistakes good cultivation and a confused riot of colour for gardening. But, for all these strictures, here is a unique mode or form of gardening which might once again be exemplified on a scale large enough to attract some of the millions of tourists who set out each year to look at the wider world. Such a garden should be on a large scale for several reasons. First, to be able to absorb crowds and so to earn an income adequate for its upkeep, and secondly to give ample space for the spectacular effects which, quite understandably, are needed to win the admiration of a crowd.

The nearest approach to this type of garden are the Savill Gardens in Windsor Great Park, the astonishing achievement of Sir Eric Savill who has quietly, over the years, transformed acres of Windsor's woodland into a gardener's dreamland. These are private gardens, although always hospitably open to those who know and care to seek them out. The scale and nature of their planting makes them the best existing example of current English gardening and perhaps the most important contribution to landscape gardening in twentieth-century Britain.

The breaking up of almost every extensive estate in the land and the general disappearance of the great country houses should make it easy to find an attractive property and develop a National Garden on the lines of a National Park, where British horticulture might lay out a hundred or more acres as a carefully planned succession of gardens, open from April to October, to draw flower lovers from all over the world. This would be once more the pipe dream of an enthusiast, if the economics of Keukenhof and of the Ghent and other international flower shows did not prove that gardening devised as a mass spectacle of the public can draw profits, just as surely as an international football game.

motor racing, ice hockey or any other public entertainment.

Gardening will have to follow the patterns of living which our contemporary Western civilisation imposes. The sedentary period is over. For two thousand years European civilization has been rooted to the ground. People, in the main, lived out their lives in town or village, castle, cottage or country house, embellishing these as the times and fortune permitted. The last hundred years have brought a total change. Slow as it was to gather momentum, we were scarcely aware of the change in range and tempo and the gradual redistribution of wealth until two wars speeded the processes of mechanical inventions.

CHAPTER XIII

My garden

This book could have been called *Other People's Gardens* if this title had not been used already. I have no garden of my own and what I have learned has been from the years of working on other people's ground. But I allow myself day-dreams that I one day mean to have.

I hope that it will be on land which is neither chalky nor too acid, with soil to which I can add peat or lime. I hope, too, for soil which is not heavy clay that takes years of back-breaking labour to lighten, nor a hot dry sand whose thirst for water and manure I could never assuage.

It must be a small garden and a simple one; one man's work, mine perhaps, and in any case not so large as to need an armoury of mechanical devices or a full-time mechanic to keep these in running order. However good the soil, the first thing I shall do will be to make two enclosures, for compost, each five feet wide by ten feet long and walled in to a height of three feet. Into these will go everything that in a few months will ensure me a regular supply of rich black humus, since I know no better way of having a garden relatively free from pests and diseases. There are limits to the time, trouble and money I am prepared to spend on spraying my garden with chemical preparations which can so easily destroy nature's subtle balances and, by eliminating one pest, fatally leave the door open for others.

Once I have made this, the garden's future larder, I can start to consider the site. First of all I should say that I plan to make my garden in England since, all things considered, I do not know a better country. I would rather start with an old garden, however badly arranged and however neglected, since a few mature trees, an old wall and even a few square yards of good soil will give me the advantage of a twenty year start, all the more so as I shall be so late a starter. First I shall take out all the rubbish, elder bushes, nettle beds and any trees which are ugly and misshapen or too crowded. I shall thin out old shrubberies without pity and prune back any specimens which I may wish to keep and, later perhaps, transplant. All soft green rubbish will go to the compost heaps, the rest I shall burn and save the wood ash where I can. Only when I have cleaned the garden and ridded it of everything I know I will not want, shall I make a careful survey on paper as a basis for an eventual plan.

My garden will be very simple. There will be no herbaceous borders, no rose garden and no complicated formal layout with all the bedding out, edge trimming and staking which these forms of gardening involve. A ground-floor room in the house or a converted outbuilding will be my workroom, part library for garden books and catalogues, part studio for drawing board and painting materials, part tool shed for all the small tools, string, raffia, tins of saved seed and all the odd extensions and aids to the gardener's two hands.

I see my workroom with one wall all window, and below it a wide work table running its whole length with a place to draw and a place to write. Walls will be whitewashed, the floor of brick, there will be a fireplace and chairs for talk, and at least one wall lined with books.

This room will open south or westwards on to my working garden and I shall design this just like one of those black-japanned tin boxes of water-colours. I see this working garden as a rectangular space as large as I can afford and manage. With luck or good management or both, high walls will protect it to east and north and I shall enclose the other two sides with a low wall or a five feet yew or box hedge. Under the walls I shall make a three or four feet wide bed for climbing plants and others which like the warmth and shelter that a wall at their back will give them. I shall then divide the rest into small beds, perhaps four and a half feet or five feet square, separated by eighteen inch paths of bricks on edge or stone or even pre-cast cement flags of a good texture and colour and set, like the bricks or stone, in a weak cement mixture so that no weeds can grow. The number of beds and their exact dimensions will depend on the area of my ground but they must be small enough to be easily accessible from the paths surrounding them. In working out my simple criss-cross pattern I shall surely find it useful to have a few beds as double units, nine feet by four foot six or ten feet by five feet. In fact this garden will closely resemble the " system garden " of an old botanical garden whose small beds are each devoted to growing numbers of the different plant families. I shall use this garden as paint box, palette and canvas, and in it I shall try out plants for their flower colour, texture of foliage and habit of growth. In some beds I shall set out seedlings for selection, in others bulbs, in others plants combined for essays in colour. Each bed will be autonomous, its own small world in which plants will grow to teach me more about their æsthetic possibilities and their cultural likes and dislikes. I shall make no attempt at a general effect, for this will be my personal vegetable museum, my art gallery of natural forms, a trial ground from which I will always learn. I may use a flowering tree here or there above some of my postage-stamp squares in places where I want to grow plants which appreciate a dappled shade, and I may hollow out a square or two as pools for water lilies or *Iris kaempferi*.

So, close to my workroom, I shall have my palette, changing from year to year and season to season and accessible and work able in any weather. I see already a square with tufts of white and coral-feathered, scarlet and rose-pink tulips whose foliage as it dies off will be covered by the new leaves, blue-grey, green or yellow-green striped with white, of the various hostas, and camassias with their sober flowers of lavender grey. In another square will grow *Euphorbia wulfenii* and hellebores and perhaps some long spurred aquilegias. There will be lilies too and lavender, some of the old-fashioned roses and all the garden pinks I can find. Perhaps I shall have a square or two of delphiniums, plants I like only in an enclosed garden. Here I shall test kurume azaleas for their colours as seen in sun or shade; primula species, rodgersias, moraeas and meconopses will grow in squares of specially moist and peaty soil, helianthemums and cistus in others which are sandy and dry. Here, I shall find, living and growing, the coloured expansions of my pleasures as a painter and gardener, as well as an addict of catalogues and dictionaries.

Only in an enclosed garden would I want to grow plants in this apparently chaotic way. Even so, any elaborate design, with axes and central features and with differing proportions of beds and paths of grass and water, would destroy the charm and defeat the purpose and meaning of this garden. This is why I shall make my plan a repetition of small units so that it will resemble the neatly partitioned drawers of a numismatist's cabinet or more exactly, a page from a stamp collector's album.

I do not find it easy to envisage my future garden without its house—it is like drawing a body without a head. But whether the house is large or small, its walls will be covered with climbing plants and below them there will be growing things. Against the house, in full sun and sheltered from the wind, there will be a wide paved space and perhaps to one side a few rectangular flower beds edged with box or lavender. I am a tulip addict and will not be able to deny myself a bed or two of tulips and pansies, forget-me-nots, wallflowers and bachelor's buttons in spring. In summer I shall plant these beds with thick patches of half-hardy annuals. Only a prophet can know which to plant each year. In a wet summer zinnias will be a failure, (and I love white zinnias and white tobacco flowers near a house); or I shall try a particoloured bed of *Phlox drummondii* only to see them wither to nothing in a scorching season. But I am willing to try my luck rather than forgo petunias and fuchsias, ageratums, dwarf dahlias, hardy chrysanthemums—all gaudy flowers whose place is near the house.

As with the house, I cannot predict my future landscape.

I should like a stream, and a fast running one too, at least for part of its course through the garden. If it drops in level three or more feet, I shall arrange to dam it in three or four places with stones artfully placed to give each little fall of water a different note, for one of my greatest pleasures is the sound of falling water. I would do little more by way of water gardening, as I do not care much for bog and waterside gardening in places where I can dispense with it. If the yellow flag iris grows there, and meadowsweet, perhaps I would replace the wild iris with the blues and whites of *Iris sibirica* and *Iris laevigata*, but discreetly and with a light hand; and if there were room I would add a few of the tall pink herbaceous *Spiraea venusta*. I should certainly try to establish *Primula rosea* along the moist part of the stream's banks because of a predilection for the bright carmine pink of this Himalayan plant, so unusual a colour in early April. In the showers and fleeting sunshine of early spring, *Primula rosea* looks as stalwart and happy as a native primrose, so vigorous and strong and so prolific that it ought, years since, to have naturalised itself down half a hundred English streams. As far as I know it never has, but I shall be satisfied to go on trying to encourage it. I may, too, allow myself a clump or two of *Primula florindae*. I know it is coarse compared with the lovelier *P. sikkimensis*, but, coming in July, its tall heads of drooping cowslip yellow flowers look native and it establishes itself easily. So much for my stream. I hope it will be shaded along its course just for the faint mystery it evokes as it emerges from shadow into sunlight and for this I may want to aid and plant a simple native tree or two.

The main part of my garden will take the shape of a pool of lawn, which may run level away from the house or perhaps rise or fall. It may extend from the house thirty yards or sixty or a hundred, but whether it is wide or long, whether it runs up hill or down, I shall try to give it a shape complete in itself. It will be the vital open space which links and gives meaning to everything else—house and hedges, trees and plantings, the clear or cloudy sky. To enhance them all I shall try to give this open space a definite but not rigid form. As I do not see the house as an architectural gem demanding a formal treatment, I shall avoid a formal shape and define it nearest the house with curving hedges or some simple and unified planting scheme. Farther away I shall try to outline its shape by light and shade, rather than underline it by a rigid and brightly coloured planting. I shall think of this, the centre of my composition, as an enclosure rather than as a glade. Glades, at least as they are used to-day, suggest a succession of irregular capes and bays with carefully planted groups of flowering shrubs. In a curious way these imply dispersion, a theme which best suits large properties where you are thus drawn farther and farther into the garden to discover new walks and vistas. But mine will be a small garden and my theme should suggest containment. If there is a view I will try to frame it in, so that it too contributes to the central open space which, for all its apparent emptiness, will still be a focus and centre. For here the vibrations, the intentions and qualities of all the different elements of the rest of the garden will meet and mingle to give the whole its unity.

Since I have chosen the English landscape as my setting, I shall avoid pushing any abstract forms too far. I would not try to merge house and garden in the Californian manner, as the climate will make this an uncomfortable anomaly, nor would I aim to embody the abstractions of my concept in a wilfully exotic way. The mood I seek above all is one of relaxation given by a garden, easy and untortured, in which plants, however rare and strange, will grow and take their place naturally and discreetly.

In the back of my mind lurks the picture of some native growth of trees, a few beech or oaks or birch perhaps or Scots fir, some form of little copse with hazel stools or a few wild hollies. Or if this is an old garden there may be a few good trees or an overgrown orchard, so that some good part of my garden has a canopy of leaves and the silhouettes of trees to break the skyline. If there are spruce and fir, out they will come: most small gardens are better without them. I might spare a fine isolated horse-chestnut or sycamore but I should remove both at once if they were in any place which I intended to plant: the chestnuts because they make a dank and sour shade in which even ivy can scarcely grow and the sycamores for their graceless youth and their unlovely foliage, usually blackened with disease by July. Canadian poplars would share the same fate.

Perhaps my main grass area will reach as far as the foot of the nearest trees. If so, I will define its edge by fairly compact drifts of large shrubs chosen for their effectiveness as mass and texture rather than for the colour of their flowers. These might be box or yew or perhaps rhododendrons or viburnums or cotoneasters. As they will mark the far limits of the lawn, I would not have them too brightly coloured. The scarlet or strong rose pink of certain rhododendrons, for instance, would falsify the whole perspective. Whether in the open or in shade, I would frame my lawn with carefully modulated greens and use clear pale colours—cream, pale yellows, soft pinks and blue mauves in sunshine and much white with clear mauve and accents of coral pink in the half light and shadows. I like white flowers, especially camellias, roses, rhododendrons, viburnums and hydrangeas, the silky whites of *Romneya coulteri*, the mauvy white satin of wood anemones and philadelphus "Belle Etoile," the icy snow-white of certain camellias and of the double white rugosa rose. By juxtaposition you can underline and bring out these different tonalities of white or enhance them by contrast and reflection.

I shall have to work warily with flower colour in such a small garden and avoid all the sensational and too dramatic effects of brilliant colouring, unless there is enough room to hide an occasional explosion of colour—reds and salmons and scarlets, black purple and orange—in places where they would not disrupt the pervading quiet harmony.

But the garden's most usual livery is, after all, green and I shall make it my main task to handle my plants and arrange them in their own terms of green. If I can succeed in groupings good in their form, textures and differing tonalities, I shall be sure of harmony throughout the yearly rhythm of the garden. Then only I will consider flower colour as an added study and delight.

At this point I have to warn myself quickly against the anæmic approach of certain modern purists who have pushed the theory of understatement in planting to ridiculous lengths, planting one bulrush and one *Caltha palustris*, for example, in a formal pool in the patio of some elaborate modern house, or else thinking that a patch of marram grass and a few tufts of osier will enhance the bright *avant-garde* conceits of a pavilion at an exhibition. Such aridities, and they are increasingly frequent, are a bleak denial of all the pleasures of gardening.

If I am prejudiced I am also tolerant and ready to understand a garden designer's revolt against the popular passion for bright flower colour at all costs. I remember a vast fan design of beds, a hundred square yards perhaps, solid with scarlet salvias spilling out over a rough grass slope in a public park in Geneva—a vulgar and thoughtless splash of colour, all the more surprising as it lies within a few yards of one of Europe's better rose gardens. At the other end of the same scale I think of a small English inland garden, often cited as a model of good planting and planning. Here under a grey and clouded sky I saw flower borders planted with infinite love and trouble in a most carefully thought-out scheme of purple and crimson and orange. Purple berberis and rhus, cascades of *Clematis jackmanii*, groups of *Phlox paniculata* in Tyrian purples and royal crimsons and well grown clumps of tiger lilies all combined to create a garden picture as strident as it was oddly funereal.

Between these two extremes of under and over-statement we have to tread carefully. I see my green lawn and its surroundings as the one part of my garden which I shall design entirely as scenery. Large or small, this link between the house and its surroundings will be an exercise in landscape composition.

I should like to keep my pool of lawn, and the planting which rings it, free from the hard intrusion of a path. I would rather make a path as an outer ring lying well behind the plantings that fringe and shape the lawn, and as a main line of communication linking all the parts of the garden. It will start somewhat formally, passing to one side of the house between flower beds. Here it

may be of brick or stone, but as it passes round and through
each part of the garden its material will change accordingly. To
make sure that it dries quickly and is practicable in all weathers,
I will give it a foundation of at least nine inches of broken stones
or brick rubble and three inches of ashes or coarse gravel above
that. Only then will I surface it with good binding sand and
perhaps fine sieved and washed pea-gravel. Pea-gravel is better
than crushed gravel or stone whose sharp edges will ruin even the
stoutest shoes.

The path will make its way from the slightly formal arrangement of flower beds next the house through a series of secondary
garden pictures, all lying outside and invisible from the central
part of the garden. These will be as elaborate or simple as the
nature of the garden and my own possibilities allow. Perhaps
I shall be able to bring my path through plantings of flowering
shrubs, large enough, maybe, to need narrow paths breaking
away from the main one to rejoin it later. Here I would use
sub-shrubs that I like and could make grow to break the edges of
the paths—lavenders and pontentillas, ceratostigma and caryopteris, leonotis and phlomis, cistus and helianthemum, and
heaths, not all, nor all together, for my choice will depend on
soil and site. I see all this as garden-planting, grouped harmoniously surely, but intimate and designed as garden and not as
landscape. These small shrubs will be like foothills for the higher
mounds of all the larger shrubs I might want to grow informally.
I say informally as, if I have room, the lilacs and philadelphus,
laburnums and other domesticated flowering shrubs will need
another and slightly more formal setting in an enclosure which
would include such roses too as I might want to grow. These
are the roses which may be left to grow into large bushes with
only an occasional pruning to remove dead wood and keep them
in shape. I have a catholic taste and would happily mix the
stronger-growing floribunda types, " Queen Elizabeth " for
instance, with shrub roses like " Fruhlingsgold," *R. nevada*,
R. gallica versicolor as well as damask roses and *R. centifolia* and
the lovely free-flowering perpetuals like " General MacArthur,"

"Ulrich Brunner" and "Caroline Testout." Nor would I leave out hybrid musk roses, such as "Penelope" and "Pax". In this part of the garden I see, amongst the bushy roses, thick clumps of perennials, too coarse-growing for my "system" garden, but which I would not like to be without: herbaceous paeonies and thalictrums and a dozen varieties of *Phlox paniculata* for their fresh colours and the honey sweetness they bring in late summer and all the Japanese anemones I could lay hands on. I would have crown imperials and *Galtonia candicans*, *Lilium candidum* and deeply planted clumps of certain tulips, cottage and Rembrandt, left in place to come up each year. In this way, although the individual flowers will be smaller, the clumps will increase and make great bouquets growing larger every year. Between all these will run my path primly bordered with London Pride or alchemilla or with the handsome foliage of bergenia or hostas.

At this point in our imaginary walk we might pause and consider the question of the kitchen garden. I have to think of it as a luxury—it would be my modest equivalent of the rich man's yacht or racing stable. I would want its produce but not at the cost of working it myself. But for the moment I will imagine myself with a neat kitchen garden divided by the path into four quarters, all neatly edged with box. For all it harbours slugs, needs cutting and is, in general, the working gardener's bane, I would not care for a kitchen garden without box edges and, as well, neatly pruned espaliers and cordons of apples and pears. In my four quarters I will grow only those vegetables whose taste is ruined if more than an hour elapses between their being culled and cooked—like asparagus, green peas, new potatoes and baby carrots. If ever I have this kitchen garden I shall make it an even costlier adventure by making all the paths in asphalt with gravel rolled into the final coat of bitumen or, of well-roughened concrete with wooden laths set in flush every three feet as expansion joints and to prevent crazing. Weeding paths is an appalling waste of time and the use of weedkillers means the death of anything growing along the edges.

We have wandered so far beyond the limits of our modest garden dream that we might just as well let our path, as it comes to the kitchen garden, pass into the shade of a nut walk, an old and lovely gardening convention which is simple enough to realise. Here the path will be about five feet wide; on either side I shall plant hazel nuts spaced about six feet apart. In a few years these will make clumps of dark brown stems arching upwards and outwards and joining overhead. Hazels and hazel shade are companionable to plant life and here at their feet will grow a whole company of plants which thrive in just such conditions, primroses and particularly the double mauve one if I can find it, polyanthus, *Anemone appennina*, *A. blanda*, *A. fulgens*, hepatica, helleborus, *Anchusa myosotidiflora*, foxgloves perhaps, dwarf campanulas and as many dwarf daffodil and tulip species, scillas, muscari, chionodoxa and other small bulbs as I can afford.

At this point we must trace our way back, pass through the flowering shrubs and plunge into the shade of a little wood. Under the trees the path will change. I will surface it here with sand and leave it to become moss-grown and strewn with fallen leaves which an occasional raking will keep in order. If the foundations are solid enough, only dwarf weeds or grass will grow which will give no trouble for coarse weeds need a richer nourishment than they will find here. In the Eastern United States you constantly see woodland garden paths thickly coated with pine needles or tan bark or a mixture of the two. These make an agreeable walking surface and keep down weeds very effectively.

Here in the wood out of sight of the main view from the house, I can experiment with shade-loving plants: rhododendrons, for instance, or azaleas, or hydrangeas in as brilliant or modulated a range of colours as I choose. My choice of plants will depend on the nature of the wood. Perhaps the tree boles will be better left unobscured by busy plants and I will keep my plantings low. I may choose *Gentiana asclepiadea*, the willow gentian, in drifts, kirengeshoma and smilacina and tiger lilies, dog's tooth violets, trilliums and ferns which will all do well if

the soil is deep and moist and slightly acid. In drier and sandier
soil I might prefer to make groups of carefully selected white and
clear pale pink foxgloves. But whatever species or combinations
I choose, I shall try to keep the planting very simple, grow only
a few varieties but exploit these to the full, for I have seen too
many shady woods and copses ruined by over-complicated and
fidgety plantings.

By now we will have come through the wood into open
meadowland where any definite path will look altogether out of
place. Even so I shall not abandon my foundation but again sand
the surface and let the grass gain on this as it will. The path will
still drain quickly and give a good walking surface which an
occasional mowing will keep in order.

Here perhaps I shall find the stream I hope for or at least a
pond which I should handle with the same reticence as the
stream. In the grass I should like to try and establish two meadow
plants. One is the wild blue geranium which makes clouds of soft
blue where the sloping meadows of the Yorkshire dales drop
away to pebbly, alder-shaded becks in which dippers and water
wagtails dart from stone to stone in the singsong chatter of broken
and falling water. For these I will clear and dig a space large
enough to hold a hundred plants in the hope that they will thrive
and naturalise themselves: if they do not I shall not insist.
Salvia superba, the purple meadow sage, is another wild plant I
should like to grow among the meadow grasses as naturally as it
does, along with the yellow tansy and milky-blue chicory, on the
open roadsides of the Ile de France.

By now I have hopefully pictured an ambitious garden but
one still without a small greenhouse where I could grow plants
from seeds and cuttings and winter geraniums and fuchsias and
other potted plants. I like pot gardening and would use plants in
pots on steps, low walls and on my paved terrace space, grouping
them in simple flower pots of all sizes. I should use cannas and
yuccas and hedychium, *Francoa ramosa*, tigridias, yellow and
white lantanas clipped into balls, and the dwarf pomegranate,
which grows so easily from seed and whose neat foliage and

orange scarlet flowers are an exact miniature of the ordinary pomegranate.

Part of the greenhouse I shall save for the pale blue *Plumbago capensis* and especially for *Jasminum polyanthum* so that through the winter months I can cut sprays of its brown-red buds and intensely fragrant white flowers. I shall have to find room too for bowls and dishes set with bulbs of narcissus " PaperWhite " to bring into the house for Christmas, for a few Roman hyacinths and scented creamy freesias and other spring flowers; there would always be enough for one small vase to relieve the dark days of winter. If I have two heated frames next to the greenhouse they will be enough to grow half-hardy annuals for my flower beds in good time for me to set out sturdy plants towards the third week in May.

Wherever I make my garden the main elements will not change: in front of the house a deliberately composed " landscape," so quietly arranged that one would not tire of it; nearby a working garden; and subsidiary to both of these, such additional features as the landscape, the soil and the site would indicate and as I could afford. To try and describe the structure of a nonexistent garden is, I fear, but to make a rusty catalogue. Walls, paths, trees, shrubs, lawns and terraces, lists of plant names, tool sheds, greenhouse, parking space and all the rest are like the separate pieces in a box of toys to be put together to make the structure and fabric of a garden. If that were all, it would be a slow and arid process, the mere application of technique and experience towards changing the external appearance of one tiny plot of ground—an infinitesimal point on the planet's surface—a pastime like another, as constructive, no more nor less, as playing patience or doing jigsaw puzzles.

A garden really lives only insofar as it is an expression of faith, the embodiment of a hope and a song of praise. These are high-sounding words but wherever I set my aim, high or low, the achievement, by the very nature of things as they are, is bound to fall far short of them and a too modest aim may well result in an insignificant achievement. I use the word aim perhaps

too loosely, for I will surely have many aims in connection with
every garden I attempt; the first perhaps quite simply is to leave
a place more beautiful than I find it. By itself this is a subjective
aim, one for my personal satisfaction and related to my own
inevitably subjective ideas about beauty. So, at once, I have to
expand or add to my aim and endeavour to understand the point
of view of others. Will my garden spell for them the message it
has for me? So my aim widens to include some understanding
of my fellows. Nor can that be all or enough. I have to understand too the nature of all the processes that will go to make the
garden, the rhythm of activities and where in each process this
rhythm checks and falters and can resume only with the application of a stimulus at an exact moment. These are the rhythms also
of all human as well as all vegetable processes: men, like trees,
can be moved at certain moments and not at others. I draw and
draw, searching for a composition which will come right in its
own time only, perhaps at once, perhaps after hours and days of
work. Of course the answer is inherent in the problem, and I
find the solution only as soon and as clearly as I see all or enough
of the factors which compose the problem. So now my aim
includes my own necessity for clearer thinking. You see now to
where this leads, for a finer quality of thinking comes only with
a wiser heart and where must I look to find the heart's wisdom?
All these I must remember as I struggle with problems of drawing
and composing on paper, with the spadework of calculations and
lists, the difficulties of construction, the chance vagaries of
behaviour of plants and men, soil and weather for which I have
to remember to make allowances.

I am forced to a life-long discipline and a necessary and
constant awareness so that eagerness may not turn into ill-temper
and hopes not well based on facts founder in useless despair or
wither into a frivolous cynicism.

When I come to build my own garden it can scarcely take
another form than the one which is a reflection of its maker. If
I want it to be " ideal," then I too must set myself my own
ideal, my own aim. Now, as for a painter or a sculptor or any

artist comes the test—what values does the garden-maker try to express? It seems to me that to some extent he has the choice. He may choose the easy way and design a garden as a demonstration of his technical skill and brilliance, go all out for strong effects or see the problem as one of good or bad business and so plan accordingly. Or he may try to make his garden as a symbol and set up as best he can a deliberate scaffolding or framework which nature will come to clothe with life. Perhaps circumstances will help him to decide that his garden theme should be devoted to water and so he will devote his garden to showing all the aspects he can of water: still and quiet water to reflect the soft green shade of summer trees, the purple greys of a coming storm or the brightness of white clouds crossing a clear blue sky, or shallow water running shining over a pebble bed or breaking into white foam where it falls. He may want to show water making lacy patterns against stone or bronze or use it in a hundred other ways to demonstrate its manifold aspects and attributes.

I can see another garden with another theme, one where the texture and shapes of foliage would be all important, a green garden which the eye would explore as it would an Altdorfer forest, layer upon layer of leaves sombre or caught in sunlight or in dappled silhouette. I remember a sequence in the Japanese film, " *Rashomon*," when the camera " travelled " with its lens focused upwards to the topmost branches of a forest set against the sky. As the endless succession of leafy patterns flickered across the screen, each with its definite shape and nature, one felt part of the world of trees and leaves and light and this, in quite another medium, gave to me at least a newly felt understanding of a whole dimension of the gardener's art.

In my garden I might choose to try and illuminate more especially one aspect of the force of nature. I could consider the growing point, the nose of a bulb of snowdrop or scilla and the strength and the heat it generates to force its way through the frozen earth, and then its symmetrical expansion of leaves and flower, in controlled and lovely explosion. So often these and all the natural phenomena of spring pass unnoticed. We take them for granted and hardly look. Why should I not devise my garden deliberately as an act of appreciation to the forces which bring about this ardent growth? Why not design and plant some part of it to focus my attention and perhaps so widen my understanding of just this one aspect of nature?

After aconite and snowdrop the crocus next pierce through and then the early daffodils usher upwards all the spears of spring hyacinths and the orderly regiments of tulips. The fat buds of crown imperials come with the unfolding rosettes of *Lilium regale* and the deep red-brown knobs of paeonies which soon unfurl the elaborations of their young spring foliage. From the black mud burst the incredible spathes of *Lysichiton camtschatcense* and arisaema and under the trees two more modest aroids, our native Lords and Ladies and the mousetail Arisarum pierce the woodland floor. Ferns no sooner break through the spring moist earth than the uncurled spring of each young frond uncoils with all the ogival curves and volutes of a Gothic crozier, and the blue-grey spear heads of flag iris burst from the ground sharp with the urgency of growth.

Those are the rites of spring, the earth turns and in a few sun-warmed hours the ice recedes and the soldanella's fringed lilac flower shines in a dark earth pocket against the snow.

My imaginary garden thus takes many forms and each of its forms has many aspects. Sometimes I see it as a sandy hollow ringed with dunes planted with marram grass against the shifting winds. Beyond the dunes the grey blue sea rolls and thunders on till the rhythm changes and it recedes leaving the long level reaches of sand glistening in the sun. My garden repeats in vegetable forms the shapes and colours of the waves with brakes of the silvery sea-buckthorn, *Hippophae rhamnoides*, and sea-green mounds of atriplex to protect wide plantings of blue-grey echinops and eryngium, static *Veronica hulkeana*, teucrium, silvery santolina and cistus and *Buddleia alternifolia*, senecios, *Cineraria maritima* and seakale; all plants armoured in silver to meet the challenge of the sandy soil in this sunny and airy garden.

Like clouds moving across the sky dissolving and re-forming

now in towering rounded masses, now in long streamers or curling wraiths, now jagged and torn or neatly spread in fish scale pattern over the sky, my garden's patterns shape and re-shape themselves. A leaf or a twig, the feel of a stone step under one's tread, a trickle of water, the musky smell of a cyclamen plant set in a pot that you have but to tap to know from the sound whether it needs watering or not, such transient impressions as these can open a door and set in motion a whole world of garden pictures. Each second is new and in each second are implicit a hundred gardens. In one it is sunset and suddenly there is a chattering in the pine trees and in the moment of evening's hush eight magpies wing through the air, drop down for a moment among the short grasses where the harebells flower and then, calling to each other, disperse and whirl severally back into the trees. Elsewhere the butterflies, peacocks and red admirals, settle thickly on the purple honey-scented panicles of buddleia. Below the great stone house is a lawn squarely hedged with dark green yew, where a white peacock spreads the splendour of his tail and sets his wing quills drumming. Where a russet brick bridge spans the moat, an old Persian lilac makes a mound of blossom to hang over the moss-green water where later the dragonflies will seem to tease the golden carp.

So, as in a kaleidoscope, the brightly coloured trifles shift and at each turn comes a new garden picture, dimensioned in time as well as space; where each leaf, though long since dead and withered, burgeons again and the gossamer web for ever catches the dew of a morning long since past.

Sometimes my garden seems like a mirage always receding but if ever this intermittent vision becomes a reality, wherever it is, whatever its size and shape it will be satisfying for like all gardens it will be a world for itself and for me.

Index

Index

Index

Index

Index

Index

About the Author

RUSSELL PAGE, who died in 1985, attended The Slade School, University of London, and studied painting in Paris. He began gardening professionally in 1928, and there are examples of his work in England, Belgium, France, Italy, Switzerland, Spain, Egypt, Iran and the United States, from Long Island to Texas. At the end of his life, he was spending time annually in the United States, where he was working on the Pepsico gardens in Purchase, New York.